Exploring European Identities

The Open University

Exploring European Identities

EDITED BY Cristina

Chimisso

This publication forms part of an Open University course AA300 *Europe: Culture and Identities in a Contested Continent*. Details of this and other Open University courses can be obtained from the Course Information and Advice Centre, PO Box 724, The Open University, Milton Keynes MK7 6ZS, United Kingdom: tel. +44 (0)1908 653231, e-mail ces-gen@open.ac.uk

Alternatively, you may visit the Open University website at http://www.open.ac.uk where you can learn more about the wide range of courses and packs offered at all levels by The Open University.

To purchase this publication or other components of Open University courses, contact Open University Worldwide Ltd, The Open University, Walton Hall, Milton Keynes MK7 6AA, United Kingdom: tel. +44 (0)1908 858785; fax +44 (0)1908 858787; e-mail ouwenq@open.ac.uk; website http://www.ouw.co.uk

The Open University
Walton Hall, Milton Keynes
MK7 6AA

First published 2003. Reprinted 2005.

Edited, designed and typeset by The Open University

Printed and bound in the United Kingdom by The Bath Press, Bath

ISBN 0 7492 9609 7

1.2

26787B/aa300b1prei1.2

Contents

Contributors

Cristina Chimisso, Lecturer in European Studies, Philosophy Department, the Open University

Clive Emsley, Professor of History, the Open University

Lorna Hardwick, Senior Lecturer in Classical Studies, the Open University

David Herbert, Lecturer in Religious Studies, the Open University

Audrey Linkman, Visual Resources Manager, Arts Faculty, the Open University

Mark Pittaway, Lecturer in European Studies, History Department, the Open University

Robert Wilkinson, Senior Lecturer in Philosophy, the Open University

Readings

The readings that appear in this book are extracts from the following works.

Chapter 1

Virginia Woolf, *Three Guineas*

Luigi Pirandello, *One, No One and One Hundred Thousand*

Colin MacInnes, *Absolute Beginners*

Atvar Brah, *Cartographies of Diaspora*

Judith Butler, *Gender Trouble*

Pierre Bourdieu, *State Nobility: Elite Schools in the Field of Power*

Chapter 2

Turgot, 'A philosophical review of the successive advances of the human mind'

Condorcet, *Sketch for a Historical Picture of the Progress of the Human Mind*

Jean-Jacques Rousseau, *Discourse on the Origins and the Foundation of Inequality among Men*

Jean-Jacques Rousseau, *Emile*

Chapter 3

L'Encyclopédie (Denis Diderot)

Giuseppe Mazzini, *The Duties of Man*

František Palacký, 'Letter to the Frankfurt parliament'

Leopold Ranke, 'The great powers'

Introduction

CRISTINA CHIMISSO

The title of this book, *Exploring European Identities*, invites authors and readers alike to undertake an exciting and challenging project. Identity has become a central concept in the social sciences and humanities, and indeed questioning 'what we are' is increasingly important for many individuals and groups. The authors of this book believe that the concept of identity also provides an extremely useful analytical tool in the study of modern Europe. The focus on identities (in the plural) allows the student to approach Europe from the perspective of its inhabitants, rather than its institutions and political events. It also avoids any temptation to adopt simple definitions of Europe and Europeanness and to suppress diversity. Although studies of particular identities present in Europe abound, it has been far rarer to approach European identities as an interactive, diverse and often contradictory whole. Moreover, publications and courses on 'Europe' are often about the European Union, or about either western or eastern Europe. This separation is overcome by examining realities in the whole continent, and indeed questioning different representations of Europe.

The authors did not attempt a definitive study of European identities; this would have been impossible, for identities are not only too complex and subjective to be fully described but they are also in a continuous process of change and redefinition. The *explorations* carried out in this book do not, of necessity, cover all possible aspects of European identities and their interactions. Rather, they examine the fundamental mechanisms of identity formation, focusing on various types of cultural identities to be found in Europe. The aim of the book is primarily to provide the intellectual tools necessary to grasp the complex and changing reality of cultural identities in Europe. This is done, however, by examining numerous concrete examples. The case studies presented here are not only illustrations of mechanisms by which identities are formed, negotiated, perceived and performed. They also analyse important aspects of European history, societies and cultures.

Culture here is defined as the totality of symbols and artefacts produced by human beings. This encompasses modes of thinking, feeling and behaving as much as values, customs, traditions and norms. On the basis of this conception of culture, the study of cultural identities carried out in the book has an extremely broad angle. The symbols and artefacts through which the authors investigate European identities range from modern performances of Greek tragedies to eighteenth-century philosophical texts, from nineteenth-century nationalistic writings and monuments to current expressions of religious faith, from contemporary analysis of gender and 'race' to eastern world views. The importance attributed to visual culture is reflected in the central role of the images and in the inclusion of a full visual essay, 'Portraying identities, portraying conventions', which describes the ways in which identities have been represented in early photographic portraiture. Far from being a collection of disparate studies, this book aims to recompose aspects of culture that all too often are kept artificially separate by the current organization of the academic disciplines.

No single discipline could offer the variety of approaches necessary for the study of European identities, hence the authors' choice of a genuinely interdisciplinary perspective. Although attention is focused mainly on the present, the recognition that identities are historically formed has called for discussion of their historical roots, hence the analyses of, for instance, nineteenth-century nationalism, the Enlightenment idea of progress, and theatre performances in ancient Greece. This book's focus is on society rather than institutions, but it would have been naive to overlook the impact of the latter on identities. This is why the role of the state, and the roles of educational and religious institutions, among others, are also examined.

Chapter 1, 'What is identity?', provides a theoretical discussion of the concept of identity and of European identities in particular. In this chapter I draw my interpretative categories from both philosophy and sociology, and discuss a variety of texts, including extracts from a polemical essay (Virginia Woolf's), novels (Luigi Pirandello's and Colin MacInnes's) and theoretical works (Atvar Brah's, Judith Butler's and Pierre Bourdieu's). The chapter also introduces some of the themes that are discussed in depth in the following chapters: the relationship between history and identity (Chapters 2 and 3), and the role of language (Chapter 4) and religion (Chapter 5) in the formation of identities.

Chapters 2 and 3 discuss two very important ways in which Europeans have conceived of world history, themselves and their place in history. Chapter 2, 'History and identity: the Enlightenment idea of progress', examines the idea of progress as a prominent example of the role played by historical reconstructions in the formation of identities. I have chosen the idea of progress because it has been particularly crucial in Europeans' self-perception, and in their representations of other peoples. This chapter focuses on the eighteenth-century roots of the idea of progress, through a discussion of the French Enlightenment and in particular the writings of Turgot, Condorcet and Rousseau.

Chapter 3, 'Nation, nation-state, nationalism and Europe', investigates one of the most important identities in Europe: national identity. Clive Emsley links national identity to central events in European history. He examines first of all the formation of nation-states, and especially the conceptions of nation put forward by historians. Following a discussion of the Enlightenment conceptions of nation and Europe, he concentrates on nineteenth-century theories of nation and national history. The readings included in this chapter are primary sources: extracts from Diderot and D'Alembert's *L'Encyclopédie*, and the writings of Giuseppe Mazzini, František Palacký and Leopold von Ranke.

This examination of national identity is developed further in Chapter 4, 'Language, identity and nation'. Here, Mark Pittaway focuses in particular on the role that language plays in the formation, perception and transmission of national identity. Like Chapter 3, this chapter draws examples from both western and eastern Europe. The extracts analysed range from an ethnographer's account of the use of language in her interviews (Milena Hübschmannová), to the linguist Karl Vossler's 1920s discussion of language communities, and the Czech historian Miroslav Hroch's views on the nation-building process in Europe.

Chapter 5, 'Religion and European identities', consists of three integrated parts. In the first part, David Herbert outlines the European religious landscape and debates the most important issues concerning religious identity in contemporary Europe. The long reading appended to this part illustrates a recent religious movement, that of 're-Christianization', which has been especially active in France during the past two decades. The second and third parts of the chapter are case studies. The former examines the actions of the European Convention for the Protection of Human Rights in specific religious controversies. The other case study deals with the complex interactions of religious identities in Bosnia, and with the role of religious organizations during and after the conflict that affected the region in the 1990s.

Following the discussion of the most important aspects of cultural identities in Europe in Chapters 1 to 5, Chapter 6 invites the reader to take a step back and reflect more generally on what makes this very concept of identity viable in European culture. In 'East is east and west is west: on the fundamentals of the European and eastern world views', Robert Wilkinson focuses in particular on the eastern outlook known as 'non-dualism', according to which reality is ultimately an undivided whole. Non-dualism prevents the development of the concept of personal identity as analysed in this book. Through an examination of non-dualism and its consequences for all aspects of thought, behaviour and even artistic expression, the author shows that the European conception of the self and the world is far from being universal.

In Chapter 7, 'Ancient Greek drama on the modern European stage: identities and performance', Lorna Hardwick approaches the debates about identities and politics from the point of view of dramatic performances. Her analysis of modern 'interventionist' performances of ancient Greek plays sheds light on the complex questions of the multiple readings of identities and of the appropriation of the past as a means by which to intervene in the present. The chapter includes an analysis by J. Michael Walton of the dramatic context, staging and theatrical qualities of Aeschylus' *Agamemnon*. This play is the object of the case study that constitutes the last part of the chapter.

This is the first of four books in the series *Europe: Culture and Identities in a Contested Continent* which form the main texts of an Open University level 3 course of the same name.

1

What is identity?

CRISTINA CHIMISSO

Introduction

Who are the Europeans? Does it make any sense to speak of European identities? If it does, have these identities changed through time? The name 'Europe' is problematic in itself, being taken by different people to mean sometimes the European continent (its many islands included), sometimes the European Union, and sometimes by some British people to mean the rest of Europe, from which they exclude their own country. This confusion does not exist just in common parlance. 'Europe' is often used by politicians and the media as a synonym for the European Union. You might have had a similar experience to mine: on a flight from the United States to London, the crew advised the passengers that those of us who held 'a British *or* European passport' did not need to fill in a landing card. They did not mean that a Bulgarian or Russian passport would exempt its holder from filling in the card. What they meant by European passports was in fact European Union passports; in this case, though, British passports are a subset of EU ones, rather than something different. 'Europeans' is an even more problematic term than Europe for it implies a European identity, or a set of European identities. Before setting out to explore European identities and cultures, it is necessary to analyse the concept of identity itself. Identity is a complex concept, employed in such disciplines as philosophy, sociology and history, in politics and in everyday speech. It is increasingly more pervasive, and perhaps elusive.

This chapter provides a theoretical framework which will help you to analyse particular case studies and indeed your own experiences and the situations you may observe. You will become familiar with some of the ways in which the concept of identity has been employed and explained in a variety of contexts. You will be guided to reflect on the complexity of the concept of cultural identity in general and European identity in particular. Although definitions and descriptions will be provided, you will learn that none of these is uncontroversial and definitive: all are ideas of particular authors, which can be accepted, challenged or improved. You will learn not only to be critical towards academic discourse but also to reflect upon, analyse and possibly challenge common assumptions, including your own, about cultural identities, their supposed immutability, and their foundations in territory, history, language and religion.

You will form your own ideas about this difficult topic by reading texts taken from works of different genres: a polemical essay (Virginia Woolf's), two novels (Luigi Pirandello's and Colin MacInnes's) and three academic texts (Atvar Brah's, Judith Butler's and Pierre Bourdieu's). In this way, you will learn how to use the conceptual tools provided in the chapter to analyse different types of text.

The chapter is divided into three main parts. The first, 'Conceptions of identity', introduces the idea by presenting the modern challenges to a long-lived concept of personal identity which we will call Cartesian, after the philosopher René Descartes. The second part, 'Identity building', analyses the processes by which identities are socially constructed and focuses on some crucial elements in this construction: history, geography, religion and language. The third part, 'Types of identity', proposes three 'ideal types' of identity that, taken together, provide an analytical tool; it also introduces some preliminary reflections on which type of identity Europeans may have. The concepts and distinctions set out in this chapter, then, are intended to provide you with effective techniques that will enhance your consideration of the question of European identities and cultures, not to limit it. You are encouraged to reflect on, and possibly challenge, the proposed theoretical framework itself.

Conceptions of identity

The term 'identity' suggests that something is *identified* (in other words, that it is made or considered identical to something else). To talk about identity in relation to human beings means answering one of the questions 'What are we?' or 'What makes us human?' or 'What makes me who I am?' The concept of identity has a long history, having been first employed in philosophy. Personal identity, in the western tradition, has been grounded in the act of thinking by the philosopher René Descartes (1596–1650).

Cartesian identity and its critics

For Descartes, the individual had a sense of her or his own identity as a 'thing that thinks'. How did he arrive at this conclusion? In his *Meditations* he set out to find the foundations for an infallible method to achieve true knowledge, believing that in order to achieve this all knowledge should be subjected to radical critique. Descartes decided to doubt any item of knowledge, including that acquired through the senses, for he was aware that his senses had deceived him on many occasions. However, he found that he could not doubt that he existed, because in order to doubt and in general to think, he had to exist. After proving his existence, Descartes wondered which type of thing he was and, since the only thing beyond doubt was his thought, concluded that he was a 'thing that thinks'. In his words:

> Thinking? At last I have discovered it – thought; this alone is inseparable from me ... I am, then, in the strict sense only a thing that thinks; that is, I am a mind, or intelligence, or intellect, or reason ...
>
> A thing that thinks. What is that? A thing that doubts, understands, affirms, denies, is willing, is unwilling, and also imagines and has sensory perceptions.
>
> (Descartes [1641] 1986, pp. 18, 19)

Descartes identified the self with thought: thinking is essential to what we are, while other characteristics and activities are contingent, or dispensable. The sense of the self is in this way inextricably linked to a mental act, rather than, for example, to the body or to relationships with others.

Note that the expression 'Cartesian identity' has become a label for the conception of identity that I shall analyse below. It does not directly refer to the work of the seventeenth-century philosopher, whose concerns were obviously far removed from present-day discussions on identity. This label is used because later scholars, particularly from the 1950s onwards, regarded some characteristics of Descartes' conception of human beings as an enduring legacy of European culture. You may find that some critics talk of the **Enlightenment** conception of human beings with a very similar meaning. Again, the reference is to an enduring conception of identity that these critics regard as rooted in the Enlightenment and in the cultural framework of the French Revolution, seen as the application of the views exemplified by Descartes. These labels refer to a universal conception of human beings, one which does not consider their particular social and historical circumstances, nor acknowledge cultural differences. This universalistic conception has been very important for European culture, and has been the intellectual underpinning for the advocating of universal rights, universal suffrage and equality before the law.

However, this conception has been challenged in many ways, generally along the lines that it is a projection of a particular identity and does not take into account the real diversity of experience, culture and social class, **gender** and '**race**'.

Conceptions of identity which oppose a Cartesian one regard identity as the product of interactions between subject, history and society.

The concept of Enlightenment is discussed in detail in Chapter 2, for example in the section 'What is Enlightenment'?

Gender and 'race' are here conceived as socially constructed. See the section 'Identity building', below, and in particular Atvar Brah's text for 'race' and Judith Butler's for gender. I have placed 'race' in inverted commas to emphasize that its use here is not intended in the original biological sense, which is nowadays discredited. This problem does not arise for gender, as one can distinguish between sex as a biological reality and gender as a social one.

Sociology, psychology and anthropology have investigated such types of identity that are grounded in history and society. Psychoanalysts have challenged the perfectly conscious character of the Cartesian thinking **subject**. In recent years, feminists have also criticized the universality and the disembodied character of the Cartesian subject. Some of these challenges are examined in more detail below.

Am I my body?

The Cartesian subject is a *mind*: the body does not form personal identity. In his *Meditations* Descartes declared, 'I am not that structure of limbs which is called the human body' (Descartes [1641] 1986, p. 18). Indeed he regarded mind and body as two distinct entities. This is what is called mind–body dualism: a human being is formed of two parts, a mind and a body; the mind is her or his essence, whereas the body is a 'possession' of the mind. This distinction between mind and body has been called into question; it has been argued that the body is much more meaningful for a sense of self than is suggested by a Cartesian view of identity. What we are is also the product of the discipline imposed on our bodies by others and by ourselves, in terms of how we behave, move, look after our bodies, and at which times and in which places we perform certain activities. The body also plays an important role in the social interactions that are constitutive of the self. For example, the appearance of the body, including dress, grooming and adornment, communicates or expresses a variety of information about a person's identity, such as gender, 'race', approximate age, social status, occupation, lifestyle, and possibly political convictions and sexual preferences (see Figures 1.1–1.3). The body conveys social and cultural meanings. In late modernity, projects of the self can also involve a shaping of the body, through exercise and diet, as well as through surgery which can change not only the body's shape but also its sex.

For Descartes there is an absolute distinction between subjects (thinkers) and objects (what they think about). Subjects are conscious of being the authors of their thoughts. As you will see in this chapter, Michel Foucault argued that with the emergence of the human sciences at the beginning of the nineteenth century subjects (human beings as authors of thoughts and actions) also became objects – as the objects of scientific study. You will also see below that many sociologists (including Anthony Giddens) regard people's ability to think about themselves (and therefore to be *objects* of their own thoughts) as the core characteristic of modernity (see the note, below, on 'reflexivity').

Figure 1.1 Hagia Sophia mosaic, in Istanbul, Turkey, depicting the Virgin and Child in the middle, with Emperor John XI and Empress Irene on either side. This is an example of sacred art in which conventions in representing the body are used to identify personages. Even with no particularly sound art education it is possible to identify the Virgin and infant Jesus in this mosaic. Medieval art in particular was aimed at a largely illiterate public, and images had to express most, and often all, of the information. Photo: Art Directors/Trip/Turner

Figure 1.2   Master of the Judgement of Solomon (fl. 1620–5) *The Philosophers*, oil on canvas, Musée de l'Hotel Sandelin, Saint Omer, France. The conventions employed in visual representations of the human (or divine, as in Figure 1.1) body have often lasted centuries (see the colour plates section, 'Portraying identities, portraying conventions'). The representation of the philosopher as a bearded man reading or holding a book (or roll) dates back to hellenistic sculpture and lasted well into the twentieth century. These conventions, however, carry hidden meanings. In the case of the philosopher they perpetuated the idea that there exists a link between wisdom and masculinity. Bearded philosophers also recall the image of God the Father, their beard commanding the respect that F/fathers, real or symbolic, enjoy in a patriarchal society (see Chimisso, 2001, Chapter 1). Musée de l'Hotel Sandelin, Saint Omer, France. Photo: Bridgeman Art Library

Figure 1.3   This photograph is an example of the expression of a chosen identity. The individuals portrayed convey their choice of an alternative lifestyle through their grooming (note the person with dreadlocks in the bottom right-hand corner), their clothing and their choice of musical instrument. Photo: Format/Sue de Jong

However, the choices that people make regarding food, exercise and general care of their bodies are not free individual choices, but are linked to income, occupation and level of education. For instance, in many parts of Europe working-class people consume cheaper, fatty food which impacts not only on their body weight but also on their likelihood of developing coronary diseases. By contrast, the middle classes are more likely to eat leaner food, and less of it, and to have a regime that allows them to have a body shape that is valued in their milieu. It would be a mistake to regard choices in lifestyle as simple and direct effects of income level. Taste depends on culture, and different social classes have developed different cultures which they express in preferences for certain types of food (and music, films, clothes, furniture, art). The sociologist Pierre Bourdieu (1930–2002) argued that 'they [agents] have a taste for what they are anyway condemned to' (Bourdieu, 1989, p. 178). People on a low income do not eat cheap food only because they cannot afford expensive food but because they like it. Indeed it would be absurd to argue that people eat burgers, fish and chips or pizzas because they cannot afford caviar and champagne.

Am I an island?

The Cartesian subject is *isolated and self-sufficient*: she or he does not need others in order to have a sense of self. A challenge to this view comes from those who ground personal identity in relationships with others. Psychoanalysts have argued that the formation of the self in children is a slow and difficult learning process, which can develop only in interaction with other selves. For them, childhood experiences and relationships are of great importance in the shaping of the individual. Indeed in the view of the founder of psychoanalysis, Sigmund Freud (1856–1939), children introject part of their parents' personality: for Freud, children internalize parental authority at around the age of five or six years, and in so doing they start to develop a part of their personality – called the super-ego – which acts as a moral agency. Whereas in the very first years of our existence control over our behaviour is completely external, exercised by parents who forbid and correct, later the super-ego plays the parent's role, creating a sense of guilt and ultimately morality. The process of formation of the self is seen as never completed.

Other scholars (sociologists in particular) have also emphasized the importance of social relationships in the formation of personal identity. In this view, it is society that bestows identities and transforms them. The sociologist Stuart Hall argues that 'the subject still has an inner core or essence that is "the real me", but this is formed and modified in a continuous dialogue with the cultural worlds "outside" and the identities which they offer' (Hall, 1992,

p. 279). Hall expresses a balanced position in the spectrum of possible views, which ranges from the representation of identity as completely independent of social setting to the view that individuals are purely the product of social structures.

Movements such as structuralism, which were particularly popular in the 1960s and 1970s, went a long way towards denying human beings any autonomy. Structuralism was inspired by research in linguistics, led by that of Ferdinand de Saussure (1857–1913), who argued that language is an autonomous system of signs which organizes its components without direct reference to an external reality. Although many authors have refused the label of structuralist, generally the semiologist Roland Barthes (1915–80), the psychoanalyst Jacques Lacan (1901–81), the anthropologist Claude Lévi-Strauss (1908–) and the Marxist philosopher Louis Althusser (1918–90) are regarded as leading structuralists. What these different scholars have in common is that they argue that human beings are not the free authors of their thoughts and actions, for behind the sense that they give them lie hidden structures that establish the framework of these words and actions. In order to understand society, history, relations between people and their behaviour, structuralists believe that it is necessary to uncover and analyse these hidden structures. Thus Barthes analysed the structures of literary texts, rather than studying them from the point of view of their authors. Lacan employed structural analyses to make sense of the **unconscious**, which, according to him, exhibits the same structure as language. Lévi-Strauss focused on kinship, isolating the types of familiar relationships that always occur in human societies and that create a system of obligations and interdictions. Althusser developed a 'science of history' founded, in his view, by Karl Marx, that analysed history not in relation to human agency but in terms of economic, ideological and political structures.

What interests us here is that all these theories regard human beings not so much as the originators of these structures (language, the unconscious, kinship, history) but rather as their product. Therefore the human being cannot be conceived independently of these structures, let alone as an isolated individual.

Whether or not the philosopher Michel Foucault (1926–84) was a structuralist has been the topic of hot debate, resulting in numerous articles and books; what his work has in common with the philosophies described above is its emphasis on structures rather than human beings. In his *Order of Things*, Foucault outlined a philosophical history of the ways in which the human being has been conceived. Let us start with Descartes. As discussed above, Descartes defined the human being as a 'thing that thinks' and 'doubts, understands, affirms, denies, is willing, is unwilling': he is always the

In psychoanalysis the unconscious is that part of the mind whose content is not present to us: 'We call a psychical process unconscious whose existence we are obliged to assume – for some such reason as that we infer it from its effects – but of which we know nothing' (Freud). Psychoanalysis is aimed at accessing the unconscious. Freud believed that the most effective way of investigating the unconscious was through the interpretation of dreams.

subject of an action. The Cartesian subject is a spectator of the world, and can represent it objectively. Descartes did not observe and describe the human being, as one would with a natural object. At the beginning of the nineteenth century, Foucault argued, this approach was to change, with the emergence of the human sciences (Foucault, 1970). A drastic reorganization of knowledge took place, and as a consequence there emerged the

> individual who lives, speaks, and works in accordance with the laws of an economics, a philology, and a biology, but who also, by a sort of internal torsion and overlapping, has acquired the right, through the interplay of those very laws, to know them and to subject them to total clarification.
>
> (Foucault, 1970, p. 310)

In this phase human beings became an object of scientific study, thus acquiring specific characteristics that the Cartesian subject lacked. Foucault, however, thought that this conception of the human being was also transitory. As noted above, he believed that the emergence of 'man' as opposed to the abstract Cartesian subject was the result of a reorganization of knowledge. In his view, just as the structures of knowledge had created man, so they could eliminate him (when study of the 'sciences of man' began in the nineteenth century, gender awareness was rather weak). Indeed Foucault argued that not only is man a recent invention, but he is also on his way out. He welcomed the 'death of man':

> It is comforting ... and a source of profound relief to think that man is only a recent invention, a figure not yet two centuries old, a new wrinkle in our knowledge, and that he will disappear again as soon as that knowledge has discovered a new form.
>
> (Foucault, 1970, p. xxiii)

All these critiques of the isolated Cartesian subject make us aware of the importance of human interactions, society and culture in the formation of identity. Note, though, that structuralists and Foucault go much further than recognizing that the human being cannot be understood in isolation. They undermine the very idea of any autonomy of the individual. Foucault expected 'man' to disappear from our system of knowledge. It was noted earlier that the sociologist Stuart Hall has argued that there is a continuous interplay between a 'real me' and the 'outside'. Foucault would have rejected this idea of a 'real me', even if understood in conjunction with his or her environment.

Are we all the same?

The Cartesian subject is *universal*; he or she is a thinking being without any further connotations. In its aspiration to equality the Enlightenment promoted the notion of the universal subject, and this conception of identity has since been crucial for social and political thought. However, since the 1960s new social movements have challenged the notion of universal subject by claiming that it is in fact the idealization of a white, middle-class *man*. Feminist, gay liberation, black activist and other movements have pointed out that, far from being universal, the proposed subject has been representative of a small, although powerful, minority. These movements often advocate a recognition of different identities, which the realization of this type of universalism has oppressed and transformed into mere 'deviations'. Their politics are described as identity politics, for they appeal to the identities of their supporters (feminism to women, gay liberation movements to gay men and lesbians, black activism to black people). In addition to these movements, identity politics are characteristic of religious and ethnic minorities too.

All these different critiques point to the conclusion that a subject as universal and abstract as the Cartesian one is not useful in an analysis of European identities, because by definition such identities belong only to specific groups of people. Moreover, in this book European identities are analysed in the context of their historical and social formation and development, rather than presented as something immutable. The concept of identity reflected on here is better understood as the *identification of an individual with a certain group or community*. These groups or communities do not have to be empirically observable or homogeneous; they only need to be real for individuals, or imagined by them to be homogeneous. It is in this sense that Benedict Anderson talks of 'imagined communities' in order to describe nations (Anderson, 1991).

Classic examples of this concept of 'identity as belonging' are *class* and *nation*. A class or national identity can exist in the sense that an individual may regard her sense of self as inextricably connected with a certain class (for example, working class), or nation (such as French). Class identity has been central in Marxist and socialist political movements. National identity has been particularly important in Europe since the nineteenth century, as well as in anti-colonial struggles around the world. In Chapter 3 of this book, Clive Emsley explains how 'nations' have emerged in Europe and how they have become an almost universal model for conceiving of identities and history.

In this book European identities are conceived of as cultural identities. This simply means that the identification of one individual with a group consists, in more specific terms, in her identification with the culture of this group. For instance, if an individual has a French identity they consider themselves to be part of French culture. What does culture mean in this context? The term has been defined in a very great variety of ways. (Two anthropologists, Alfred L. Kroeber and Clyde Kluckholn, have listed over 150 definitions in their book *Culture: a Critical Review of Concepts and Definitions*; see Kroeber and Kluckhohn, 1978.) The meaning that is of interest here is that according to which culture is the totality of symbols and artefacts produced by human beings. Modes of thinking, feeling and behaving are part of culture, as are values, customs, traditions and norms. Any human being obviously has culture, but when we talk about cultural identities we imply that individuals identify with a particular culture, rather than with a universal human culture.

To go back to my example, some 60 million people may identify themselves as French. Obviously they are all different from each other, as they are individuals, and they will all have other identities besides this particular one. Imagine a French woman called Simone. As a woman, she has her gender in common with half of the world's population, but not with half of all French people. Simone is also heterosexual, black, secular, a parent, a journalist, a member of the Socialist party, and she has a hearing impairment. The relation she entertains with the imagined communities of women, heterosexual people, parents, media workers and so on may vary greatly from that of other women, heterosexual people, parents and so on. *A certain identity does not have the same meaning for all persons who share it.* Simone could be very active in groups of people with hearing impairments, committed to the diffusion of sign language and of the specific culture connected with it, while another person might regard his hearing impairment as a feature which is not crucial to his sense of self. The specific meaning and importance of Simone's identities depend on a number of factors, including to a certain extent personal choice, but crucially on the interaction of these identities with each other. For instance, the importance of national identity can vary greatly from one person to another, covering a spectrum that ranges from xenophobic nationalism at one extreme, to the rejection of national identity, or cosmopolitanism, at the other extreme. In Simone's case, the fact that she is black is very likely to interact with her French national identity, because she will be aware of the political stance of racist nationalists (like those of the National Front, a far right party), because she will probably have experienced racism from other French people, and because, if her black identity is strong, this may create for her a very significant link with non-French black people. *Identities interact with one another and affect one another.*

Individuals may be comfortable with their different identities; however, in other situations these identities can conflict with one another. For instance, the children of migrants can experience discomfort at being part of different cultures that might be at odds with each other in terms of a number of proposed aspirations and models of behaviour. Sometimes participation in one community can be refused because of one's belonging to another community; from a Marxist point of view, for example, workers' solidarity opposes national identities, which would undermine it. A parallel argument has been used in relation to women. For instance, the writer Virginia Woolf (1882–1941) declared, 'as a woman, I have no country'. These words appear in the third part of her *Three Guineas*, written by Woolf in 1938 in reply to a letter from the secretary of an anti-fascist association in which he asked her to do something to prevent the coming war (that is, the Second World War). Note that in this extract Woolf uses the term England as a synecdoche for the United Kingdom as a whole.

When he [a man] says, as history proves that he has said, and may say again, 'I am fighting to protect our country' and thus seeks to rouse her patriotic emotion, she [a woman] will ask herself, 'What does "our country" mean to me an outsider?' To decide this she will analyse the meaning of patriotism in her own case. She will inform herself of the position of her sex and her class in the past. She will inform herself of the amount of land, wealth and property in the possession of her own sex and class in the present – how much of 'England' in fact belongs to her. From the same sources she will inform herself of the legal protection which the law has given her in the past and now gives her. And if he adds that he is fighting to protect her body, she will reflect upon the degree of physical protection that she now enjoys when the words 'Air Raid Precaution' are written on blank walls. And if he says that he is fighting to protect England from foreign rule, she will reflect that for her there are no 'foreigners', since by law she becomes a foreigner if she marries a foreigner. And she will do her best to make this a fact, not by forced fraternity, but by human sympathy. All these facts will convince her reason (to put it in a nutshell) that her sex and class has very little to thank England for in the past; not much to thank England for in the present; while the security of her person in the future is highly dubious. But probably she will have imbibed, even from the governess, some romantic notion that Englishmen, those fathers and grandfathers whom she sees marching in the picture of history, are 'superior' to the men of other countries. This she will consider it her duty to check by comparing French historians with English; German with French; the testimony of the ruled – the Indians or the Irish, say – with the claims made by their rulers. Still some 'patriotic' emotion, some ingrained belief in the intellectual superiority of her own country over other countries may remain. Then she will compare English painting with French painting; English music with German music; English literature with Greek literature, for translations abound. When all these comparisons have been faithfully made by the use of reason, the outsider will find herself in possession of very good reasons for her indifference. She will find that she has no good reason to ask her brother to fight on her behalf to protect 'our' country. '"Our country,"' she will say, 'throughout the greater part of its history has treated me as a slave; it has denied me education or any share in its possessions. "Our" country still ceases to be mine if I marry a foreigner. "Our" country denies me the means of protecting myself, forces me to pay others a very large sum annually to protect me, and is so little able, even so, to protect me that Air Raid precautions are written on the wall. Therefore if you insist upon fighting to protect me, or "our" country, let it be understood, soberly and rationally between us, that you are fighting to gratify a sex instinct which I cannot share; to procure benefits which I have not shared and probably will not share; but not to gratify my instincts, or to protect either myself or my country. For,' the outsider will say, 'in fact, as a woman, I have no country. As a woman I want no country. As a woman my country is the whole world.' And if, when reason has said its say, still some obstinate emotion remains, some love of England dropped into a child's ears by the cawing of rooks in an elm tree, by the splash of waves on a beach, or by English voices murmuring nursery rhymes, this drop of pure, if irrational, emotion she will make serve her to give England first what she desires of peace and freedom for the whole world.

(Woolf [1938] 1977, pp. 195–8)

EXERCISE _____

1   Why, for Woolf, do women not have, and should not have, a national identity? Do you share her view?

2   Woolf wrote this text in 1938: does her argument still apply to contemporary society?

DISCUSSION _____

1   Woolf's main argument is contained in the lines '"Our country" ... throughout the greater part of its history has treated me as a slave'. In other words, women should not have a sense of loyalty towards institutions that they were not allowed to build or influence, and that sanction or promote their marginality. Woolf expands her argument to show the absurdity of the sense of superiority on which she thinks any nationalism is based.

2   It could be argued that since these words were written the position of women in the UK has changed greatly, and that women today may think that they 'own' the country where they were born much more than they did in Woolf's time. Their access to education (especially), and to the professions has never been so open. On the other hand, despite the vastly improved opportunities there are very few women in positions of power, in government, the judiciary, or management in industry and finance, not to mention senior ranks of the military.

Woolf attacks national sentiment and identity from the point of view of a gender identity. This is an example of the deployment of identity as a political argument in the context of social critique. Marginal or oppressed groups may argue, as Woolf does, that their identity is at odds, indeed in open conflict, with the world view and aspiration of the dominant group. This may lead to political action or civil disobedience. You might notice that when Woolf talks about 'being a woman' she implies a political consciousness of female identity. In other words, she does not claim that women actually have no national identity, or are not nationalistic, but that reflection on their identity would lead them to reject nationalism.

_____

I have already discussed how a particular conception of identity (Cartesian or Enlightenment identity) that pointed to a sense of self as a human being, without any other specific criteria, has been criticized on many fronts. All these various critiques uphold the notion that the Cartesian conception of identity erases social and cultural differences. The concept of identity employed in this book is that of the identification of one individual with a group and its culture. It should not be forgotten, though, that the shared identity within a group or community does not have the same meaning and value for all those who identify with it. Moreover, since each individual has more than one cultural identity, these various identities interact with and may change each other.

Figure 1.4 Clash of identities: in the foreground the policemen represent the state, while the demonstrators represent the women's movement. This was 1972, and the demonstrators had gone to support a woman who was being tried for having had an abortion when this was still illegal in France (the 'Bobigny trial'). The gender identity of the 1970s women's movement was a political one: it meant fighting for women's rights. Many women did not share this identity. As you can see in the photograph, however, there were some men who supported the women's struggle. Note that the state is wholly represented by men. Photo: Rex Features

Why has identity become so central in the modern world? Some possible explanations are considered below.

The multiplicity of identities in the modern world

Identity has become central in modern times precisely because of the multiplicity of models and choices offered to the individual. In traditional societies the identity of an individual is not regarded as something that she or he constructs, but to a certain extent as something acquired at birth; changes of identity, for instance from adolescence to adulthood, do not depend on the individual's choice – they are clear-cut, and often marked and thus objectified by a rite of passage. Today, however, a much wider range of real or imagined lives is now open to an individual. In modern societies children no longer automatically follow the same occupation as their parents; women can choose whether or not to have children; adults can to a certain extent exercise choices about their religion, sexuality, education, habitation, leisure activities, dress and grooming, and so on. Certainly, 'equality of opportunities' is generally more of a slogan than a reality even in the wealthy societies of the west. However, if you compare the choices available to you with those you would have had if you had lived even one century ago, the difference is clear.

Not only are social roles less fixed than in the past, but people also have access to a multiplicity of personal stories offered by the media. Through newspapers, magazines, radio, television, cinema and the internet you can obtain information about people you would not otherwise have met or known about. Many different lifestyles are presented through these media, one alongside the other. Throughout history people have always migrated from one area to another, but today the speed and relatively low cost of transport have also made it possible to visit far-away places and people without permanently uprooting yourself from your home. More dramatically, the information technology revolution has made physical proximity unnecessary for the fast exchange of information. Individuals are able to question their own identity in relation to these other identities, which are seen not necessarily as 'other' but possibly as alternative suggestions or models. For instance, the young daughter of farmers might aspire to become a pop singer, even though she has never met one personally. She will have seen a great number of pop singers on television, read about them in magazines and perhaps seen some of them perform. Similarly, a stockbroker living in a major European city might decide that city life is too much for him and so move to the countryside, or to rural India for a life of meditation (of course India has large, modern cities, but many Europeans will have seen it represented only as a place of ancient ways of living).

According to the sociologist Anthony Giddens, this awareness of different identities, and of the possibility of changing one's own, has led to individuals reflecting on their own identities. He argues that 'the altered self has to be explored and constructed as part of a reflexive process of connecting personal and social change' (Giddens, 1991, p. 32). He supports his claim of modern people's **reflexivity** on 'what they are' with reference to the increasing recourse to therapy, or to self-help manuals. These encourage patients/readers to analyse their behaviour, feelings, desires and so on, in order to change their self. For Giddens, the diffusion of pedagogical theories and the recourse to child psychologists or educators are further proofs of reflexivity.

The wealth of real or often only hypothetical opportunities with which the individual is presented could be destabilizing, as it creates

'Reflexivity is the process of referring back to oneself ... Reflexivity refers to the human ability to think of and refer to ourselves as if we were someone else. The statement "I like myself", for example, is reflexive because I am both the subject of the verb and its object and thereby refer to myself just as I might to someone else, as in "I like Nora". Reflexivity is a crucial human ability that [according to some sociological theories] makes possible the development of the self and the ability to participate in social life in relation to others' (Johnson, 2000, pp. 255–6). Note, however, that Michel Foucault thought that reflexivity (as expressed in the human sciences) was only a short episode in the history of knowledge.

a loss of certainty and calls for difficult, even impossible, choices. The loss of one well-defined identity has been expressed often in recent European literature and art, especially in the first decades of the twentieth century. Luigi Pirandello (1867–1936), Sicilian novelist and playwright, put at the centre of virtually all his works the theme of the loss of such an identity. Pirandello's characters lose their individuality in the realization of the virtually infinite multiplicity of identities. In one of his plays, *Six Characters in Search of an Author*, one character expresses this feeling quite plainly:

> Think of yourself as you once were, sir, and the illusions that you had, the way you saw the world around you and inside you! That *was* the world for you, in those days, sir! Now, thinking back on those lost illusions, on all that vanished seeming world which once was the world for you, don't you feel something give way beneath your feet, not just these boards but the very ground of your existence? Knowing that in just the same way the 'you' of today, which feels like reality here and now, is destined to seem an illusion tomorrow?

(Pirandello [1921] 1988, p. 57)

Antonio Gramsci (1891–1937) (politician, philosopher and contemporary of Pirandello) commented on Pirandello's perspective by saying that his work was the application of the dialectic of modern philosophy against the 'objective reality' of what he called 'the Aristotelian–Catholic world-view' (Gramsci [1930–2] 1975, p. 705). Gramsci meant that Pirandello represented reality as the fluid result of interactions between ideas, points of view and people, rather than as ordered and immutable. Pirandello, however, went decisively down the road of **relativism** (much more than Gramsci approved of), by dispensing altogether with any objective version of reality: for him, each version of the self, relative to a particular point of view and moment, was equally valid. In this way, Pirandello completely destabilized the subject. The reading below is taken from the beginning of his novel *One, No One and One Hundred Thousand*, originally written in 1913 but published in 1926. In this extract the protagonist, Moscarda, starts to wonder who he is.

Relativism is the view according to which there are no universal truths. Any truth is then *relative* to certain premises, culture or point of view. In Pirandello any account of the self is relative to a specific point of view; consequently there is no 'true self'.

Book One

I   My wife and my nose

'What are you doing?' my wife asked, seeing me linger, unusually, in front of the mirror.

'Nothing,' I replied. 'Just looking at myself, at my nose, here, inside this nostril. When I press it, I feel a little pain.'

My wife smiled and said: 'I thought you were looking to see which way it tilts.'

I wheeled around like a dog whose tail has been stepped on.

'Tilts? My nose?'

And my wife said, serenely: 'Of course, dear. Take a good look. It tilts to the right.'

I was twenty-eight years old, and until then I had always considered my nose – if not actually handsome – at least quite decent, like all the other parts of my person generally. So it was easy for me to accept and assert what is usually accepted and asserted by all those who haven't had the misfortune of being given a deformed body: namely, that it is foolish to be vain about one's own features. Hence the sudden and unexpected discovery of this flaw irritated me, like an undeserved punishment.

Perhaps my wife saw much deeper into that annoyance of mine and she added at once that, if I had the reassuring notion that I was without defects, I could dispel the thought because, not only did my nose tilt to the right, but also –

'What else?'

Oh, lots of other things! My eyebrows stood over my eyes like two circumflex accents, ^^ my ears were badly placed, one protruded more; and there were other shortcomings ...

'Other – ?'

Yes, other ones; my hands, the little finger; and my legs (no, not actually crooked, the right one a bit more curved than the left: just a little, at the knee). After a careful examination, I had to acknowledge the existence of all these defects. And finally my wife, surely mistaking for grief and dejection the wonder I felt, immediately after my irritation, sought to console me, telling me not to take it to heart since, even with these flaws, all things considered, I was still a good-looking man.

Who wouldn't be irritated, on receiving as a generous concession what had previously been denied him as a right? I blurted out a venomous 'thanks' and, sure of having no cause for grief or for dejection, I attached no importance to those slight defects, but a great, exceptional importance to the fact that I had lived all these years, without ever changing noses, always with that one, and those eyebrows, and those ears, those hands, and those legs; it wasn't till I had taken a wife that I found out that these were all defective.

'Why so surprised?! We know all about wives! They were born to discover their husband's defects.'

Mm, yes, wives: I agree. But I, too, if I may say so, was made to plunge, at every word addressed to me, at every gnat I saw flying, into abysses of reflection and consideration that burrowed deep inside me and hollowed my spirit up, down, and across, like the lair of a mole, with nothing evident on the surface.

'Obviously,' you say, 'you had a great deal of spare time.'

Well, no. It was my nature. But for that matter, true, it was also my idleness, I admit. Rich, I had two faithful friends, Sebastiano Quantorzo and Stefano Firbo, to handle my affairs after the death of my father, who, though he tried in every way, had never succeeded in making me accomplish anything; except taking a wife, of course, when I was very young; perhaps in the hope that I might soon have a son who wouldn't resemble me in the least; but, poor man, he wasn't able to obtain even this from me.

Not, mind you, that I had any objection to following the path on which my father set my feet. I followed all paths. But when it came to advancing, I wouldn't advance. I would pause at every step; I took care to circle every pebble I encountered, first distantly, then more closely; and I was quite amazed that others could pass ahead of me paying no heed to that pebble, which for me, meanwhile, had assumed the proportions of an insuperable mountain, or rather, a world where I could easily have settled.

I had remained arrested like that at the first steps of so many paths, my spirit filled with worlds – or pebbles: it's the same thing. But I never felt that those who had gone past me and had covered the whole length of the path actually knew any more than I did. They had passed ahead of me, no doubt about that, and they were all foaming at the mouth like so many horses; but then, at the end of the path, they had found a cart, their cart; they had hitched themselves to it with great patience, and now they were pulling it along. I wasn't pulling any cart, no, not I; and so I had neither reins nor blinders; I saw certainly more than they; but as for moving ahead, I didn't know where to go.

Now, to get back to the discovery of those slight defects, I plunged totally, immediately, into the reflection – was this possible? – that I didn't know well even my own body, my most personal possessions: nose, ears, hands, legs. And I began looking at them again, to re-examine them.

This was the beginning of my sickness. The sickness that would quickly reduce me to conditions of spirit and body so wretched and desperate that I would surely have died of them or gone mad, if I had not found in the sickness itself (as I will tell) the remedy that was to cure me of it ...

VIII So?

So, nothing. Just this. And doesn't it seem like a lot to you? Here is a first list of the ruinous reflections and the terrible conclusions derived from the innocent, brief satisfaction my wife Dida chose to give herself. I mean, by pointing out to me that my nose tilted to the right.

Reflections:

1st – that I was not for others what I had till then believed I was for myself;

2nd – that I could not see myself live;

3rd – that, being unable to see myself live, I remained an outsider to myself, namely one whom the others could see and know, each in his own way; and I couldn't;

4th – that it was impossible for me to confront this outsider, to see him and know him; I could see myself, but could not see him;

5th – that my body, if I observed it from outside, was for me like a dream apparition; something that didn't know it was living, and stayed there, waiting for someone to take it;

6th – that, just as I took this body of mine to be on occasion as I wanted myself and as I felt myself, so it could be taken by anyone else who would give it a reality in his own fashion;

7th – that finally this body in itself was so much a nothing and a nobody that a puff of air could make it sneeze, today, and carry it off tomorrow.

There were, for the moment, these two conclusions:

1st – that I began at last to understand why my wife Dida called me Gengè;

2nd – that I decided to discover who I was at least for those closest to me, my so-called acquaintances, and to amuse myself by dismantling spitefully the me that I was for them.

Book Two ...

VII   A parenthesis, necessary for all

Marco di Dio and his wife Diamante had the misfortune of being (if I remember rightly) my first victims. I mean, the first designated for the experiment of the destruction of a Moscarda.

But what gives me the right to talk about it? What right have I to give an aspect and a voice to others outside myself? What do I know of them? How can I talk about them? I see them from outside and, naturally, as they are for me, that is to say, in a form in which they surely would not recognize themselves. And am I not doing to others the same wrong of which I complain so? Yes, of course; but with one little difference: the fixations I mentioned at the beginning; that certain way in which each wants himself, constructing himself this way or that, according to how he sees himself and sincerely believes himself to be, not only for himself, but also for the others. A presumption, in any case, for which the penalty must be paid.

But you still refuse to give up, I know, and you exclaim: 'What about the facts? For God's sake, aren't there the facts?'

'Yes, there are.'

To be born is a fact. To be born in one period rather than another ... and of this or that father, and in this or that condition; to be born male or female; in Lapland or in central Africa; and handsome or ugly; with a hump or without: *facts*. And if you lose an eye, it's a fact; and you can even lose both, and if you're a painter it's the worst fact that can happen to you.

Time, space: necessity. Fate, fortune, chance: all snares of life. You want to be, eh? There's this catch: in abstract, you cannot just be. The being must be trapped in a form, and for some time it has to stay in it, here or there, this way or that. And every thing, as long as it lasts, bears the penalty of its form, the penalty of being this way and of no longer being able to be otherwise. That freak there seems a jest, a joke that can be tolerated perhaps for a minute, and then no more; then up he'll get, erect, quick, agile, tall ... But no! He will always be like that, for a whole life, and we only live once, and he has to resign himself to spending all, all of it like that.

And as it is with forms, so it is with actions.

When an act has been performed, it's that; it can no longer be changed. When a man, however, has acted, even if afterwards he doesn't feel or find himself in the actions performed, what he has done remains: like a prison for him. If you have taken a wife, or more materially, if you have stolen and been discovered; if you have killed, the consequences of your action enfold you like coils and tentacles; and on you, around you, like thick, stifling air, hangs the responsibility you have assumed for those actions and their consequences, unwanted, unforeseen. And how can you then free yourself?

All right. But what do you mean by this? That acts, like forms, determine my reality or yours? And how? Why? They are a prison: no one can deny that. But if you want to assert only this, take care not to assert anything against me, because I say and affirm exactly that: they are a prison and the most unjust prison imaginable.

Good heavens, I thought I had proved this to you! I know X. According to my knowledge of him, I assign X a reality: for myself. But you also know X, and surely the one you know isn't the same one I know, because we each know him in our way and, in our way, we assign X a reality. Now also for himself X has as many realities as the people he knows, because he knows himself in one way with me and in another with you and another with a third, or a fourth, and so on. Which means that X is really one for me, one for you, another for a third, another for a fourth, and so on, though he –

more than anybody else – also has the illusion of being one for all. This is the problem; or the joke, if you prefer to call it that. We perform an act. We believe in good faith to be all in that act. We realize unfortunately that this is not so, and that the act, on the contrary, is always and only performed by the one of the many things we are or can be, and then, through a most unfortunate circumstance, we suddenly remain as if hooked and suspended: we realize, I mean, that we are not all in that act, and therefore it would be a horrible injustice to judge us from that alone, to keep us hooked and suspended from it, pilloried, for an entire existence, as if this were all summed up in that single act.

'But I am also this, and this other, and this other still!' we start shouting.

Many others, ah, yes; so many who were not included in the act of that one, and who had nothing or very little to do with it. And, besides, that one self, that reality we gave ourself in one moment and performed the act, often has totally vanished a moment later; so the memory of the act remains in us, if it does remain, as an anguished, inexplicable dream. Another, ten others, all those others that we are or can be, rise one by one in us to ask how we could have done this; and we are no longer able to explain it.

Past realities.

If the facts are not so serious, these past realities we call undeceivings. Yes, agreed; because truly every reality is a deceit. That same deceit that now makes me say to you that you have another in front of you.

'You're mistaken!'

We are very superficial, you and I. We don't delve deeply into the joke, which is more profound and rooted, dear friends. And it consists in this: the human being acts necessarily through forms, the appearances he creates for himself, to which we give the value of reality. A value that changes, naturally, according to how the being appears to us, in that form, in that act.

And it must always necessarily seem to us that the others are mistaken, thinking that a given form, a given act is not this and is not thus. But inevitably, a little later, if we shift one degree, we realize we were also mistaken, and it isn't this and it isn't thus; so in the end we are obliged to recognize that it will never be this or thus in any stable, sure way; but first one way, then another, and at a certain point all will seem to us mistaken, or all true, which amounts to the same thing; because a reality wasn't assigned to us and doesn't exist, and we have to make it ourselves, if we want to be: and it will never be one for all, one forever, but continuously and infinitely changeable. The capacity for deluding ourselves that today's reality is the only true one, on the one hand, sustains us,

> but on the other, it plunges us into an endless void, because today's reality is destined to prove delusion for us tomorrow; and life doesn't conclude. It can't conclude. Tomorrow if it concludes, it's finished.
>
> (Pirandello [1926] 1990, pp. 3–5, 21–2, 59–63)

EXERCISE

How does Pirandello represent Moscarda's loss of identity?

Why do the 'one hundred thousand' versions of oneself amount to 'no one', as the title suggests?

Do you think Pirandello's relativism is extreme?

DISCUSSION

Moscarda's problem consists in the realization, sparked by his wife's remark about his nose, that our identity is different for different people, and that we have no control over other people's representations of us. Moscarda sets out to 'kill' all the other versions of himself. Yet he finds that this task is not only impossible, it is also useless – for Moscarda realizes that even he does not perceive himself as one, but rather as different selves depending on circumstances, moments and the people with whom he interacts. In this sense in Pirandello's presentation identity is not just the result of interaction with other people, but indeed consists in other people's view of our identity. Thus it is not the case that Moscarda has a well-defined identity, which is variously interpreted by other people; rather, the way he represents himself is linked to the role he is playing at any given moment (husband, friend, whatever). There is no real Moscarda beyond and above the many versions of him that exist for other people. He is not one, but one hundred thousand; to be one hundred thousand individuals, however, amounts to being no one in particular. Moscarda illustrates the condition of the modern person who has lost a traditional world view which supported his or her sense of self, and has found one hundred thousand possibilities open to him or her. The result of this modern 'reflexivity' seems to be displacement, confusion and ultimately madness.

In works such as those of Pirandello, the self loses its identity in the sense of sameness: it is fragmented, for it can no longer be said to be one, always identical to itself; and it is confused, for it has lost its reflexive sense of being one as different from others.

Local identities as a reaction to modernity?

If, on the one hand, people's choices of lifestyle, work and education appear to have dramatically increased, on the other the fast exchanges of information and goods around the world are narrowing differences between the lifestyles to which individuals aspire. In other words, although sharp economic differences make certain goods or lifestyles easily achievable for some individuals and impossible for others, they still cross borders. Moreover, in a very broad sense, globalization is not a new phenomenon, in either institutional or cultural terms. Structures such as Christianity, Islam, Buddhism, colonial administrations, transnational corporations and world banking have always been global; trade, travel, migration and the cultural exchanges that go with them have always existed. However, in the last few decades the trend has accelerated dramatically. This is perhaps most obvious in the globalization of popular culture, including music, cinema and television, fashion and body language (during the 2000 Olympic games Chinese gymnasts, when satisfied with their performance, would exchange the 'high-five', which was originally an Afro-American greeting). Industries have also become global, so that one can be a Ford employee in the US, Germany, the UK or India, for example.

According to such sociologists as Alain Touraine and Manuel Castells, it is precisely this sense of cultural homogeneity that encourages individuals to seek their own specificity in more local, or 'old', cultural identities. In this view, the distance between increasingly globalized centres of power and the individual who does not belong to the elite has become progressively wider. Civil society, seen as a place of mediation between the private citizen and state institutions, is disappearing (Castells, 1997, pp. 11ff). Touraine claims that it has become increasingly difficult in a globalized society to conceive of oneself wholly as a citizen, a worker, or a parent. He argues:

> Under these conditions, individuals are either reduced to being mosaics of behavioural patterns that are so diverse that they cannot generate any unitary personal principle, or seek that unity in a cultural heritage, a language, a memory, a religion or even libido which is as impersonal as a culture, but which does supply a principle around which a personality can be built. Hence the central paradox of our society: at the very time when the economy is being globalised and transformed rapidly by new technologies, the personality is no longer being projected into the future, and is looking, on the contrary, to the past or to an historical desire for support.
>
> (Touraine, 2000, p. 39)

Figure 1.5 At the annual Braemar Highland Gathering, Braemar, Scotland, 2000. Traditional dress is worn in order to assert and express local identity. Globalization is never far away, though: note the Tesco carrier bag on the right-hand side. Photo: Scotland in Focus

Castells uses very similar terms to locate the upswelling of nationalisms, religious fundamentalisms, and a range of new identities founded on ethnicity and local history, heritage and language.

Identity building

The historical character of identities

Identities are not social roles or indeed activities. Most people would not describe being 'computer users' as an identity, however important the use of computers is in their lives (although to be a hacker dedicated to the sabotage of multinational corporations may well be). For one person to be a parent may be a social role; for another it could be an identity, if being a parent is an important self-definition for him. When a certain behaviour or activity becomes an identity, it is perceived either as permanent, or very difficult to change. We can envisage even radical changes in our behaviour, preferences, job, the language we speak on a daily basis, the country we reside in and our passport. By contrast, if we 'are' heterosexual or homosexual, town or country people, intellectuals or manual workers, English or Portuguese, it seems more difficult to change and become something else. This does not mean that identities are in fact immutable, but only that they are often perceived as such, especially with regard to other people. National stereotypes rest on the assumption that there is something intrinsic about being, say, German or Greek, which not only accrues to all members of that 'community' but is also permanent in time. However, generally people would not accept being reduced to a national stereotype constructed by others.

Both personal and collective identities are subject to evolution and change. Moreover, cultural identities are not inscribed once and for all: they emerge in specific times and places; they develop, change and can disappear. To be a knight at the service of one's sovereign might well once have been a powerful identity, but this notion has now disappeared.

Identities that might appear to many people as timeless are in fact relatively recent, and by no means universal. The view of childhood as a way of being, as it were, rather than just a stage on the road to adulthood and therefore in a sense incomplete, is a modern phenomenon. Even more recent is the development of the teenage identity, complete with a specific lifestyle, outlook on life and possession of certain consumer goods. In other times, this specific phase between childhood and adulthood did not exist.

The writer Colin MacInnes has celebrated the emergence of teenage identity in 1950s London in *Absolute Beginners*. The following reading is taken from the beginning of this novel.

In June

It was with the advent of the Laurie London era that I realized the whole teenage epic was tottering to doom.

'Fourteen years old, that absolute beginner,' I said to the Wizard as we paused casually in the gramophone section to hear Little Laurie in that golden disc performance of his.

'From now on,' said Wizard, 'he's certainly Got The Whole World In His Hands.'

We listened to the wonder boy's nostrils spinning on.

'They buy us younger every year,' I cried. 'Why, Little Mr L.'s voice hasn't even dropped yet, so who will those tax-payers try to kidnap next?'

'Sucklings,' said Wizard.

We climbed the white stair to the glass garden under the top roof of the department store, and came out on the glorious panorama, our favourite rendezvous.

I must explain the Wiz and I never came to this store to buy anything except, as today, a smoke-salmon sandwich and ice coffee. But in the first place, we have the opportunity to see the latest furnishings and fabrics, just like some married couple, and also to have the splendid outlook over London, the most miraculous I know in the whole city, and quite unknown to other nuisance-values of our age, in fact to everyone, it seems, except these elderly female Chelsea peasants who come up there for their elevenses.

Looking north you don't see much, it's true, and westward the view's entirely blocked up by the building you're inside. But twisting slowly on your bar stool from the east to south, like Cinerama, you can see clean new concrete cloud-kissers, rising up like felixes from the Olde Englishe squares, and then those gorgeous parks, with trees like classical French salads, and then again the port life down along the Thames, that glorious river, reminding you we're on an estuary, a salt inlet really, with crazy seagulls circling up from it and almost bashing their beaks against the circular plate glass, and then, before you know it, you're back again round a full circle in front of your iced coffee cup.

'Laurie L.,' I said, ''s a sign of decadence. This teenage thing is getting out of hand.'

The Wiz looked wise, like the middle feller of the three old monkeys.

'It's not the tax-payers,' he said, 'who are responsible. It's the kids themselves, for buying the EPs these elderly sordids bribe the teenage nightingales to wax.'

'No doubt,' I said, for I know better than ever to argue with the Wizard, or with anyone else who gets his kicks from an idea.

Mr Wiz continued, masticating his salmon sandwich for anyone to see. 'It's been a two-way twist, this teenage party. Exploitation of the kiddos by the conscripts, and exploitation of themselves by the crafty little absolute beginners. The net result? "Teenager"'s become a dirty word or, at any rate, a square one.'

I smiled at Mr W. 'Well, take it easy, son,' I said, 'because a sixteen year old sperm like you has got a lot of teenage living still to do. As for me, eighteen summers, rising nineteen, I'll very soon be out there among the oldies.'

The Wizard eyed me with his Somerset Maugham appearance. 'Me, boy,' he said, 'I tell you. As things are, I won't regret it when the teenage label's torn off the arse pockets of my drip-dry sky-blue jeans.'

What the Wiz said was at any rate partially true. This teenage ball had had a real splendour in the days when the kids discovered that, for the first time since centuries of kingdom-come, they'd money, which hitherto had always been denied to us at the best time in life to use it, namely, when you're young and strong, and also before the newspapers and telly got hold of this teenage fable and prostituted it as conscripts seem to do to everything they touch. Yes, I tell you, it had a real savage splendour in the days when we found that no one couldn't sit on our faces any more because we'd loot to spend at last, and our world was to be our world, the one we wanted and not standing on the doorstep of somebody else's waiting for honey, perhaps.

I got off my stool and went and stood by the glass of that tottering old department store, pressed up so close it was like I was out there in the air, suspended over space above the city, and I swore by Elvis and all the saints that this last teenage year of mine was going to be a real rave. Yes, man, come whatever, this last year of the teenage dream I was out for kicks and fantasy.

But my peace was shattered by the noise I heard of Wizard in an argument with the conscript behind the counter bar.

I should explain the Wiz has for all oldies just the same kind of hatred psychos have for Jews or foreigners or coloureds, that is, he hates everyone who's not a teenager, except for short-pant sperms and chicklets, whom I suppose he regards as teenagers in bud. The Wiz just doesn't like the population outside the teenage bracket, and takes every chance he gets to make the oldies conscious of their hair-root dyes, and sing out aloud the anthem of the teenage triumph.

Wiz has the art of clawing the poor tax-payers on the raw. Even from where I stood I saw the barman's face was lurid as a point steak, and as I approached I heard that sharp, flat, dry little voice the Wizard has, was needling him with, 'Oh, I suppose you're underpaid, boy, that's what's the matter with you. Don't like your work up here with these old hens.'

'You'd best settle up and op it,' said the conscript.

The Wizard turned to me. '"Op it," he says – just listen! This serf speaks authentic old-tyme *My Fair Lady* dialect.'

The Wizard's tactic always was to tempt the enemy to strike him which, because he's small, and seems so slender and so juvenile, arouses sympathy of other oldsters, the born aunts among them especially, who take his side and split the anti-teenage camp wide open. He often succeeds, because I can tell you he's completely fearless, a thoroughly vicious, dirty little pugilist, and only fails when sometimes they laugh at him, which makes him beside himself with rage.

The present argument, as I expected, was about the bill, which Wizard, when he's in the mood, will query even if it's for an item like a cup of tea. And often, even when he's loaded, he'll make out he's completely skint and say to them well, there you are, I've got no money, what you going to do about it? And this with the left breast pocket of his Continental casual jacket stuffed with notes and even visible, but his face so fierce and come-and-kill-me that it frightens them, and even me. It usually seems to work, because they say get to hell out, which he does in his own time, and at his own speed, as if it was an eight course meal he'd had and paid for, not just bounced a bill.

I paid for him, and Wiz didn't mind my paying, only laughed that little ha-ha laugh of his as we walked down the white and silver metal stair. 'Boy,' he said, 'you're a born adult number. With your conventional outlook, you just can't wait to be a family man.'

I was vexed at him, but answered, 'Don't be like that, Wizard. We all know you're loaded, so why do you play that kindergarten game?'

Which is a fact, I mean his being loaded, because the Wiz, in spite of his tender years, is, for his age, the number one hustler of the capital, his genius being in introducing A to B, or *vice versa*, that is to say, if someone has an article to sell, and someone else desires it, Wiz has a marvellous instinct for meeting them both and bringing them together. But, you might answer, that's what shops are for, which is exact. But not for exchanging the sort of article the Wizard's customers are interested in which, as you've guessed, are not so legal, and when I say 'article', I mean it may be the kind of services which might make you call the Wiz a pimp, or a procurer if you wanted to, not that it would worry him particularly.

(MacInnes, 1959, pp. 9–13)

EXERCISE _____

1   Do you agree that young people did not have a specific cultural identity before the 1950s or 1960s? If you are not old enough to compare your pre-1960s experience with that of young people nowadays, you might want to ask somebody older and compare lifestyles. You might also want, if you can (and have the time), to watch 1940s and 1950s films and observe how adolescents are represented, what clothes they wear and what activities they engage in.

2   Does existence of this identity differentiate Europe from other areas?

DISCUSSION _____

1   You might find that before the 1950s, and in many places the 1960s, adolescents were represented more as children or as young adults, rather than as having a specific identity. You might also find that they were much less of a focus of attention for film-makers; and that they were not specifically targeted as consumers of products, from fashion to magazines and literature.

2   We cannot say that teenage culture is specifically European. The United States is an important model here, while young Japanese people, for example, also participate in this culture, which is becoming more and more global. However, a teenage culture implies that young people get married and start working relatively late, and that they have enough money to buy consumer goods, as pointed out in the extract from _Absolute Beginners_. In other words, the possibility of being a teenager is linked to economic expansion and is probably lacking or less marked in poorer countries. However, a detailed study might reveal regional differences in the teenage identity as in any other identity, depending on the other identities with which it interacts and on specific social circumstances.

_____

I now turn to another identity present in Europe: black identity. The idea that human beings could be distinguished as different 'races' on the basis of somatic, or physical, differences emerged at the beginning of the nineteenth century. Before then the term 'race' indicated a familial unity of the ruling class and had no connections with physical characteristics. This does not mean that there were no strong ideas of human inequalities between peoples, but there was no 'scientific' classification of human groups based on somatic traits. Nowadays, biologically human beings are regarded as all part of just one race. However, the term 'race' is still used to indicate groups of human beings, and identities connected with 'race', such as black identity, play an important role in modern societies. It is important not to confuse social and cultural identities with biological ones. This confusion is very common. Colette Guillaumin, author of *Racism, Sexism, Power and Ideology*, a study on the construction of racist and sexist ideologies, reports that a scientist 'recently' (presumably in the early 1990s) stated that sickle cell anaemia is 'a (genetic) trait ... specific to Blacks, but strangely enough it is also found in India, among white people' (quoted in Guillaumin, 1995, p. 83). (Incidentally, sickle cell anaemia is also common around the Mediterranean.) It is clear that this scientist unreflectively assumes that blacks (and whites) constitute a genetically homogeneous group, even though ironically his own research does not support such an idea. Who is black? Where does this category come from? Does the same person count as black in different countries, and in different social contexts? Let us reflect on these issues in the context of contemporary Britain.

In recent years there has been a debate around the use of the very term black in Britain, in particular over whether this term can be used to indicate persons of Asian descent (I use the term Asian here in the British sense, referring to people who trace their origins to present-day India, Pakistan, Bangladesh or Sri Lanka). The reading below, from Atvar Brah's *Cartographies of Diaspora*, provides a glimpse of such debate. This extract should be read as an illustration of the main topic of this section, which is that cultural identities emerge, develop, change and may disappear, and that this process depends on historical and social circumstances. In this reading you will also see how identities are shaped by political strategies. First, however, a few words about the author, who thought it was important to sketch her own biography in her book's introduction. Atvar Brah was born in Punjab. At the age of five she moved with her family to present-day Uganda or, as she puts it, 'what used to be known as British East Africa' (Brah, 1996, p. 1). She then went to the United States to pursue a university degree. Finding herself in Britain on her way to visit her family at the time when Asians were expelled from Uganda, she stayed. She now teaches at Birkbeck College, London.

What's in a Name? What's in a Colour?

Over the past few years the usage of the term 'black' to refer to people of African-Caribbean and South Asian descent in Britain has been the subject of considerable controversy. It is important to address some of these arguments, as they often centre around notions of 'difference'.

The African-Caribbean and South Asian people who migrated to Britain in the post-war period found themselves occupying a broadly similar structural position as workers performing predominantly unskilled or semi-skilled jobs on the lowest rungs of the economy. They were then commonly described in popular, political, and academic discourses as 'coloured people'. This was not a simple descriptive term. It had been the colonial code for a relationship of domination and subordination between the coloniser and the colonised. Now the code was re-worked and re-constituted in and through a variety of political, cultural and economic processes in post-war Britain. In other words, the African-Caribbean and Asian groups experienced the racialisation of their gendered class positioning through a racism which foregrounded their 'non-whiteness' as a common thematic within the discourse of 'coloured people'. Although the precise ways in which these heterogeneous sets of people were racialised were not identical, the condensation of the binary white/non-white in this discourse constructed equivalence and similarity of experience, as they faced racist practices of stigmatisation, inferiorisation, exclusion, and/or discrimination in arenas such as employment, education, housing, media, the criminal justice system, immigration apparatus, and the health services. These relations of equivalence created the conditions under which a new politics of solidarity became possible.

The concept of 'black' now emerges as a specifically political term embracing African-Caribbean and South Asian peoples. It constitutes a political subject inscribing politics of resistance against colour-centred racisms. The term was adopted by the emerging coalitions amongst African-Caribbean and South Asian organisations and activists in the late 1960s and 1970s. They were influenced by the way that the Black Power movement in the USA, which had turned the concept of 'black' on its head, divested it of its pejorative connotations in racialised discourses, and transformed it into a confident expression of an assertive group identity. The Black Power movement urged black Americans to construe the 'black community' not as a matter of geography but rather in terms of the global African diaspora. Eschewing 'chromatism' – the basis of differentiation amongst blacks according to lighter or darker tone of skin – 'black' became a political colour to be claimed with pride against colour-based racisms. The African-Caribbean and South Asian activists in Britain borrowed the term from the Black Power movement to foster a rejection of chromatism amongst those defined as 'coloured people' in Britain.

Class was an important constitutive element in the emergence of the concept of 'black' as a political colour. The project is best understood as part of the British New Left. A number of organisations active in this political movement defined themselves as workers' organisations; for instance, the Indian Workers Association and the Black Peoples Alliance. Major political publications of the period, such as *Race Today* and *Race and Class*, addressed the articulation between racism and class relations. The journal *Race and Class* is still going strong in the 1990s as a leading journal committed to challenging global racisms and class inequities. The new political subject produced by the politics of 'black' transformed class politics by interrogating political discourses which asserted the primacy of class.

The politics of solidarity between African-Caribbean and South Asian activists of the period were also influenced by the memory of recent anti-colonial struggles and decolonisation in Africa, Asia and the Caribbean. Some were also involved in the agitation against the war in Vietnam, the Campaign for Nuclear Disarmament, and other similar protest movements. The discourse of 'Afro-Asian' unity in Britain resonated with the call of anti-colonial liberation movements for unity among the colonised. Moreover, as Mercer (1994) argues, the sign 'black' was mobilised also as a displacement for the categories 'immigrant' and 'ethnic minority' which, throughout the 1960s and 1970s had come to denote racialised re-definitions of belonging and subjecthood. The fusion of these various influences in the formation of a project concerned to address the social condition of post-colonial experience in the heart of the British metropolis meant that the concept of 'black' has been associated with rather distinctive and somewhat different meanings in Britain as compared with the USA.

British usage of the term 'black' has been criticised by commentators like Hazareesingh (1986) and Modood (1988). They argue that the 'black' in Black Power ideology referred specifically to the historical experience of people of sub-Saharan African descent, and was designed to create a positive political and cultural identity among black Americans. When used in relation to South Asians the concept is *de facto* emptied of those specific cultural meanings associated with phrases such as 'black music'. The concept can incorporate South Asians in a political sense only, and they therefore conclude that it denies Asian cultural identity. Clearly there is some force in this argument. It is certainly the case, as we have already noted, that the Black Power movement's mobilisation of the term 'black' was an attempt to reclaim an African heritage that had been denied to black Americans by racism. But, as a historically specific political project located in the socio-political and economic dynamics in the USA, the Black Power ideology did not simply reclaim a pre-given ancestral past. In that very process, it also constructed a particular version of this heritage.

Given that cultural processes are dynamic, and the process of claiming is itself mediated, the term 'black' does not have to be construed in essentialist terms. It can have different political and cultural meanings in different contexts. Its specific meaning in post-war Britain cannot be taken to have denied cultural differences between African, Caribbean and South Asian people when cultural difference was not the organising principle within this discourse or political practice. The concrete political struggles in which the new meaning was grounded acknowledged cultural differences but sought to accomplish political unity against racism. In any case, the issue of cultural difference cannot be posed purely in terms of differences between South Asian and African-Caribbean cultures. There are, for example, many differences between African and Caribbean cultures (which also include the cultures of people of South Asian descent). Cultures in the diasporas always have their own specificity. In other words, even when the use of the term 'black' is restricted to sub-Saharan Africa and its diasporas, it can be said, within the parameters of the terms set by the critics, to deny the cultural specificities of these diverse groups ...

The point I wish to stress through this foray into the debate surrounding the use of the term 'black' in Britain is how 'difference' is constructed differently within these competing discourses. That is, the usage of 'black', 'Indian' or 'Asian' is determined not so much by the nature of its referent as by its semiotic function within different discourses. These various meanings signal differing political strategies and outcomes. They mobilise different sets of cultural or political identities, and set limits to where the boundaries of a 'community' are established. This debate has to an extent been echoed within feminism.

References

Hazareesingh, S. (1986) 'Racism and cultural identity: an Indian perspective', *Dragon's Teeth*, 24.

Mercer, K. (1994) *Welcome to the Jungle*, London: Routledge.

Modood, T. (1988) '"Black" racial equality and Asian identity', *New Community*, 14(3).

(Brah, 1996, pp. 96–99, 102)

EXERCISE _____

1   What changes has the term black undergone in Britain, according to Brah's account?

2   According to Brah, is black identity constructed in the same way in Britain and the US?

3   What, for Brah, determines the referent of the term black?

4   After answering the questions above, consider how, if at all, the reading addresses issues which have been discussed in this chapter so far, such as the historical character of identities and the relational character of identities.

Figure 1.6   The British comedy *Bahji on the Beach* shows the complex interactions of identities in individuals. Note the woman standing on the right-hand side: she lives in Britain and consciously expresses her Indian identity by wearing a sari. This is not necessary for her relative (wearing sunglasses), for she does not need to come to terms with migration: she lives in India and her style of dress is western. The younger Asian British women in the photograph are also in western dress. Another identity explored in the film is that of gender. The younger woman who has organized the trip sees it as an occasion to have some 'female fun'. Her feminist identity, however, cannot be shared by the older women. One of the younger women has a relationship with a young black man: from her perspective, he shares the cultural space she inhabits outside her home, but she is aware that for her parents he is the 'other' and definitely not a desirable prospective son-in-law. Photo: BFI Collections/Channel 4

DISCUSSION _____

1   In Brah's account, one can pick out three phases that the term
     black has undergone in Britain:

     ● immediately after the Second World War, indicating 'African-
        Caribbean and South Asian peoples' recently migrated to Britain;

     ● in the 1960s and 1970s, as a political term adopted by
        political organizations within the British new left, indicating
        African-Caribbean and South Asian peoples (in this sense,
        black identity was strictly connected with class identity);

     ● in recent years, when the term has become controversial as it
        has been criticized for its application to people who are not
        of African descent.

2   In the 1960s and 1970s black identity was adopted as a political
     identity in Britain after the example of the Black Power
     movement in the US. However, Brah claims that this 'constructed
     a particular version of [African] heritage'; she implies that in
     Britain black identity has acquired a different political and
     cultural meaning.

3   First of all, the term black acquired its meaning in the context of
     colonial domination: black people were the colonized and
     subordinate people. As part of their experience of migration, they
     came to occupy a similar social position ('on the lowest rungs of
     the economy'). People from different parts of the world and
     cultures found themselves in the category of black because of the
     binary distinction of white/non-white existing in Britain, and as a
     consequence had similar experiences of exclusion and
     discrimination. Historical, social and economic circumstances
     determined who was black. Later on, when this identity was
     vindicated by political movements, the referent did not change, as
     it referred to the same people, but its sense shifted; it became a
     positive identity, one that was chosen rather than imposed, and
     implying political projects. More recently, the word black may
     indicate either persons of African, Caribbean and Asian descent,
     or, more restrictively, persons of African or African-Caribbean
     descent, depending on different political views. In this extract
     from her book, Brah only offers a schematic account of how a
     diverse group of people came to be called black. As we know from
     her own biography, and as some of us may know from experience,
     not everyone who migrated either to Britain or to other European
     countries from outside the European continent really belonged
     'on the lowest rungs of society'. A minority belonged to the
     middle classes in their own countries; others were students, writers
     or artists. However, this difference would have hardly counted in
     terms of how white people regarded them. Moreover, some black

people have not migrated in recent times but belong to families who have been in Europe for many generations. However, they would all too often be identified as migrants.

4   The reading does address these themes. The historical character of identities is exemplified when Brah shows how black identity emerged at a certain time as a consequence of colonial relationships, and how its meaning has altered in recent decades because of social change and political action. She describes black identity as relational, for it was created by colonial relations between peoples and by economic relations between migrants and their host society. There also appears to be a reference to Foucault, in the final paragraph of the reading, when the usage of 'black', 'Indian' or 'Asian' is said to be determined by 'its semiotic function within different discourses'.

Models of production of identities

Despite the fact that identities are socially constructed, they can be 'naturalized'. In other words, they can be presented and felt as 'given' prior to any social construction. Following Stuart Hall (Hall, 1990), we can distinguish two models of the production of identities.

1   The first model assumes that there is something intrinsic, 'essential', to a particular identity. Proponents of the 'authentic' identity model deny the identity's social and historical construction. This model can be seen at work, for instance, in some versions of feminism and black nationalism. Struggle against an identity's negative image results in a reinterpretation which renders the identity positive.

2   The second model recognizes that identities are always incomplete, that they are in a constant process of formation and alteration. Moreover, this second model acknowledges that identities are always relational. This means that an identity defines itself in relation to other identities. With a change in circumstances and relation between identities, the identities will change as well. For example, gender identities are different nowadays compared with even a few decades ago, for social relations have changed. Analogously, they are not the same in different societies, or in different sectors of a society; for instance, they are different in fundamentalist Muslim, Jewish or Christian communities and in secular communities.

EXERCISE

From the individual's point of view, all cultural identities have to be *learned, performed and reproduced.* Nobody is born with a certain identity; an identity is not something abstract, but takes shape in interaction; and it has to be transmitted to others in order to survive. Reflect on your own cultural identities (for instance, you might regard your nationality, gender, occupation, political conviction or life outlook as important cultural identities). Try to trace a tentative, and by necessity very rough, history of it. Who performed the same type of identity when you were still growing up? How were cultural identities performed around you when you were young? For instance, if your chosen identity is your gender, you might want to reflect on how you learned gender roles, how you reflected on them (if you did) and how your gender affected your interaction with other people. Moreover, you might want to answer the question of how this identity links you with other individuals who share it. Some of these persons will also have identities which you do not share. In the example here, clearly you do not share all identities with all women (or all men) in the world. Does this make your own identity different from theirs? Is it the same to be a woman (or a man) in Edinburgh as it is in Kabul? Is it the same to be a heterosexual, homosexual or bisexual woman (or man)?

In the reading above from Woolf's *Three Guineas*, gender identity is not presented as something biological, but as social and political. Woolf emphasizes the disadvantageous social position that historically has led women to be indifferent to national sentiment. However, since Woolf's times the problematization of the categories of 'men' and 'women' has been greatly developed. One of the best-known theorists who have challenged traditional gender categories is Judith Butler. The reading below is the beginning of the piece anthologized as 'Subjects of sex/gender/desire', which is an extract from the introduction of Butler's book *Gender Trouble*, published in 1990.

(T)here is the political problem that feminism encounters in the assumption that the term *women* denotes a common identity. Rather than a stable signifier that commands the assent of those whom it purports to describe and represent, *women*, even in the plural, has become a troublesome term, a site of contest, a cause for anxiety. As Denise Riley's title suggests, *Am I That Name?* is a question produced by the very possibility of the name's multiple significations.[1] If one 'is' a woman, that is surely not all one is; the term fails to be exhaustive, not because a pregendered 'person' transcends the specific paraphernalia of its gender, but because gender is not always constituted coherently or consistently in different historical contexts, and because gender intersects with racial, class, ethnic, sexual, and regional modalities of discursively constituted identities. As a result, it becomes impossible to separate out 'gender' from the political and cultural intersections in which it is invariably produced and maintained.

The political assumption that there must be a universal basis for feminism, one which must be found in an identity assumed to exist cross-culturally, often accompanies the notion that the oppression of women has some singular form discernible in the universal or hegemonic structure of patriarchy or masculine domination. The notion of a universal patriarchy has been widely criticized in recent years for its failure to account for the workings of gender oppression in the concrete cultural contexts in which it exists. Where those various contexts have been consulted within such theories, it has been to find 'examples' or 'illustrations' of a universal principle that is assumed from the start. That form of feminist theorizing has come under criticism for its efforts to colonize and appropriate non-Western cultures to support highly Western notions of oppression, but because they tend as well to construct a 'Third World' or even an 'Orient' in which gender oppression is subtly explained as symptomatic of an essential, non-Western barbarism. The urgency of feminism to establish a universal status for patriarchy in order to strengthen the appearance of feminism's own claims to be representative has occasionally motivated the shortcut to a categorial or fictive universality of the structure of domination, held to produce women's common subjugated experience.

Although the claim of universal patriarchy no longer enjoys the kind of credibility it once did, the notion of a generally shared conception of 'women', the corollary to that framework, has been much more difficult to displace. Certainly, there have been plenty of debates: Is there some commonality among 'women' that preexists their oppression, or do 'women' have a bond by virtue of their oppression alone? Is there a specificity to women's cultures that is independent of their subordination by hegemonic, masculinist cultures? Are the specificity and integrity of women's

---

[1] See Denise Riley, *Am I That Name?: Feminism and the Category of 'Women' in History* (New York: Macmillan, 1988).

cultural or linguistic practices always specified against and, hence, within the terms of some more dominant cultural formation? If there is a region of the 'specifically feminine', one that is both differentiated from the masculine as such and recognizable in its difference by an unmarked and, hence, presumed universality of 'women'? The masculine/feminine binary constitutes not only the exclusive framework in which that specificity can be recognized, but in every other way the 'specificity' of the feminine is once again fully decontextualized and separated off analytically and politically from the constitution of class, race, ethnicity, and other axes of power relations that both constitute 'identity' and make the singular notion of identity a misnomer.[2](...)

Is the construction of the category of women as a coherent and stable subject an unwitting regulation and reification of gender relations? And is not such a reification precisely contrary to feminist aims? To what extent does the category of women achieve stability and coherence only in the context of the heterosexual matrix? If a stable notion of gender no longer proves to be the foundational premise of feminist politics, perhaps a new sort of feminist politics is now desirable to contest the very reifications of gender and identity, one that will take the variable construction of identity as both a methodological and normative prerequisite, if not a political goal.

(Butler [1990] 1997, pp. 278–9)

EXERCISE _____

Find in Butler's text passages that support, imply or contradict what you have read so far, either in the main text of this chapter or in the readings.

DISCUSSION _____

These are some of the possible examples.

1 'If one "is" a woman, that is surely not all one is; the term fails to be exhaustive, ... because gender intersects with racial, class, ethnic, sexual, and regional modalities of discursively constituted identities.' This claim supports what I have said about the fact that identities interact with one another and affect one another.

---

[2] See Sandra Harding, 'The Instability of the Analytical Categories of Feminist Theory', in Sandra Harding and Jean F. O'Barr (eds.), *Sex and Scientific Inquiry* (Chicago: University of Chicago Press, 1987), 283–302).

2   'Is the construction of the category of women as a coherent and stable subject an unwitting regulation and reification of gender relations?' This rhetorical question implies that identities (in this case gender identities) are constructed. Moreover, the implicit criticism of the view which sees identities as stable confirms what has been said, following Stuart Hall, about identities being in a constant process of formation and alteration.

3   The political assumption that there must be a universal basis for feminism, one which must be found in an identity assumed to exist cross-culturally, often accompanies the notion that the oppression of women has some singular form discernible in the universal or hegemonic structure of patriarchy or masculine domination. The notion of a universal patriarchy has been widely criticized in recent years for its failure to account for the workings of gender oppression in the concrete cultural contexts in which it exists.

Does this argument contradict Woolf's motto 'as a woman, I have no country'? Although Woolf talks only about 'English' women, she does not draw any distinction within this group (according to class, sexual orientation and so on). She indeed seems to assume a homogenous category of 'women'.

If identities are always constructed, through what processes are they formed? It can easily be seen that the 'material' with which identities are constructed varies. I shall propose here four elements that are very relevant in Europe to the formation of some cultural identities: history, geography, religion and language. These elements are particularly important for national and local identities and for those identities that are more comprehensive than national ones, such as European, central European or western identities.

History

History is often a powerful element in the construction of identities; the sense of a shared past or of a collective memory functions as a social cement. A community becomes like an individual, whose accumulated experience and memory make her what she is. In order for history to serve as identity-building material, a continuity between events in the past and the present state of affairs must be postulated or argued. The vindication of one's past contains a project for the future. This has been the common strategy of the construction of identities in Europe since the Renaissance: a continuity from ancient Greece, to ancient Rome, Renaissance Italy, Enlightenment France and so on has been constructed. In each country dominant representations have articulated strong links with a prestigious past, even if this past took place outside its geographical boundaries. It must be borne in mind that these representations vary from country to country because of different nationalist agendas. This lineage has also been adopted in the United States, where, for example, college courses in 'western civilization' retrace the European narratives and add American history at the end of it. In this context, the recent battle over ancient Egypt is interesting. Traditionally ancient Egypt has been conceived by Europeans as part of their own past, and the British Museum, the Louvre and hundreds of other large and small museums in Europe are full of objects brought from there. In recent decades, however, groups of African Americans have claimed ancient Egypt as their own past. The controversial work *Black Athena: the Afroasiatic Roots of Classical Civilisation* by Martin Bernal (Bernal, 1987) has given this enterprise an academic platform and indeed positioned African Egypt at the origins of Greek civilization.

An interesting example of how a national identity has been built on history is provided by Greece. Greek national identity has attracted the attention of scholars because it has been constructed on a distant past, that of ancient Greece, and largely on the image of it formed by outsiders. During the Renaissance, in western Europe ancient Greek culture was presented as the roots of European civilization. Whether there was a Greek identity in ancient Greece (as opposed to Athenian, Spartan, Theban identities) is a moot point. However, what is most interesting in the case of modern Greek identity is that by the time it started to take shape in the eighteenth century, continuity with ancient Greece had been severed several times, especially with the integration of Greece into the Ottoman empire (fifteenth century to 1829). The eighteenth century was also the period, though, when Greece became peripheral to western Europe, particularly in commercial terms. An identity built on ancient Greece made modern Greece western; indeed modern Greece was presented as the most direct continuation of Europe's prestigious 'beginnings', when allegedly the foundations of democracy, science, philosophy and literature were laid (Friedman, 1994, Chapter 8).

This linear and progressive model of historical development is itself a specific way of looking at history. In Chapter 2 I shall examine the character of this European way of regarding one's past and envisaging one's future.

Geography

Geography can also be an important element, as identities may be formed around the inhabiting of a certain territory. Maps provide an image of one's own 'place' on earth; and they have been used to express power, projects and national identity. Once put down on paper, boundaries, for instance, appear sanctioned and even natural. It is no coincidence that in most European countries during the nineteenth century geography became a compulsory subject in the emerging primary schools that were open to all: it was thought that in order to develop a national identity it was necessary to identify the territory of the nation (García-Ramon and Nogué-Font, 1994, pp. 206–7). European identity may also have a geographical basis, but the *limits of Europe* are not universally accepted; for example, Europeans disagree on where the eastern borders of Europe lie.

Inhabiting a certain type of territory can be a key element of one's identity too, for it implies a certain set of experiences and values, and a lifestyle. Hence the traditional (stereotypical) differences that are held to exist between people inhabiting mountainous territories, those living near the sea, and those in places perceived as wild, or cold, or hot – and of course the most general differentiation, that between country people and city people. Over 75 per cent of western Europeans live in cities, but there are strong differences between, for instance, Belgium which is almost totally urbanized (97 per cent) and Greece which is relatively more rural (60 per cent are city people) (see United Nations website). Landscapes have provided strong elements of national identities in a very explicit way, being used in the symbolic representation of countries and almost invariably mentioned in national anthems.

The English countryside is a key symbol of Englishness, even though it is far from being the setting of the lives of most people living in England (the United Kingdom as a whole is among the most urbanized countries in the world: 90 per cent of its inhabitants live in cities; see United Nations website). In a contribution to a volume dedicated to geography and national identity, David Lowenthal argues that the English landscape is seen as the embodiment of English history and of values of decor and order that belong to the aristocracy and landed elite (Lowenthal, 1994). This landscape is tamed and artificial, a place where nature has not been left wild but rather has been ordered by human intervention. However, as such intervention has been a steady process over time, it manages to convey the idea of a long history – even the idea of the old-fashioned character both of the landscape itself and of the activities which take place in it. One difference between England and other parts of Europe is that in England the elite has retained its rural residences; indeed 'the English have always regarded the countryside as the proper place for proper people to live in' (Howard Newby quoted in Lowenthal, 1994, p. 16). Often, country people present themselves as those who preserve Englishness, in contrast to modern, multicultural urbanites.

Some nations are part of larger countries, and for them too geography plays an important role. Against an English identity rooted in a gentle landscape, for instance, has been opposed the highlander identity, chosen in some quarters (notably by Hollywood) to represent Scottish identity in general. Geography has also played a major role in the promotion and preservation of Catalan identity, especially in the period when it was most repressed, during Franco's dictatorship (1939–75). Located in the northeast corner of Spain, Catalonia has its own language and a strong national identity, both

Figure 1.7 John Constable, *View of Osmington Village with Church and Vicarage*, 1816, oil on canvas. Constable's landscapes have come to represent the quintessentially English countryside – tame and safe. The church and vicarage are not only religious symbols but two of the main focuses of village life. Photo: Bridgeman Art Library/Yale Centre for British Art, Paul Mellon Collection, USA

nowadays protected by laws and institutions. Geographers were involved in the promotion of its identity, by pushing for the introduction of the study of the Catalan territory and society in schools, and by promoting the map-making of the region. Moreover, they were active in the two Catalan hiking societies, founded towards the end of the nineteenth century, which also attracted geologists, botanists, historians, archaeologists, ethnologists and even writers and poets. Hiking in Catalonia was an activity with strongly nationalistic overtones, as expressed in 1904 by a member of one of the hiking societies, the poet Joan Maragall:

> our hiking is neither a sport nor a pleasure or a work: it is love and not merely an abstract love for nature as a whole but for our nature ... Hence we can proudly say that the soul of our hiking movement is the love for Catalonia.
>
> (Quoted in García-Ramon and Nogué-Font, 1994, p. 202)

The French, meanwhile, feeling that their country did not have one single type of landscape, celebrated its diversity instead: the Alps and the Mediterranean, hills and plains. This stereotype is so strong that the famous French historian Fernand Braudel (1902–85) found himself repeating it at a conference in Germany. As Braudel himself narrated, his audience protested that Germany's landscapes were as diverse as France's; and he realized that he was just repeating a familiar point almost mechanically, for of course he 'knew all along that Germany, Italy, Spain and England were just as diverse' (Claval, 1994, pp. 53–4). Indeed, most landscapes are not unique to any one country, and conversely most countries have a variety of them; but generally, for historical and social reasons, one type of landscape is elected to be a national symbol.

Religion

Religion has played a significant part in the formation of identities, although nowadays its importance varies within Europe, as it provides a strong source of identity for some Europeans but is not very meaningful for others. Christianity has certainly long lain at the core of a sense of community shared by people in Europe, especially in contrast with people who did not share their religion; during the Middle Ages, for instance, the 'Christian lands' regarded themselves as besieged by Islam on their eastern and southern borders. A good example is provided by the Iberian peninsula, parts of which were governed by Arab rulers between the eighth and the fifteenth centuries, where the opposition between Christianity and Islam has been employed as an element of modern Spanish identity. In the era of overseas exploration and settlement, Europeans came into contact with other non-Christian people too, and colonization and the spread of Christianity all too often went hand in hand. Within Europe, however, it was Islam, especially in the form of the Ottoman (Turkish) empire, that was perceived as the potential source of conflict. From the fifteenth century onwards, the identification of Europe and Christianity became standard. Pope Pius II (1458–64), for example, calling the European states to unite in a joint defence against the perceived Turkish threat, employed 'Europe' and 'Respublica christiana' as synonyms (den Boer, 2000, pp. 34–5). However, in reality 'Christian Europe' was greatly fragmented politically, and indeed its religious unity was problematic: a schism had already split the church in the eleventh century (this resulted in the division between the western and the Orthodox churches); heresies were always springing up; finally the Reformation made the differences between Protestants and Catholics more important than their similarities. Moreover, adherents of other religions, notably Judaism, have always been present in Europe, although marginalized and even, as we know, the targets of pogroms and genocide. Nevertheless, Europe as the Christian continent has been a powerful idea. Nowadays the picture appears to be complex and the label 'Christian Europe' would not have a universal appeal among Europeans, largely because a significant minority of Europeans are secular (out of a total population of around 729 million, 106 million describe themselves as 'non-religious' and 23 million as 'atheists'; see Table 1.1). According to the British Social Attitudes poll conducted in November 2000, 44 per cent of British people, including two-thirds of 18–24 year olds, have no religious affiliation (see BBC news website).

In most European countries today the distinction between state and church is either institutionally or *de facto* accepted. The relation between Europe and Christianity, or indeed between Europe and religion generally, is nevertheless seen in different terms in different parts of Europe. In one draft of the European Charter of Fundamental Rights which was approved in October 2000 by the European Union, a sentence about the 'Jewish–Christian heritage' of Europe had been inserted, then changed to 'religious heritage'. The French delegate protested, as he put it 'for political, philosophical and constitutional reasons' (France is a lay state by constitutional law; the division between church and state and the lay character of the latter are important elements of French national identity). The adjective 'religious' was then changed to 'spiritual' (*Il Manifesto*, 20 September 2000; for the text of the Charter and how it was drawn up, see European Union website).

Moreover, over 40 million Europeans profess other religions, notably Islam (31 million people in Europe are of Islamic faith; see Table 1.1, below). Since the majority of Muslims in western Europe are immigrants or immigrants' children, religion might in some cases become an identity of resistance, in reaction to discrimination or to policies of forced integration. As David Herbert discusses in Chapter 5, the case in 1989 of the French girls prevented by their teachers (who were enforcing an existing law) from wearing the *foulard* (headscarf) at school immediately sparked a fierce debate and turned the *foulard* into a symbol of resistance.

Table 1.1 shows some of the most important religious groups and the number of atheists and non-religious people in Europe in mid-2000:

Table 1.1   Religious practice in Europe, 2000

Europe's total population	**728,887,000**
Christians	559,643,000
Affiliated Christians	536,832,000
Roman Catholic	285,978,000
Orthodox	158,105,000
Protestants	77,529,000
Anglicans	26,637,000
Nonreligious	106,841,000
Muslims	31,566,000
Atheists	22,922,000
Jews	2,527,000
Buddhists	1,547,000

(Adapted from *Britannica Book of the Year*, 2001, p. 302)

Statistics like those above make us aware of social realities, such as the numbers of people who are not affiliated to Christian churches in the supposedly 'Christian continent'. However, they do not tell us much about the role played by religion in the formation of European *identities*. Cultural and social identities are phenomena that are too complex to be studied solely from a quantitative point of view. Rather, what is needed is an approach that considers the complexities of culture, society, history, and that takes into account the subjective perceptions of and responses to one's milieu.

Language

Language is another important element on which identities are often based. It is generally assumed that people have a special relationship with one language, their mother-tongue. Moreover, people might find a sense of communality with others with whom they can easily communicate, who share the same language. The way an individual

Figure 1.8 Religious identity is often expressed through clothing and grooming: in this photograph it is easy to identify the two men on the left-hand side as Jewish. This is the Parisian neighbourhood of Belleville, which has experienced a steady influx of new residents – many of them Jewish and Arabic – during the past century. The French writer Daniel Pennac has given a humorous portrait of multicultural Belleville in his novels. Photo: Magnum/Kalvar

personally lives their relationship with the languages they speak might of course vary – and here you might want to reflect on your own relationship with your mother-tongue. There are many ways that people's relationship with a language may differ. For instance, an individual might speak a language that is the official language of her country alone (such as Hungarian or Polish), or that of many countries (English or Spanish, say); or her country might have more than one official language (as in Switzerland or Belgium). Moreover, the language used at home might not be the same as the language of one's social life or education. And within a language, a particular accent might indicate belonging to a certain social class or a regional origin. Even the latter is often not free of a value judgement, for the language of some parts of a country might be perceived as more or less 'prestigious' than others.

Language has often been at the core of the building of national identity. But how is it that modern European countries have distinct languages that are spoken by all of their citizens? The answer is that they acquired these national languages through historical processes. Generally speaking, one particular language or variety of a language acquired a hegemonic position because it was spoken by the ruling class, or was the preferred written language. Italian is an interesting example. Italy was unified only in 1860 and, as Clive Emsley recalls in Chapter 3, the claim to a single Italian language was one of the key arguments of Italian patriots who intended to assert and promote the 'Italian nation'. Most Italians nowadays perceive their language uncontroversially as their mother-tongue, and by studying the history of literature at school they acquire a sense of the long history of that language (Italian literature is a compulsory subject in all schools and is tested at *maturità*, the final exam taken at secondary school).

Where does the Italian language come from? In the Middle Ages spoken Latin slowly underwent transformations which resulted in the formation of different languages in present-day Portugal, Spain, France, Italy, Romania and parts of Belgium and Switzerland. In the Italian peninsula a multitude of different idioms emerged. Between the fourteenth and the sixteenth centuries, however, the educated classes started to employ a communal language in their public and private writings: Italian. This was a literary version of the Tuscan dialect, the lexicon, grammar and style of which had been established by the works of Dante Alighieri (1265–1321), Francesco Petrarca (Petrarch) (1304–74) and Giovanni Boccaccio (1313–75). For centuries, Italian was largely a language used by the elite sectors of society, in writing or on solemn or official occasions. Only in Tuscany and Rome was it used more broadly. In Tuscany Italian was used because it was, to all intents and purposes, the Tuscan dialect; in Rome the reasons for its use were more complex. During the seventeenth century Rome's work opportunities attracted a high number of immigrants. This followed a period of scarce population as a result of extensive pillage and destruction by Emperor Charles V's armies in 1527 (known as 'the sack of Rome'). The new inhabitants of Rome tended to use as their communal language an idiom closer to Tuscan, and therefore closer to Italian, than the original Roman dialect. Another factor in Rome's use of Italian was that the papal court was formed by individuals from different areas of what is now Italy and beyond. Because they did not speak the same idiom, they used Italian to communicate with one another and with the rest of the Roman population (see De Mauro, 1963, pp. 25-6).

At the time of the unification of Italy only a tiny percentage of Italians spoke Italian: 2.5 per cent according to more restrictive evaluations; 8–10 per cent according to more generous ones which include people from central Italy generally, rather than from only Tuscany and Rome (De Mauro, 1993, p. 17). The so-called dialects of Italy were in fact different languages, each with a distinct vocabulary and grammar: a speaker of a dialect of the northeast, for instance, would have been totally incomprehensible to a speaker of a dialect of Sicily. Some of these dialects had their own literature and theatre, as in the case of Venetian, Neapolitan and Milanese; in Venice the dialect was used by the judiciary, in Naples at the royal court. The linguistic unification of Italy occurred only in the 1950s, thanks to the spread of television and newspapers, to universal schooling and to internal migration from the countryside to the cities and from the south to the industrialized north (De Mauro, 1963, p. 116). Thus the nineteenth-century patriots' appeal to a single language can be interpreted as being just a project or aspiration, rather than a description of reality; or it may have been a rhetorical device. It can also be explained as a conscious or unconscious reference not to all Italians but only to the educated ones who regarded the written language of Italian literature as a meaningful part of their identity.

EXERCISE

Reflect on one of your own cultural identities (this time you might want to choose national, local or regional identity) in order to understand what it consists of, and to assess whether history, language, geography and religion might have contributed to form it or whether other elements are more important. You may want to repeat the same exercise in relation to other identities that you do not regard as your own. When assessing the importance of each element, ask yourself why and how it came to be significant. For instance, if you are analysing the role of history, you might want to reflect on how you got to know the history of your country (or people, city, or the like) and how you formed your own evaluation of it. An obvious answer is that you learned this history at school, but there are many other possible channels: references in the media or in conversation, films, symbols, festivities and so on. How did you come to feel (or not feel) connected with people who lived centuries ago, in places you perhaps have never seen? If you choose to reflect on language, you may (or may not) detect different levels of identity rooted in language; for instance, language can be linked to a national identity, to a local identity (through a local language, dialect, or simply accent), to a certain age group (through the use of certain terms) and very personally to the use of a particular vocabulary that links you to your childhood experiences and your family. The role of history, language and religion are analysed in more depth in Chapters 3, 4 and 5, so consider your own reflection at this stage as preliminary. You may want to keep records of your thoughts in order to work on them later.

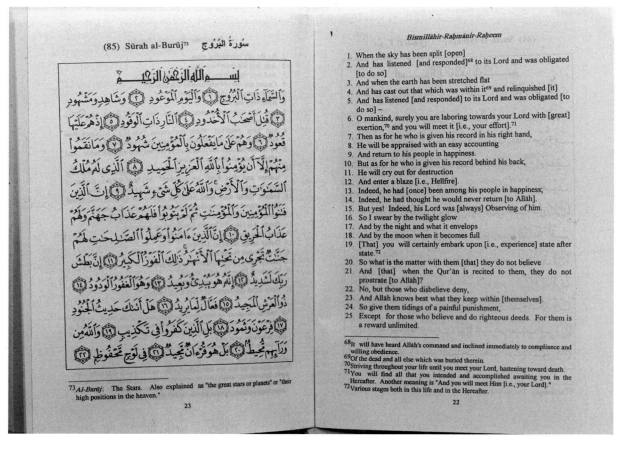

Figure 1.9 Muslim family reader by Dr Saidi J. L. El-Liwaru and Maishazojat El-Liwaru, published 1988, American Trust Publications, with English on the right-hand page and Arabic on the left. For many people language is part of their national identity; however, for many others it is part of their religious identity. Classical Arabic, which is the language of the Qur'ān, unifies Muslims who speak different versions of Arabic as well as those who speak completely different languages. Photo: Art Directors/Trip/Helen Rogers

Education and the shaping of identities

Identities can be, and often are, promoted; this is particularly evident in the process of nation building. The linguistic unification of a country is certainly a powerful means of achieving this; education is also a very important way. The teaching of history has been highly significant in the promotion of national identity; the type of history traditionally taught in many schools (political history) and the type of narrative it proposes (focused on the nation or on the nation-to-be) are particularly suited to making pupils identify with this past and present imagined community. It has already been noted how geography can also be employed in education in order to build a sense of nationality. Literature is often very important in this context too – it has been mentioned that for Italian pupils the history of Italian literature is a compulsory subject until they are nineteen years of age; one could argue that studying literary history can give them a sense of a long national history that pre-dates the creation of their nation-state.

However, the shaping of national identities and other cultural identities through education extends to most subjects. French pedagogical literature has been particularly explicit on the aim of shaping the identity of the pupil. Throughout the twentieth century literature on school reform, parliamentary speeches and the *Encyclopédie française* (the French encyclopaedia, corresponding to the *Encyclopedia Britannica*) repeatedly made the point that education is to be managed by the state because it is aimed at the formation of the citizen. This objective is best pursued, pedagogues and politicians alike have argued, not so much through one particular subject but rather through a comprehensive culture. In a pamphlet on school reform published in 1922, the philosopher Léon Brunschvicg, professor at the Sorbonne, introduced his proposals with the rhetorical question, 'Do we want France's continued existence, *yes or no?*' (Brunschvicg, 1922, p. 51). For him, as for many intellectuals, the future of France depended on good schools. School textbooks in the interwar period explained how to be a good citizen, parent and spouse; these were not presented simply as social roles, but rather as the realization of an individual's humanity. Even science textbooks, which at first sight might appear less likely places for moral lessons, presented the behaviour of such national heroes as Louis Pasteur (1822–95) as examples of disinterestedness, hard work and unselfishness. The aim of education was to shape Frenchmen and women.

Education might promote national identities and models of behaviour, and define worthwhile life targets and social roles, but whose ideals are those proposed in schools? The sociologist Pierre Bourdieu, who carried out research on education for over thirty years, had no doubts: the culture and values of school education are those of the dominant classes. Indeed, he believed that education reproduces social differences and hierarchies. So, it is not just that social and cultural identities are imparted to pupils, but that the very identities proposed in schools reflect those of the dominant classes. Education mirrors and reproduces existing social structures. Bourdieu's research was focused on French education, but although the details of his accounts might not be transferable to other contexts the substance of his argument seems to me to have a far more general validity. The reading below is taken from his *State Nobility: Elite Schools in the Field of Power* (Bourdieu, 1998). In this particular extract

Bourdieu examines the relationship between the preference for a subject of study and social class, and the social meaning of academic precocity. (His arguments are backed up by a wealth of statistics that are not reproduced here.)

The disciplining of minds ...

Academic subjects assumed to require talent and gifts and associated with the possession of considerable inherited cultural capital (such as philosophy, French, and, in its place, mathematics) contrast with those that are seen to require primarily work and study (such as geography and the natural sciences, with history and modern or ancient languages occupying an intermediate position) ... The major differences between the two types have to do with indices of the modality of their relationship to what it means to be educated. On the one side lie disciplines that discourage willingness and academic zeal, as much through the nebulous and imprecise nature of the tasks they involve as through the vagueness and uncertainty of the signs of success or failure they offer, disciplines that require often undefinable previous knowledge ('you have to have read a lot'). On the other lie disciplines that involve research that suits the taste for work 'well done' and that appears 'safe' and 'profitable' because one knows where to direct one's efforts and results are easily measured ...

'Talent subjects', which offer the most profitable investment to inherited cultural capital – that is, to so-called 'independent' (as opposed to 'academic') culture and to the familiar rapport with culture that can only be acquired through the diffuse teachings of familial education – recruit at a higher social level than those subjects that give students from the dominated regions of social space the occasion to exhibit just those ethical dispositions whose compensatory function is liable to be more fully realized here than in other areas ...

Given that the same taxonomies that serve both to classify academic disciplines and to determine the personal qualities they require also organize the perception and appreciation that 'disciplined' students (who will have to choose among them) have of their own qualities, it is not surprising that academic verdicts should have the power to determine one's 'vocation' and that statistical analysis should uncover just as rigorous a connection between the properties socially conferred on the different disciplines and the dispositions of those who excel in them (or teach them). Disciplines choose their students as much as students choose their disciplines, imposing upon them categories of perception of subjects and careers as well as of their own skills.

The privilege of ease

Differences among disciplines both cover up and recover social differences. The canonical disciplines, such as French or classics and mathematics or physics, socially designated as the most important and most noble, consecrate students who come most often from well-positioned families with abundant cultural capital, correspondingly more of whom have followed the royal path of lycées and classical tracks from the *sixième* to the *terminale* and skipped grades in the course of their secondary schooling, and who are better informed about possible vocations and careers. This should come as no surprise if the academic hierarchy of disciplines coincides with the hierarchy established according to the average age of the prizewinners, a hierarchy extending in the sciences from mathematics to physics and the natural sciences and in the humanities from French or classics to history and geography or modern languages.

One of the clearest attestations of the privilege that is granted to charismatic values, leading the educational institution to disregard strictly scholastic learning, is the cult of precocity, valued as an indicator of 'gifts' ...

Through the near miraculous speed of her learning, the precocious student (the extreme example of which is 'the child prodigy' or, as we would say today, 'the exceptionally gifted child') demonstrates the extent of the natural gifts that enable her to avoid the slow work ordinary individuals must perform in order to learn. In fact, *precocity* is but one of the many academic retranslations of cultural privilege ... what we call precocity, and what is in reality a manifestation of cultural heritage, is closely related to all indicators of success ...

In fact, precocity is but one of the indices of the mode of cultural acquisition favored by the educational institution – but a particularly reliable one. If the systems of manners set apart by academic taxonomies (whatever their degree of refinement) always refer back to social differences, this is because the way education is acquired lives on in what is acquired in the form of a certain way of using the acquisition. The *modality* of the relationship an individual maintains with the school, with the education it transmits, and with the language it uses and requires depends on the distance between her family milieu and the academic world and on her generic chances for survival in the system – or, in other words, on the probability of her acceding to a determined academic position that is objectively attached to her group of origin. Thus, when, in the indefinable nuances that define 'ease' or 'natural' talent, we think we recognize behavior or ways of speaking considered authentically 'cultured' because they bear no mark of the effort and no trace of the work that go into their acquisition, we are really referring to *a particular mode of acquisition*: what we call ease is the privilege of those who, having imperceptibly acquired their culture through a gradual familiarization in the bosom of the family, have academic culture as their native culture and can maintain a familiar rapport with it that implies the unconsciousness of its acquisition ...

The ambiguities of competence ...

Granting an academic title is ... a legitimate juridical act of categorization, through which the undoubtedly most determinant *attribute of one's social identity* is conferred (along with the occupation that this attribute largely determines). Given that this social identity is always ... social difference, distinction (positive or negative), it is indissociable from the differentiation of groups separated by magical boundaries ...

Academic judgments, through their 'Oedipal effect,' are nowadays undoubtedly one of the crucial factors in the construction of personal identity. Children, especially the least well endowed, have no recourse, no authority to which to appeal in response to these verdicts (which are usually absolute and blunt, whether in praise or in condemnation, and nearly always repeated and reinforced by their peer group and especially by their family) – except child psychologists and psychiatrists. Social magic manages to transform agents in a real way by getting everyone – hence the interested parties themselves, who cannot but be affected by the consequences of this proclamation – to be aware of and to recognize an expectation or, better still, a prediction about their identity that, invested as it is with the prophetic authority of the group, becomes their destiny. 'Become who you are.' The certificate, which assigns an essence, produces what it certifies as much as it ratifies it. In a reversal of cause and effect characteristic of social alchemy, the educational institution confers, not just a certificate of technical competence giving one the right to a particular job, but a pass to a job in which the major portion of the necessary technical competence is often acquired on the job. The magic of the academic title rests on a power held and exploited by all groups, the power to act upon bodies through the symbolic efficacy of signs. Whether dignifying or dubious distinctions, public

> criticism or praise, the solemn verdicts of socially recognized
> authorities, as predictions vested with the authority of officialdom,
> tend to produce what they predict, both benedictions and
> maledictions being equally fatal.
>
> (Bourdieu, 1998, pp. 11, 14–15, 19–21, 117–18)

EXERCISE

Briefly summarize and assess the reading above, following these
questions.

- How do the differences between the types of performance
  required in different school subjects reflect social differences in
  Bourdieu's account?

- What do precocity and 'ease' really amount to for Bourdieu?

- Is Bourdieu's analysis relevant for a reflection on the formation
  of identities?

DISCUSSION

Bourdieu argues that students are directed towards different
disciplines as a result of their social background. Some subjects (such
as literature and philosophy) require the type of knowledge and skills
which are most often found among the dominant classes, and are not
directly acquired in schools. As a result, it is easier for middle-class
young people to excel in these subjects, for they can 'spend' the
cultural capital that they have unwittingly accumulated at home. They
also tend to perceive these subjects as their own vocation, and are
confirmed in their belief by the academic institutions. By contrast, in
those subjects which require a more definite set of skills and
knowledge that are acquired though specific training, working-class
young people are at less of a disadvantage. They are more likely to
excel in these subjects, and to perceive them as their personal
vocation. Social differences are thus perceived as individual
differences. The same is true, in Bourdieu's account, for academic
precocity and natural talents. Abilities that appear to be natural gifts
– because they have not been acquired through specific training – are
actually acquired in the extra-scholastic environment. Since the
abilities that schools value are those belonging to the dominant
classes, young people from the dominant classes tend to exhibit
them, and be rewarded for having them. A young person from the
dominant classes is statistically much more likely to demonstrate
academic excellence and so be selected for an elite school and then
for an elite occupation. Through this circular process, schools help to

reproduce social differences and social and cultural identities. Not only do educational institutions exercise power in determining a student's position in society, they also reproduce social and cultural values and shape the perception that people have of their own abilities and realistic aspirations, and of those of their children.

Types of identity

Three forms of identity

It is worth trying to distinguish identities according to their origins and the mechanisms by which they are formed. Manuel Castells (Castells, 1997, p. 8) locates three forms and origins of identity building.

1   Legitimizing identity. This has its origins in institutions. A very powerful institution in this sense is the state which grants citizenship. Other institutions and groups are also extremely important in the creation of legitimizing identities, such as churches, trade unions, political parties, cooperatives and other associations of citizens. These associations occupy an intermediate position between the state and citizens: they are rooted in civil society, but at the same time reproduce the structure of the state. For this reason, legitimizing identities can be seen both as empowering people, in that they enable them to change the state, and as dominating and controlling people.

2   Resistance identity. Groups of people who find themselves in a marginalized and de-legitimized position in society can develop identities that differ from the dominant one. Resistance identity leads to the formation of communities which exclude those who have excluded the members of these communities from central positions in society. Resistance identity is typical of radical separatist feminism or ethnic nationalism. For instance, some black nationalists in predominantly white societies advocate the separation of their own community from the wider, and oppressive, society, together with the creation of alternative black institutions and cultural and social networks.

3   Project identity. This identity is constructed around the shared project of seeking to change existent identities and realities. Project identities bind together social actors who intend to redefine their position in society and seek a transformation of the overall structure of society. This is the identity of members of some political movements and parties.

EXERCISE _____

Recall (or re-read) the readings presented in this chapter and see if in some (or all) of them the identities discussed can be fitted into one or more of the three types above.

DISCUSSION _____

The identities produced by educational institutions as described by Bourdieu seem to fit the definition of legitimizing identities, for they reproduce the identities which rationalize and legitimize social domination. In the extract from Brah's work some of the stages of black identities described can be read as resistance and project identities. She talks of the formation of a black identity as constituting resistance to the socially disadvantaged position that migrants from outside Britain came to occupy. Black identity, as Brah describes it, appears to be not only a resistance identity but also and above all a project identity, for she links it tightly with political projects within the left. Similar comments can be made about Butler's text, in relation to gender identity. She demonstrates the complexity of the construction of a resistance identity in the case of women. She points out that gender identity interacts with other identities that the individual has, which might be other resistance identities, but also might be legitimizing identities. Butler also discusses the ways in which resistance identities are constructed and turned into projects.

European identities/identities in Europe

The concepts, categories and themes that have been introduced here will help you to analyse European identities. However, there is still a problem to address: what are the identities to consider – which identities are European? They might be regarded in one of the following three ways:

1   as identities of people living in Europe;

2   as identities which are specific to Europe;

3   as one of the identities that some people have, when they declare that they are or that they feel European.

These three ways of considering European identities are not mutually exclusive, but they are different. It is useful to take a little time to think about the implications of these different angles.

1   The first perspective, looking at the identities of people living in Europe, involves the examination of diverse, complex and

interrelated identities. Despite its complexity, this approach is indispensable for an understanding of European identities and cultures. The approach is descriptive rather than normative. In other words, rather than having a preconceived idea about what European identities are, and then using it to judge which identities are European, the aim is to understand the identities of the groups and persons forming the societies of Europe. If the characters of identities that have been described above (in the section on 'Identity building') are accepted, the description of identities cannot be set in stone once and for all. The historical character of identities has been pointed out: it cannot be taken for granted that identities which existed in the past are still important for people nowadays, or that they have the same meaning. Similarly, it cannot be assumed that what is observed today will necessarily be valid in the future. Social, economic, political and cultural changes are likely to impact on how people regard themselves and others. Indeed, it has been noted that Foucault argued that the very conception of human beings as autonomous authors of their thoughts and actions, and as an object of study among others, is a product of modern discourse. In a far less radical manner, Giddens sees reflection on cultural identity as a product of the choices at one's disposal in the modern world. I have also pointed out that identities are relational. Identities in Europe are no exception to this; no identity can be considered as if it exists in complete isolation. As a consequence, the emergence or evolution of some identities will very likely have an effect on others.

2   The second way of looking at European identities, as specific to Europe, perhaps presents more theoretical difficulties than the first. In a general sense, the cultural identities mentioned so far could not be said to be exclusive to Europe. However, even apparently universal identities, such as gender, may play out very differently in different societies. Butler's text gives a glimpse of how some intellectuals involved in gender studies are discussing this issue. She points out that gender identity always exists alongside other identities, and is therefore shaped in relation to one's other identities. Analogously, the extract from Brah provides an example of how black identity has developed differently in British and North American society, and in successive periods. The historical and relational characters of identities opens up the possibility that some identities, or combinations of identities, may be specifically European. However, this cannot just be assumed to be so; this conclusion can be reached (or not) only as a result of study. Whether some identities are shared across Europe and are not present in a

similar way in other parts of the world is a question to investigate, rather than a fact to assume.

3 Finally, European identity can also be discussed as one identity that some people feel to be their own. Unlike the first sense of European identities delineated above, but similar to the second, this is something to be investigated rather than assumed. It is a less difficult question than that of whether specific European identities exist. Indeed empirical research studies have been conducted to find out whether people would list European identity as one of their identities. Some of these studies have employed quantitative methods, including one that was carried out in twenty-five secondary schools in six countries of the European Union (England, France, Germany, Italy, the Netherlands and Spain). To the question 'Do you think of yourself as European?' year 10 pupils (or the equivalent in mainland Europe) in different countries and of different 'ethnic' origins gave different answers, as shown in Table 1.2.

Table 1.2 Do you think of yourself as European?

	Not at all (%)	Only partly (%)	Yes, totally (%)
England	39.8	41.6	18.6
France	17.4	41.0	41.6
Germany	10.5	26.3	62.6
Italy	4.3	41.0	54.7
Netherlands	2.6	7.0	90.4
Spain	6.4	25.1	68.4

	Afro-Caribbean (%)	Asian (%)	White (%)	Other (%)
Not at all	55.0	46.5	20.2	9.8
Only partly	40.0	43.4	31.8	46.2
Yes, totally	5.0	10.1	47.9	43.9

(Convery et al., 1997, pp. 32, 31)

Although such data are useful, they cannot be taken at face value. For instance, it is not at all clear what 'to feel European' means; certainly while some people would have different views on this, others would have no view or interest in the question at all. This question has also become more complicated because 'Europe' may be taken to be an economic–political project, and to refer to the European Union rather than to Europe in a cultural sense.

Any statistical analysis of this problem, such as the one presented above, has therefore to be taken with a pinch of salt, because it tends to overlook the fact that 'European' can have a variety of meanings and connotations for different people. Moreover, there may be different views on the interaction of European identity and national identity. For instance, a survey carried out among a sample of British and Italian university students concluded that for the majority of the British students interviewed, British and European identities were in conflict, whereas the Italian students tended to see Italian and European identities as compatible (Cinnirella, 1997, p. 25). Perceptions of Europe and its parts of course vary greatly not only between one country and another; different views may also depend on age, social class, personal experiences and outlook.

Like any other identity, European identity in this sense has limits; indeed it is constructed against the 'other', that is what is *not* European. This exclusionary aspect of identities is inescapable and problematic at the same time. It can lie at the root of racism and social exclusion. However, to have a European identity may also mean to overcome eurocentrism, a European-centred cultural outlook. In many European cultural expressions, including literature, philosophy and anthropology, European writers have assumed themselves to be presenting the 'neutral' point of view. A European identity is only one possible identity among many, and in this sense is more circumscribed than the universality that many Europeans ascribe to themselves.

European identities can be usefully explored in their cultural expressions. In this book these cultural expressions are explored through the 'routes', and not just the roots, of European identities: how these identities have been constructed and expressed in different times, places and social circumstances. This is accompanied by analysis of whether these European identities are also project identities, and motors of change.

References

Anderson, B. (1991) *Imagined Communities: Reflections on the Origin and Spread of Nationalism*, 2nd edn, London, Verso.

BBC news website: http://news6.thdo.bbc.co.uk/hi/english/uk/newsid%5F1043000/1043986.stm

Bernal, M. (1987) *Black Athena: the Afroasiatic Roots of Classical Civilisation*, vol. 1: *The Fabrication of Ancient Greece 1785–1985*, London, Free Association.

Bourdieu, P. (1989) *Distinction: a Social Critique of the Judgment of Taste*, transl. R. Nice, London, Routledge.

Bourdieu, P. (1998) *The State Nobility: Elite Schools in the Field of Power*, with the collaboration of M. de Saint Martin, transl. L. C. Clough, Cambridge, Polity.

Brah, A. (1996) *Cartographies of Diaspora: Contesting Identities*, London/New York, Routledge.

Britannica Book of the Year 2001 (2001) Chicago, Encyclopedia Britannica.

Brunschvicg, L. (1922) *Un Ministère de l'éducation nationale*, Paris, Plon.

Butler, J. [1990] (1997) 'Subject of sex/gender/desire', in S. Kemp and J. Squires (eds), *Feminisms*, Oxford, Oxford University Press.

Castells, M. (1997) *The Power of Identity*, Oxford, Blackwell.

Chimisso, C. (2001) *Gaston Bachelard: Critic of Science and the Imagination*, London/New York, Routledge.

Cinnirella, M. (1997) 'Towards a European identity? Interactions between the national and European social identities manifested by university students in Britain and Italy', *British Journal of Social Psychology*, vol. 36, pp. 19–31.

Claval, P. (1994) 'From Michelet to Braudel: personality, identity and organisation of France', in D. Hooson (ed.), *Geography and National Identity*, Oxford, Blackwell.

Convery, A., Evans, M., Green, S., Macaro, E. and Mellor, J. (1997) *Pupils' Perceptions of Europe*, London, Cassell.

De Mauro, T. (1963) *Storia linguistica dell'Italia unita*, Bari, Laterza.

De Mauro, T. (1993) 'Gli obiettivi della ricerca', in T. De Mauro, F. Mancini, M. Vedovelli and M. Voghera (eds), *Lessico di frequenza dell'italiano parlato*, Milan, Etaslibri.

den Boer, P. (2000) 'Europe to 1914: the making of an idea', in K. Wilson and J. van der Dussen (eds), *The History of the Idea of Europe*, London/New York, Routledge/Open University.

Descartes, R. [1641] (1986) *Meditations on First Philosophy, with Selections from the Objections and Replies*, transl. J. Cottingham, Cambridge, Cambridge University Press.

European Union website, European Charter of Fundamental Rights: http://europa.eu.int/comm/justice_home/unit/charte/index_en.html

Foucault, M. (1970) *The Order of Things: an Archaeology of the Human Sciences*, London, Tavistock.

Friedman, J. (1994) *Cultural Identity and Global Process*, London, Sage.

García-Ramon, M. D. and Nogué-Font, J. (1994) 'Nationalism and geography in Catalonia', in D. Hooson (ed.), *Geography and National Identity*, Oxford, Blackwell.

Giddens, A. (1991) *Modernity and Self-identity*, Cambridge, Polity.

Gramsci, A. [1930–2] (1975) 'Quaderno 6' (Notebook 6), *Quaderni dal carcere* (Prison notebooks), vol. 2, ed. V. Gerratana, Edizione critica dell'Istituto Gramsci, Turin, Giulio Einaudi.

Guillaumin, C. (1995) *Racism, Sexism, Power and Ideology*, London/New York, Routledge.

Hall, S. (1990) 'Cultural identity and diaspora', in J. Rutherford (ed.), *Identity: Community, Culture, Difference*, London, Lawrence & Wishart.

Hall, S. (1992) 'The question of cultural identity', in S. Hall, D. Held and T. McGrew (eds), *Modernity and Its Futures*, Cambridge/Milton Keynes, Polity/The Open University.

Johnson, A. G. (2000) *The Blackwell Dictionary of Sociology: a User's Guide to Sociological Language*, 2nd edn, Oxford, Blackwell.

Kroeber, A. L. and Kluckhohn, C. (1978) *Culture: a Critical Review of Concepts and Definitions*, Millwood, NY, Kraus.

Lowenthal, D. (1994) 'European and English landscapes as national symbols', in D. Hooson (ed.), *Geography and National Identity*, Oxford, Blackwell.

MacInnes, C. (1959) *Absolute Beginners*, Harmondsworth, Penguin.

Pirandello, L. [1921] (1988) *Six Characters in Search of an Author*, in *Collected Plays*, vol. 2, transl. F. Firth, London, Calder.

Pirandello, L. [1926] (1990) *One, No One, and One Hundred Thousand*, transl. and intro. W. Weaner, Boston, MA, Eridanos.

Touraine, A. (2000) *Can We Live Together?*, transl. D. Macey, Cambridge, Polity.

United Nations website: http://www.un.org

Woolf, V. [1938] (1977) *Three Guineas*, London, Hogarth.

2
___

History and identity:

the Enlightenment idea of progress

CRISTINA CHIMISSO

Introduction

An understanding of the idea of progress is crucial in the study of European identities and cultures for two reasons. The first is that the study of this idea enables us to reflect on reconstructions of history and on their role in the formation of identity. In Chapter 1 history was indicated as an important element in the formation of identity. Progress is a particularly important way of reading history because it provides a framework to interpret not only the past, but also the future. As a consequence, it may be connected with the 'project identity' discussed in Chapter 1: in other words, in most versions of the theory of progress human beings have to work towards the realization of an improved life, or greater knowledge.

The second reason why progress is particularly important in the analysis of European identities and cultures is that the idea has been elaborated in Europe and has proved a powerful idea for centuries. As discussed below, during the eighteenth century this idea was employed and developed with particular conviction. Since that time it has played a part, in different versions, in diverse European ways of looking at history and knowledge. The idea of progress has been employed in political doctrines, has been the main framework for the interpretation of scientific knowledge, and has been used to justify a wide range of actions, attitudes and policies. It has also inspired strong reactions, for instance on the part of those who have regarded tradition as a more reliable guide instead. Nowadays the idea of progress remains firmly attached to the way we regard the development of science and technology. In this context, progress today has a mixed reputation. On the one hand, it is seen as desirable and unstoppable; for example, in the way we expect it to bring cures for currently incurable illnesses, or more powerful computers or faster trains – all consequences that are expected and generally welcomed. On the other hand, we are only too well aware of the risks that scientific progress may entail. Although the benefits that science and technology have brought to humankind are obvious, nowadays many people are also concerned with the potentially destructive consequences of many types of technologies. During the cold war, the most obvious concern of this kind was the risk of a nuclear holocaust. Some years down the line, although nuclear armaments still exist in abundance, the current major issues in the majority of the world at least seem to belong to fields such as genetics and ecology. The ability to modify plants and animals genetically raises strong concerns, and as a response to consumers' pressure many supermarkets in the UK (for example) now sell GM-free products. The most serious concern of all applies of course to the possibility of modifying or even cloning human beings. At the same time, many people (although crucially not the current US president, George W. Bush) are convinced that there is a link between climate changes and the emissions of so-called greenhouse gases as a consequence of industrial and agricultural activities.

The idea of progress has also contributed to shaping European identities in relation to the 'other', that is non-Europeans. Eighteenth-century authors elaborated upon the idea that Europeans were more advanced in terms of progress than peoples in the rest of the world. Since then this belief, in a more or less explicit form, has played a crucial and often unfortunate role in shaping both European identities and European attitudes towards the rest of the world.

This chapter analyses the link between the idea of progress and the position that some Europeans attributed to themselves in the world, as evidenced in eighteenth-century texts, or in other words when such ideas were first established. Primary sources for these ideas are analysed below. However, in order to tackle such sources effectively it is first necessary to reflect on some of the theoretical issues concerning the idea of progress, and to discuss the fundamental ideas underlying the Enlightenment, the cultural movement to which eighteenth-century advocates of progress belong. The structure of this chapter is as follows. The first section ('History, time and progress') analyses the idea of progress according to its key components, by focusing on the particular representation of historical time that it presupposes. There follows a presentation of the main theoretical and historical characteristics of Enlightenment ideas in these respects. There is then a discussion of the theories of 'Progress in the age of the Enlightenment' by specific French authors, including readings from Turgot's and Condorcet's demonstrations of historical progress. I shall pay particular attention to these authors' conception of Europe and its connection with the idea of progress. Their evaluation of progress is contrasted with Rousseau's, with an analysis of the latter's version of history and his criticism of the connection between progress in the sciences and arts on the one hand and moral progress on the other. Finally, the conclusion proposes some themes for reflection on the role of the idea of progress after the Enlightenment.

History, time and progress

Few definitions of progress seem to capture all the different doctrines, attitudes and programmes that have theorized, prophesized or promoted the idea. John Bury, who is often viewed as the most distinguished twentieth-century scholar of progress, wrote that progress 'means that civilization has moved, is moving, and will move in a desirable direction'(Bury, 1955, p. 2). This very general definition provides a starting point to reflect on what progress has meant and continues to mean for people who believe, hope or intend to promote it. In Bury's definition the first thing that is apparent is the temporal dimension: progress is presented as the movement of civilization in the past, present and future which involves an (undefined) improvement. In order to talk of progress, it seems that we need to represent history as a movement which follows a linear trajectory, like an arrow.

Past   Future

Is this an obvious way to portray historical time? This representation involves two presuppositions: one is that time is linear and continuous; the second is that it has a direction. The first presupposition appears intuitive, and may indeed be taken for granted in contemporary Europe; the second is perhaps less popular nowadays than it has been in the past. Each element should be examined in turn. As to the first, although the belief that time is linear and continuous may appear obvious to us nowadays, this has not always been the case. The idea that time was cyclical was in fact common in antiquity; more recently, the notion was revived by the philosopher Friedrich Nietzsche (1844–1900). According to this model, human civilization follows the same cycles – such as expansion followed by decadence – over and over again.

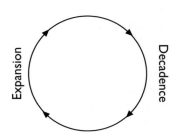

The idea that time is continuous has not always seemed obvious either. Indeed the ancient Greeks before the fifth century BCE had no such view of historical time. It is generally agreed that we can prove this by looking at the *Iliad* and the *Odyssey*. These epic poems, regarded as marking the beginnings of Greek literature, were probably composed in the eighth century BCE but were drawn from earlier traditional material referring to the Mycenaean period (1600–1200 BCE). These works did not only establish lasting literary conventions; for the Greeks they also represented accounts of their own past. The narratives they tell, however, are very different from those of modern histories. In the *Iliad*, for example, which is the story of the Greeks' conquest of Troy, no dates are given and the heroes are timeless models: their great deeds do not belong to any specific era. Analogously, the future is foreseen by oracles. Past and future events are isolated happenings rather than points on a continuous line.

Most scholars think that by the fifth century BCE the Greeks had developed an idea of continuous time, although they deny that classical civilizations held to any real idea of progress. But this opinion does not go unchallenged. Robert Nisbet, for instance, has argued that there is evidence that among the Greeks and Romans there did indeed exist the idea of development from a less civilized period to increasingly better times (Nisbet, 1980). However, Nisbet does admit that other conceptions of history were also very popular – such as the notion of degeneration. The first written model of history as degeneration is *Works and Days* (c. 700 BCE). Its author, Hesiod of Ascra, proposed a view of history as a succession of ages of gradual decadence. *Works and Days* starts with the Golden Age, when people lived like gods, with no care or pain, and then describes increasingly less desirable times, running from the Silver Age to the Bronze Age to the Age of Heroes (the time of the Trojan wars narrated in the *Iliad*) and concluding with the current Iron Age, which Hesiod regarded as an age of misery and injustice.

Literally 'the writing of history', historiography means both the theory and the practice of history writing.

The idea of a Golden Age existing at the beginning of time has been a powerful image throughout European history. It passed on to Christianity as the Eden where Adam and Eve lived without knowing pain or labour. As in *Works and Days*, in the Bible there is also a fall from grace. The difference between a 'pure' **historiography** of degeneration and the Christian one, however, is that the latter envisages another Golden Age arising at the end of history. Indeed in Christian thought it is this very promise of paradise to come that gives sense to history. In fact it was the cyclical model of history, derived from Greek philosophy, that was adopted by the first Christian philosophers, although Christian history was never represented as a series of cycles totally without direction. In this interpretation, everything comes from God and goes back to God; this journey can be represented circularly, but it happens only once. Eventually, however, Christian representations of history settled for a linear model. According to this, human history and time have a beginning (the fall from grace), a central event (the life of Jesus Christ) and an end still to come (marked by the last judgement).

Thus on the one hand Christian historiography has in common with classical theories of degeneration the theme of a Golden Age that existed at the beginning of times; while on the other hand it shares with the theories of progress the idea of a Golden Age to come at the end of time – in this case heaven, although it is not open to all. The most important difference between secular theories of progress and Christian theories of history is of course that the Christian Golden Age exists outside history, while for secular theories it exists within it. Secular theorists of progress have often presented a perfect future as the ultimate goal of history or of human efforts. Whereas this perfect future may be viewed as something that is actually achievable, or as a utopian state that can be approximated, in either case an ideal state is still a necessary condition to give sense to the whole process. In other words, in order to claim that history is progressing towards a better state of affairs, this progress has to be measured against some idea of what is desirable. For instance, to say that to have more equality or freedom constitutes progress must imply that an ideal or real state of complete equality and freedom is desirable.

To sum up, in very general terms, a theory of progress rests on two basic assumptions: that time is linear and that it carries civilization towards a perfect state of affairs. It follows from this that history has an overall meaning, which the philosopher can uncover. In this view all events, actions, achievements and apparent setbacks are to be interpreted as part of a general, progressive grand narrative. Obviously there may be other grand narratives that are not theories of progress; for instance, a theory of decadence would give an overall sense to history without, by definition, being a theory of progress. Christian historiographies have also conferred a general significance to human history, without necessarily presenting it as progressive. In these historiographies, the motor of history is providence, or a divine plan.

What about secular theories of progress? What determines the movement of history according to these theories? Broadly speaking there are two answers here: the unfolding of history and the activities of human beings. In the former view, there is a mechanism according to which history proceeds; according to the latter it is human beings who bring about change. For instance, the philosopher Georg Wilhelm Friedrich Hegel (1770–1831), a strong believer in history as a process governed by inherent laws, argued that individuals are only the means by which world history progresses. Such 'heroes' as Caesar and Napoleon, although apparently moved to action by their own passions or ambitions, unwittingly brought about stages in history which depended on history's unfolding rather than their own individual designs (Hegel, 1857, pp. 29–31). However, very often there is a cross-over in the views that progress is realized either according to the laws of history or through the conscious actions of people. Even those who believe in historical laws of advancement generally still call for human action.

Let me recall Bury's claim that progress 'means that civilization has moved, is moving, and will move in a desirable direction'. Bury intends 'civilization' to signify an undivided whole. Nowadays it is rare to encounter doctrines of progress 'of civilization'; the term 'progress' is more often applied to specific enterprises, especially in science and technology. While it is still relatively common to read or to hear people talk about scientific and technological progress, it is comparatively rare to find arguments aimed at demonstrating aesthetic or moral progress. As discussed below, even eighteenth-century advocates of progress often thought that different human enterprises progressed at different speeds; indeed some of them expressed scepticism about the possibility of progress in particular areas.

There is an even more fundamental problem with the idea of the progress of 'civilization'. It suggests that there is only one world civilization, and that its advancement can be seen in world history. How can the history of different peoples who had little contact with each other be seen as one? Some ways in which this was done are described below. On the whole in the eighteenth and nineteenth centuries there was no need to justify this attitude, as Europeans regarded their own civilization as civilization in general, and their own history as world history. This idea of a world civilization corresponds to the universal identity discussed in Chapter 1. The 'Cartesian' universal identity has been criticized for being in fact the identity of European white men belonging to the upper layers of society. Analogously, the general idea of world history and of its progress has been criticized for being in fact the history of Europeans, and in particular of prominent European men.

Enlightenment

Many scholars agree that the eighteenth century is the period when the idea of progress was first consistently formulated; others believe that this idea was present in former periods, even in antiquity. Either way, it is unarguable that in the eighteenth century the idea of progress was elaborated upon and employed in order to generate historical accounts, to explain events, to justify courses of action and to exhort to action in an unprecedentedly wide way. Although not all Enlightenment authors supported the idea of progress, Enlightenment and progress do appear to be closely interlinked. Why is this so? Here it is necessary to take a step back and consider some general characteristics of the Enlightenment, in order to establish why the idea of progress was so much at the heart of it.

What is Enlightenment?

'Enlightenment' is a term used to indicate either a cultural movement which took place in the eighteenth century, or a general philosophical attitude which can be assumed in any historical time. In the latter sense it indicates, broadly speaking, a trust in the power of reason to create objective and universal knowledge (in other words, knowledge that is applicable to any situation) as opposed to tradition, religion, common sense and prejudice. These two meanings of the term enlightenment are obviously connected, but you should be careful not to confuse them. For instance, discussions about 'enlightenment values' or criticism of 'enlightenment abstract reason' refer to general attitudes (that is to enlightenment as a general philosophical attitude). These attitudes are perceived to be the legacy of the Enlightenment (as a specific eighteenth-century cultural movement), but are often not to be found in the same form in eighteenth-century texts. This section is concerned with Enlightenment as a specific eighteenth-century cultural movement.

For some of the strongest critiques of Enlightenment abstract reason, see the reading in Chapter 5 by Gilles Kepel.

What is Enlightenment? This very question was already a matter of debate in the eighteenth century, and it has not found a unanimous response since. In 1783 a Berlin newspaper, the *Berlinische Monatsschrift*, invited contributions to this debate and received in reply three essays, from the dramatist Gotthold Lessing (1729–81) and the philosophers Moses Mendelssohn (1729–86) and Immanuel Kant (1724–1804). All three agreed that Enlightenment was a process, far from completed, of the education of man in the use of his own reason (Outram, 1996, p. 1). Kant's response has since become a classic text, and its beginning is almost invariably quoted in discussions on the Enlightenment. I shall not depart from this convention:

> Enlightenment is man's release from his self-incurred tutelage. Tutelage is man's inability to make use of his understanding without direction from another. Self-incurred is this tutelage when its cause lies not in lack of reason but in lack of resolution and courage to use it without direction from another. *Sapere aude!* [Dare to know!] 'Have courage to use your own reason!' – that is the motto of Enlightenment.
>
> (Kant [1784] 1950, p. 286)

EXERCISE

What is the most important message of the Enlightenment, according to Kant?

DISCUSSION

The passage above is an exhortation to readers to take responsibility for their own opinions and actions. Kant represents this process as a coming of age. By relying on authority – whether this be other people, written texts, customs or tradition – human beings are like children who rely on others to guide their understanding. However, whereas a child needs guidance because its faculty of judgement is not yet formed, for Kant an adult who does not use his or her reason only lacks the courage to do so. Enlightenment is not defined as a doctrine or a theory, but rather as an attitude towards authority and as an assumption of responsibility for one's own judgement and choices.

For Enlightenment authors the function of reason was that of a radical critique of all items of knowledge and all fields of experience, including politics and religion. This critique did not stop at reason itself; indeed one of the most important philosophical contributions of the eighteenth century lies in the investigation of the capabilities and limits of reason, notably in the works of Kant and of the philosopher David Hume (1711–76). Enlightenment thinkers on the whole did not believe that reason was all-powerful, although later critics have sometimes represented them as believing so. The teaching of experience was crucial in their philosophy, and they thought that both reason and experience should guide our knowledge.

The full exercise of an individual's reason requires the freedom to express and debate opinions and may imply a criticism of political and religious authorities. Where did the Enlightenment stand on the issues of freedom of speech and tolerance? The answer is that views obviously varied, especially because of the different political and social circumstances of different countries. It is, however, a fair generalization to say that Enlightenment authors presented themselves as advocates of freedom and tolerance. The limits of freedom and tolerance, however, were difficult to set. In *What is Enlightenment?*, for example, after the passage quoted above Kant went on to defend the duty of public obedience to one's prince.

The Enlightenment has been regarded as the basis of modern conceptions of political freedom, tolerance and universal human rights. However, it has also been deemed to be at the root of intolerance and despotism. This controversy cannot be easily resolved, if at all, but it is worth keeping in mind when discussing Enlightenment views of progress and of the role of Europe. Particularly important for the discussion of identity here is the

Enlightenment conception of uniform human nature. Using the modern terms that were employed in Chapter 1, it can be said that most Enlightenment thinkers subscribed to the notion of a universal human identity. This conception has constituted the basis of a defence of the principles of equality and universal rights. Some commentators, however, are of the opinion that this same concept is intolerant of cultural differences.

Where and 'who' was the Enlightenment?

Broadly speaking, the Enlightenment was a European phenomenon. In different places, however, it displayed different characteristics; for this reason you will often find the word prefixed by a geographical indication – hence English, French, Scottish, German and Neapolitan Enlightenment, for instance. You will also find German (*Aufklärung*), Italian (*Illuminismo*) and French words (*Lumières*) employed to indicate the specific types of Enlightenment that developed in those parts of Europe (in the eighteenth century France was one country, whereas Germany and Italy were divided into many states, hence the more frequent use of terms such as the 'Milanese' or 'Venetian' rather than 'Italian' *Illuminismo*). In the geography of the Enlightenment, we must also include the (former) American colonies of European countries. The cultural links between European settlements in the Americas and European countries were strong enough to include those settlements within a European cultural space. The French, English and Scottish Enlightenments were points of reference for all other types of Enlightenment; however, while in North America there were direct links with France, England and Scotland, Spain was 'the main channel or filter until 1808 through which the Enlightenment reached Spanish America' (Whitaker, 1971, pp. 21–2).

Here the emphasis is on French authors, because they elaborated the most explicit theories of progress. I have used the word 'authors' because it is difficult to identify them precisely in modern terms; they called themselves 'philosophers' but, as Roy Porter points out, 'they were men of the world: journalists, propagandists, activists, seeking not just to understand the world but to change it' (Porter, 1990, p. 3). This difference from current academic philosophers is the reason why eighteenth-century 'philosophers' are often referred to by the French term *philosophes*. To be a *philosophe* was for many not just an occupation (some of them did receive salaries), but an identity which defined a way of being, a way of conceiving society and of conducting one's affairs and one's relations with other people.

For a long time, critics concentrated on a relatively small number of *philosophes*, such as Voltaire, Condorcet, Turgot and Rousseau, about whom there is a very extensive literature. More recently, scholars have distinguished between a 'High Enlightenment' and a 'Low Enlightenment' and have investigated the latter through the great number of publications, often in the form of pamphlets, that circulated in France in the eighteenth century. Robert Darnton argues that it was the 'Low Enlightenment' writers who produced the more daring arguments, expressing their hatred for the *ancien régime* – the monarchical regime which was swept away by the French Revolution (note that the term *ancien*/old carries negative connotations, in line with the theory of progress). Indeed, Darnton thinks that it was in the 'pamphleteering of Grub Street' that the revolution found its voice (Darnton, 1982, pp. 39–40).

In general, the Enlightenment, in its different expressions, was not a movement limited to a small elite; rather it was sustained by a large number of often obscure thinkers, and by the printers and publishers who took the risk, for money or conviction, of publishing works that might displease the censors and cause very serious trouble. These two versions of the Enlightenment, however, were not separate, and the authors of the 'Low Enlightenment' read and knew the works of the 'High Enlightenment' authors.

Progress in the age of the Enlightenment

The historian and philosopher of science Georges Canguilhem (1904–95) wrote 'according to the philosophy of progress, the progress of reason dispelled prejudices just as the sun dispelled darkness' (Canguilhem, 1998, pp. 322–3). In the metaphor of the light of reason dispelling the darkness of prejudices, the illumination is progressive, that is it takes place stage by stage. The Enlightenment's promotion of critical reason went hand in hand with a theory of history. First of all, the past ceased to be an authority; ancient authors were no longer revered but were rather submitted to criticism as any other source might be. Enlightenment philosophers thought that their own time was by and large more 'enlightened' than previous epochs had been, and there was therefore no reason for submitting to any authority, least of all to that of people who had lived in the past. At the same time, great emphasis was put on the future, as a 'realm of unrealised possibilities' (Gay, 1969, p. 92). What linked past, present and future was progress. Progress was the unifying principle of history: historical events received their significance from the idea that improvements had taken and would take place. Enlightenment authors judged the past from the point of view of their own ideals; only by doing so could they construct a progressive history. For instance, a typical *philosophe* would have had a positive view of any rational inquiry into nature and would have opposed reliance on tradition and the teaching of the established religion. He or she would then have judged past epochs or different cultures by examining the state of the study of nature in that time or place, together with its reliance on the weight of tradition and religion. Based on these assessments, the *philosophe* would now have been in a position to create a hierarchy of epochs, ranging from the most 'backward' to the most 'advanced'. Such hierarchies generally corresponded to historical time: the more remote the epoch, the more backward the culture. However, most *philosophes* regarded the Middle Ages as less advanced than ancient Greece; in their eyes this did not disprove the theory of progress but only showed that there could be setbacks in the overall advancement.

In the Enlightenment, at least for the French authors considered here, history became a thoroughly human affair; its development was generally explained without recourse to God or divine providence.

Moreover, the Christian dogma of original sin was rejected: for Enlightenment authors, human beings were naturally inclined to virtue, and had a 'faculty of perfectibility' as Jean-Jacques Rousseau (1712 (Geneva) – 78 (Paris)) put it. Progress included advancement in the knowledge of nature, refinement of art, music and letters, and social and indeed moral improvement, guided by better self-understanding. For Enlightenment philosophers, human beings were able not only to expand their knowledge of nature, but also to increase their own happiness by means of moral improvement.

History was conceived primarily as moral and cultural history; the emphasis was on human beings' progressive understanding of the natural world and of themselves, and on their creativity as expressed in the arts and the sciences. François-Marie Arouet, alias Voltaire (1694–1778), in his *Essay on the Manners, Customs, and the Spirit of Nations* (Voltaire [1754] 1963) outlined human history as the history of progressive enlightenment. Voltaire did not believe that human nature changed, but rather that human beings were increasingly successful in dominating their passions. Such passions were in his view responsible for all the horrors of history, which he described so vividly in the *Essay* that many interpreted his work as an

Figure 2.1 Maurice Quentin de la Tour (1704–88), portrait of Voltaire, engraving. Private Collection. Photo: Bridgeman Art Library

ironic presentation of human vices. The *Essay* is in fact a narration of the rise of modern Europe, which Voltaire regarded as incomparably richer, more civilized and more enlightened in his time than it had ever been before (Voltaire [1754] 1963, tome 2, p. 810).

On the whole, Enlightenment authors thought that past ages were ridden with prejudice and errors. Why then were they preoccupied with history? One reason was that they thought the knowledge of the unhappiness that prejudices and irrational behaviour had brought about in the past constituted a warning for the present: if people fully realized the consequences of prejudices, they would be more likely to follow the path of rationality, tolerance and justice. For instance, in his *History of Charles XII* (Voltaire [1731] 1733) Voltaire aimed to show that that ruler's pursuit of glory resulted in his subjects' unhappiness. In such ways the writing of history could be an instrument of progress.

Figure 2.2   Clément Belle, *Minerva Hands Hercules the Decree Abolishing the Vices of the Former Government*, model for the tapestry ordered by the count of Angiviller in 1788 for the Gobelins factory, oil on canvas. Moral progress was at the core of much of Enlightenment historiography. Here is a symbolic abolition of the vices of the *ancien régime*. For the revolutionary use of classical mythology see Chapter 3. Louvre, Paris. Réunion des Musées Nationaux

Many *philosophes* also wrote history for another reason: they intended to uncover the laws that they believed were inherent in historical development. For them, history was not just a chronicle but exhibited an overall logic, and historical events were linked by relations of cause and effect that had to be found out. By understanding the logic of history, it would be possible to decide on future actions, or even predict future events. The *philosophes* were not interested in all past events but only in those that were relevant to the understanding of history as a whole. Their histories, as exemplified below in the extracts from Turgot's and Condorcet's works, were grand narratives aimed at showing the progression of human civilization and, more specifically, the effects of cultural events such as the invention of writing on the overall direction of history. The *philosophes* derived the idea that there are laws which govern phenomena from Isaac Newton (1642–1727). In his *Principia* (full title *Philosophiae naturalis principia mathematica*, or *Mathematical Principles of Natural Philosophy*, 1687), Newton formulated a very general law on what held the solar system together: universal gravitation. This law, according to which every particle of matter is attracted to every other by a force that varies directly as the product of their masses and inversely as the square of their distance from each other, was mathematically precise and had universal application. The *philosophes* turned to human affairs and sought similar laws in the unfolding of history.

Founded in 1257 as a theological college for poor students, the Sorbonne has become the symbol of the University of Paris. Nowadays three of the thirteen colleges of the University of Paris are called Sorbonne (Paris I, III and IV). Theology remained the Sorbonne's core teaching for centuries. It has not been taught in French state universities, including the Sorbonne, however, since 1886 (nor is it taught in some other European countries, such as Italy). This is a consequence of the secular character of French education, which is largely run by the state.

Turgot on progress

The characteristics of the Enlightenment idea of progress outlined above are very general, and do not always apply to the specific convictions of individual authors. To appreciate this it is necessary to turn to eighteenth-century texts in which the idea of progress is more explicitly presented and defended. The reading below is from Turgot's 'A philosophical review of the successive advances of the human mind' (Turgot [1750] 1975). Anne-Robert-Jacques Turgot, baron de l'Aulne (1727–81), was the third son of a state administrator under King Louis XV. *A Philosophical Review* is the text of a Latin lecture he delivered at the opening of the academic year of the **Sorbonne**. It was the year 1750, Turgot was twenty-three years old and he was 'prior' at the Sorbonne, which made him responsible for the supervision of theology students (Canguilhem, 1998, p. 314). He was still pursuing an ecclesiastical career, which he cut short in 1751 in favour of one in the state administration. Under Louis XVI he became naval minister and, for two years only, finance minister.

A Philosophical Review of the Successive Advances of the Human Mind

The phenomena of nature, governed as they are by constant laws, are confined within a circle of revolutions which are always the same. All things perish, and all things spring up again; and in these successive acts of generation through which plants and animals reproduce themselves time does no more than restore continually the counterpart of what it has caused to disappear.

The succession of mankind, on the other hand, affords from age to age an ever-changing spectacle. Reason, the passions, and liberty ceaselessly give rise to new events: all the ages are bound up with one another by a succession of causes and effects which link the present state of the world with all those that have preceded it. The arbitrary signs of speech and writing, by providing men with the means of securing the possession of their ideas and communicating them to others, have made of all the individual stores of knowledge a common treasure-house which one generation transmits to another, an inheritance which is always being enlarged by the discoveries of each age. Thus the human race, considered over the period since its origin, appears to the eye of a philosopher as one vast whole, which itself, like each individual, has its infancy and its advancement.

We see the establishment of societies, and the formation of nations which in turn dominate other nations or become subject to them. Empires rise and fall; laws and forms of government succeed one another; the arts and the sciences are in turn discovered and perfected, in turn retarded and accelerated in their progress; and they are passed on from country to country. Self-interest, ambition, and vainglory continually change the world scene and inundate the earth with blood; yet in the midst of their ravages manners are softened, the human mind becomes more enlightened, and separate nations are brought closer to one another. Finally commercial and political ties unite all parts of the globe,

Figure 2.3 Anon. (French School), portrait of Anne-Robert-Jacques Turgot, eighteenth century. Château de Versailles. Photo: Bridgeman Art Library

and the whole human race, through alternate periods of rest and unrest, of weal and woe, goes on advancing, although at a slow pace, towards greater perfection ...

[N]atural resources and the fertile seeds of the sciences are to be found wherever there are men. The most exalted mental attainments are only and can only be a development or combination of the original ideas based on sensation, just as the building at whose great height we gaze in wonder necessarily has its foundation in the earth upon which we tread. The same senses, the same organs, and the spectacle of the same universe, have everywhere given men the same ideas, just as the same needs and inclinations have everywhere taught them the same arts.

Now a faint light begins occasionally to penetrate the darkness which has covered all the nations, and step by step it spreads. The inhabitants of Chaldea, closest to the source of the original traditions, the Egyptians, and the Chinese apparently lead the rest of the peoples. Others follow them at a distance, and progress leads to further progress. The inequality of nations increases; in one place the arts begin to emerge, while in another they advance at a rapid rate towards perfection. In some nations they are brought to a standstill in the midst of their mediocrity, while in others the original darkness is not yet dissipated at all. Thus the present state of the world, marked as it is by these infinite variations in inequality, spreads out before us at one and the same time all the gradations from barbarism to refinement, thereby revealing to us at a single glance, as it were, the records and remains of all the steps taken by the human mind, a reflection of all the stages through which it has passed, and the history of all the ages.

But is not nature everywhere the same? – and if she leads all men to the same truths, if even their errors are alike, how is it that they do not all move forward at the same rate along the road which is marked out for them? It is true that the human mind everywhere contains the potential for the same progress, but nature, distributing her gifts unequally, has given to certain minds an abundance of talents which she has refused to others. Circumstances either develop these talents or allow them to become buried in obscurity; and it is from the infinite variety of these circumstances that there springs the inequality in the progress of nations ...

With the passing of time new peoples came into being ...

The Phoenicians, inhabitants of a barren coast, had made themselves the agents of exchanges between peoples. Their ships, spread out over the whole Mediterranean, began to reveal nation to nation.

Astronomy, navigation, and geography were perfected, one by means of the other. The coasts of Greece and Asia Minor came to be filled with Phoenician colonies. Colonies are like fruits which cling to the tree only until they have reached their maturity: once they had become self-sufficient they did what Carthage was to do later, and what America will one day do.

Out of the intermingling of these colonies, each independent of the others, with the ancient peoples of Greece and with the remnants of all the swarms of barbarians who had successively ravaged her, there arose the Greek nation, or rather that family of nations comprised of a large number of small peoples ...

Happy centuries, in which all the fine arts spread their light on every side, and in which the passion of a noble emulation was swiftly transmitted from one city to another! Painting, sculpture, architecture, poetry, and history grew up everywhere at the same time, as we see in the expanse of a forest a thousand different trees springing up, growing, and being crowned together ...

While the Athenians, the Spartans, and the Thebans are in turn arrogating to themselves superiority over the other cities, the Macedonian power, unnoticed, like a river which overflows its banks, slowly extends into Greece under Philip, and violently inundates Asia under Alexander ...

But for several centuries already, Rome, in Italy as if in a world apart, had been advancing by a continual succession of triumphs towards the conquest of the world. Victorious over Carthage, she appeared suddenly in the midst of the nations. Peoples trembled and were brought into subjection: the Romans, conquerors of Greece, became aware of a new empire, that of intellect and learning. Their austere uncouthness was tamed. Athens found disciples, and soon rivals, among her conquerors ...

The laws of Rome, created to govern one city, sank under the burden of the whole world: Roman liberty was extinguished in waves of blood. Octavius alone finally gathered in the fruit of the civil strife. Cruel usurper, temperate prince, he gave tranquillity to the earth. His enlightened protection stimulated all the arts. Italy had a Homer, less productive than the first, but wiser, more equable, just as harmonious, and perhaps more perfect. Sublimity, reason, and the graces united to create Horace. Taste was perfected in every sphere ...

From this time until the fall of the Empire, we see nothing but a general decadence in which everything is plunged ...

Soon the Empire, abandoned to the caprices of an insolent militia, becomes the prey of a host of tyrants, who, in the process of seizing it from one another, bring desolation and havoc to the provinces. Military discipline is destroyed, the northern barbarians penetrate on every side, peoples fall upon peoples, the cities become deserted, the fields are left uncultivated, and the western Empire, weakened by the transference of all its power to Constantinople, ruined everywhere by so many repeated ravages, at last suddenly collapses, and the Burgundians, Goths, and Franks are left to quarrel over its far-flung ruins and to found kingdoms in the different countries of Europe.

Could it be, in this sanctuary, that I should pass over in silence that new light which, while the Empire was proceeding towards its ruin, had spread out over the world – a light a thousand times more precious than those of letters and philosophy? Holy religion, could it be that I should forget you? Could I forget the perfecting of manners, the dissipation at last of the darkness of idolatry, and the enlightenment of men on the subject of the Divinity! ...

But the wounds of the human race were too deep; centuries were necessary to heal them ...

[N]evertheless, from the midst of this barbarism, perfected arts and sciences will one day rise again ...

Germany, Denmark, Sweden, and Poland through the efforts of Charlemagne and the Othos, and Russia through trade with the Greek empire, cease to be uncultivated forests. Christianity, in bringing together these scattered savages, in settling them in towns, is going to dry up forever the source of those inundations which have so often been fatal to the sciences. Europe is still barbarous; but the knowledge brought by her to even more barbarous peoples represents for them immense progress. Little by little the customs introduced by Germany into the south of Europe disappear. The nations, amid the quarrels of the nobles and the princes, begin to fashion for themselves the principles of a more stable government, and to acquire, in accordance with the different circumstances in which they find themselves, the particular character which distinguishes them. The wars against the Mussulmans in Palestine, by giving a common interest to all Christian states, teach them to know one another and to unite with one another, and sow the seeds of that modern political state of affairs in which so many nations seem to comprise nothing but one vast republic. Already we see the royal authority reviving again in France; the power of the people establishing itself in England; the Italian towns constituting themselves into republics and presenting the likeness of ancient Greece; the little monarchies of Spain driving the Moors before them and little by little joining up again into one whole. Soon the seas, which have hitherto separated the nations, come to be the link between them through the invention of the compass. The Portuguese in the east and the Spaniards in the west discover new worlds: at last the world as a whole is known ...

The time has come. Issue forth, Europe, from the darkness which covered thee! Immortal names of the Medici, of Leo X, of Francis I, be consecrated for ever! May the patrons of the arts share the glory of those who cultivate them! I salute thee, O Italy! – happy land, for the second time the homeland of letters and of taste, the spring from which their waters have spread to fertilise our territories ...

Time, spread your swift wings! Century of Louis, century of great men, century of reason, hasten! Already, even amidst the turmoil of heresy, the long-disturbed fortunes of states have ended by settling down, as if as the result of a final shock. Already the unremitting study of antiquity has brought men's minds back again to the point where its progress was arrested; already that host of facts, experiments, instruments, and ingenious exercises which the practice of the arts has accumulated over so many centuries, has been rescued from obscurity through printing; already the productions of the two worlds, brought together before our eyes as the result of a far-flung commerce, have become the foundation of a natural philosophy hitherto unknown, and freed at last from alien speculations; already on every hand attentive eyes are fixed upon nature: the remotest chances, turned to profit, give birth to discoveries. The son of an artisan in Zealand brings together for amusement two convex glasses in a tube; the boundaries of our senses are made to recede, and in Italy the eyes of Galileo have discovered a new firmament. Already Kepler, seeking in the stars for the numbers of Pythagoras, has discovered those two famous laws of the movements of the planets which one day in the hands of Newton will become the key to the universe. Already Bacon has traced out for posterity the road which it must follow.

Who is the mortal who dares to reject the learning of all the ages, and even those notions which he has believed to be the most certain? He seems to wish to extinguish the torch of the sciences in order to relight it all on his own at the pure fire of reason. Does he wish to imitate those peoples of antiquity among whom it was a crime to light at other fires that which was made to burn on the altars of the Gods? Great Descartes, if it was not always given to you to find the truth, at least you have destroyed the tyranny of error ...

At last all the shadows are dispelled: and what a light shines out on all sides! What a host of great men in every sphere! What a perfection of human reason! One man, Newton, has subjected the infinite to the calculus, has revealed the properties of light which in illuminating everything seemed to conceal itself, and has put into his balance the stars, the earth, and all the forces of nature. And this man has found a rival. Leibnitz encompasses within his vast intellect all the objects of the human mind. The different sciences, confined at first to a small number of simple notions common to all, can no longer, when as a result of their progress they have become more extensive and more difficult, be envisaged otherwise than separately; but greater progress once again unites them, because there is discovered that mutual dependence of all truths which in linking them together illuminates each through the other; because, if each day adds to the vast extent of the sciences, each day also makes them easier, because methods are multiplied with discoveries, because the scaffolding rises with the building.

O Louis, what majesty surrounds thee! What splendour thy beneficent hand has spread over all the arts! Thine happy people has become the centre of refinement! Rivals of Sophocles, of Menander, and of Horace, gather around his throne! Arise, learned academies, and unite your efforts for the glory of his reign! What a multitude of public monuments, of works of genius, of arts newly invented, and of old arts perfected! Who could possibly picture them? Open your eyes and see! Century of Louis the Great, may your light beautify the precious reign of his successor! May it last for ever, may it extend over the whole world! May men continually make new steps along the road of truth! Rather still, may they continually become better and happier!

(Turgot [1750] 1975, pp. 41, 42–3, 47, 50, 51, 52, 52–3, 53, 55, 56–7, 57, 57–8, 59)

EXERCISE _____

1   What is, for Turgot, the difference between the 'phenomena of nature' and 'the succession of mankind'?

2   At the end of the second paragraph of the extract Turgot claims that 'the human race, considered over the period since its origin, appears to the eye of a philosopher as one vast whole, which itself, like each individual, has its infancy and its advancement'. How does Turgot show this idea in his narration of human history?

3   Turgot's ideal journey through history is also a geographical journey, as he wanders from one part of the earth to another. Can you see a general geographical direction?

DISCUSSION _____

1   Turgot contrasts the cyclical movement of nature with the linear history of humankind. Although individual animals and plants are born and die, these events only maintain nature as it is, so creating a cycle of renewal which is always the same. Here Turgot is just stating a point which had been widely accepted since antiquity, when time was conceived as cyclical. Especially in temperate areas like Europe, the succession of seasons has stood as a display of nature's continuous repetition of the same pattern. For Turgot, human history exhibits new events, rather than an endless repetition. He claims that these new events are produced by 'Reason, the passions, and liberty', while nature is 'governed ... by constant laws'. This contrast between human beings' liberty and nature's laws should not be interpreted as a suggestion that there is no pattern to human history. Indeed Turgot regards historical events as linked by a relation of cause and effect. In this way, he can claim that history has a direction, rather than being just a meaningless succession of events.

2   Turgot's outline of human history presents various civilizations – Egyptian, Chinese, Phoenician, Greek and so on – as successive stages of one and only one civilization. Thus it is not important in this history to narrate what occurred, for instance, in Egypt or China in the fifteenth or sixteenth centuries, because, for him, in this period advancement in civilization took place in 'Europe' and in particular in 'Italy'. In _A Philosophical Review_ the progress of human civilization is seen as parallel to the growth of an individual in that it is a development from a state of ignorance, lack of sophistication and superstition towards increasingly greater knowledge, refinement and rationality.

3   Turgot starts with Chaldea (a region of ancient Babylonia, today southern Iraq), Egypt and China, and then (with the Phoenicians) moves on to what Europeans now call the Middle East. From the next step (represented by the Greeks) onwards most of Turgot's story is set in Europe, and on the whole is westbound. The direction of world civilization in *A Philosophical Review* is based on the view that the civilization of some parts of Europe is the most advanced in the world, while the past of all human history is read in hindsight as an advancement towards this. In this way, ancient Egyptians and Greeks become the ancestors of eighteenth-century French people, and to a certain extent of Euro-Americans as a whole, while the modern inhabitants of Egypt and Greece drop out of history.

Figure 2.4   The name of Turgot lives on at the Louvre in Paris for tourists and passers-by to see. Photo: B. W. Alleyne

Turgot's representation of history displays the characteristics which were described above (in the section 'History, time and progress') as being judged necessary to theories of progress: it is linear and continuous. Moreover, as in Bury's definition, it is the progress of world civilization, rather than that of a particular people. Like the other *philosophes*, Turgot regarded humankind as a whole. However, this does not mean that in his view all peoples advanced together; rather, in different times, different regions of the world were the setting for the newest developments. Turgot thought that in his time Europe was at the forefront of the process of enlightenment, and as such it carried the responsibility of enlightening peoples in other parts of the world. So conceived, 'Europe' is not only a geographical space but also a historical moment. From Turgot's outline of human history, it also follows that for him Europe had not always occupied the most advanced stage of human history.

Turgot regarded human history as exhibiting a clear progressive character. In his view progress characterized all aspects of human life, but not in the same way and at the same speed. He isolated four types of progress, each applying to a different area of human activity (Turgot actually used the plural of the term 'progress'): technology, speculative science, moral behaviour and artistic expression (Manuel, 1962, p. 36). Of these, he viewed technological progress as the steadiest type; the great number of people practising mechanical arts meant that development in this field was rapid and likely to continue. Unlike most of his contemporaries, he acknowledged the importance of medieval technical inventions and believed that they played an important role in the advancement of Renaissance speculative science. However, he expected a great expansion of speculative science in his own time, increasingly independent of technology. As for moral progress, he believed it would eventually bring about the end of cruelty and war. Finally, in *A Philosophical Review* Turgot does hint at progress in the arts, but later in his life he lost confidence in this idea, for it seemed to him that ancient authors were not inferior to modern ones.

Does nature have a history?

To a modern reader acquainted with the theory of evolution, Turgot's assumption that nature does not exhibit changes might appear peculiar. Obviously Turgot could not have been aware of the theory of evolution as presented by Charles Darwin, who was born in 1809 and published *On the Origin of the Species* in 1859. In the eighteenth century, however, several theories started circulating that suggested the earth had not always existed in its present form, but rather had originated at a certain point in time and gradually evolved. Georges-Louis Leclerc, comte de Buffon (1707–88), a French naturalist who became keeper of the Jardin du Roi (the royal botanical garden, now the Jardin des Plantes), argued on the basis of the study of fossils that nature had a history. Indeed he put forward the theory that the earth originated from a rock torn from the sun. Kant also elaborated a theory of the origin of the earth, the so-called nebular hypothesis, according to which the solar system originated from a nebula (cloud) of dust and gas. Before these theories were expounded the received view, based on the biblical story of the creation, was that the earth had been created in its present form (between about 6000 and 4000 BCE), and that all animal and vegetable species had always existed as we see them now.

At the beginning of the nineteenth century the French naturalist Jean-Baptiste de Lamarck (1744–1829), who had been Buffon's pupil, proposed a theory of evolution of the various species. He called his theory 'transformism', because in his view the different species underwent transformations as a reaction to their environment. These transformations occurred in individual creatures and, gradually over long periods of time, became permanent in each species. According to Lamarck's theory, the different species were not created once and for all exactly as they are now, but rather were the result of a series of long and never-ending transformations. This view of nature can be read as a type of progress, for species evolve from being 'less perfect' to being 'more perfect' (meaning 'better adapted to their environment and more complex'). This was indeed the way in which Lamarck's doctrine was read in nineteenth-century Britain. While at best ignored at Oxford and Cambridge, Lamarckism was very popular in socialist and radical circles, for it offered a scientific theory of perfectibility which could be transferred to society. It was argued that just as species are transformed by the natural environment, human beings can also be improved upon by changing their social environment. Education and a change of social and material circumstances would thus bring about progress. The **Owenite socialists** in particular employed Lamarck's doctrine as scientific support for their own doctrine of social perfectibility and their programme of constructing a secular, scientifically based cooperative society (Desmond, 1987; 1989).

The novelty of attributing a history to nature cannot be overestimated. Indeed the philosopher Michel Foucault has claimed that the idea that nature undergoes change and has a history marks a fundamental difference between the philosophy of the Enlightenment and that of previous periods (Foucault, 1970). Turgot's view of nature was on its way out, and 'by the end of the [eighteenth] century it had become impossible to sustain the calm and stable view of nature left by many theologians' (Outram, 1996, p. 59).

Followers of Robert Owen (1771–1858), a Welsh utopian socialist. Owen aimed to transform society through the foundation of industrial and agricultural cooperative communities. The philosophical assumption that supported his plans was that the character of human beings is formed by circumstances, hence his great emphasis on the creation of a favourable environment and on education.

Condorcet on progress

Figure 2.5   Anon. (French School), portrait of Marie-Jean-Antoine-Nicolas Caritat, marquis de Condorcet, eighteenth century, pastel. Château de Versailles et de Trianon. Réunion des Musées Nationaux

A political group in revolutionary France. It seized power in June 1793 and stepped down just over a year later. Its most famous member, Robespierre, exercised great influence over the Parisian club (the group was subdivided into many clubs) and the revolutionary government while the Jacobins were in power.

In many of the *philosophes*' writings, the ideas of Europe, Enlightenment and progress are intimately connected. A very good example is provided by Condorcet's *Sketch for a Historical Picture of the Progress of the Human Mind* (Condorcet [1794] 1979), one of the most explicit presentations of a theory of progress in successive stages. This work was written in remarkable conditions: its author was in hiding. Antoine-Nicolas Caritat, marquis de Condorcet (1743–94), had been Turgot's disciple and had known such other famous *philosophes* as Voltaire and Jean d'Alembert (1717–83) (Gay, 1969, p. 112). However, unlike them, he had lived to see and take part in the French Revolution. In 1791 he was elected a member of the legislative assembly and the following year became a member of the Convention (the constitutional and legislative assembly which wrote the first republican constitution). During this period he drafted a project for the constitution and a plan for the reorganization of the educational system. However, his disagreements with the **Jacobins** in power became irreconcilable, and in 1793 a warrant was issued for his arrest.

He went into hiding and it was then that he wrote the *Sketch*. Eventually captured, he died in prison (Manuel, 1962, p. 58).

Despite his difficult situation, Condorcet advocated the principles of the revolution and foresaw an enlightened future. The *Sketch* is divided into an introduction and ten parts, each corresponding to a stage of human history. As its title suggests, this work is a history of

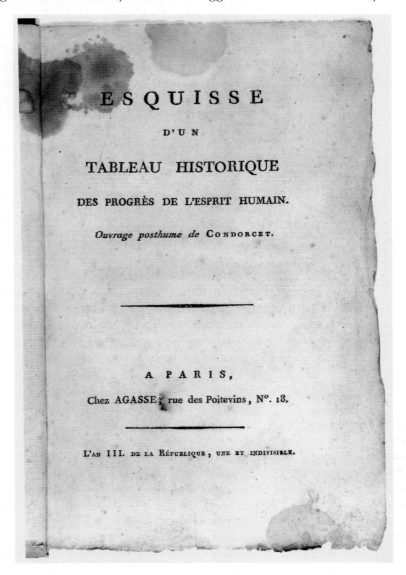

Figure 2.6 Title page of one of Condorcet's *Esquisse d'un Tableau historique des Progrès de l'Esprit humain*. Bodleian Library, University of Oxford, Vet E5 e.238

'the human mind'. Indeed, in Condorcet's view history was formed by human genius and creativity. As a result, the arts and technology are the protagonists of Condorcet's story, rather than kings and battles. The passages from one stage to another are not marked by political changes but rather by cultural events, such as the invention of agriculture (second epoch), the invention of writing (third epoch) and Aristotle's organization of the sciences (fifth epoch). In the *Sketch* progress does not proceed smoothly, indeed it experiences setbacks. This is because, in Condorcet's view, the 'forces of Enlightenment' had continuously to fight the 'forces of obscurantism', that is those people who place obstacles in the way of the free use of reason, either in the name of religion, or because of their own philosophical systems, or because of a lust for power (Manuel, 1962). However, Condorcet had no doubt that the forces of Enlightenment would prevail. His certainty was such that he concluded his *Sketch* with a presentation of the future, or the tenth epoch of the human mind.

How could Condorcet justify his prediction of the future state of affairs in the concluding chapter of the *Sketch*? Anticipating such an objection, he offered an answer in the first paragraphs of the tenth epoch, as reproduced in the reading below.

The Tenth Stage

The future progress of the human mind

If man can, with almost complete assurance, predict phenomena when he knows their laws, and if, even when he does not, he can still, with great expectation of success, forecast the future on the basis of his experience of the past, why, then, should it be regarded as a fantastic undertaking to sketch, with some pretence to truth, the future destiny of man on the basis of his history? The sole foundation for belief in the natural sciences is this idea, that the general laws directing the phenomena of the universe, known or unknown, are necessary and constant. Why should this principle be any less true for the development of the intellectual and moral faculties of man than for the other operations of nature? Since beliefs founded on past experience of like conditions provide the only rule of conduct for the wisest of men, why should the philosopher be forbidden to base his conjectures on these same foundations, so long as he does not attribute to them a certainty superior to that warranted by the number, the constancy, and the accuracy of his observations?

Our hopes for the future condition of the human race can be subsumed under three important heads: the abolition of inequality between nations, the progress of equality within each nation, and the true perfection of mankind. Will all nations one day attain that state of civilization which the most enlightened, the freest and the least burdened by prejudices, such as the French and the Anglo-Americans, have attained already? Will the vast gulf that separates these peoples from the slavery of nations under the rule of monarchs, from the barbarism of African tribes, from the ignorance of savages, little by little disappear?

Is there on the face of the earth a nation whose inhabitants have been debarred by nature herself from the enjoyment of freedom and the exercise of reason?

(Condorcet [1794] 1979, pp. 173–4)

EXERCISE

1   On which conviction does Condorcet base his belief in the possibility of predicting the future?

2   What is the relationship between history and natural sciences expressed in the extract?

DISCUSSION

1   Condorcet bases his prediction of the future stage of human history on the conviction that history is regulated by laws. We can find out these laws, or the general trend of history, he argues, by studying the past. A prediction can then be made, based on the mechanisms observed in the past. However, Condorcet calls his prediction for the future 'hopes' and intends, as he later goes on to say (Condorcet [1794] 1979, p. 175), to show that 'nature has set no limits to the realization of our hopes'. It is clear that progress, for Condorcet, is something desirable to promote, not just a disinterested observation of the laws of history. Moreover, he only claims that nature has set no limits, rather than demonstrating the inevitability of progress. Going beyond the very 'scientific' opening of this extract, I believe that in Condorcet the two ideal types of progress – the result of the unfolding of history and the result of human activities – are both present.

2   Condorcet opens 'The tenth stage' by comparing the natural sciences and the writing of history, claiming that history can be founded on the same methods as the natural sciences. By doing this Condorcet implicitly claims that nature and history are similar, as both are governed by laws which can be discovered. Unlike his mentor Turgot, he emphasizes the similarities rather than the differences between history and nature.

The eighth epoch of the *Sketch* is marked by the invention of printing. This was a recurrent theme in the literature of the Enlightenment; the diffusion of ideas made possible by the easy reproduction of texts was seen as the necessary means of enlightening minds and therefore effecting progress. At the same time, along with his discussion of printing, Condorcet also starts to employ the word 'Europe' rather than the term 'Christian West' that he had used up to the seventh epoch, which corresponds to the end of the Middle Ages. In the *Sketch*, Europe is conceived as an intellectual and moral community which the circulation of printed texts has made possible. Voltaire had already linked the invention of printing with the creation of a European intellectual commonwealth. In his *Remarques sur l'histoire*, he claimed that printing had turned Europe into a kind of 'immense republic' and compared it with ancient Greece (Coutel, 1997, pp. 44–5; Pomeau, 1991, p. 246). Ancient Greece represented a time and place of remarkable intellectual achievements even for Enlightenment thinkers who generally favoured the present and the future over the past. For them, its lack of political unity made it similar to Europe in their own times. The historian Paul Hazard (1878–1944) argued that the *philosophes* regarded Paris as the model for Europe, as it 'was like a great drawing-room, a great *salon*, in which it was a delight to talk, to shine, or merely to listen' (Hazard, 1965, p. 470).

Condorcet presented Europe as the most enlightened part of the world, although not uniformly so, as he placed France at the most advanced point of progress thus far; he also included European settlements outside Europe, especially the North American colonies which had recently won their independence from Great Britain and had formed the United States of America. Europe was clearly ahead of any other part of the world in the sciences and technologies. For the *philosophes*, including Condorcet, there was no doubt that Europe was also more advanced in moral and political terms. They believed that it was in Europe that the ideals of freedom and equality were being realized, and regarded Europeans as intellectually, morally and culturally superior to all other peoples, but not by virtue of an intrinsic superiority. Indeed they firmly believed that human nature was one and the same all over the world. However, they thought that for various reasons Europeans had found themselves at the head of the line of the progress of human history. For Condorcet, this privileged position in the unfolding of history was what it meant to be European; we could say that it constituted European identity (of course he did not use the term 'identity', which in this sense is a modern use).

Figure 2.7   In 1989 France celebrated the
bicentenary anniversary of the revolution. This
stamp portraying Condorcet was issued that year
to commemorate one of the most convinced, if
unlucky, supporters of the revolution. Vincennes
Philatelic, Paris

The Enlightenment was above all a project, and it comes as no
surprise that Condorcet concluded his *Sketch* with a presentation of
the future. The reading below is another extract from 'The tenth
stage' of the *Sketch*.

If we glance at the state of the world today we see first of all that in
Europe the principles of the French constitution are already those
of all enlightened men. We see them too widely propagated, too
seriously professed, for priests and despots to prevent their gradual
penetration even into the hovels of their slaves; there they will
soon awaken in these slaves the remnants of their common sense

and inspire them with that smouldering indignation which not even constant humiliation and fear can smother in the soul of the oppressed.

As we move from nation to nation, we can see in each what special obstacles impede this revolution and what attitudes of mind favour it. We can distinguish the nations where we may expect it to be introduced gently by the perhaps belated wisdom of their governments, and those nations where its violence intensified by their resistance must involve all alike in a swift and terrible convulsion.

Can we doubt that either common sense or the senseless discords of European nations will add to the effects of the slow but inexorable progress of their colonies, and will soon bring about the independence of the New World? And then will not the European population in these colonies, spreading rapidly over that enormous land, either civilize or peacefully remove the savage nations who still inhabit vast tracts of its land?

Survey the history of our settlements and commercial undertakings in Africa or in Asia, and you will see how our trade monopolies, our treachery, our murderous contempt for men of another colour or creed, the insolence of our usurpations, the intrigues or the exaggerated proselytic zeal of our priests, have destroyed the respect and goodwill that the superiority of our knowledge and the benefits of our commerce at first won for us in the eyes of the inhabitants. But doubtless the moment approaches when, no longer presenting ourselves as always either tyrants or corrupters, we shall become for them the beneficent instruments of their freedom ...

These vast lands [Africa and Asia] are inhabited partly by large tribes who need only assistance from us to become civilized, who wait only to find brothers amongst the European nations to become their friends and pupils; partly by races oppressed by sacred despots or dull-witted conquerors, and who for so many centuries have cried out to be liberated; partly by tribes living in a condition of almost total savagery in a climate whose harshness repels the sweet blessings of civilization and deters those who would teach them its benefits; and finally, by conquering hordes who know no other law but force, no other profession but piracy. The progress of these two last classes of people will be slower and stormier; and perhaps it will even be that, reduced in number as they are driven back by civilized nations, they will finally disappear imperceptibly before them or merge into them ...

The progress of these peoples is likely to be more rapid and certain than our own because they can receive from us everything that we have had to find out for ourselves, and in order to understand those simple truths and infallible methods which we have acquired only after long error, all that they need to do is to follow the expositions and proofs that appear in our speeches and writings ...

The time will therefore come when the sun will shine only on free men who know no other master but their reason; when tyrants and slaves, priests and their stupid or hypocritical instruments will exist only in works of history and on the stage; and when we shall think of them only to pity their victims and their dupes; to maintain ourselves in a state of vigilance by thinking on their excesses; and to learn how to recognize and so to destroy, by force of reason, the first seeds of tyranny and superstition, should they ever dare to reappear amongst us.

(Condorcet [1794] 1979, pp. 175–6, 177, 178, 179)

EXERCISE

1   What is Condorcet's view of the future?

2   What is, for Condorcet, the relation that Europeans should enter into with the peoples of Africa and Asia? What is the connection between Condorcet's view of the matter and his theory of progress?

DISCUSSION

1   Condorcet believes that progress towards justice, equality and brotherhood is unstoppable, because the ideals of the Enlightenment, embodied in the French revolutionary constitution, have spread widely around the world. The enemies of progress – whom he identifies with priests and despots – will not be able to reverse this trend. Condorcet's vision, like that of the other *philosophes*, is worldwide: all peoples and all nations, for him, must be liberated from tyranny and must be able to exercise their freedom. In his view, the means of implementing such liberation vary according to different circumstances: in some cases reforms introduced by existing governments will be sufficient, while in other cases nothing short of revolution will do. He is confident that eventually all men will be free, and tyranny and religion will 'exist only in works of history and on the stage'.

2 Condorcet distinguishes quite sharply between the execrable behaviour that Europeans adopted towards Africans and Asians in the past and their present mission. In his view, Europeans have not always occupied their current position of the most enlightened people in the world; in previous times they were guilty of 'murderous contempt for men of another colour or creed'. However, now enlightened Europeans are the most advanced in respect of progress and have the responsibility of bringing other peoples up to their own level. Condorcet envisages a brotherhood between non-Europeans and Europeans, but thinks that the peoples of Africa and Asia will be Europeans' 'pupils'. According to Condorcet, there is only one world history and one desirable course of it. Therefore, for him there is no doubt that at the time he is writing European civilization is superior to other civilizations, and the latter can only gain by becoming more similar to the former. In Condorcet's intentions this assimilation of non-Europeans is aimed at bringing them justice, freedom and happiness. However, his theory of progress does not acknowledge cultural differences other than as differences in levels of development. Unequal relationships between different cultures must therefore follow from Condorcet's theory.

Rousseau on progress

It was noted above (in the section 'Turgot on progress') that Turgot distinguished four types of progress: in technology, the speculative sciences, moral behaviour and the arts. Condorcet similarly discussed progress in different areas of human activity. Both of them regarded advances in one area as being connected with progress in another, and ultimately foresaw and advocated progress in all sectors of human life (although, as mentioned earlier, Turgot did develop doubts about progress in the arts). Other *philosophes*, however, were more sceptical about the connection between different types of progress. Nowadays we might be more likely not to see a connection between, say, scientific and moral progress or artistic progress. Moreover, the awareness of the possible problems that scientific and technological advances carry is increasingly stronger today. Our attitude towards progress of any kind has changed greatly over the last 200 years or so. However, it should not be assumed that everybody in the eighteenth century subscribed to this belief in progress, or even that everybody was an incurable optimist. Turgot's and Condorcet's works are in many ways the most convinced 'demonstrations' of progress, but even in their writings there is an awareness of the difficulties that such advances may encounter and the risk that they may entail (Gay, 1969, pp. 108–11).

One of the most celebrated eighteenth-century philosophers, Jean-Jacques Rousseau, developed these concerns about the evil consequences of civilization. Rousseau is particularly interesting in an investigation of the Enlightenment idea of progress, because he did not deny the possibility of such advances but nevertheless presented a rather bleak picture of human history. As mentioned above, he firmly believed in the perfectibility of human nature and devoted a large part of his writings to how to improve human life. However, he thought that progress in the sciences, arts and technology had not brought about moral progress, but rather decadence. This idea should be examined in more detail.

Like Turgot and Condorcet, Rousseau composed an outline of the history of civilization – in his *Discourse on the Origins and the Foundation of Inequality among Men* (Rousseau [1754] 1984). This outline is similar to those of Turgot and Condorcet in that it is a world history, taken as a whole. Rousseau also shared with the other two *philosophes* the view that to a certain extent the direction of human

Figure 2.8 Maurice Quentin de la Tour (1704–88), portrait of Jean-Jacques Rousseau, pastel. Musée Antoine Lécuyer Saint-Quentin. Réunion des Musées Nationaux. Photo: Gérard Blot

civilization is inevitable: given certain conditions, certain consequences will follow, unless human beings consciously and decisively struggle to change the course of history. Moreover, Rousseau too was interested in the future as well as the past; indeed his main concern was to build the best possible future. His political treatise *The Social Contract* (Rousseau [1762] 1997) is a recipe for a just society, while his *Emile* (Rousseau [1762] 1993) is a pedagogical work aimed at the development of the best possible moral being. However, a crucial difference separates Rousseau from Turgot and Condorcet. For Rousseau, the advancement of technology, the development of trade and the evolution of forms of government had caused inequality, injustice and unhappiness. Indeed in his view civil society inevitably bore the germ of inequality. As he explained in the *Discourse*:

> The first man who, having enclosed a piece of land, thought of saying 'This is mine' and found people simple enough to believe him, was the true founder of civil society. How many

Figure 2.9 Albert-Ernest Carrier-Belleuse (1824–87), sculpture of Jean-Jacques Rousseau, terracotta. Château Musée Nemours. Réunion des Musées Nationaux. Photo: R. G. Ojeda

crimes, wars, murders; how much misery and horror the human race would have been spared if someone had pulled up the stakes and filled the ditch and cried out to his fellow men: 'Beware of listening to this impostor. You are lost if you forget that the fruits of the earth belong to everyone and that the earth itself belongs to no one!'

(Rousseau [1754] 1984, p. 109)

From the establishment of private property, according to Rousseau, inequality and injustice had progressively increased. Inequality in turn had corrupted human beings:

> From the extreme inequality of conditions and fortunes, from
> the diversity of passions and talents, from useless arts,
> pernicious arts and foolish sciences would arise a mass of
> prejudices, equally contrary to reason, happiness and virtue.
>
> (Rousseau [1754] 1984, p. 134)

The conclusion to be drawn is that progress in the sciences does not
go hand in hand with moral progress; indeed it is at odds with it. In
the *Discourse*, Rousseau outlined human history from the state of
nature to its current situation, going through the stages of
'civilization' in turn. It is implicit in the text that only Europe – which
Rousseau regarded as 'more continuously and better civilised than
other parts of the world' (Rousseau [1754] 1984, p. 116) – had in fact
gone through all these stages. By contrast, he mentioned peoples
such as the 'Caribbean Indians' as examples of human beings
existing in the state of nature, prior to the formation of civil society.
Like Condorcet and Turgot, Rousseau compared non-Europeans with
Europeans of previous times. Thus native Americans are not
examples of a different culture, but human beings who have not
developed any culture and have failed to progress. Once again,
progress is a model that explains differences between peoples and
cultures.

Rousseau's view of civilization was negative. As he represented native
Americans as human beings in their natural state, prior to civilization,
it might be concluded that he therefore proposed the native
American way of life as a model. Was this really the case? Form your
own opinion by reading the following four extracts; the first two
come from Rousseau's *Discourse on Inequality*; the second two from his
Emile. The latter, as you know, is Rousseau's treatise on education,
describing the ideal education of the young Emile. The first extract
from *Emile* comes from the beginning of the book; in the second
Rousseau refers to his (imaginary) work as an educator – 'doing too
much or too little' refers to this educational task.

> [Who] does not see that everything appears to remove the savage
> man both from the temptation to quit the savage condition and
> from the means of doing so? His imagination paints no pictures;
> his heart yearns for nothing; his modest needs are readily supplied
> at hand; and he is so far from having enough knowledge for him
> to desire to acquire more knowledge, that he can have neither
> foresight nor curiosity. The prospect of the natural world leaves
> him indifferent just because it has become familiar. It is always the
> same pattern, always the same rotation. He has not the intelligence
> to wonder at the greatest marvels; and we should look in vain to

him for that philosophy which a man needs if he is to know how to notice once what he has seen every day. His soul, which nothing disturbs, dwells only in the sensation of its present existence, without any idea of the future, however close that might be, and his projects, as limited as his horizons, hardly extend to the end of the day. Such is, even today, the extent of the foresight of a Caribbean Indian: he sells his cotton bed in the morning, and in the evening comes weeping to buy it back, having failed to foresee that he would need it for the next night.

(Rousseau [1754] 1984, p. 90)

I know we are constantly being told that nothing is more miserable than man in the state of nature; and if it is true, as I think I have proved, that it is only after many centuries that man could have had either the desire or the opportunity to quit that state, this is a charge to bring against nature and not against him whom nature has so constituted. But if I understand correctly the term 'miserable', it is a word that has no meaning or signifies only a painful deprivation and state of suffering in body or soul. Now I would be pleased to have it explained to me what kind of misery can be that of a free being whose heart is at peace and whose body is in health? I ask which – civilized or natural life – is the more liable to become unbearable to those who experience it? We see around us people who nearly all complain and several of whom indeed deprive themselves of their existence as far as they are able; and the joint sanction of divine and human law hardly suffices to halt this disorder. I ask if anyone has ever heard of a savage in a condition of freedom even dreaming of complaining about his life and killing himself? Let it be judged with less pride on which side the real misery lies. Nothing, on the contrary could be as miserable as a savage man dazzled by enlightenment, tormented by passions, and arguing about a state different from his own. It is thanks to a very wise Providence that the faculties which were potential in him should have become actual only with the opportunity of using them, so that they were neither superfluous nor onerous before their time, nor late in appearing and useless when the need arose. In instinct alone man had all he needed for living in a state of nature; in cultivated reason he has what is necessary only for living in society.

(Rousseau [1754] 1984, p. 97)

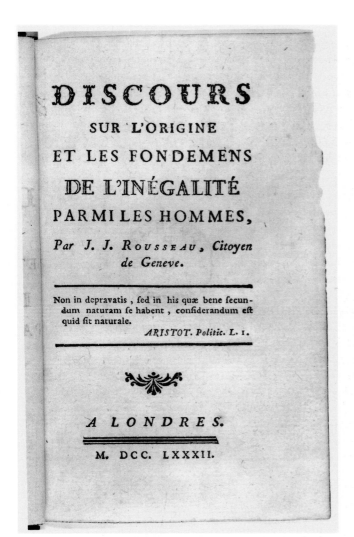

Figure 2.10 Two eighteenth-century editions of Rousseau's *Discourse on Inequality*, one published in London and the other in Amsterdam. Note that the author is 'Rousseau, citizen of Geneva'. Alone among the authors of the so-called French Enlightenment discussed in this chapter, Rousseau was not actually French. He was born in the independent republic of Geneva, which he left when he was sixteen years old. Geneva was annexed to France in 1798 but has been part of the Swiss confederation since 1814. Rousseau arrived in Paris at the age of thirty, after spending time in Savoy and Piedmont. There, through his friend Diderot, who commissioned him to write several articles for *L'Encyclopédie* (see Chapter 3), he met the most illustrious exponents of the French Enlightenment. He dedicated his *Discourse* to the citizens of Geneva, in tribute to their government. Bodleian Library, University of Oxford, Vet E5 f.162

God makes all things good; man meddles with them and they become evil. He forces one soil to yield the products of another, one tree to bear another's fruit. He confuses and confounds time, place, and natural conditions. He mutilates his dog, his horse, and his slave. He destroys and defaces all things; he loves all that is deformed and monstrous; he will have nothing as nature made it, not even man himself, who must learn his paces like a saddle-horse, and be shaped to his master's taste like the trees in his garden.

Yet things would be worse without this education, and mankind cannot be made by halves. Under existing conditions a man left to himself from birth would be more of a monster than the rest. Prejudice, authority, necessity, example, all the social conditions into which we are plunged, would stifle nature in him and put nothing in her place. She would be like a sapling chance sown in the midst of the highway, bent hither and thither and soon crushed by the passers-by.

(Rousseau [1762] 1993, p. 5)

It is not easy for a man to begin to think; but when once he has begun he will never leave off. Once a thinker, always a thinker, and the understanding once practised in reflection will never rest. You may therefore think that I do too much or too little; that the human mind is not by nature so quick to unfold; and that after having given it opportunities it has not got, I keep it too long confined within a circle of ideas which it ought to have outgrown.

But remember, in the first place, that when I want to train a natural man, I do not want to make him a savage and to send him back to the woods, but that living in the whirl of social life it is enough that he should not let himself be carried away by the passions and prejudices of men; let him see with his eyes and feel with his heart, let him own no sway but that of reason. Under these conditions it is plain that many things will strike him; the oft-recurring feelings which affect him, the different ways of satisfying his real needs, must give him many ideas he would not otherwise have acquired or would only have acquired much later. The natural progress of the mind is quickened but not reversed. The same man who would remain stupid in the forests should become wise and reasonable in towns, if he were merely a spectator in them. Nothing is better fitted to make one wise than the sight of follies we do not share, and even if we share them, we still learn, provided we are not the dupe of our follies and provided we do not bring to them the same mistakes as the others.

(Rousseau [1762] 1993, pp. 260–1)

Figure 2.11 Two illustrations from Rousseau's *Emile*, 'Emile as a gardener' (left) and 'The race for the cakes' (right). Bibliotèque Nationale de France

EXERCISE

In order to form your view on whether Rousseau is proposing the native American way of life as a model, try first to answer the following questions (I shall employ 'man' to mean 'human being', because this is the term Rousseau uses).

- In the first two extracts, how does Rousseau describe man in the state of nature? Does 'primitive' man have the use of reason?

- In the second two extracts, can a man go back to the state of nature? Can he stop himself from using reason? What is Rousseau's aim in the education of Emile?

DISCUSSION _____

It does not seem that Rousseau believes that a return to the state of nature is either possible or desirable. In his view, man in the state of nature is indeed happy; however, this is because he has no use of reason, but only of instinct. He has neither imagination nor expectations; he lives only in the present. In many ways, he seems more like an animal than a human being. By contrast, Rousseau argues, 'cultivated reason' is needed to live in society. Instinct is not enough to have social life, which is the type of life people now have. For Rousseau, when the use of reason has been reached there is no way back: 'Once a thinker, always a thinker.' Therefore the best course of action consists in making the best use of reason in order to have a critical understanding of the corruption and vices that civilization has created. In this way, one can learn from social life without being corrupted by it. Rousseau's aim is to reform human beings and society; he is not proposing to return to a state of nature, which is happy and innocent but ultimately not fully human.

_____

For Turgot and Condorcet human capability for self-improvement had borne good fruits, while for Rousseau it had become an instrument of self-destruction. However, Rousseau was no pessimist: he believed that human capability for self-improvement could be turned to a good end by means of political reform and education. In this sense, for Rousseau a happy and just future was possible and highly desirable; however, unlike Turgot and Condorcet, he thought that this would not take place unless people fought for it against the course that history had taken and the corruption engendered by progress in the sciences, arts and trade.

Conclusion

This chapter has shown how historical time has been represented in different ways; for instance as cyclical, as linear and showing decadence, and as linear and showing progress. The manner in which historical time is represented is inextricably connected with the way that people regard their past and their lives, with the expectations and hopes they might have for the future, and ultimately with their identity.

The representation of history as progress has been remarkably important in Europe. During the eighteenth century theories of progress were put forward in an unprecedentedly decisive and influential way. The earlier sections of this chapter analysed the general character of the Enlightenment, the cultural movement out of which these theories emerged. The *philosophes* placed great emphasis on the critical use of reason and on the *progressive* defeat of prejudices. They interpreted history as this progressive process of enlightenment, and as a consequence depreciated the past in favour of the future.

Turgot and Condorcet both thought that humanity was advancing in successive stages towards greater knowledge and greater happiness. Although Turgot still distinguished between the cyclical movement of nature and the linear advancement of human history, it was during the eighteenth century and at the very beginning of the nineteenth that the first theories which attributed a history to nature emerged – thanks to Buffon, Kant and Lamarck. Condorcet regarded both history and nature as processes whose features could be identified and rationalized, concluding that the future of human history could be predicted just as the natural sciences can predict material phenomena. He claimed that future progress could be predicted by studying the past; in this way he defended the conception of progress as the unfolding of history. However, it has been noted that he did not exclude human initiative as a cause of progress.

Enlightenment theories of progress regarded human history as one single enterprise, following one progressive path. The differences between various civilizations were explained as the differences between successive stages on the same line of progress. Europeans were viewed as the most advanced of all, and as such they were believed to be charged with the duty of enlightening other peoples. Condorcet, Voltaire and other *philosophes* defined Europe as an intellectual space that emerged during the Renaissance as a result of the invention of printing, which facilitated the circulation of ideas. In this way European identity was based on the 'more advanced' level of European culture, defined as the ideas produced by the relatively small number of people who published their work.

Turgot and Condorcet regarded progress in the fields of technology, science, moral behaviour and the arts as proceeding at different speeds, but ultimately interlinked. This view, however, did not go unchallenged; Rousseau, for example, believed that it was advances in the arts and sciences that had multiplied prejudices and brought about unhappiness and corruption.

Theories of progress always encountered resistance from those who believed rather in the decadence of historical development, or who aimed to preserve traditions and the existing political order. However, even those who advocated the conservation of traditional ways of life had to confront the theory of progress in its many versions, for it was an extremely important way of interpreting history and directing actions. The idea of progress was fundamental to the ways in which

A philosophical doctrine elaborated by Auguste Comte (1798–1857) that in the second half of the twentieth century assumed diverse forms in all western countries. In general, positivism exalts science and technology, and regards any inquiry beyond observable phenomena and the laws governing them as outdated metaphysical speculation. Scientific, technological and social progress is at the core of the positivistic interpretation of history.

many Europeans interpreted history and their own place within it until the beginning of the twentieth century. Nineteenth-century philosophical doctrines, such as **positivism**, interpreted history according to a progressive scheme. The theory of progress was also combined with the theory of evolution, to justify the belief that Europeans were more 'advanced' because they had reached a higher level of evolution than other 'races' (Bowler, 1989) (at that time there was a widespread belief that several distinct human 'races' existed). Various versions of socialism, and notably Marxism, also regarded history as progressive, sometimes emphasizing the role of the laws of history, sometimes that of human actions, and often appealing to both.

During the nineteenth century life changed rapidly for many Europeans. Many areas were being industrialized, and as a consequence the rate of urbanization grew rapidly and steadily – not only in England and Wales but also in large parts of the rest of Europe. Some cities grew extraordinarily quickly. The number of people living in Vienna increased from 400,000 in 1846 to 700,000 in 1880; between 1849 and 1875 the population of Berlin grew from 378,000 to almost a million and that of Paris from 1 million to 1.9 million; while London's rose from 2.5 million to 3.9 million between 1851 and 1881 (Hobsbawm, 1975, p. 211). Railways started to criss-cross the richest countries, while steamships traversed the oceans. Not everybody, of course, welcomed these changes and expected the future to be better than the past. There were many sceptical voices who, rather than denying the existence of scientific progress, pointed out the corrupting effects that this progress could have on society. In nineteenth-century Britain some people gave new currency to the cyclical view of history, arguing that their civilization could decline just as the great classical civilizations had done. This view was reinforced by the risks that technological progress seemed to imply (Bowler, 1989, p. 9). Progress, however, seemed to be unstoppable and to be happening everywhere, and to most people its promises on the whole appeared to outweigh its dangers.

The belief in progress was fuelled by spectacular advances in science and technology. The new marvels were exhibited in the great urban centres of Europe and the US. The French started to hold national displays of industrial and craft produce in 1797, shortly after the revolution. Similar exhibitions were also held in several British cities, and in Munich, Ghent, Stockholm, Tournai, Haarlem, Dublin, Madrid, New York, Moscow, St Petersburg and Brussels. The first international 'Great Exhibition' took place in London in 1851. The size of this exhibition was incomparably greater than any that had been held previously. It was the Crystal Palace in Hyde Park that housed this great display of goods, which were admired by 6 million visitors. The 1851 exhibition also marked an internationalization of cultural life for, unlike previous events, the exhibits were not limited to those of the host country: half of the space was assigned to guest countries 'and their empires', and half to Britain and its empire. Other cities soon started planning their own exhibitions. In 1853 two were held in Dublin and New York; Paris responded in 1855 with its own *exposition universelle*, which accorded more space to the fine arts than London had done. New events followed in London in 1862 and Paris in 1867. A great number of international exhibitions were organized throughout the nineteenth century, in many European countries, including Switzerland, Belgium, the Netherlands, Sweden, Germany, Poland, Italy, Spain and Portugal, as well as in the US and Australia. Exhibitions were also arranged well into the twentieth century, whose beginning was celebrated with the Paris *exposition* of 1900. Some of the titles of twentieth-century exhibitions made very clear what they sought to celebrate, such as the Chicago exhibition of 1933, entitled 'Century of Progress'.

In the nineteenth century many Europeans (though by no means all) regarded the future as holding the promise of a better life. So the First World War came as a shock to most people. Its horrors were perpetrated with the aid of technology rather than prevented by it, and these horrors took place largely in Europe, rather than in some distant land. The rest of the twentieth century had much more in store for Europe, including genocide and a Second World War. Today it is widely held that the belief in progress was crushed under these events. In academic philosophy, the notion of laws governing the development of history became increasingly less popular. Without this notion, views of progress such as those held by Condorcet and Turgot become unsustainable. However, as we know, there are many different versions of the idea of progress, which can be applied to different realms of experience and reality. Thus the idea has survived the twentieth century, though in less systematic and comprehensive forms than before. For instance, progress has often lain at the core of political programmes, especially those of socialist and social democratic parties. Moreover, Europeans did not renounce all their expectations of a better future, even after the disaster of the Second World War. Indeed the postwar period, and especially the 1960s when western Europe experienced great economic expansion, was arguably quite an optimistic time. In the last quarter of the twentieth century and the beginning of the twenty-first, however, belief in the overall progress of human civilization has been widely questioned. Sociologists such as Jonathan Friedman see the evidence of this disillusion with progress in the numerous 'new cultural movements, from cults and religious revival to primitivism, a new traditionalism, a striving for the re-establishment of a new culturally defined identity' (Friedman, 1994, p. 78).

Although disillusion with progress is a very important feature of recent European culture, the idea of progress is still a powerful legacy of the Enlightenment. Even though it may have been watered down, the notion is still implicit in many European ways of looking at the world. For instance, majority world countries are often represented as being 'behind' in terms of economic development, and frequently in terms of political and even cultural development too. Such representations imply a progressive view of history which, crucially, is inextricably linked with scientific and technological knowledge. But it is not obvious that knowledge should be seen as progressive: early medieval scholars, for instance, considered the great classic texts (along with sacred texts) as their source of authority and did not regard their own work as equal, let alone superior, to them. Yet today the idea that scientific knowledge is progressive seems so obvious that many fail to see that this way of judging it is an embodiment of the idea of progress itself. It is precisely the perceived inevitability of this idea of progress that creates fears and reactions to it. The link between technological and social progress has proved to be one of the most controversial ideas of the Enlightenment, but at the same time one of the most important in European culture.

References

Bowler, P. J. (1989) *The Invention of Progress: the Victorians and the Past,* Oxford, Blackwell.

Bury, J. B. (1955) *The Idea of Progress: an Inquiry into its Origins and Growth,* New York, Dover.

Canguilhem, G. (1998) 'The decline of the idea of progress', *Economy and Society,* vol. 27, pp. 313–29.

Condorcet, A-N. de [1794] (1979) *Sketch for a Historical Picture of the Progress of the Human Mind,* transl. J. Barraclough, Westport, CT, Hyperion.

Coutel, C. (1997) *Lumières de l'Europe: Voltaire, Condorcet, Diderot,* Paris, Ellipses.

Darnton, R. (1982) *The Literary Underground of the Old Regime,* Cambridge, MA/London, Harvard University Press.

Desmond, A. (1987) 'Artisan resistance and evolution in Britain, 1819–1848', *Osiris,* vol. NS 2, pp. 72–110.

Desmond, A. (1989) *The Politics of Evolution: Morphology, Medicine and Reform in Radical London,* Chicago, University of Chicago Press.

Foucault, M. (1970) *The Order of Things: an Archaeology of the Human Sciences*, London, Tavistock.

Friedman, J. (1994) *Cultural Identity and Global Process*, London, Sage.

Gay, P. (1969) *The Enlightenment: an Interpretation. The Science of Freedom*, New York, Vintage.

Hazard, P. (1965) *European Thought in the Eighteenth Century*, Harmondsworth, Penguin.

Hegel, G. W. F. (1857) *Lectures on the History of Philosophy*, transl. J. Sibree, London, Bohn.

Hobsbawm, E. (1975) *The Age of Capital, 1848–1975*, London, Weidenfeld & Nicolson.

Kant, I. [1784] (1950) 'What is Enlightenment?', in L. B. Beck (ed.), *Foundations of Metaphysics and Morals: What is Enlightenment?*, Chicago, University of Chicago Press.

Manuel, F. E. (1962) *The Prophets of Paris*, Cambridge, MA, Harvard University Press.

Newton, I. (1687) *Philosophiae naturalis principia mathematica*, London, Streater.

Nisbet, R. (1980) *History of the Idea of Progress*, London, Heinemann.

Outram, D. (1996) *The Enlightenment*, Cambridge, Cambridge University Press.

Pomeau, R. (1991) *L'Europe des Lumières: Cosmopolitisme et unité européenne au XVIIIe siècle*, Paris, Stock.

Porter, R. (1990) *The Enlightenment*, Basingstoke/London, Macmillan.

Rousseau, J-J. [1754] (1984) *A Discourse on Inequality*, transl. and intro. M. Cranston, Harmondsworth, Penguin.

Rousseau, J-J. [1762] (1993) *Emile*, transl. B. Foxley, London, Everyman.

Rousseau, J-J. [1762] (1997) *The Social Contract and Other Later Political Writings*, transl. V. Gourevitch, Cambridge, Cambridge University Press.

Turgot, A-R-J. [1750] (1975) 'A philosophical review of the successive advances of the human mind', in R. L. Meek (ed.), *Turgot on Progress, Sociology and Economics*, Cambridge, Cambridge University Press.

Voltaire [1731] (1733) *The History of Charles XII King of Sweden*, London, Davis and Lyon.

Voltaire [1754] (1963) *Essai sur le mœurs et l'esprit des nations et sur les principaux faits de l'histoire depuis Charlemagne jusqu'à Louis XIII* (Essay on the manners, customs, and the spirit of nations), Paris, Garnier Frères.

Whitaker, A. P. (1971) 'Changing and unchanging interpretations of the Enlightenment in Spanish America', in O. A. Aldridge (ed.), *The Ibero-American Enlightenment*, Urbana, IL, University of Illinois Press.

3

Nation, nation-state, nationalism and Europe

CLIVE EMSLEY

Introduction

National identity is one of the most obvious identities acknowledged by individual people. It is not a uniquely European phenomenon though, arguably, given the impact of Europeans in shaping the world during the nineteenth and twentieth centuries the modern world of nation-states is, at least in significant part, a European creation. To be a member of a nation, and/or to be a citizen of a nation-state, generally involves, among a variety of other things, acceptance of a national heritage and recognition of a shared past. Much history, whether presented by professional historians, teachers, the media or politicians, focuses on the nation and the nation-state. It seems to be commonly accepted that while nation-states are the creation of past events and have been physically created by individuals or groups of individuals, the nations themselves have always existed. Yet nations have also been created, and there are continuing debates about the significance of, for example, language, geography and the acceptance of a shared past and culture in the evolution of national identity.

EXERCISE _____

The title of this chapter includes three related concepts – nation, nation-state and nationalism. Before proceeding any further you should try to clarify in your own mind the meanings of these concepts. I would suggest that you do this by first noting down your ideas and then turning to the following discussion.

DISCUSSION _____

There are no hard and fast definitions of these concepts, and indeed the definition of each one is the subject of academic debate. Broadly, we might regard a nation as a group of people who share a common culture and, sometimes, a common territory. A nation is a unity identified by historians, politicians or others. It is different from 'national identity', which is people's actual identification with 'their' nation. While groups of people sharing language, religion and so forth have always existed, the concept of national identity has not always existed.

A nation-state, by contrast, is a legally defined entity which may or may not be coterminous with a nation; and of course it is possible for a 'state' to exist without any single 'nation' within it. Remember too that 'state' is also a concept whose precise meaning is open to debate, though most people would probably accept the current definition of it as a set of institutions, generally at the centre of a geographically bounded territory, that monopolize rule over, and on behalf of, that territory. To the extent that they were legal entities with their own frontiers and their own independent administrative and legal structures, the city-states of the classical and medieval worlds, as well as empires such as that of Napoleon and that of the **Habsburg** family (which continued until the end of the First World War), might all be defined as 'states'. While many (perhaps most) contemporary nations aspire to having their own nation-states, in some instances it might be argued that it was the nation-state itself, rather than any shared ethnicity, which gave rise to a common culture and history (for example, in the United States, Australia and New Zealand).

Nationalism is probably the most contentious of the three concepts. A leading analyst of the subject, John Breuilly, begins his book on nationalism by noting how others have treated it: as a state of mind, as the expression of national consciousness, as a political doctrine elaborated by intellectuals (Breuilly, 1993). Probably the most commonly held assumption – shared by these approaches – is that nationalism arises ultimately from some sort of national identity or that it is the search for such an identity. Breuilly sets out to show that this 'is a very misleading idea'; in his estimation, 'nationalism is best understood as an especially appropriate form of political behaviour in the context of the modern state and the modern state system' (Breuilly, 1993, p. 1).

The Habsburgs were one of the oldest noble families in Europe. They first came to prominence in the twelfth century and monopolized the crown of the Holy Roman empire from the fifteenth century. In 1806, when this empire was formally ended, they became rulers of a vast 'Austrian', and from 1867 'Austro-Hungarian', empire that covered most of central and eastern Europe.

This chapter takes an enormous chronological sweep and has three principal aims: it seeks to introduce you, first, to the way in which Europe's nation-states emerged and, secondly, to the ways in which, especially in the nineteenth century, historians and others understood nations and national developments; finally, it seeks to encourage you to recognize that much of our understanding of the world, and of the identities of people in it, has been constructed from a European perspective.

The emergence of Europe's states

If states, particularly nation-states, are now perceived as the natural order of international organization, this was not always the case. The manner in which states emerged in late medieval and early modern Europe was unique. Elsewhere in the world during these centuries, and long after, there were empires and tribal structures, many of which were to fall to European imperialism. Some of these empires were considerable – such as the Aztec, Maya, Inca, Chinese, Mogul and Ottoman empires (the latter extending into Europe itself). Europe during the medieval period was more commonly described as Christendom, and Christendom was divided between the Byzantine empire, centred on Constantinople, and the territories to the west which, in theory at least, were under the spiritual authority of the pope and the temporal authority of the **Holy Roman emperor**. This separation of authority was unique; it was impossible in Islam where the caliph combined both political and religious (but not spiritual) authority. The contrast can be seen to some extent in the roots of the words for religion. The English word 'religion' comes from the Latin term *religio*, which was originally used to describe the cults of pagan Rome and the traditional honours paid to the gods by the state. The Islamic equivalent, *din*, was originally Arabic and the cognate words in other semitic languages, such as Aramaic and Hebrew, mean 'law'.

The Holy Roman empire lasted formally from 962, with the coronation of Otto I of Saxony in Rome, until 1806 when, following the onslaught of Napoleon, the Emperor Francis II renounced his Holy Roman title to become Emperor Francis I of Austria. The empire, though occasionally spreading into Italy as well as elsewhere, had always been strongest in the German lands, but its unity depended on the strength of its ruler and his ability to keep his subordinate kings and princes in check.

The states of Europe were formed only gradually. They were established by war, treaty, dynastic marriage, even accident. They generally began by being centred on a prince and his court rather than as a clearly defined, single territory; and they slowly undermined the authority of the Holy Roman empire whose spiritual and secular authorities were, respectively, the pope and the emperor. At the centre of medieval and early modern states were princes and elites who might occasionally speak in terms of 'nation', but whose understanding of the word was different from our own. Anyone familiar with Shakespeare will know how the noun 'France' is equated with the king of France, 'Egypt' with the queen of Egypt and so forth. Almost a century after Shakespeare's death Louis XIV expressed this understanding authoritatively when he declared, 'In France the nation is not a separate body, it dwells entirely within the body of the King' (quoted in Breuilly, 1993, p. 76).

The majority of a prince's subjects never figured in this concept of nation, though they were encouraged to recognize and celebrate national figures and symbols; while in the aftermath of the Reformation they were expected, and occasionally required, to adopt the religion of the prince: *cuius regio, eius religio* (he who rules has the right to determine religion) was the famous phrase coined at the *Diet* of the Holy Roman empire in 1526. Even those princes who remained Catholic were jealous of the existence of a supranational institution on their territories and increasingly encroached on both imperial and papal authority. The stronger the prince, and the more extensive his territories, the more independence he acquired.

The unity of Christendom was further undermined by what has been termed 'print capitalism' (Anderson, 1991). During the Middle Ages Latin was the language of intellectuals and it was the only language taught seriously in places of learning. Latin was also the language of most forms of written literature. Writing in vernacular languages developed from the eleventh century onwards, particularly with the production of a few long, versified narratives and subsequently with the growing use of the vernacular by state administrations. Print capitalism built on the increasing use of the vernacular but it also fuelled that demand with the mass production of books employing the new technology of printing. Moreover, print capitalism coincided with the Reformation, and among the printed books and pamphlets of the period were copies of the Bible and of religious pamphlets in languages other than Latin. The resulting close links between religion, politics and national sentiment were unique to the European experience, and were to be central to the subsequent development of nations and nation-states. England, for example, began to be portrayed in national propaganda as a Protestant island, particularly favoured by Providence as the fierce defender of Protestantism against the Catholic powers of Spain and France. In turn, propaganda in Spain portrayed the nation – in the sense of the prince and the ruling elite – as triumphant missionaries and exemplars of Catholicism, though papal authority was kept firmly at arm's length. Alongside these inward-looking national developments the concept of Christendom ceased to have much meaning while that of Europe was rarely mentioned, except for a brief period at the end of the seventeenth and beginning of the eighteenth centuries when it was deployed particularly by English and Dutch propagandists in the wars against Louis XIV. William of Orange became the *handhaver der Europese vrijheid* (preserver of the liberty of Europe), while the English parliament regarded his Grand Alliance against Louis XIV as aimed at 'preserving the Liberties of *Europe* and reducing the exorbitant Power of *France*' (quoted in Schmidt, 1966, pp. 174, 177).

Many of the leading thinkers of the seventeenth century continued to write their books and treatises in Latin; they even, on occasions, used that language to write to each other. During the Enlightenment, however, French increasingly became the language of culture, of the courts and of diplomacy. Ministers in European courts and officers in European armies were not necessarily born subjects of the prince they served. The main exception here was England where, although from 1714 the royal family originated in Germany and spoke German as its first language, ministers were always native-born.

L'Encyclopédie, prepared under the principal direction of the French man of letters Denis Diderot (1713–84), was one of the most imaginative projects of the eighteenth-century Enlightenment. The two readings below are translations of its articles on 'Europe' and 'Nation'.

The daughter of Agenor and sister of Cadmus was Europa who, in the Greek myth, was seduced by the god Zeus when he disguised himself as a bull.

EUROPE, a large region of the inhabited world. The etymology of the word is most likely a derivation from the Phoenician *urappa* which means *white face*, an epithet that could have been given to the **daughter of Agenor, sister of Cadmus**, but which suits Europeans who are neither bronzed like the people of the Middle East nor black like Africans.

Europe has not always had the same name nor has it always been similarly divided by the people who live there; these sub-divisions are the result of impossible details and historians have failed to provide a thread capable of exploring this labyrinth.

But, rather than exploring the *Europe* which the ancients knew and for which we have their writings, here I will only delineate its limits.

Europe extends at its longest from Cape St Vincent in Portugal and the Algarve, on the coast of the Atlantic Ocean, to the mouth of the Obi in the Northern Ocean, a distance of 1200 French leagues, and of 20 degrees, or 900 German miles. Its greatest breadth, from Cape Matapan in the Morea to the North Cape in the most northern part of Norway, is roughly 733 French leagues, similarly 20 degrees, or 550 German miles. It is bordered in the east by Asia, in the south by Africa, from which it is separated by the Mediterranean Sea, in the west by the Atlantic or Western Ocean and in the north by the Glacial Sea.

I do not know if it is right to divide the world into four quarters, of which Europe is one; this division does not seem right as it excludes the territories of the Arctic and Antarctic which, although less well known than the rest, none the less exist and merit empty spaces on globes and maps.

L'Esprit des lois (The spirit of the laws) was written by Baron Montesquieu, one of the most influential thinkers of the Enlightenment in France.

Nevertheless, *Europe* is always the smallest quarter of the world; but, as the author of **L'Esprit des lois** remarked, it has achieved such a measure of power that history can show almost nothing comparable when one considers the immensity of its finances, the size of its commitments, the number of its troops and the cost of their upkeep, even if they have no other use but ostentation.

Besides, it matters little that *Europe* is the smallest quarter of the world since it is the biggest of all in terms of commerce, navigation, fruitfulness, in the enlightenment and industry of its peoples, in their knowledge of arts, sciences and crafts, and, most important, because of Christianity and its moral benevolence which brings happiness to society. In the government we owe to this religion constitutional law, and in war we owe to it the rights of individuals that human nature would not otherwise recognize; in appearing only to offer bliss in another life, it also brings our joy in this one.

(Translation by Clive Emsley from *L'Encyclopédie*, 1751–80, vol. vi, pp. 211–12)

NATION, collective word used to describe a large number of people who inhabit a particular expanse of country enclosed within certain limits, and who obey the same government.

Each *nation* has a particular character: it is proverbial to use terms such as frivolous as a Frenchman, jealous as an Italian, solemn as a Spaniard, malicious as an Englishman, vainglorious as a Scot, drunk as a German, lazy as an Irishman, cunning as a Greek, etc.

The word *nation* is also used in some universities to distinguish their members or fellows by the various lands from which they originate.

The University of Paris is composed of four *nations*; those of France, Picardy, Normandy and Germany: each of these nations, except for that of Normandy, is subdivided into tribes and each tribe has its own dean, sub-dean, bursar, proctor and his attendants and beadles.

The German nation includes all foreign *nations*, English, Italian, etc.

The titles which they employ in their assemblies, acts, notices, etc. are, for the French nation, *honoranda Gallorum natio*; for Picardy, *fidelissima Picardorum natio*; Normandy is indicated by *veneranda Nomanorum natio*; and Germany by *constantissima Germanorum natio*. Each has its own regulations for elections, honours, ranks and, in a word, for everything that concerns their management. These are sanctioned in the law courts and have the force of law.

(Translation by Clive Emsley from *L'Encyclopédie*, 1751–80, vol. xi, p. 36)

EXERCISE _____

As you answer the following questions try to be critical of the extracts, looking, for example, for any internal discrepancies.

1   How is Europe defined?

2   How is a nation defined?

3   Does the definition of 'nation' given here differ from your own?

4   Are you surprised that there is no cross-linkage between the two extracts?

DISCUSSION _____

1   The definition is geographical, but Europe is also considered to be the most powerful and prosperous quarter of the world.

2   The nation is defined as people living in a particular territory and obeying the same government, though, as my discussion of question 3 suggests, the text does not always stick to its own definition.

3   What, I think, we might expect to see commented upon in modern definitions are, first, some reference to ethnicity; secondly, some recognition that a nation might exist across state frontiers; and thirdly, some mention of what we might call sub-national groups – are, for example, Bretons and Prussians members of separate Breton and Prussian 'nations'? Rather more than half of the article on 'nation' is devoted to the division of the University of Paris into 'nations'. This implies acceptance of the idea of France itself being divided into 'nations' (France – which here means the region around Paris known as l'Île de France – Picardy and Normandy), with everyone else being lumped into the German nation. This division might also be said to reflect an assumption of French importance.

4   An entry on 'Europe' in a modern encyclopaedia might be expected to include some reference to nations or nation-states – note that the entry here refers simply to complex 'subdivisions'. Similarly a modern entry on 'nation' might be expected to include some comment on the history of the term and its relations with 'nation-state' and 'nationalism', both of which might require some reference to Europe.

Nineteenth-century nationalism: western Europe

There is debate about whether nationalism is a phenomenon of the modern world or whether the concept can realistically be used to describe sentiments and behaviour that were present in the medieval period. That said, however, many theorists of nationalism regard the French Revolution as having made a significant contribution to the development of the concept, even though they differ over whether nationalism was an ideology largely constructed to conceal class identities (Hobsbawm, 1990), emerged as an appropriate means of conducting politics in the modern world (Breuilly, 1993), or arose from any one of a half dozen or more other reasons.

At the beginning of the French Revolution concerns were expressed that French was not the first language of every citizen, for many spoke local languages such as Auvergnat, Breton, Gascon or Flemish. But, perhaps more important, at the outset of the revolution the 'nation' replaced the 'king' at the top of the state hierarchy. Laws were now drafted by a *national* legislature at the behest of the *nation*; the king, as long as he lasted, was merely the executive authority. The politically active took pride in being French and in creating, as they saw it, a new world order in which the rights of man were given due recognition. There was no heritage or tradition to which they could turn for this, so they constructed what one historian has called a 'mythic present', the instant creation of a new community, the sacred moment of a new consensus. The ritual oaths of loyalty taken around a liberty tree or sworn en masse during many revolutionary festivals commemorated and re-created the moment of social contract; the ritual words made the mythic present come alive, again and again (Hunt, 1984, p. 27).

When a legitimizing past was sought, particularly for images and symbols, the revolutionaries turned to the classical world. This was a world well known to and venerated by the progressive, forward-looking thinkers and actors of the Enlightenment. While, as noted above, French had increasingly become the leading language of eighteenth-century Europe, Latin and classical Greek, as well as classical thought, were central to elite education and the classical world was seen as a common heritage providing a common frame of reference within which ideas could be debated and projected. Radicals in the early stages of the revolutionary French republic envisaged Hercules as the representative of the French people; the image of Liberty on official documents was depicted grasping the *fasces* of the Roman republic. And when Napoleon Bonaparte usurped the revolution he continued the appropriation of classical images, most notably in his use of the imperial eagle.

The *fasces* were a bundle of elm or birch rods surrounding an axe. They were an emblem of authority carried before magistrates in ancient Rome.

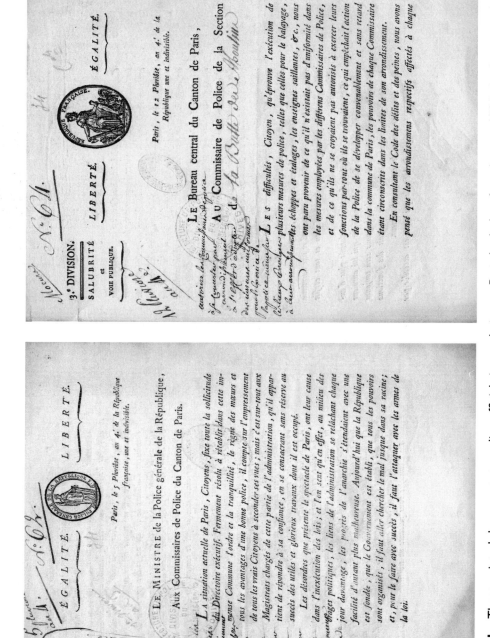

Figure 3.1   These printed documents to police officials in revolutionary Paris both date from January 1796. At the top each shows a representation of Liberty; it might also be a personification of the republic. Note that in each case 'she' has a classical costume and carries a *fasces*. The cockerel, at the feet of the seated figure, is another national emblem of France. Musée des Collections Historiques de la Prefecture de Police

Figure 3.2 Jacques-Louis David (1748–1825), *Napoleon Distributing the Eagles*. This painting represents Napoleon distributing the flags to his regiments three days after his coronation as emperor in August 1804. The flagpoles had a classical eagle at their top, hence the standards were known as 'Eagles'. David's original version was to have a winged victory showering laurel wreaths on the soldiers swearing their oath of allegiance – a very classical allusion. But at Napoleon's request this was removed. The Empress Josephine was similarly removed since, by the time David finished the painting (in 1810), Napoleon had divorced her. Chateau de Versailles et de Trianon. Réunion des Musées Nationaux/Peter Willi

There is debate about the extent to which the example of France and the experience of the revolutionary and Napoleonic wars fostered nationalism and national sentiment elsewhere in Europe. For the English the wars could be understood in a similar way to earlier conflicts against French hegemony, though for English loyalists in the new context England was less the Protestant island protected by Providence and rather the beacon of liberty and sanity – first against an atheistic and destructive, levelling creed, and then, following the rise of Napoleon, against a rapacious, imperial tyrant. Yet there remains controversy about the extent to which the conflict furthered the idea of being 'British' and the extent to which the component parts of Britain each took different national sentiments and images from it.

On the Italian peninsula the protagonists of *Italia* tended to be sympathetic to the French, while the 'German War of Liberation' (*der Befreiungskrieg*) (1812–13) was fought against the French. The Congress of Vienna, which in 1814–15 redrew state boundaries after the upheaval of the Napoleonic wars, set out to create a balance of power on the continent so as to ensure that no single state was strong enough to threaten international (that is European) security. In consequence several of the states created by Napoleon in the west of Germany were maintained under their new rulers, and in the aftermath of the wars the rulers of these states – notably Baden, Bavaria and Württemberg – sought to create their own distinctive national identities. By contrast, the Rhineland, which had been incorporated into Napoleon's empire, was made Prussian. The diplomats at Vienna reasoned that a strong Prussia, on the banks of the Rhine, would be a good counterbalance to a resurgent France. Catholic Rhinelanders and Lutheran Prussians may have spoken versions of German but they did not particularly like each other; and many Rhinelanders made little secret of their preference for French laws (which they were eventually allowed to keep) and administration.

The 'Germany' which emerged from the Congress of Vienna consisted of thirty-nine independent states of varying size; it was united in a confederation and overseen by a *Diet*, under the presidency of Austria, but there was no central administration or executive. Post-Napoleonic Italy was similarly divided, but without a confederation where the states met. In 1831 Giuseppe Mazzini (1805–72), one of the leading Italian nationalists of the period, founded Young Italy (*La giovine Italia*), a nationalist pressure group, which he subsequently sought to develop into an internationalist Young Europe movement. Mazzini set down his nationalist/ internationalist ideas in a variety of publications of which *The Duties of Man*, first published as newspaper articles in the early 1840s, is among the best known. The following reading consists of an extract from this pamphlet.

Duties to Country

But what can *each* of you, with his isolated powers, *do* for the moral improvement, for the progress of Humanity? You can, from time to time, give sterile expression to your belief; you may, on some rare occasion, perform an act of *charity* to a brother not belonging to your own land, no more. Now, *charity* is not the watchword of the future faith. The watchword of the future faith is *association*, fraternal co-operation towards a common aim, and this is as much superior to *charity* as the work of many uniting to raise with one accord a building for the habitation of all together would be superior to that which you would accomplish by raising a separate hut each for himself, and only helping one another by exchanging stones and bricks and mortar. But divided as you are in language tendencies, habits, and capacities, you cannot attempt this common work. The *individual* is too weak, and Humanity too vast. *My God*, prays the Breton mariner as he puts out to sea, *protect me, my ship is so little, and Thy ocean so great!* And this prayer sums up the conditions of each of you, if no means is found of multiplying your forces and your powers of action indefinitely. But God gave you this means when he gave you a Country, when, like a wise overseer of labour, who distributes the different parts of the work according to the capacity of the workmen, he divided Humanity into distinct groups on the face of our globe, and thus planted the seeds of nations. Bad governments have disfigured the design of God, which you may see clearly marked out, as far, at least, as regards Europe, by the courses of the great rivers, by the lines of the lofty mountains, and by other geographical conditions; they have disfigured it by conquest, by greed, by jealousy of the just sovereignty of others; disfigured it so much that to-day there is perhaps no nation except England and France whose confines correspond to this design. They did not, and they do not, recognise any country except their own families and dynasties, the egoism of caste. But the divine design will infallibly be fulfilled. Natural divisions, the innate spontaneous tendencies of the peoples will replace the arbitrary divisions sanctioned by bad governments. The map of Europe will be remade. The Countries of the People will rise, defined by the voice of the free, upon the ruins of the Countries of Kings and privileged castes. Between these countries there will be harmony and brotherhood. And then the work of Humanity for the general amelioration, for the discovery and application of the real law of life, carried on in association and distributed according to local capacities, will be accomplished by peaceful and progressive development; then each of you, strong in the affections and in the aid of many millions of men speaking the same language, endowed with the same tendencies, and educated by the same historic tradition, may hope by your personal effort to benefit the whole of Humanity.

To you, who have been born in Italy, God has allotted, as if favouring you specially, the best-defined country in Europe. In other lands, marked by more uncertain or more interrupted limits, questions may arise which the pacific vote of all will one day solve, but which have cost, and will yet perhaps cost, tears and blood; in yours, no. God has stretched round you sublime and indisputable boundaries; on one side the highest mountains of Europe, the Alps; on the other the sea, the immeasurable sea. Take a map of Europe and place one point of a pair of compasses in the north of Italy on Parma; point the other to the mouth of the Var, and describe a semicircle with it in the direction of the Alps; this point, which will fall, when the semicircle is complete, up on the mouth of the Isonzo, will have marked the frontier which God has given you. As far as this frontier your language is spoken and understood; beyond this you have no rights. Sicily, Sardinia, Corsica, and the smaller islands between them and the mainland of Italy belong undeniably to you. Brute force may for a little while contest these frontiers with you, but they have been recognised from of old by the tacit general consent of the peoples; and the day when, rising with one accord for the final trial, you plant your tricoloured flag upon that frontier, the whole of Europe will acclaim re-risen Italy, and receive her into the community of the nations. To this final trial all your efforts must be directed.

Without Country you have neither name, token, voice, nor rights, no admission as brothers into the fellowship of the Peoples. You are the bastards of Humanity. Soldiers without a banner, Israelites among the nations, you will find neither faith nor protection; none will be sureties for you. Do you beguile yourselves with the hope of emancipation from unjust social conditions if you do not first conquer a Country for yourselves; where there is no Country there is no common agreement to which you can appeal; the egoism of self-interest rules alone, and he who has the upper hand keeps it, since there is no common safeguard for the interests of all. Do not be led away by the idea of improving your material conditions without first solving the national question. You cannot do it. Your industrial associations and mutual help societies are useful as a means of educating and disciplining yourselves; as an economic fact they will remain barren until you have an Italy. The economic problem demands, first and foremost, an increase of capital and production; and while your Country is dismembered into separate fragments – while shut off by the barrier of customs and artificial difficulties of every sort, you have only restricted markets open to you – you cannot hope for this increase. To-day – do not delude yourselves – you are not the working-class of Italy; you are only fractions of that class; powerless, unequal to the great task which you propose to yourselves. Your emancipation can have no practical beginning until a National Government, understanding the signs of the times, shall, seated in Rome, formulate a Declaration of Principles to be the guide for Italian progress, and shall insert into it these words, *Labour is sacred, and is the source of the wealth of Italy.*

(Mazzini, 1907, pp. 51–4)

EXERCISE _____

Consider the following questions.

1   What, for Mazzini, is the problem with Europe?

2   What is the problem for Italians?

3   How should peoples draw their frontiers?

4   What is common to the people within the frontiers of Italy?

5   Mazzini uses one 'nation' as a model for those without a country. Which nation is this?

DISCUSSION _____

1   The problem for Europe is that God's design has been thwarted by bad governments (kings and privileged castes).

2   God has given every individual a country, but bad governments have disfigured his design. God allotted the Italian people a well-defined country, but unfortunately it is no longer united and, until unity is achieved, it will be impossible for the people to achieve real progress.

3   In Mazzini's estimation the peoples of Europe do not have to draw frontiers; God did this when he divided national territories by rivers and mountains.

4   Mazzini insists that within the God-given frontiers the Italian language is spoken and understood.

5   The 'nation' that Mazzini uses as a model is the 'Israelites'.

Mazzini hoped for a Europe of republican nation-states which, confidently settled behind their natural frontiers, would live together in peace, progress and harmony. The idea of natural frontiers went back to the Enlightenment and had been one of the war-cries of French revolutionaries who insisted that their original conquests were merely to restore France's 'natural frontiers' – the sea, the Rhine, the Alps, the Pyrenees. But it is important to recognize that the ability to draw precise lines of state frontiers was relatively new. One reason why the princes of the Middle Ages and the early modern period were the focal points of their 'nations' was because the peripheries were fluid. Moreover, each prince frequently had title to lands some distance away from the bulk of his state, often surrounded by the state territories of another prince. The decisions of the diplomats at the Congress of Vienna put an end to most of these vagaries, particularly in the west of Europe, by consolidating the territories of the leading princes.

See the section on language in Chapter 1.

Mazzini's insistence that the Italian language was spoken and understood within the natural frontiers of Italy requires considerable qualification – the point was made above that even in 'united' France at the outset of the revolution, a mere fifty years before Mazzini was writing, there was concern that not everyone spoke French as their first language, and this situation continued throughout the nineteenth century. Nevertheless, language became central in much of the debate about nations and nationalism in nineteenth-century Europe. Before Mazzini was born the German philosopher Johann Gottfried von Herder (1744–1803) had stressed that language was what separated humanity from the animals and made people human. Language and the power to name, Herder maintained, were synonymous with thought, and made both personality and community possible. Language could only be learned in a community, and it followed from this that each community had its own system of thought, while language was the most distinctive expression of a people's identity. These ideas led Herder to embark on his quest for national folktales and literature, seeking out the essence of the living organism of the *Volk* (people, or nation). For Herder the proper role of history was to trace the culture of the *Volk* in its art, its religion and, above all, its use of language. These ideas were taken up and developed during the wars with Napoleon and were given a much sharper edge by men such as Ernst Moritz Arndt (1769–1860) and Johann Gottlieb Fichte (1762–1814) who, understandably perhaps given the violent context in which they wrote, began to see the state and politics as far more central than Herder had. The Germans were regarded as fortunate to be an original *Volk* – Tacitus was cited to show how they had resisted the Romans – with a language that was particularly pure.

Rulers had always been keen to cement their legitimacy by using history and the early nineteenth century saw significant developments in this discipline which appeared to give it a greater 'scientific' validity. The work of German historians was of particular importance for the way in which the discipline was shaped. Johann Gustav Droysen (1808–84) distinguished between aspects of the past that he considered to be significant as history, which he called *Geschichte* (the German word for history), and aspects that he thought to be largely irrelevant transactions (*Geschäfte*), which had no place in the grand narratives that were the concerns of historians. *Geschichte* dealt with politics, elites and the powerful; *Geschäfte* were the dealings of common, uninfluential people. Leopold von Ranke (1795–1886), probably the best-known historian in Europe in the mid nineteenth century, stressed that good history required the seeking out and the critical analysis of archival sources – skills that are still regarded as central to the modern discipline. In Europe the period during which history became a research-orientated, academic subject coincided with the growth of the modern concept of nationalism and the modern nation-state. As men of their time nineteenth-century historians were generally patriotic, perceived a linear process in historical development, and considered that European civilization was leading the way for less fortunate, more 'backward' peoples. They saw no conflict between their national and European bias and their scientific professionalism. They also tended to see the nineteenth-century state formulations as having emerged during the Middle Ages. Huge collections of primary sources were assembled and published to indicate how the nation and particularly the nation-state had their origins in the distant past – the *Monumenta Germaniae Historia* was begun in 1824, *Documents inédits sur l'histoire de France* in 1833 and the Rolls series, in Britain, in 1838. Historians, increasingly claiming the professionalism of experts and ensconced within the walls of universities, wrote narratives tracing the story of their nation. Historical explanations were provided for national differences. Thus the Norwegian historians Peter Andreas Munsch (1810–63) and Rudolf Keyser (1803-1864) demonstrated that Norwegians were quite different from their fellow Scandinavians the Danes and the Swedes. The Norwegians, they maintained, had migrated to their country from the north when Germanic tribes split; the Danes and Swedes, by contrast, were part of a southern migration. The consequence of this was that earlier unions between these peoples were doomed to failure.

History, as interpreted by these new professional historians, showed a forward movement, and national histories were written emphasizing national progress. 'The English state ... in what direction and towards what goal has that been advancing?' asked the Regius professor of history at Cambridge in 1883. 'The words which jump to our lips in answer are Liberty, Democracy!' (Seeley, 1895, p. 8). Ranke himself was not an advocate of a German nation-state, but other German historians did manifest such an aspiration and this led to them putting particular emphasis on the rise of Prussia, the power which seemed best able to achieve their dream and which, in 1871, did indeed establish a unified German empire with the king of Prussia as its emperor or *Kaiser*. But such nationalism was not always rooted in notions of the pure *Volk*. Many recognized that contingency had been significant in making up the citizenry of nation-states.

The English philosopher John Stuart Mill (1806–73) stressed how much more beneficial it was for the individual Breton or Basque to be a member of the French nation, or for the Scot or Welshman to be a Briton, rather than sulking as 'the half savage relic of past times, revolving in his own little mental orbit, without participation or interest in the general movement of the world' (quoted in

Hobsbawm, 1990, p. 34). The French historian Ernest Renan (1823–92) criticized ideas of *Volkish* purity thus: 'The noblest countries – England, France, Italy – are those whose blood is most mixed. Is Germany an exception in this regard? What an illusion! The entire south was Gallic. The east, after the Elbe, is entirely Slavic' (quoted in Woolf, 1996, p. 53). For Renan the nation was an agreement about a shared heritage uniting people in the present with their past, and an agreement between people to live together and share that heritage.

EXERCISE

An agreement to live together and to share a heritage is rather like the old notion of a social contract being signed by people to come together and establish a governmental system. Do you consider that there are any prerequisites for people to accept a national heritage?

Figure 3.3 W. Hauschild, *Siegfried lasst sich das Schwert 'Gram' schmieden*, c. 1880, fresco. Schloss Neuschwanstein. Bildarchiv Preussischer Kulturbesitz. Photo: Alfredo Dagli Orti

Figure 3.4 Ferdinand Keller, *Kaiser Wilhelm der Siegreiche*, oil on canvas, 500 x 700 cm. Berlin National Gallery/Bildarchiv Preussischer Kulturbesitz. Photo: Klaus Göken

Figures 3.3 and 3.4 show two images reflecting different elements that fed into nineteenth-century German nationalism. The strong underpinning of ideas of the *Volk* fostered a fascination with Volkish myths. The fresco from Neuschwanstein Castle in Bavaria portrays a moment from the medieval epic the *Nibelungenlied* when the great German hero, Siegfried, oversees the forging of his sword. The Siegfried story was taken up by Wagner for his massive *Ring Cycle*. The painting by Keller shows the Prussian King Wilhelm who, with the unification of Germany in 1871, became emperor (*Kaiser*) of the new German empire. Wilhelm was the modern hero of the unification; the title of the painting is 'Wilhelm the Victor', but rather than Volkish celebration, Keller opted for a bizarre mixture of classical chariot and figures with angels and cherubs. The figure holding the laurel wreath over Wilhelm's head might suggest one reason for Napoleon's reservations about David's plans (see Figure 3.2).

DISCUSSION _____

It is at least arguable that people need to be able to envisage that they have things in common (a heritage if you like) with a large number of other individuals. We recognize that there are millions of others across the world who share our individual gender or who share the opposite. We are aware of being atheist, agnostic, Anglican, Catholic and so on by recognizing that there are others who share our beliefs. We are aware of being English, French or German, similarly by recognizing that there are others who 'share' our nationality and others who do not. The recognition of national membership therefore requires some understanding of others who share that nationality and of some limits to that nationality – not necessarily state frontiers. It is impossible for our putative English, French or German person to know every other English, French or German person; but they have to be able to envisage that there are others to whom they are linked. This is why the anthropologist/ historian Benedict Anderson has stressed that nationalism is really about 'imagined communities' (Anderson, 1991). Members of nations have to be able to imagine their national community and also its limits.

EXERCISE _____

1   Can you think of any identity that might have displaced a national identity during the late nineteenth and early twentieth centuries?

2   Can you think of any communities that would have no conception of belonging to a nation or sharing a national heritage?

3   Thinking back over what you have read in this chapter so far, can you think of any such communities existing in nineteenth-century Europe?

DISCUSSION _____

1   I would suggest that there were two particular ideologies that could have provided significant alternative identities: religion and international socialism.

2   Examples might be isolated communities that have little or no idea of what exists beyond their immediate locality, and little or no desire to find out.

3   I have not clearly identified any such communities above, but I have mentioned people living in France at the time of the great revolution who did not speak French as their first language. I have also queried Mazzini's assertion about the understanding of the Italian language, and discussed Rhinelanders who were incorporated into the Prussian state and who may, in a very broad sense, have considered themselves German but who preferred the short-lived heritage of a French occupation to the system that was imposed on them by fellow, but Prussian, Germans.

Europe's nation-states and empires were extremely jealous of their authority. International socialism, which urged working people to prioritize their class identity, was bound to antagonize national and imperial governments. With hindsight it is apparent that, when the chips were down in 1914, national and imperial identities proved stronger than those of class; but neither governments nor the socialist leaders, who believed that they had the key to the progressive pattern of history, could have known this beforehand. As for religion, in the late nineteenth and early twentieth centuries governments could also clash with the church, particularly the Catholic church with its long international reach. The pope disapproved of the new Italian state – not surprisingly, since it had expropriated his territories and left him 'the prisoner in the Vatican' – and instructed good Italian Catholics to have nothing to do with it. Meanwhile, Bismarck's Prussia enacted legislation specifically to limit the influence of the Catholic church. The radical republicans of the Third Republic in France were similarly suspicious of the church and ultimately, in 1905, succeeded in separating church and state, but France also provides interesting examples of how both Catholics and republicans could claim to be patriotically French and could clash over how to interpret national icons. How, for example, was a staunch radical republican, hostile to the church and all its works, to interpret Joan of Arc? The issue became one of national debate at the turn of the century when a republican schoolmaster criticized a pupil for writing that '[Joan] is one of religion's glories, not some pagan goddess of patriotism ... She saw in the king only Christ's lieutenant, and she came to lead France back to Christ.' As far as the schoolmaster was concerned, 'Miracles should not be introduced into history. As a historian, I am not required to believe in God, who is not a historical personality. Joan did not come to conquer France for Christ, she was a very natural character, a decent peasant girl.' And her 'voices'? According to the

Figure 3.5 Sebastien-Melchior Cornu, *The Republic*, 1848, sketch, 72.8 × 59.5 cm. Musée de Besançon

Figure 3.6 Honoré Daumier, *The Republic*, 1848, oil on canvas, 73 × 60 cm. Musée d'Orsay. Réunion des Musées Nationaux/Hervé Lewandowski

Two contrasting images of the French republic from the mid nineteenth century. Sebastien-Melchior Cornu's *The Republic* is rather bland and traditional, incorporating many of the old revolutionary symbols (see Figures 3.1 and 3.2), especially when set alongside Honoré Daumier's powerful vision. While it won no prizes and was startling for its time, Daumier's concept of *The Republic* nourishing and educating her children increasingly became the self-vision of nineteenth-century European states and their apologists.

eminent republican historian Ernest Lavisse (1842–1922), 'she *thought* she heard voices from heaven, and they spoke to her of France's misfortunes', though this in no way diminished the great deeds that she performed for France (Ferro, 1984, pp. 106–7).

At the beginning of the nineteenth century the majority of people living in continental Europe were peasants. They lived on the land and most made their living directly from it. The prince might be regarded as good, but his state was commonly disliked for its exactions, notably taxes and military conscription. During the nineteenth century the peasantries were gradually incorporated into the nation. In some instances this occurred as part of a general process of economic change that was not always positively developed by state governments. The growth of national markets, the cutting of new and better roads and the development of railways all contributed to a situation in which the peasant could 'imagine' his or her nation rather than the local community. At the same time state actions, such as conscripting young men to serve in national armies, the development of national educational systems, the settling of national legal systems in the countryside in the form of petty courts and state police officials, provided both direct and indirect opportunities for state functionaries to educate the peasantry about their nation. Such developments were most obvious in the new nation-state of Italy, where the government and its agents had to transform Calabrians, Piedmontese, Romans, Sicilians and so on into Italians. But the historian Eugen Weber has forcefully argued that the same was true in France, where Auvergnats, Bretons, Gascons and so on were only properly transformed into French people and fully integrated into what was, essentially, the official culture of Paris during the half century before the First World War.

> Roads, railroads, schools, markets, military service, and the circulation of money, goods, and printed matter provided [the significant] experiences, swept away old commitments, instilled a national view of things in regional minds, and confirmed the power of that view by offering advancement to those who adopted it.

(Weber, 1976, p. 486)

Nineteenth-century nationalism: east and southern Europe

The historian Larry Wolff has argued that during the eighteenth-century Enlightenment the cultural elite of the west, particularly the *philosophes* such as Voltaire, Diderot and Rousseau, invented the idea of eastern Europe. This was a complementary other half to their own, civilized world. Eastern Europe was distinct from the orient, yet it was backward compared with the west. Eighteenth-century travellers took up and developed these ideas when they described feelings of 'leaving Europe' and entering territories that were familiar, yet unfamiliar, as they crossed into Poland, for example (Wolff, 1994). Whether or not Wolff is correct – and others have set the division of Europe into east and west far earlier, with contrasting attitudes to serfdom and different legal principles (Rady, 1993) – the political structures of these two halves of Europe were very different in the aftermath of the Napoleonic wars. While the west was a region of developing nation-states, in the east there were three great empires – Austrian, Russian and Ottoman – and within each of these there was a variety of different ethnic and religious groups. These groups were intermingled across the territories of the empires, partly as a result of successive invasions from the early Middle Ages, partly because of the chaos left behind in the wake of struggles against the Ottoman invasions since the fourteenth century. During the nineteenth century many of these ethnic groupings experienced cultural revivals that were spurred on by members of their elite who had been educated in German universities and imbued with the ideas of men like Herder. Occasionally there were nationalist risings as well.

Poland had been partitioned between Austria, Prussia and Russia in the final third of the eighteenth century. The Congress of Vienna re-created a 'Poland', but this was a province of the tsarist empire, and many other Poles lived in the east of the kingdom of Prussia or in

Figure 3.7 Diètrich Monteu, *Farewell of the Poles to their Fatherland*, 1831–2, oil on canvas, 44.2 x 52.4 cm. This work shows a group of Polish soldiers leaving their country in the wake of the 1831 insurrection against the Russians. The painting oozes romanticism: tragic, weeping heroes; no blood, no mud; still glorious uniforms, and the only tatters on the flag. Nevertheless images such as this inspired the intellectual Polish elite in exile, and fostered the perception of the martyred nation and country. Berlin National Gallery/Bildarchiv Preussischer Kulturbesitz. Photo: Klaus Göken

Austrian Galicia. Throughout the nineteenth century the idea of an independent Poland was kept alive by a cultural elite, often living in exile. The idea was underpinned by Polish Catholicism, adherence to which, in addition to ethnicity, was a way for the Poles to distinguish themselves from Orthodox Russians and Lutheran Prussians. Poets such as Adam Mickiewicz (1798–1855) and Zygmunt Krasiński (1812–59), fired by a messianic romanticism, portrayed their native land as a Christ-like martyr. Insurrections against tsarist rule in 1830 and again in 1863–4 were ruthlessly put down. During the Europe-wide revolutions of 1848 a Hungarian uprising against Austrian rule was also bloodily suppressed, but within twenty years the Hungarians achieved a significant degree of autonomy and, from the *Ausgleich* (compromise) of 1867, the empire became commonly known as the Austro-Hungarian empire. Within a few years the Hungarians, concerned about being a minority in their 'own' land and anxious about their language, set about imposing restrictions on the Croats, Romanians, Serbs and others in their territories.

However, independence regardless of others was not the aspiration of every nationalist in east-central Europe during the nineteenth century. Between the Germans of the Austrian heartland around Vienna and the Poles of Galicia lay Bohemia, a territory principally occupied by ethnic Czechs. The Czech historian František Palacký (1798–1876) was in the forefront of the Czech cultural revival in the early nineteenth century. When the German revolutions of 1848 brought about the creation of a German assembly in Frankfurt, Palacký was invited to join it as a representative of the three provinces of Bohemia, Moravia and Silesia. He declined.

The next reading is an extract from Palacký's reply to this invitation.

I am a Czech of Slavonic blood, and with all the little I possess and all the little I can do, I have devoted myself for all time to the service of my nation. That nation is a small one, it is true, but from time immemorial it has been a nation of itself and based upon its own strength. Its rulers were from olden times members of the federation of German princes, but the nation never regarded itself as pertaining to the German nation, nor throughout all the centuries was it regarded by others as so pertaining ...

The second reason which prevents me from taking part in your deliberations is the fact that, according to all I have so far learned of your aims and intentions as publicly proclaimed, it is your irrevocable desire and purpose to undermine Austria as an independent empire and indeed to make her impossible for all time to come – an empire whose preservation, integrity and consolidation is, and must be, a great and important matter not only for my own nation but also for the whole of Europe, indeed, for humanity and civilisation itself. Will you be good enough to give me a brief and kindly hearing on this point too?

You know, gentlemen, what Power it is that holds the entire East of our Continent. You know that this Power, now grown to vast dimensions, increases and expands of itself decade by decade in far greater measure than is possible for the countries of the West. You know that, secure at its own centre against practically every attack, it has become, and has for a long time been, a menace to its neighbours; and that, although it has unhindered access to the North, it is nevertheless, led by natural instinct, always seeking, and will continue to seek, to extend its borders southwards. You know, too, that every further step which it will take forward on this path threatens at an ever accelerated pace to give birth to, and to establish, a *universal monarchy*, that is to say, an infinite and inexpressible evil, a misfortune without measure or bound, such as I, though heart and soul a Slav, would nonetheless profoundly regret from the standpoint of humanity even though that monarchy be proclaimed as a Slavonic one. Many persons in Russia name and regard me as an enemy of the Russians, doing me the same injustice as those in Germany who regard me as an enemy of the Germans. I am not, I would declare loudly and publicly, an enemy of the Russians: on the contrary, I observe with pleasure and sympathy every step forward which that great nation makes within its natural borders along the path of civilisation; but with all my fervid love of my own nation I always pay greater respect to the good of humanity and learning than to the national good, and for this reason the bare possibility of a universal Russian monarchy has no more determined opponent or foe than myself – not because that monarchy would be Russian but because it would be universal.

You know that in the South-east of Europe, along the frontiers of the Russian Empire, there live many nations widely differing in origin, in language, in history and morals – Slavs, Wallachians, Magyars and Germans, not to speak of Turks and Albanians – none of whom is sufficiently powerful itself to bid successful defiance to the superior neighbour on the East for all time. They could only do so if a close and firm tie bound them all together as one. The vital artery of this necessary union of nations is the Danube. The focus of power of such a union must never be diverted far from this river, if the union is to be effective and to remain so. Assuredly, if the Austrian State had not existed for ages, it would have been a behest for us in the interests of Europe and indeed of humanity to endeavour to create it as soon as possible.

Why is it, however, that we have seen this State, which by nature and history is predestined to be the bulwark and guardian of Europe against Asiatic elements of every possible type – why is it that we have seen it at a critical moment lacking help and almost devoid of counsel in the face of an advancing storm? It is because, in the unhappy blindness that has long afflicted her, Austria has long failed to recognise the real juridical and moral basis of her existence, and has denied it: the fundamental rule, that is, that all the nationalities and all the religions under her sceptre should enjoy complete equality of rights and respect in common. The rights of nations are in truth the rights of Nature. No nation on earth has the right to demand that its neighbours should sacrifice themselves for its benefit, no nation is under an obligation to deny or sacrifice itself for the good of its neighbour. Nature knows neither dominant nor underyoked nations. If the bond which unites a number of diverse nations in a single political entity is to be firm and enduring, no nation can have cause to fear that the union will cost it any of the things which it holds most dear. On the contrary, each must have the certain hope that in the central authority it will find defence and protection against possible violations by neighbours of the principles of equality. Then will every nation do its best to confer upon that central authority such powers as will enable it successfully to provide the aforesaid protection. I am convinced that even now it is not too late for this fundamental rule of justice, this *sacra ancora* for a vessel in danger of foundering, to be publicly and sincerely proclaimed in the Austrian Empire and energetically carried out in all sectors by common consent. Every moment, however, is precious; for God's sake do not let us delay another hour with this! ...

When I direct my gaze beyond the frontiers of Bohemia, natural and historical considerations constrain me to turn, not to Frankfurt but to Vienna, to seek there the centre which is fitted and predestined to ensure and defend the peace, the liberty, and the rights of my nation. But *your* endeavours, gentlemen, seem now to me to be directed ... not only towards ruinously undermining, but even utterly destroying, that centre to whose authority and strength I look for salvation for the Czech lands and not alone for them. Or do you think that the Austrian State can continue to exist when you forbid it in its hereditary domains to maintain an army of its own independent of Frankfurt as the joint head? Do you think that the Austrian Emperor or any sovereign who succeeds him will be able to maintain his position if you impose upon him the duty of accepting all the most important laws from your Committee, and in this manner make the imperial Austrian

Parliament and the provincial Diets of the united Kingdoms mere shadows without substance and power? And suppose that Hungary, following her own instincts, should sever her connection with the State, or what is much the same thing, should withdraw within herself – would such a Hungary as refuses to hear of racial equality within her borders be able to maintain herself free and strong in the future? Only the just is truly free and strong. A voluntary union of the Danubian Slavs and Wallachians, or even of the Poles themselves, with a State which declares a man must first be a Magyar before he can be a human being is wholly out of the question; and much more so is a compulsory union. If Europe is to be saved, Vienna must not sink to the rôle of a provincial town. If there exist in Vienna people who ask to have your Frankfurt as their capital, we can only cry: Lord, forgive them, for they know not what they ask!

Finally, there is a third reason for which I must decline to take part in your deliberations: I regard all the attempts hitherto made to give the German Reich a new system of government based on the will of the people as impossible of achievement and as unstable for the future, unless you decide upon a real life-or-death surgical operation. By this I mean the proclamation of a German Republic, even if only in temporary form. All the draft schemes attempted so far for a partition of power between the semi-sovereign princes and the sovereign people recall to my mind the theory of the Phalansteries, which was likewise based on the fundamental rule that the persons concerned would act like arithmetical figures and would not seek any other application than that allocated to them by the theory. It is possible that my opinion is unfounded, that my conviction is at fault – but I really hold that conviction, and may not for a moment let that compass leave my hand unless I wish in the storms of the present day to perish without help. As to the establishment of a republic in the German Reich – this is a matter wholly outside my competence, so that I have no desire even to express my opinion on it. I must, however, reject expressly and emphatically in advance the idea of a republic within the frontiers of the Austrian Empire. Think of the Austrian Empire divided up into sundry republics, some considerable in size and others small – what a delightful basis for a universal Russian monarchy! ...

In conclusion, to sum up these somewhat lengthy but only general remarks, I must briefly express my conviction that those who ask that Austria (and with her, Bohemia) should unite on national lines with Germany, are demanding that she should commit suicide – a step that has neither moral nor political sense. It would, on the contrary, be much more justifiable to demand that the

German Reich be attached to the Austrian Empire, that is to say, that Germany should be incorporated in the Austrian State on the conditions above referred to. As that, however, is not in accord with German national sentiment and opinion, nothing remains but for the two Powers – the Austrian and German Empires, to organise themselves on an equality side by side, to convert their existing ties into a permanent alliance of defence and defiance.

(Palacký [1848] 1947–8, pp. 304–8)

EXERCISE _____

When you have read the extract, answer the following questions.

1   What reasons did Palacký give for turning down the invitation?

2   Why did Palacký consider it essential to preserve the Austrian empire?

DISCUSSION _____

1   Palacký declined to attend on the grounds that he was Czech rather than German, and his nation had never been considered to be a part of Germany; that the assembly's plans would undermine the Austrian empire which he considered essential for Europe, for 'humanity and civilization'; and that the assembly's plans were impractical and likely to destabilize Germany.

2   Palacký considered the Austrian empire to be the bulwark of Europe against 'Asiatic elements of every possible type', though he singled out the Russians as the main threat. He considered that the union of the different peoples within the empire was the best protection for all the individual nations both from external threat and from the threat of a dominant group within any single province (for example, the Magyars in Hungary).

Palacký's letter formulated the concept that was subsequently called Austro-Slavism. This aspired, essentially, to put the subject Slav peoples (or nations) of the Austrian empire on an equal footing with the dominant Germans (and, after 1867, the Magyars). The problems for Austro-Slavism were, first, getting all of the different Slav groups within the empire to agree with each other and, secondly, what to do with those Slavs who lived outside the empire but who demanded recognition, such as **Galician Poles** whose homeland lay in Prussia and radical Russians who opposed the tsarist regime. There were also

Galicia was a region of Poland which was divided principally between the Habsburg and Russian empires.

139

large numbers of Slavs in the Balkans; their territories bordered the Austrian empire, but even in the mid nineteenth century they were still at least technically part of the Ottoman empire.

In 1832, having won their independence from the Ottomans, the Greeks established a monarchy to rule their new kingdom. The Greeks are not Slavs, but their Slav neighbours to the north, many of whom possessed a considerable degree of autonomy within the Ottoman empire, aspired to follow their example. Montenegro achieved independence in 1859. Following war, and a European peace congress in Berlin, Bulgaria, Romania and Serbia all achieved full independence in 1878. Albania followed in 1913. The squabbles between these new states, and their continuing hostility to the Turks, led to new wars shortly before 1914. The Austrians occupied Bosnia-Herzegovina, the most Muslim of the Ottoman's Balkan lands, in 1878; in 1908 they annexed it, much to the fury of the Serbs who saw the territory as their outlet to the Adriatic and a link to their Montenegrin allies. It was the diplomatic fall-out from the assassination, by Bosnian Serbs, of the Austrian Archduke Franz Ferdinand which brought about the First World War. The aftermath of that conflict saw the creation of the little republics that Palacký feared would fall prey to Russia. After the Second World War this is precisely what did happen, though that does not necessarily confirm Palacký as a prophet.

European identity and other identities

Europe is not a nation. Nor is it an entity with which people in the mass have identified when forming a sense of themselves. Very few people have fought and died for Europe as they have for a religious faith, for a sovereign, for a national cause, or even for the international proletarian revolution. It has no symbols, and no cultural artefacts and ideologies in any way comparable with those of nationality and nationalism. Histories of Europe, while they may implicitly or explicitly compare the peoples and their cultures, the economies, the technologies of Europe with those of elsewhere, are also always conscious of the internal contrasts and conflicts between the states and the nations, and the consequent shifting frontiers. That said, however, it remains the case that the European cultural elite has commonly had a view of 'Europe' as different from the rest of the world, and since the Enlightenment at least has regarded Europe as the more 'civilized' part of the world. This view, moreover, has been popularized well beyond the educated elite.

While he held a chair at the University of Berlin and was appointed 'Prussian Historiographer' by King Frederick William IV in 1841, Ranke always saw himself as writing European history. His last, unfinished work, *Weltgeschichte* (World history), was planned as an account of Europe from the concluding centuries of the Roman empire to the Middle Ages. This in itself is indicative of how Ranke perceived 'Europe' and 'the world'. The next reading is an extract from a relatively early essay of his on 'The great powers'.

Let the reader imagine the condition of Europe around the year 1680. France, so suited and so long accustomed to keeping Europe in a ferment, had a king [Louis XIV] who understood perfectly how to rule her. His nobles, finally subdued after long obstinacy, served him with equal zeal at court and in the army, and his clergy had allied themselves with him against the Pope. France was more unified and more powerful than ever before ...

But the state of Europe was no less imperiled. If there were to be a supreme authority, it should at least be a legally determined one. This arrogated supremacy, which was constantly disturbing the peace, threatened to destroy the foundations of European order and development. It is not always recognized that the European order of things differs from others that have appeared in the course of world history by virtue of its legal, even juridical nature. It is true that world agitations now and again destroy this system of law and order. But after they have subsided, it is reconstituted, and all exertions aim only at perfecting it once more.

Nor was this the only danger. A no less considerable one lay in the fact that under such decided domination by one nation, the other could hardly achieve an independent development, particularly not when this domination was supported by a preeminence in literature. Italian literature had already run its full course, English literature had not yet risen to general significance, and German literature did not exist at this time. French literature, light, brilliant, and animated, in strictly regulated yet charming form, intelligible to everyone and yet of an individual, national character, was commencing to dominate Europe. It may seem irrelevant to point out that the dictionary of the Academy, which set the standards for speech, abounds particularly in hunting and military expressions which were current at court. But it is undeniable that French literature completely corresponded to the state and helped the latter to attain its supremacy. Paris was the capital of Europe. She wielded a dominion as did no other city, over language, over custom, and particularly over the world of fashion and the ruling classes. Here was the center of the community of Europe. Yet it is remarkable that the French should already have boasted to all the world of their constitution, calling it 'the happy condition of well-protected submission in which France finds herself, under a prince who, above all others, deserves to rule the world by his courage and wisdom and to bring true unity to it' ...

But against such an increase in strength and in political predominance the lesser powers could band together. And they did indeed form alliances and associations. The concept of the European balance of power was developed in order that the union of many other states might resist the pretensions of the 'exorbitant' court, as it was called ...

In great danger one can safely trust in the guardian spirit (*Genius*) which always protects Europe from domination by any one-sided and violent tendency, which always meets pressure on the one side with resistance on the other, and, through a union of the whole which grows firmer from decade to decade, has happily preserved the freedom and separate existence of each state ...

If the main event of the hundred years before the French Revolution was the rise of the great powers in defense of European independence, so the main event of the period since then is the fact that nationalities were rejuvenated, revived, and developed anew. They became a part of the state, for it was realized that without them the state could not exist.

It is almost generally held that our times tend towards and are capable only of dissolution. Their only significance lies in the fact that they are putting an end to the unifying or shackling institutions left over from the Middle Ages. They are striding towards this goal with the certainty of an innate impulse. It is the end-product of all great events and discoveries, of our entire civilization, in fact. It also explains the irresistible inclination towards democratic ideas and institutions, which of necessity produces all the great changes which we are witnessing. It is a general movement, in which France merely preceded the other countries.

All this is an opinion which can of course lead only to the gloomiest prospects for the future. We believe, however, that it cannot be supported against the truth of the facts. Far from being satisfied only with negation, our century has produced the most positive results. It has achieved a great liberation, not wholly in the sense of dissolution but rather in a creative, unifying sense. It is not enough to say that it called the great powers into being. It has also renewed the fundamental principle of all states, that is, religion and law, and given new life to the principle of each individual state. In just this fact lies the characteristic feature of our time.

In most epochs of world history it has been religious ties that have held the peoples together. Yet occasionally there have been other periods, which can be better compared with ours, when several larger kingdoms and free states existed side by side, linked by one political system. I shall only mention the period of the Hellenistic kingdoms after Alexander. It provides many similarities to our own, a highly developed common culture, military science, and action and interaction of complicated foreign relations, also the great importance of the trading interests and of finance, rivalry of industries, and a flowering of the exact sciences based on mathematics. But those states, produced by the enterprise of a conqueror and the dissension among his successors, had neither possessed nor been able to attain any individual principles of existence. They were based upon soldiers and money alone. It was for that very reason that they were so soon dissolved and at last entirely disappeared. It has often been asked how Rome could overcome them so quickly and completely. It happened because Rome, at least as long as she had enemies of importance, held to her principle of existence with admirable firmness.

With us it also appeared as if only the extent of our possessions, the power of the troops, the amount of wealth, and a certain share in the general civilization were of value to the state. If there were ever events qualified to dispel such an illusion, it is those of our own time. They have finally made the public aware how important moral strength and the sense of nationality are for the state. What would have become of our states if they had not received new life from the national principle upon which they were based? It is inconceivable that any state could exist without it.

(Ranke [1833] 1950, pp. 182–3, 187–8, 189, 215–17)

EXERCISE

1 What made the threat to Europe from Louis XIV's France all the greater?

2 Which element does Ranke see as central to the modern state, an element of which people have only recently become aware?

3 Which system has evolved to preserve Europe?

4 Have you come across a view of nationality similar to that of Ranke elsewhere in this chapter?

DISCUSSION _____

1   The danger from Louis XIV's France was all the greater because of the domination of the French language in the period. (Think back to the ideas of Herder on the significance of language for a *Volk*.)

2   Ranke stresses the importance of nationality for the modern state. This point is made, in particular, in the concluding sentence of the extract.

3   The self-regulating machinery of Ranke's Europe is the balance of power.

4   Implicit in this extract is a view of Europe not greatly dissimilar from that of Mazzini; the ideal is a stable Europe in which a balance of power is maintained between states, and those states themselves should be founded on nationality.

_____

Europe, for Ranke, was a cultural unit bound together by its Christian character. In the aftermath of the Reformation he believed that each nation had resolved the relationship between temporal and spiritual power in its own way and because of its own attributes. Europe thus became a unique cluster of sovereign states bound in a diplomatic system. Other historians, notably the Frenchman François Guizot (1787–1874), believed that it was the rivalry between Europe's states which had given the region its dynamism and world dominance; and even contemporary historians have been tempted towards similar explanations.

But what of large cultural units which went different ways? Do they commonly share the kind of identities perceived in Europe? It was noted at the beginning of this chapter that divisions between temporal and religious authority were unknown in the Islamic world. In 1917 a grand vizier of the Ottoman empire could declare, 'The Fatherland of a Muslim is wherever the Holy Law of Islam prevails' (Lewis, 1993, p. 136). The Ottoman empire spread far wider than its territories in southern Europe. At the same time that it came under threat from its Balkan peoples it also experienced the first stirrings of Arab nationalism; indeed the break-up of the empire in the wake of the First World War saw the emergence of new Arab states in what had once been Ottoman territory. But Arab nationalism was different from Balkan nationalisms. In the Balkans people identified themselves as Albanians, Bulgars, Greeks, Macedonians, Montenegrins, Serbs and so on, and they each had their own language. Arabs were spread across North Africa and the Middle East; they were mainly Muslim and they shared the Arabic language. This language had two forms: *fusha,* the standard, classical language used in religious discourse and among the *ulema* (religious leaders); and *amiyyas,* the dialect versions spoken in different regions in day-to-day discourse. *Fusha* was a sacred language, like medieval Latin. It was the language of the *Qur'ān* which provided the laws and rules for the Islamic Ottoman empire and its Muslim predecessors, as well as for an individual Arab's ordinary behaviour. Not only had the Arab/Islamic world never seen a spiritual/secular divide as there had been in Christendom, its view of history was also different from that of Europe. History was Allah's plan to save humanity as expounded in the vision of the Prophet Muhammad, and as far as knowledge of historical personages and events was concerned most Arabs, wherever they came from, would have had some knowledge of the Prophet, his family and his immediate descendants. The Arab nationalist movement emerged in the mid nineteenth century from among a new educated elite, rather than the *ulema*. Many members of this new elite were Christian Lebanese and Syrians who had been exposed to European ideas and technology, particularly the printing press. Moreover, western influence had contributed significantly to a linguistic revival of Arabic in the early nineteenth century. There was no growth of print capitalism comparable with that in Europe three centuries earlier, but new political and 'national' ideas did spread, in printed Arabic, along the Mediterranean trade routes and beyond thanks to the new elite and the printing press. The first influential Arabic newspaper, *al-Jawa'ib,* for example, was printed by a Lebanese of Christian descent in Constantinople, and was noted as being read not only in all the major cities of Egypt and the Near East, but also by Arabian merchants as far away as Bombay.

Arab nationalism may have appeared a significant force within the Ottoman and European empires at the end of the nineteenth and beginning of the twentieth centuries, but many Muslims preferred to look to their community of believers and considered that a revival of the faith and a restoration of the Holy Law promised a better way into the future. The first notable group of this type to establish itself during the twentieth century was the Muslim Brothers (*al-Ikhwan al-Muslimun*), founded in Egypt in 1928. Since then such groups have engaged in charitable, educational, religious and social work; they have also preached and acted, sometimes violently, against the infidel west and against what they see as the infidels' puppets and surrogates who run the 'nation-states' of the Islamic world now that the foreigners have left. They think in terms of a single Islamic polity that transcends western concepts of nation and country. In a stimulating essay comparing Europe and Islam Bernard Lewis has argued that while his subjects may appear asymmetrical – a geographical expression contrasted with a religion – 'this asymmetry is more

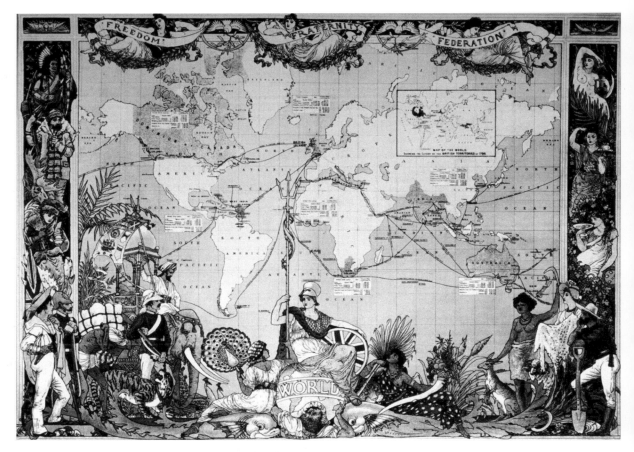

Figure 3.8 *Imperial Federation: the British Empire in 1886.* An international agreement signed in 1884 agreed finally to make Greenwich the prime meridian. This settled Europe at the top, in the centre of the overwhelming majority of maps of the world. It was, for obvious reasons, especially popular with the British who were in the process of creating their world empire on which 'the sun never set'. This map glories in Britain's centrality in the world and in the development of her empire. Flora, fauna and people of the empire sweep round to frame the map and to highlight the image of Britannia seated on the globe. The Mansell Collection/Timepix/Rex Features

apparent than real since both terms ... represent a primary civilizational self-determination of the entities which they designate' (Lewis, 1993, pp. 3, 5).

Europe was an invention of Europeans to set themselves apart from others. Africans and Asians did not know that they were 'Africans' and 'Asians' until Europeans created the terms, identified the 'continents' and then informed their peoples. By the same token America, both north and south, and Australasia too were found, conceived as 'new' and labelled by Europeans. Within Europe, Europeans also sought to set themselves apart from each other;

particularly in the nineteenth century, building on a variety of cultural, ethnic and linguistic traditions, the concept of the nation-state was established and became the key idea by which Europeans sought to divide their civilized world – the uncivilized world remained for them to enlighten and develop. For nineteenth-century Europeans, History appeared to be moving in a linear direction; there was a great chain of being, and different peoples occupied different points along the line of development. Indeed, this linear path of history and civilization appears significant, though rarely as clearly articulated in many contemporary quarters; as such it continues to muddy understanding of ethnic and national identities.

References

Anderson, B. (1991) *Imagined Communities: Reflections on the Origin and Spread of Nationalism*, 2nd edn, London, Verso.

Breuilly, J. (1993) *Nationalism and the State*, 2nd edn, Manchester, Manchester University Press.

L'Encyclopédie ou Dictionnaire Raisonné des Sciences, des Arts et des Métiers ... par M. Diderot et M. d'Alembert (1751–80) Paris.

Ferro, M. (1984) *The Use and Abuse of History, or How the Past is Taught*, London, Routledge & Kegan Paul.

Hobsbawm, E. J. (1990) *Nations and Nationalism since 1780*, Cambridge, Cambridge University Press.

Hunt, L. (1984) *Politics, Culture and the French Revolution*, Berkeley, LA/London, University of California Press.

Lewis, B. (1993) *Islam and the West*, New York/Oxford, Oxford University Press.

Mazzini, [G.] J. (1907) *The Duties of Man*, transl. E. Noyes, London, Dent.

Palacký, F. [1848] (1947–8) 'Letter to the Frankfurt parliament', *Slavonic and East European Review*, vol. 26, pp. 304–8.

Rady, M. (1993) 'Core and periphery: eastern Europe', in M. Fulbrook (ed.), *National Histories and European History*, London, UCL Press.

Ranke, L. [1833] (1950) 'The great powers', in T. H. von Lane (ed.), *Leopold Ranke: the Formative Years*, Princeton, NJ, Princeton University Press.

Schmidt, H. D. (1966) 'The establishment of "Europe" as a political expression', *Historical Journal*, vol. 9, no. 2, pp. 172–8.

Seeley, Sir J. (1895) *The Expansion of England*, 2nd edn, London, Macmillan.

Weber, E. (1976) *Peasants into Frenchmen: the Modernization of Rural France, 1870–1914*, Stanford, CA, Stanford University Press.

Wolff, L. (1994) *Inventing Eastern Europe: the Map of Civilization on the Mind of the Enlightenment*, Stanford, CA, Stanford University Press.

Woolf, S. (ed.) (1996) *Nationalism in Europe, 1815 to the Present: a Reader*, London, Routledge.

4

Language, identity and nation

MARK PITTAWAY

Introduction

Language forms a central plank of cultural identity – it is simultaneously both a means of communication and a key 'marker' of identity. It is also one of the ways in which individuals identify with others; membership of a linguistic group allows communication between members of that group. It is therefore a means of inclusion, yet it also forms a means of exclusion. The existence of a variety of languages spoken by different groups separates and differentiates. It marks individuals even within language groups from each other, however. Language, as sociolinguists have shown us, can be a marker of class and status within groups. Although much of the above may seem obvious, it focuses attention on the way that language defines and shapes personal identity. On another level it is one of the most obvious fields in which European cultural diversity is manifested. A European Community passport issued during the early 1990s before the EC was renamed the European Union and then expanded to include Austria, Sweden and Finland contained nine languages. With the accession of the last two countries to the EU in 1995 two further official languages were added. Europe is, however, commonly recognized to be more than the European Union. The eastern part of the continent is similarly marked by linguistic diversity, from the Slav languages of Russia and east-central Europe, to **finno-ugric** Magyar and Latin Romanian.

Finno-ugric refers to a non-Indo-European language family that is largely made up of languages spoken on the Eurasian plain. Magyar, Finnish and Estonian are the most prominent European examples of finno-ugric languages.

Even this summary understates the complexity of the patterns of linguistic diversity. Languages act as markers of national difference in contemporary Europe, yet language does not unproblematically define the 'natural' borders of Europe's nation-states. Transnational languages exist – German, for example, is spoken not only in Germany, Austria and Switzerland but by ethnic minorities in Belgium, Denmark, Hungary, Italy, Romania and Russia. Language can also divide nation-states. In Belgium Flemish, French and German are officially recognized, but disputes over the status of official languages, especially Flemish, have shaped political conflict in the country since the 1960s. In 1987 a difference over language in

149

one village led to the fall of the national government. These disputes have also forced the pace of constitutional reform in the country, leading to substantial devolution to regional entities in Flanders, French-speaking Wallonia and multilingual Brussels in 1993. Linguistic barriers, therefore, are not the same as political barriers. Since the nineteenth century, however, there have been concerted attempts by political elites to build unified nations through the pursuit of policies of linguistic assimilation. The tensions created by this process have profoundly reshaped language and its use across the continent.

This chapter introduces you to some of the issues involved in thinking about the relationships between language and identity in Europe. Reading it should give you some appreciation of the difficulties involved in thinking about the way identity is expressed and shaped by language. You should also acquire some idea of the politics of language in Europe during the past 200 years. I shall discuss the ways in which political elites have sought to build linguistically unified nation-states on their territories, and the mechanisms through which linguistic assimilation has actually occurred. You should also gain some awareness of the limits of this process that has shaped persisting patterns of linguistic diversity in contemporary Europe. This chapter is not a comprehensive treatment of the subject; it merely suggests issues that you may want to think about, rather than answering every question that may arise. In this sense it is very much a sketch.

I want to start by examining – in an introductory fashion – the relationships between language and cultural identity, before moving on to consider how the rise of nation-states has shaped the way that language has been used across the European continent during the past two centuries. I shall do this by considering how nation-building elites endeavoured to reshape the linguistic map of the territories they sought to transform. I shall then discuss the processes of linguistic assimilation, before going on to discuss their limits.

Language and cultural identity

How might language be defined? The definition I suggest here should be used only as a model; as with all models, reality is much more fluid. Languages are systems of signs that enable us to represent our environment. A language therefore gives us a powerful tool which enables us to articulate our experience of what is around us, define our relationship to it and thus communicate with others who share the same language – if you like, the same system of signs. By 'sign' I mean nothing more than the fact that languages give names to objects, things or thoughts. Producing a sign, or signifying, is nothing more than recognizing that a given object or thought is different from another and therefore requires a different sign, so that the difference can be represented and communicated through language. The relationships between different objects, thoughts and deeds are represented in language through systems, or 'grammars', that allow languages to relate different signs to each other. Language allows us to identify our own place in the world and our own subjectivity.

The implications of such a definition are far-reaching for the way in which we think about language. Is it a structure that each individual has to accept and master in order to articulate and communicate their experience? Or is it a liberating device, a product of human ingenuity that can be shaped, and reshaped by the individual using that language? This is a debate which has preoccupied linguistics for a century – it is also one which is not of direct concern here, though some of the discussion below will help you think about these issues. For the moment it is sufficient to note that an individual language is a system which a user must master in order to communicate effectively in that language. It is also important to recognize a far less practical point – that languages are human creations, and are both a powerful tool and a part of culture. I use the term culture here to mean 'a system of shared meanings, attitudes and values, and the symbolic forms in which they are expressed and embodied' (quoted in Burke, 1978, prologue). In other words, a language is the product of the collective attitudes and values of a particular group. Languages are not, however, given and fixed for all time; they are continually reshaped by the historical experiences of the groups that use them. Often this is a product of contact and exchange between different linguistic groups as words and signs are borrowed across linguistic boundaries. An obvious example might be the spread of terms from English into other European languages associated with recent developments in information technology; on a recent visit to a provincial Romanian town my eye was constantly drawn by billboards prominently displaying English words to advertise computer hardware, software and internet services. There is little that is new in this phenomenon; Magyar, the official language of Hungary, has assimilated vocabulary derived from Turkish, from German, and from both the north and south Slav languages of the territories that have surrounded the country. This reflects the adaptation of language to historical experience; Turkish influence, for example, stems from Ottoman occupation during much of the sixteenth and seventeenth centuries. Other influences reflect the strongly multilinguistic nature of the territories – by no means only the territory of contemporary Hungary – where Magyar is spoken.

I want to leave that last point for the moment, though I shall return to it. Please do bear in mind, however, that languages are never fixed. Linguistic diversity means that there are many different systems of signs, which allow people to represent their environment and experience. This raises a fundamental question over the extent to which human beings can understand each other's experiences and cultures across linguistic boundaries. Only by mastering the conventions of another language can any individual cross linguistic 'borders'. Alternatively, users of one language can communicate with users of another language through translation – in other words, meaning as conveyed in one language can be transferred into another, thus allowing communication between two cultures. Yet translation has its limits, for concepts expressed in one language often cannot be straightforwardly transferred to another because the systems through which concepts are expressed are different. Translation might result, however, in the creation of entirely new meanings that enrich the original. But if concepts that can be articulated in one language or culture cannot be expressed straightforwardly in another then this creates further barriers to communication. It also raises fundamental questions about cultural identity: if certain experiences can be expressed in one language and not so easily in another, this marks out those cultures as different – and that difference helps to define identity.

In order to focus your thinking about the relationship between language and cultural identity, it is necessary to consider how language carries cultural identity in more concrete terms by thinking about issues of translation. The first reading below is an extract from the writings of a Czech ethnographer, Milena Hübschmannová. Hübschmannová recorded the experiences of a Slovak Gypsy, Ilona Lacková, over an extended period in order to gain an insight both into Lacková's own remarkable life and into the culture of the east European **Roma**. Hübschmannová recorded and then transcribed Lacková's oral testimony, transferring it first into a radio series and then into a book. Lacková's life story was recorded in Romani and not in Slovak, though Lacková herself spoke fluent Slovak. In this extract Hübschmannová discusses the issues involved in recording Lacková's oral testimony and the way in which her bilingualism raises issues about the communication of her identity and culture.

Roma is the collective term used to refer to central European gypsies.

I began going to see Ilona again in 1976 when I was forced (but also chose) to strike out on my own. I found that Ilona was a widow. She was also on her own – in other words, retired. She was doing piece work for the Dopleta company which, in addition to filling knitting orders, also did photographic enlargements and colorizing: wedding photos, graduation photos, photographs of sons in the army and daughters in ballroom dancing classes. Marvelous pieces of kitsch. Ilona traveled around different villages by bus with portfolios of samples and collected orders. I started travelling with her as before when I was younger, not hitch-hiking this time but in a faithful, dilapidated old car. And Ilona told stories. She told stories about things she didn't talk about when her husband was alive. Nothing bad – just a more objective evaluation of her own life. It was fantastic and I began to record it all. We recorded for whole, long evenings, a week, ten days; for the entire time I lived – understandably – at her place.

When I first put a microphone in front of Ilona, she had a tendency to speak in Slovak. She speaks excellent, cultivated Slovak, without the least 'Gypsy' accent, has a large vocabulary, and yet it wasn't quite right. When she spoke Romani, every word, every turn of phrase, every sentence reflected the way her being was saturated with the reality of which she told. Not the least little word, no note in her intonation was superfluous, empty, or out of place. And her Slovak, whether spoken or written – Ilonka, don't be angry with me, this was occasionally true – is sometimes too rich, too expressive. It was sometimes touching how those political phrases of which she had not quite got the hang, or the feeling for, mingled with the language of the popular literature that accompanied the years of Ilonka's girlhood. It had its magic, yet it was an unintended one which might have amused intellectuals but would distort Ilona's image.

As time goes on, I become more and more convinced that language – whether *gadžo* [non-Romani] speech or Romani – also works for Roma as a trigger-signal which opens the door to the *gadžo* or the Romani part of their bi-cultural personality. This is probably the way it is – not only for Roma but for any bi-lingual population. The Romani part has been developed for hundreds or thousands of years. That ordered, harmonious, beautiful *romipen* is preserved within it. In the *gadžo* part, there are inferiority complexes exorcised with self-aggrandizement and a number of received values, not yet mastered and not yet clearly grasped, all jumbled together into chaos.

A Czech who has not had the opportunity to appreciate the Romani mode of expression, to be astonished at its respectfulness, its propriety, its harmony, at the naturalness of its images and metaphors, can unfortunately judge a Rom only by his disharmonious Czech. Only a few Roma I have met know how to express themselves in a Czech that is as pleasing as their grandfathers', and perhaps their fathers', Romani once was. It may be possible to acquire the grammar and vocabulary of a language in one generation, but to acquire the cultural dimension of a foreign language is a process that takes many generations. My feeling is that those Roma who no longer know Romani (the assimilationist pressures were enormous) and still do not know Czech or Slovak are worst off of all. And, as I began to suspect earlier, linguistic impoverishment is both a cultural and an ethical impoverishment as well. The old traditional Romani stories are not told in Czech. Songs with lyrics in Romani are sung, but their texts are not what they once were: an automatic self-analysis, the synthetic confirmation of a *raison d'être*, an insistent communication which finds resonance within the community and thereby echoes its interdependence.

The mastery of another culture in its deepest dimensions is even more complex than the mastery of another language. Usually the easiest part to master is the most superficial part, the trappings. Moreover, much depends on the channels through which Roma receive *gadžo* culture. Besides mass media, particularly television, it is imparted by people who are willing to communicate with Roma – and they always were and are either people who are exceptionally enlightened (the minority) or people at the edge of *gadžo* society who do not typically convey the most cultivated of what the Czech language and culture have to offer. Naturally, what I say here does not apply equally to all Roma or to all Czech *gadže*. As soon as we begin to speak collectively of any population, nation, or group, it always leads to distorted generalizations. On the other hand, a certain general model does exist and to a lesser or greater extent, in the most varied specific forms, it flickers through in reality itself. Such a general model of a bi-cultural, bi-lingual Romani personality was also apparent when I spoke with Ilona. I always felt better, more at ease, and more inspired when she spoke Romani (I naturally never asked her how my ability to express myself in Romani affected her and whether she felt its cultural flatness to be unpleasant).

(Lacková, 2000, pp. 7–8)

EXERCISE

After you have read the extract, take notes on the following points.

1   What observations does Hübschmannová make about Lacková's use of Slovak and the use of Czech by the Roma in general?

2   How does Hübschmannová understand the relationship between
    language and culture in the case of Roma in former
    Czechoslovakia?

3   Think carefully about Hübschmannová's view of language and its
    relationship to culture. This task is more difficult than the others
    in that it is slightly more abstract. Think about Hübschmannová's
    view of bilingualism and comment on how she believes one
    acquires knowledge of another culture.

DISCUSSION

1   Hübschmannová argues that the ethnic origin of the Roma is
    visible through the use they make of both Czech and Slovak.
    What she argues is that even in the case of a bilingual Gypsy
    woman, Lacková, the effect of living in two cultures shapes the
    way in which non-Romani, or *gadžo*, language is used. Among
    Roma in general this allows non-Roma to identify Roma through
    their language, thus demonstrating the way in which a particular
    kind of command of another language can act as a social marker.
    You might have noticed that there is more than a hint of class-
    based condescension in Hübschmannová's comment that
    Lacková's use of Slovak 'wasn't quite right'. In this comment one
    can discern a university-educated ethnographer with a command
    of literary Czech and Slovak, taught through her country's
    education system, confronting a self-taught woman of both Roma
    and working-class origin. Hübschmannová's act of designating
    Lacková's Slovak as not 'quite right' illustrates the point about
    language as a social marker. This is clearly a statement about the
    superiority of one form of language over another; in making this
    statement the ethnographer asserts the superiority of her
    command of language.

2   You will have picked out the way in which language acts as 'a
    trigger-signal which opens the door to the *gadžo* or the Romani
    part of their bi-cultural personality'. Culture here is expressed
    and articulated through language, with separate languages
    defining actions in two different parts of Roma social life.
    Language not only marks identity but also carries it.

3   Though I would not deny that there is a truth in the sentence I
    have quoted in response to point 2 above, I would have noted
    that this only describes one side of the bilingual condition.
    Hübschmannová seems to argue implicitly that one 'belongs' only
    to one language. This is to deny the positive side of bilingualism,
    or for that matter multilingualism: that a wide variety of meanings
    is opened to a person who can command more than one

language. This appreciation is almost entirely missing from this extract.

Hübschmannová's argument is that of an ethnographer attempting not only to translate a story but to understand and describe another culture. Her reading of language – that individuals belong to one language – might say more about her Czech identity and the notions of language and identity contained in Czech culture than about any other influence. In order to develop this point I shall quote from a letter written in Prague in 1920. It is from Franz Kafka (1883–1924), the German-speaking Czech writer, to his Czech translator, Milena Jesenská:

> Of course I understand Czech. I've meant to ask you several times already why you never write in Czech. Not to imply that your command of German leaves anything to be desired ... I wanted to read you in Czech because, after all, you do belong in that language, because only there can Milena be found in her entirety ... So, Czech, please.

(Quoted in Sayer, 1996, p. 164)

This extract is revealing of the problems inherent in the notion that an individual 'belongs' to a language and of some of the ambiguities this notion might conceal. The letter I have quoted from was written two years after the foundation of Czechoslovakia by a German-speaking writer who could be identified by his Czech accent, who understood Czech and 'described his feel for the language', that is German, 'as that of a "half-German"' (Sayer, 1996, p. 165). It was written in a city which became the capital of Czechoslovakia in 1918, yet where German speakers had dominated the council until as recently as 1861. The gradual transformation of Prague into a Czech-speaking city – German speakers accounted for only 7.5 per cent of its population by 1900 – was accompanied by tremendous political conflict around language (Demetz, 1997, p. 317). Language formed a marker of nationality and identity. Bitter conflicts over the language of street signs in late nineteenth-century Prague were the local manifestation of the political struggle between Czech and German speakers for hegemony in the Austrian provinces of Bohemia and Moravia (Sayer, 1998, p. 101; Spector, 2000, pp. 68–92). Language acted as a marker of Czech national identity – the notion that one 'belonged' to a language formed a means of expressing a particular national identification. This relationship, I suggest, is not universal but particular and historically contingent – nation and language can have other kinds of relationships in other contexts, something I shall return to below.

Although I feel that Hübschmannová's arguments about language say more about her own identity as a Czech ethnographer studying the culture of the Roma, they should not be dismissed out of hand. She raises important questions about the nature of language and its relationship to identity. In the context of Czech and Slovak Roma, according to Hübschmannová, it both defines membership of an ethnic group and constitutes a mechanism for excluding members of that group from the majority culture around it. Because of the unusual context it raises issues of how patterns of inclusion and exclusion within language can articulate national, ethnic, regional and class differences. Though Hübschmannová's suggestion that people are at their most natural in their own language might reflect notions of language that are rooted in her being Czech, the divide between the ethnographer and her Roma subject is not one of nationality, but of **ethnicity**. In the extract above I was particularly struck by the passage where Hübschmannová describes the linguistic dimensions of Czech racism towards the Roma in Czechoslovakia in the 1980s:

> A Czech who has not had the opportunity to appreciate the Romani mode of expression, to be astonished at its respectfulness, its propriety, its harmony, at the naturalness of its images and metaphors, can unfortunately judge a Rom only by his disharmonious Czech.

This point illustrates the way in which language marks certain 'ethnic' difference, and indeed can play a part in **essentializing** those differences. It also suggests that certain notions of language help to define perceived notions of who belongs and who is outside. The Czech Roma have been the victims of considerable and often institutionalized racism. Some 25 per cent of the Roma population of Czechoslovakia (as it then was) lived in the Czech lands in 1978; many settled there after taking industrial jobs as part of the communist state's drive to industrialize during the 1940s and 1950s. In socialist Czechoslovakia the Roma suffered from considerable institutional discrimination; for example, a law passed in 1959 mandated imprisonment for those who 'persisted in a nomadic way of life', while in 1965 the regime introduced a policy of 'compulsory dispersal ... of undesirable concentrations of the Gypsy population'. Such official attitudes were reflected in popular attitudes (*Labour Focus on Eastern Europe*, 1979, pp. 6–7). Popular racism against the Roma survived the **Velvet Revolution** of 1989 and the break-up of Czechoslovakia in 1993, and persisted throughout the 1990s. Its most notorious manifestation was in 1999 when local authorities in the northern Czech town of Ústí nad Labem constructed a wall to separate the Roma from the rest of the town's population (see BBC news website). Hübschmannová's comments that attitudes towards

---

Ethnicity is a term pertaining to membership of a group defined by cultural, religious or linguistic characteristics.

For a discussion on the essentialization of identities, the first of Stuart Hall's models of identity construction, see the section 'Models of production of identities' in Chapter 1.

Velvet Revolution is a term that refers to the events in Prague in November–December 1989 that led to the fall from power of the Communist Party of Czechoslovakia (KSČ) and the subsequent beginnings of a transition to democracy in the country.

the Roma's use of Czech act as a manifestation of Czech racism towards them is revealing of the way that language can act as a marker constituting notions of ethnic difference.

What I am suggesting is that the relationship between language and cultural identity is extremely complex. It lies close to the heart of cultural identity; it shapes our perceptions and understandings of the world, yet at the same time it reflects and is reshaped by that world. Its forms, and the notions attached to it, are shaped by history and by cultural interaction. The exercise above should have given you some appreciation of the levels of complexity involved, while my discussion of Czech notions of language and identity has touched upon the issue of the relationship between language and nation. In Chapter 3 Clive Emsley describes the process of European nation building. I now want to reinforce the abstract discussion of language and cultural identity presented so far in this chapter by examining the interaction between language and nation building.

Linking language and nation

If language shapes group identities, including some and excluding others, while forming a central plank of a given culture, then it follows that language is capable of providing a key building block of political units, such as states. The notion of group identity based on a common language may provide justification for the legitimacy of a state. It can define a group – a nation – and form the basis of its claim to have a state of its own. The notion that political loyalty can be fostered by ensuring that those who are governed share a common language with the governors is far from new. For Fynes Moryson, writing during the seventeenth century, 'in general all nations have thought nothing more powerful to unite minds than the Community of language' (quoted in Burke et al., 2000, p. 1). This essentially top-down notion, that a state can secure loyalty through the dissemination of a common language among a subject population, has been complemented by a bottom-up notion of the relationship between language and state. For Johann Gottlieb Fichte, writing at the turn of the nineteenth century, 'it is beyond doubt that, wherever a separate language is found, there a separate nation exists, which has the right to take charge of its independent affairs and to govern itself' (quoted in Crowley, 1996, p. 125). This has been linked to notions of essential ethnic difference that are carried and shaped by language: for Johann Gottfried Herder in the eighteenth century, 'since the mother tongue is the best adapted to our character and fills out our mode of thought, nature, it seems, has given us ability only for our mother tongue' (quoted in Ergang, 1966, p. 151). The idea of a nation – a group of people sharing a common language and culture – claiming a common state through which that nation can govern itself came to form a key plank of the cultural and political nationalism that emerged across Europe during the nineteenth century. Before I move on to examine the development of language and nation historically I want you to think for a moment about the relationship between language and national consciousness. The reading below was written by the linguist Karl Vossler (1872–1949) in 1927 and is an extract from his writing about 'language communities', that is to say groups that share a common language.

Since at the present time we mostly see national languages around us, we have become accustomed to think of race and language as being inseparably interwoven. When a census of the races inhabiting Austria was taken, language was the sole criterion; and, in fact, there was no other reliable characteristic. Those who spoke German, that is, professed to German as their usual language, belonged to the German race; those who spoke Italian or Polish were classified as Italians or Poles in the racial, not the national sense. In doubtful cases national language is like a church – one can belong to it, and also change it. That language binds us into nations is a natural *historical* fact, but not a *law* of nature.

Not every language community is at the same time a community of peoples. A language can bring men together in a hundred different kinds of communities. Latin to begin with was the language of the Latin race. In the course of time it became the language of the Roman state, then the language of the Catholic church, and finally the paper language of scholars. Similarly there are trade languages, like English overseas, criminal languages like *Rotwelsh* (thieves' language), unnatural artificial world languages like Volapük and Esperanto, and finally as many special languages as there are special interests that bind men into castes and professions. In the Spain of the Middle Ages an artificial Galicio-Portuguese language existed beside Castilian up to the fifteenth century, but was reserved exclusively for the love lyrics of the court. King Alfonso el Sabio wrote his prose works in Castilian, his love lyrics in Galician, and a specially noble kind of love song in Provençal, according to the interests of the readers to whom he was addressing himself. How many languages fill the air of a modern city like Vienna, Constantinople, Cairo, New York, or Chicago. In such places men are bred who become as characterless in language intercourse as money is in trade. The Viennese plutocrat who hankers after money and 'culture', will speak Czech with his maid, Hungarian with his coachman, French with his mistress, Italian with his music master, English with his governess, and, if he has time and is in the mood, German with his family. This would almost lead one to believe that it is the nature of language not to have a being of its own, with its own purpose and value, but to have value merely as a medium of exchange.

In a certain sense it is true that the predominance or victory of one language over another is determined by the interplay of forces of the practical factors that arise from time to time. Research has given us numerous examples that show how language frontiers are determined and shifted by military, political, ecclesiastical, and economic needs, and how the weaker interest must always give way to the stronger. In Switzerland, a free and peaceful country, in which attempts are no longer made to advance this or that language by military or administrative compulsion, the movement of languages is determined solely by economic factors. The routes of communication decide the matter. The Gotthard railway carries German into the Tessin, the Simplon line takes Romance to the North, the federal lines and the line Basle-Biel, again, are routes along which German advances against French. In Wallis, however, French enters from the West by means of the railway, whilst German, which has to come from the East by means of the stage-coach, can make hardly any progress.

But once a people has had its sense of nationality awakened and stands guard over its national language, all trade routes, needs and necessities, and all compulsory measures of police, state, or church must fail. That was seen in Poland. When their civic freedom and unity had been taken from the Poles and shattered, they sang Polish songs. They clung to their language as their last sign, security, and symbol of their national character and unity. The more rigidly they were prohibited from using their language in public, the prouder, deeper, more war-like, and religious became their love for it. Now it showed to the full its spiritual value to the community, and it was spoken and tended for its own sake alone, for the sake of the Polish sentiment, in defiance of all external oppression. Since every word could now lead to prison or banishment, every Polish sound became part of the national fame; to the brother a greeting from the soul, a gesture of defiance to the enemy. Here we see in divine nakedness what so many politicians – and not only politicians, but even philologists – do not see: the ideal form urge, and the instinct for self-preservation that are immanent in every language, in so far as it is in any way the expression of spiritual characteristics and a spiritual community.

To many of our German brothers who have fallen under an iniquitous foreign yoke, their language has become the last, dearest, and tenderest pledge of national memories and hopes. Since its more concrete supports in every-day intercourse have been shattered or undermined, it no longer has any other value than that of focussing common hopes and aspirations. It retreats into private, family and social life; and if it is no longer tended there, it has to die. Hence the request of the German nation to German society at home and abroad, that its language must be tended and protected. It is a purely political demand, not a moral or religious one. Nevertheless it is addressed to the moral and religious forces of our conscience and our metaphysical will; for if it is to be achieved here and now, it must appeal to the forces beyond us. A demand that is made on our social behaviour without political pressure, but with metaphysical power, is called a debt of honour. The sense of honour is the spiritual instinct of self-preservation; for in the communities of men and of peoples the man who is without honour is dead.

So there is, in fact, a national, linguistic sense of honour, or at any rate there should and must be one, since and as long as there are national wars about languages and attempts at throttling them. If a man is robbed of his earthly home, he finds a spiritual home in his mother tongue, which is everywhere and always present to his senses, and can therefore at some time again become concrete and have an earthly home. This is true of national and political, as well as of religious and sectarian communities. For example, the more the Jews were persecuted, the more closely they clung to the language of their synagogue, protected the lyrical soul and the ancient writings of Hebrew as the home of their beliefs, and barricaded themselves behind them. In a similar way a poet, filled with his emotions, shuts himself off from the demands and the turmoil of the world, in order to become an inner ear to these emotions, and their purest and clearest voice. It is true of every feeling, and therefore also of national feeling, that, when it has been excluded from every other refuge, language will become the spiritual fortress from which it will break out and conquer its environment when the times are propitious. The man who denies or gives up this last refuge and sally-port of his home sentiments, is without honour; he is dead to the community in which he received his first experience of human language.

(Vossler [1927] 2000, pp. 257–9)

EXERCISE _____

Consider the following questions, taking notes as you do so.

1   What different kinds of 'language communities' does Vossler identify?

2   What observations does Vossler make about national languages and their sociopolitical role?

3   Can you spot anything mentioned by Vossler that might undermine his arguments about national language?

DISCUSSION _____

1   In the reading a number of different kinds of 'language communities' are identified by Vossler. National language communities are only one of these. You might have noticed that the membership of what Vossler calls 'racial' groups – though I actually think that he means ethnic groups – can be ascribed through language. He also mentions a range of other language communities. 'Trade' languages unify all those engaged in a particular activity; for example, the worldwide use of English in business might form one kind of language community. Another instance is medieval Latin, which, used within the confines of the Catholic church and the world of scholarship, formed a language community that was neither ethnic nor 'national'.

2   You will have noticed that Vossler privileges the 'national language' community. For him a 'national language is like a church ... That languages binds us into nations is a natural *historical* fact'. You will also have noticed that Vossler's comments about other forms of communities and about those who are inherently multilingual are quite disparaging. I want to draw your attention to the sentence:

> The Viennese plutocrat who hankers after money and 'culture', will speak Czech with his maid, Hungarian with his coachman, French with his mistress, Italian with his music master, English with his governess, and, if he has time and is in the mood, German with his family.

This situation is clearly implied to be unnatural, in contrast to the assertion two paragraphs later that 'once a people has had its sense of nationality awakened and stands guard over its national language, all trade routes, needs and necessities, and all compulsory measures of police, state, or church must fail'. The notion that once people identify with a community based upon their native language they enter their natural home and discover their sense of belonging is extremely strong in Vossler's account, which concludes with the sentence: 'The man who denies or gives up this last refuge and sally-port of his home sentiments, is without honour; he is dead to the community in which he received his first experience of human language.' You might have noted a parallel between the notion that an individual 'belongs' to a particular language in the discussion on the first exercise, and the arguments advanced by Vossler here.

3   Vossler's account is very clearly a restatement of some of the basic arguments of linguistic nationalism. He uneasily confronts a Europe which does not wholly conform to his arguments, however. For every example which bears out his case, such as Poland, there are others within his text which contradict it. Vossler spends a paragraph discussing Switzerland where, he argues, 'the movement of languages is determined solely by economic factors'. He also realizes that the inhabitants of cities 'like Vienna, Constantinople, Cairo, New York, or Chicago' were (at the time of writing) multilingual, so they too do not conform to the notion of a homogeneous national 'language community'.

As discussed above, language has played a central role in developing the concept of nation-states, even though assertions of linguistic unity do not quite conform to actual patterns of linguistic diversity. This observation leads on to the next point, the fact that 'nations' thus conceived are not 'given' natural states, or facts, but the products of historical processes. This in turn raises the question of nationalism and its evolution. In other words, what gave and still gives rise to the attempts of groups to create states based on the linguistic and ethnic unity of the populations that inhabit them?

It has been argued that national consciousness is a phenomenon that dates back to medieval and early modern Europe. Some have argued that notions of common political entities based upon language were inherent in the law; some that these ideas formed with the expansion of printed literature in the vernacular; others that the concept came from the traditions of 'national' branches of the church (Hastings, 1997). Still others have argued for the idea of the fundamental modernity of nationalism. Ernest Gellner contends that nationalism emerged out of the collapse of 'traditional' agrarian society and the advent of industrialization. In a more individualized society a sense of belonging based on shared ethnicity and language replaced the comfortable bonds of a rural community (Gellner, 1983). In Benedict Anderson's view the development of 'print capitalism' and the wider dissemination of the written word enabled greater numbers of people to join an 'imagined community' that formed the basis of national sentiment (Anderson, 1991). Miroslav Hroch has argued that nationalism and nation building stemmed initially from the attempts of political activists to create the notion of a common culture based on a unified language that then served as the basis for claiming a state (Hroch, 1996).

On one level what divides the protagonists in debates around nationalism is the question of its modernity. Anderson and Gellner, in particular, focus on the eighteenth- and nineteenth-century roots of the phenomenon, seeing it in terms of the interaction between ethnic difference and the economic, cultural and political shifts associated with either industrialization, the rise of commercial capitalism or mass politics. Those who stress nationalism's origins in medieval or early modern times emphasize the persistence over a longer period of a link between ethnicity and statehood, seeing the roots of modern nations as lying in this period. Historical debate on the modernity or otherwise of nationalism and the nation-state is much like debate on the origins of other historical forms – historians are prone to make claims for the periods in which they specialize. This is also a debate which cannot be fully resolved here; it is merely important to note that in contrast to the assertions of theorists of linguistic nationalism like Fichte, Herder or more recently Vossler there is nothing 'natural' about the link between language and nation. The emergence of nationalism and thus the notion of a link between nation and state has been a historical process. This is shown in the third reading below, which is an extract from an essay entitled 'From national movement to the fully-formed nation: the nation-building process in Europe' by the Czech historian Miroslav Hroch, originally published in English in 1993. This extract should help you to think about nationalism and nation building as a historical process.

The nation has been an inseparable accompaniment of modern European history. It is not difficult to ironize over the record of 'nationalism' in past and present, to criticize its role and to award good or bad marks to different groups, personalities or even nations, in the process. There is a public that finds this procedure to its taste, but it is not to be confused with a scientific approach to the subject. Historians are not judges; their task is to explain actual historical transformations. There has been a significant amount of new literature on nations and nationalism in recent years, much of it produced by social scientists developing theoretical frameworks, and then illustrating their generalizations with selected examples. Historians prefer to start with empirical research, and then move to broader conclusions. My own work has not sought to advance a theory of nation-building, but rather to develop effective methods for the classification and assessment of experiences of nation-building as a process set within a wider social and cultural history – treated not as so many singular and unrepeatable events, but as part of a broad transformation of society that is amenable to controlled generalizations. But it is important to stress at the outset that we are very far from being able to explain all the major problems posed by the formation of modern nations. Every historian of national movements agrees there are numerous data gaps in our understanding of them. In this sense, all defensible conclusions remain no more than partial findings, and all 'theories' should be taken as projects for further research. Polemically, one might say that at the moment we have an over-production of theories and a stagnation of comparative research on the topic.

Nation and Civil Society

This misfortune is, I think, in part due to a widespread conceptual confusion. For today the process whereby nations were formed in Europe is typically represented as the unfolding or spread of the ideas of 'nationalism'. This is perhaps especially true of recent Anglo-Saxon literature. In my view, this is a basically misleading way of looking at the subject. For the diffusion of national ideas could only occur in specific social settings. Nation-building was never a mere project of ambitious or narcissistic intellectuals, and ideas could not flow through Europe by their own inspirational force. Intellectuals can 'invent' national communities only if certain objective preconditions for the formation of a nation already exist. Karl Deutsch long ago remarked that for national consciousness to arise, there must be something for it to become conscious of. Individual discoveries of national sentiment do not explain why such discoveries recurred in so many different countries, independently of each other, under different conditions and in different epochs. Only an approach that looks for the underlying similarity of reasons why people accepted a new national identity, can shed light on this problem. These reasons may be verbalized, but below the level of 'high politics' they are often unverbalized.

Now the 'nation' is not, of course, an eternal category, but was the product of a long and complicated process of historical development in Europe. For our purposes, let us define it at the outset as a large social group integrated not by one but by a combination of several kinds of objective relationships (economic, political, linguistic, cultural, religious, geographical, historical), and their subjective reflection in collective consciousness. Many of these ties could be mutually substitutable – some playing a particularly important role in one nation-building process, and no more than a subsidiary part in others. But among them, three stand out as irreplaceable: (1) a 'memory' of some common past, treated as a 'destiny' of the group – or at least of its core constituents; (2) a density of linguistic or cultural ties enabling a higher degree of social communication within the group than beyond it; (3) a conception of the equality of all members of the group organized as a civil society.

The process whereby nations were built, around such central elements, was not preordained or irreversible. It could be interrupted, just as it could also be resumed after a long hiatus. Looking at Europe as a whole, it is clear that it went through two distinct stages, of unequal length. The first of these started during the Middle Ages, and led to two quite different outcomes, which provided contrasting starting-points for the second stage, of a transition to a capitalist economy and civil society. At that point the path to a modern nation in the full sense of the word proceeded from either one or the other of two contrasted socio-political situations (though, of course, there were transitional cases). Over much of Western Europe – England, France, Spain, Portugal, Sweden, the Netherlands – but also farther east in Poland, the early modern state developed under the domination of one ethnic culture, either in absolutist form or in a representative-estates system. In the majority of such cases, the late feudal regime was subsequently transformed, by reforms or revolution, into a modern civil society *in parallel* with the construction of a nation-state as a community of equal citizens. In most of Central and Eastern Europe, on the other hand, an 'exogenous' ruling class dominated ethnic groups which occupied a compact territory but lacked 'their own' nobility, political unit or continuous literary tradition. My own research has been concerned with this second type of situation. It is an error, however, to think that it never existed in Western Europe as well. The plight of the 'non-dominant ethnic group' has come to be identified with lands in Eastern and South-Eastern Europe – as the fate of Estonians, Ukrainians, Slovenes, Serbs or others. But there were originally many similar communities in Western and South-Western Europe too. There, however, the medieval or early modern state assimilated most of them, although a significant number of distinctive ancient cultures persisted through such processes of integration – Irish, Catalan, Norwegian and others (in Eastern Europe, the Greeks perhaps form an analogy). There was also an important set of transitional cases, in which ethnic communities possessed 'their own' ruling class and literary traditions, but lacked any common statehood – the Germans and Italians, or later (after the loss of their commonwealth) the Poles.

Now in the second type of situation, on which my own work has concentrated, the onset of the modern stage of nation-building can be dated from the moment when selected groups within the non-dominant ethnic community started to discuss their own ethnicity and to conceive of it as a potential nation-to-be. Sooner or later, they observed certain deficits which the future nation still lacked, and began efforts to overcome one or more of them, seeking to persuade their compatriots of the importance of consciously belonging to the nation. I term these organized endeavours to achieve all the attributes of a fully-fledged nation (which were not always and everywhere successful) a *national movement*. The current tendency to speak of them as 'nationalist' leads to serious confusion. For nationalism *stricto sensu* is something else: namely, that outlook which gives an *absolute priority to the values of the nation over all other values and interests*. It was far from being the case that all the patriots in the national movements of Central and Eastern Europe in the nineteenth or early twentieth century were nationalists in this, accurate sense of the word. The term can scarcely be applied to such representative figures as the Norwegian poet Wergeland, who tried to create a language for his country, the Polish writer Mickiewicz who longed for the liberation of his homeland, or even the Czech scholar Masaryk, who formulated and realized a programme of national independence after having fought all his life against Czech nationalists. Nationalism was only one of many forms of national consciousness to emerge in the course of these movements. Nationalism did, of course, often later become a significant force in this region, just as it did further west in the region of state-nations, as a type of power politics with irrationalist overtones. But the programme of the classic national movement was of another kind. Its goals covered three main groups of demands, which corresponded to felt deficits of national existence: (1) the development of a national culture based on the local language, and its normal use in education, administration and economic life; (2) the achievement of civil rights and political self-administration, initially in the form of autonomy and ultimately (usually quite late, as an express demand) of independence; (3) the creation of a complete social structure from out of the ethnic group, including educated elites, an officialdom and an entrepreneurial class, but also – where necessary – free peasants and organized workers. The relative priority and timing of these three sets of demands varied in each case. But the trajectory of any national movement was only consumed when all were fulfilled.

Between the starting-point of any given national movement and its successful conclusion, three structural phases can be distinguished, according to the character and role of those active in it, and the degree of national consciousness emergent in the ethnic group at large. During an initial period, which I have called Phase A, the energies of the activists were above all devoted to scholarly inquiry into and dissemination of an awareness of the linguistic, cultural, social and sometimes historical attributes of the non-dominant group – but without, on the whole, pressing specifically national demands to remedy deficits (some did not even believe their group could develop into a nation). In a second period, or Phase B, a new range of activists emerged, who now sought to win over as many of their ethnic group as possible to the project of creating a future nation, by patriotic agitation to 'awaken' national consciousness among them – at first usually without notable success (in one sub-stage), but later (in another sub-stage) finding an increasingly receptive audience. Once the major part of the population came to set special store by their national identity, a mass movement was formed, which I have termed Phase C. It was only during this final phase that a full social structure could come into being, and that the movement differentiated out into conservative-clerical, liberal and democratic wings, each with their own programmes.

(Hroch [1993] 1996, pp. 78–81)

EXERCISE

Now consider the following questions, making notes as you do so.

1   How does Hroch define 'the nation'?

2   Does Hroch see nation building as an essentially 'modern' or 'pre-modern' phenomenon? What argument does he use to sustain his position?

3   What does Hroch identify as the preconditions of nation building?

4   What are the barriers to the process of nation building that Hroch identifies?

DISCUSSION

1 Hroch defines the nation 'as a large social group integrated not by one but by a combination of several kinds of objective relationships ... and their subjective reflection in collective consciousness'. You will note that he denies that the nation is in any sense 'an eternal category' and sees it as fundamentally the product of history. Furthermore, in contrast to the arguments of linguistic nationalists that have been examined above, he does not regard the development of nations as either 'preordained or irreversible'.

2 For Hroch the nation-building process is not specifically the product of either modernity or of a pre-modern state, though nations come into their own with the advent of modernity – in other words with the emergence of capitalism, and a modern state based upon an unmediated relationship between state and citizen. The development of nation-states occurred at different times in different parts of Europe. According to Hroch:

> Over much of Western Europe – England, France, Spain, Portugal, Sweden, the Netherlands ... the early modern state developed under the domination of one ethnic culture ... the late feudal regime was subsequently transformed, by reforms or revolution, into a modern civil society *in parallel* with the construction of a nation-state as a community of equal citizens.

In the rest of Europe the process of the emergence of the nation-state took a different path. Intellectuals first sought to reconstruct national cultures and to persuade members of their ethnic groups to think of themselves as a nation. Once this was achieved a national movement was formed which actively sought statehood.

Karl W. Deutsch (1912–92) was a political scientist and historian. He was born in Prague in 1912 and emigrated to the United States in 1939 following the Nazi occupation of Czechoslovakia. He is best known for his book *Nationalism and Social Communication: an Inquiry into the Foundations of Nationality* (Deutsch, 1953).

3 Hroch differs from some theorists of the emergence of nationalism such as Benedict Anderson by arguing that nations cannot simply be 'imagined' but can only emerge under certain objective conditions – following **Karl Deutsch**, Hroch states that 'for national consciousness to arise, there must be something for it to become conscious of'. Examining Hroch's text closely, I would argue that although several preconditions for the emergence of national sentiment are listed, the one that seems to stand out is the existence of an ethnic community that dominates the state. According to Hroch, this allowed national consciousness to emerge at an early stage in western Europe and Poland. Likewise in east-central Europe, according to Hroch, nationalist intellectuals had to reconstruct national cultures and languages before they could begin the essentially political work of nation building.

4   The most significant constraint to the process of nation building that Hroch identifies is the existence of the 'non-dominant ethnic group'. As a historian of nineteenth-century Bohemia and Moravia, which were part of Austria prior to 1918, Hroch is particularly sensitive to this. Much commentary on nation building in Hroch's east-central Europe, of course, draws considerable attention to the conflicts of rival nationalisms in this region, but I would draw your attention to Hroch's statement that 'there were originally many similar communities in Western and South-Western Europe too', some of which have persisted up to the present. Incomplete patterns of assimilation are something to which I shall return below.

Hroch's analysis of the nation-building process is not a complete or comprehensive account, but it does alert us to several aspects of the dynamics of the process. As a starting point, he argues, a nation requires a state which is inhabited by a dominant ethnic group. This enables the people to identify with the state and to develop a claim to control that state. The people are recast as citizens and come to identify with the state. Within states there are non-dominant ethnic groups who are either assimilated into the dominant group, develop some other form of non-ethnic identification with the state, or develop a nationalism – a desire for a state, or cultural group rights, of their own. This model is crude and at best an approximation of a range of complex processes, but as a model it is useful in that it underlines several important points. First, nations are based on ethnic communities and often linguistic communities. Secondly, these ethnic and linguistic communities are not naturally pre-given, nor do they automatically form themselves into nations. Thirdly, the process of nation building stimulates forms of conflict. Fourthly, the process of nation-building requires that the populations of states are assimilated to some degree into a dominant ethnic culture – or at least develop some form of identification with the state that enables them to live comfortably within it.

Nation building as a process has profound implications for any discussion of the relationship between language and cultural identity. The implication of Hroch's analysis is that across Europe during the last two centuries a process of nation building has occurred which has generated considerable pressures for linguistic assimilation. I shall move on to discuss these processes and pressures and how they have affected both national and linguistic identities.

Processes of assimilation

If we accept Hroch's notion of the modern nation-state as a community of equal citizens, underpinned by a modern civil society, this means that both state and society had to share a common language or languages if the process of nation building was to be successful. This in turn means that citizens had to master the language or languages of the state. This was not simply a matter of assimilating linguistic or ethnic minorities, but of creating an identification between citizen and state. An assimilationist nation-state in the nineteenth century did not merely have to assimilate the speakers of other languages; it had to create a national culture out of a patchwork of overlapping, particularist cultures. In linguistic terms this means that during the late nineteenth century states began to standardize language, mostly through state-provided education. It is therefore necessary to consider the kinds of issues involved in the linguistic dimensions of the politics of assimilation.

The state attempted to standardize language as a means of integration. Such attempts were especially marked where cultures existed that were shaped by other languages. In British-ruled Ireland Tony Crowley has 'traced ... The historical emergence of a polyglot situation ... in which Irish was positioned as an inferior and subjugated language', a process which 'occurred as a result of the practices of political and cultural colonialism' (Crowley, 1996, p. 106). Education was one of the primary instruments the state used; thus at the end of the nineteenth century the British state attempted to use schooling to eliminate the use of national languages in politically subordinate nations, such as Wales (Williams, 1989). In Hungary, which achieved statehood within the **dual monarchy** after 1867, policies of Magyarization were pursued in order to build the nation. In order to encourage linguistic unity among the educated classes the state initiated drives, with uneven success, to close secondary schools that taught in a language other than Magyar (Romsics, 1999, pp. 83–4). Likewise, some of the new and expanded nation-states created in east-central Europe after the First World War sought to assimilate multi-ethnic populations through the encouragement of linguistic unity. In Romania political leaders in Bucharest sought to assimilate newly acquired territories which had diverse cultural and historical traditions through radical educational policies that aimed to achieve a high degree of linguistic unity in ethnically mixed Bukovina, Bessarabia and Transylvania (Livezeanu, 1995). However, the standardization of language was demanded not only by emergent nation-states that were characterized by multi-ethnic and multilingual populations, for even in nominally monolingual territories a high degree of linguistic diversity existed (and to some extent still exists).

Dual monarchy is the term used to describe the entity created by the constitutional settlement of 1867 between the Austrian emperor and leading Hungarian politicians – known in German as the *Ausgleich* and in Magyar as the *Kiegyezés*. Hungary gained a separate national government and sovereignty over its internal affairs, though both Austria and Hungary recognized a common sovereign and pooled sovereignty in several areas, including foreign affairs and defence. The dual monarchy collapsed as a result of Austria-Hungary's defeat at the end of the First World War.

In order to explore this theme further you should now turn to the fourth reading, below, taken from a historical monograph: Eugen Weber's *Peasants into Frenchmen* (1977). This is a classic work of social history, dealing with the attempts to create the social bases of a modern nation in rural France during the late nineteenth century. The extract talks of education and language. It provides a useful discussion of the challenges faced by those who sought to create a nation that was unified linguistically; it is also very suggestive about processes of nation building and comes to provocative conclusions about the outcomes of the politics of assimilation. As you read it, you will note that the extract addresses a number of issues in relation to language and identity that have already been raised in this chapter, as well as several other relevant points not yet touched on.

But the effects of school went further. In the first place, the literary or written language children learned in schools was as alien to the spoken tongue as spoken French itself was to their native dialect. In other words, schools began their work by propagating an artificial language, and this was true even for French-speakers. They did this largely through the discipline of dictations, 'the instrument of a learned and universal language' beyond the local ken. As a result, many students learned to express themselves freely and easily in speech, but had difficulty when it came to writing or to expressing thought in an idiom close to that of the written word. We can glimpse this best in the surviving files of gendarmerie reports, which are often drawn up in a stilted administrative style and relate even simple events in an awkward and convoluted manner.

A striking result of this (much worse in areas estranged by dialect) was that 'for months or years (the children) give no sign of intelligence, merely imitate what they see done.' Just as legislation can create crime by fiat, so education created stupidity by setting up standards of communication that many found difficult to attain. 'Our children cannot find, and indeed have no way to find, enough French words to express their thoughts,' reported a Cantal teacher. The result was a divorce between school learning, often acquired by rote, and assimilation, which helped slow down the progress of the schools. Memorization saved the trouble of 'having to translate one's thoughts into correct French.' It also divorced word from reality. Many children 'can spell, but syllables have no meaning for them; can read, but fail to understand what they read, or to recognize in writing some words they know but whose orthography is alien,' or to identify words learned in French with the objects around them. 'You will learn it, this language of well-bred people and you will speak it some day,' promised a prize-giver in Dordogne in 1897. The future tense used in such improbable circumstances suggests a possible reason why, by 1907, the number of illiterate conscripts seems to have been slightly higher than in the immediate past. The absolute banning of the native tongue, which had been helpful in teaching French as a second language, inhibited the learning of idiomatic French and impeded its full assimilation.

This is not to say that French did not make great strides forward. It did. But writing remained a socially privileged form of expression, and the French of the schools and of the dictations was an alienating as well as an integrative force. Perhaps that was what a school inspector meant when, looking back from 1897, he declared: 'Ignorance used to precede school; today on the contrary it follows schooling.'

Of course there were (from the school's point of view) positive results; and these too went beyond the immediately obvious. The symbolism of images learned at school created a whole new language and provided common points of reference that straddled regional boundaries exactly as national patriotism was meant to do.[1] Where local dialect and locutions insulated and preserved, the lessons of the school, standardized throughout France, taught a unifying idiom. In Ain, the Ardennes, Vendée, all children became familiar with references or identities that could thereafter be used by the authorities, the press, and the politicians to appeal to them as a single body. Lessons emphasizing certain associations bound generations together. The Kings of France were the older sons of the Church, time was the river that carried all in its waters, a poet was a favourite of the muses, Touraine was the garden of France, and Joan of Arc the shepherdess of Lorraine. Local saws and proverbs were replaced by nationally valid ones, regional locutions by others learned in books: castles in Spain rose above local ruins, and golden calves bleated more loudly than the stabled ones. The very mythology of ambition was now illustrated by landscapes that education had suggested, more stirring than the humbler ones at

---

[1] In a lesson given in the second year (four- to seven-year-olds), for example, children learned to interpret road signs. They began with the one all knew as a cross, then were taught to recognize it as a sign helping a person to find his way, and further, as an indication of how much better roads were in their own day ('Il n'y avait pas de routes dans le temps ...'). *Devoirs d'écoliers français*, pp. 356–60. This cross-as-signpost image, as Renée Balibar has shown (*Les Français fictifs*, Paris, 1974, p. 194), played an important role in the writing of [the socialist poet] Charles Péguy, who had undoubtedly been taught the lesson.

hand and by this time no less familiar. These are only aspects of the wide-ranging process of standardization that helped create and reinforce French unity, while contributing to the disintegration of rival allegiances.

The cultural underpinnings of rural society, already battered by material changes, were further weakened by shifting values. First of all, manual labor was devalued – or better still, the natural aversion to its drudgery was reinforced. The elementary schools, designed to form citizens, neglected producers. The school glorified labor as a moral value, but ignored work as an everyday form of culture. The well-established contrast between the plucky, mettlesome spirit of the *courageux* – and the idle *fainéant* – the one hardworking, especially or only with his hands, the other avoiding manual labor – was translated into scholastic terms. Soon, the idle boy was the one likely to be the most pressed into hard physical labor, the plucky boy the one most enterprising with his books. It made good sense, for the rewards of work now came to those not doing what had once been recognized as work. But it opened a crack – one more – in age-old solidarities.

In a great many homes, illiterate adults depended on small children to carry out what were becoming essential tasks – accounting, correspondence, taking notes, reading aloud pertinent documents or newspaper items. And new literacies at whatever level made new ideas accessible, especially to the young, to whom certain profound changes in the political climate of country districts were now attributed. In any case, the relationship between school and social claims was not ignored in their own time: 'The Republic has founded schools,' sang Montéhus, the revolutionary chansonnier, 'so that now the people have learned how to count. The people have had enough of the pauper's mite; they want an accounting, and not charity!' More important, where, as in Brittany, a determined campaign taught new generations French, 'children and parents form two worlds apart, so separated in spirit, so estranged by speech, that there is no more community of ideas and feelings, hence no intimacy. Often, as a matter of fact, any kind of relationship becomes impossible.' This is both exaggerated and suggestive of a generation gap more easily discerned in modern societies than in traditional ones. But even granting the exaggeration, the corrosive effects of one sort of education on a society based on another kind are undeniable.

Like migration, politics, and economic development, schools brought suggestions of alternative values and hierarchies; and of commitments to other bodies than the local group. They eased individuals out of the latter's grip and shattered the hold of unchallenged cultural and political creeds – but only to train their votaries for another faith.

(Weber, 1977, pp. 336–8)

EXERCISE

Consider, and make notes on, the following questions.

1   Why does Weber say that the French learned in nineteenth-century rural schools was alien to many of the pupils?

2   How successful was nineteenth-century French schooling in creating one nation unified by language?

3   Was the acquisition of competence in spoken and written French the only way in which pupils came to identify with the nation? In what other ways did formal education shape perceptions of nation and national community?

DISCUSSION

1   Weber points our attention to the fact that the language spoken in much of rural France was dialect. These dialects, effectively local languages closely related to each other, were also in many senses alien to each other and to the standard forms of French propagated in schools.

2   One might say that attempts to create a unified language were partly successful. While many of the schoolchildren involved acquired a degree of competence, particularly in the spoken language, you might have noticed that Weber's descriptions of these children's command of official French (especially written French) was not of the level to be normally expected in an individual's native language. As a result the acquisition of and competence in official French became a marker of social stratification – you might recall Weber's sentence where he states that 'writing remained a socially privileged form of expression'. This is an important point as it raises the issue of how members of far different classes, or social strata, could participate equally in national life even when the state was based upon the formal legal equality of all citizens.

3   In contrast to the claims of linguistic nationalism, the acquisition of spoken and written language was not the only way in which pupils came to identify with the nation. The acquisition of knowledge of national history, for example, is stressed by Weber

and touches on issues raised by Clive Emsley in Chapter 3. This formed part of what Weber terms a 'process of standardization' which although incomplete was marked in a number of fields, language included.

EXERCISE _____

At this point I think it is important to recap and tie together some of the issues already touched on. This is particularly important given that the extract challenges, expands and modifies some of the ideas you have encountered in the extracts from Vossler and Hroch. I want you to think about how Weber's analysis challenges and/or complements/modifies the arguments presented earlier.

DISCUSSION _____

The challenge posed to Vossler's text is profound. Vossler identifies the mother-tongue with national languages in the sense that we understand them today. This allows him to make a claim about native languages that privileges national identity. Weber suggests, however, using information from the French case, that the question of native language is infinitely more complex. You might think of dialects as a multitude of local, particular languages each shaped by local cultures and conditions, as well as by the nature of their users' experiences. The national language, according to this analysis, is something that has to be created and may be as alien to its local users as non-native languages are in Vossler's analysis. It suggests, too, that the links between national identity and language are much more complex than linguistic nationalists suggest, and, furthermore, that national sentiment can also be carried by means other than language.

Hroch's extract is less directly challenged by some of the issues raised by Weber. You might have noticed, however, that Hroch draws attention to the interplay between dominant and non-dominant ethnic groups in nation-states, arguing that they are either assimilated or develop their own nationalism. He stresses assimilation as a process, as Weber does. Although Hroch ignores the question of particularist forms of language, like dialect, there are parallels between the ways in which assimilationist education has sought to wipe out dialects and to eliminate the languages of non-dominant ethnic groups; for example, Welsh in the United Kingdom, Breton in France or Catalan in Spain. Weber also forces us to think about the limits to state-driven policies of linguistic assimilation, and in a different way Hroch's extract does this too. Among the rural French population the attempts to eliminate dialect were only partly successful, yet they did succeed in inculcating an identification with the nation-state. Among ethnic minorities the process of assimilation, according to Hroch, created a reaction that manifested itself in attempts to preserve a non-dominant culture, generating demands for cultural autonomy and possibly political separation.

The republican French state of the late nineteenth century was not the only state that sought to forge a united nation through the imposition of a standardized language, as I have shown above. Nor was France the only country divided by the prevalence of regional and even local dialects in the second half of the nineteenth century. Perhaps the best-known example of regional linguistic diversity in Europe, though by no means the only one, is Italy, which is discussed by Cristina Chimisso in Chapter 1. Both the extract from Weber and the Italian case suggest substantial pressures towards standardization and a shift away from dialect. They do, however, point to a somewhat paradoxical situation in that standardization did not proceed in the way that its architects intended. Furthermore, they suggest that beneath the trend towards standardization older forms of language persisted. When the focus is shifted to consider the effects of processes of assimilation on minority, or non-dominant, languages a more complex picture can be discerned. In some cases, though the proportion of a population using a non-dominant language has declined, that language has provided one of the pillars of a revival of a cultural, or even a national, identity. Consider the example of Wales, where 54 per cent of the population spoke Welsh in 1891, while only 37 per cent did so in 1931 and just 20 per cent by 1981. Yet since the Second World War, and more particularly since the 1960s, Welsh nationalism has increasingly provided a means of political mobilization and the issue of language has been central (Williams, 1989, p. 193). The issues involved in assessing the degree to which assimilation was successful are complex, though it is important to stress that such processes have not led towards just one conclusion but have resulted in new patterns of linguistic diversity that are shaped by a variety of contexts: historical, geographical and cultural.

Yet not all the causes of what I have characterized as a paradoxical process of linguistic standardization arose specifically from the nation-state, let alone from the expansion of state education. As Tim Williams has argued in the Welsh case, 'languages can be neither killed nor resuscitated by means of schools alone' (Williams, 1989, p. 194). This forces us to think about the social causes of linguistic assimilation and thus place the actions of the state in context. Education alone was an imperfect tool for forging a common identity based upon a shared language, as the examination of the extract from Weber makes clear for France. In the absence of detailed research on linguistic change and the role of the state it is difficult to evaluate the success of state-led attempts at linguistic assimilation in other contexts. An undoubted process of standardization has occurred, albeit unevenly across the continent, yet this may be due to factors other than the role of the state or education, as discussed below. What evidence we do have, however, suggests that the uneven progress of state-led cultural policies, visible in Weber's discussion of the French case, was replicated across Europe. In dualist Hungary, for example, the policies of Magyarization certainly improved knowledge of Magyar among the speakers of other languages, but without eliminating those languages. In 1880 some 14 per cent of the population spoke Magyar and at least one other language; by 1910 that figure had risen to 23 per cent (Romsics, 1999, p. 84).

One might stress other causes that are less explicitly connected with the intention of the governments of nation-states to achieve greater linguistic standardization within their national boundaries. While I cannot provide a comprehensive account, I can give a couple of examples that raise important issues about both language and linguistic change. Ernest Gellner has suggested that industrialization over the past 200 years has allowed a multitude of pre-modern, particularist cultures to meld together and fuse into a smaller number of national cultures (Gellner, 1983). A parallel might be drawn here between linguistic change and industrialization and the greater mobility of populations, in both social and geographical terms, fuelling the process of assimilation. Tim Williams has argued that coal-based industrialization in nineteenth-century south Wales created substantial pressures for **anglicization**. Initially the coalfields were worked by migrants from other parts of Wales, thus 'fleetingly' forming 'a Welsh-speaking labour force'. By the 1870s, however, some 40 per cent of new recruits to the mines came from the rural west of England – a massive wave of migration into south Wales from England followed. The consequences for the preservation of the Welsh language were enormous. According to Williams, 'immigration clearly added to the difficulties of transmitting the language from one generation to the next in a context in which one's neighbours, schoolfriends, drinking partners, team-mates, colleagues, comrades and lovers – in a phrase, civil society – might speak only in English' (Williams, 1989, pp. 195–6). Although mass migration was important in reshaping language use, it is doubtful that industrialization would have resulted in anglicization had English not been the official language of the state.

In multi-ethnic east-central Europe meanwhile, industrialization, migration and assimilation proceeded together during the late

Anglicization is defined by the OED as 'the action or process of making English'.

nineteenth century. Of the population of Budapest, for example, in 1851 only 22.9 per cent spoke Magyar as their mother-tongue, while 35.7 per cent spoke German and 41.4 per cent identified themselves as speakers of other languages. Between 1851 and 1910 the total population of the city increased from 172,935 to 880,371. In 1910 some 85.2 per cent of the population spoke Magyar, 6.5 per cent German and 3.3 per cent other languages (Tóth, 1998, p. 199). This linguistic shift occurred with industrialization. During its initial phase industry recruited workers from parts of the monarchy other than Hungary, especially among speakers of German and Czech. With rapid economic growth in the 1880s a major expansion occurred in the capital city's workforce. The overwhelming majority of new recruits were Magyar speakers; the linguistic shift in the balance of the population may not have been the only cause of linguistic assimilation, but it did give it tremendous impetus (Tóth, 1998). Yet the case of assimilation in Budapest reveals that this process was complex. Many of the 'new' Magyar speakers spoke a version of the language that was far from classical and was shaped by influences from other languages that had been spoken in the Hungarian capital, particularly from German before the process of assimilation. This language came to be termed the *Pesti Nyelv* (the Pest language), indicating that it was much more than a marker of a Budapester identity. Instead it marked its speakers as residents of the industrial and commercial eastern half of the city (Pest), differentiated from the western half (Buda) populated by the 'national' middle class and dependent on the state for its status (Gyáni, 1995). Not only had industrialization and assimilation created new particularist forms of language, they had provided a meeting point between different languages and thus re-shaped the language. In other words, industrialization could create pressures for linguistic standardization, especially when it threw together people who spoke a range of dialects. Although the state supplied the means for standardization through public education, industrialization and migration provided the catalyst.

Despite a lack of precise information on its effects on language, another factor worthy of mention is that of the mass media. The rise of print and a publishing industry in the eighteenth century is credited with creating a widely available set of texts that allowed linguistic groups to shape 'imagined communities' of nation (Anderson, 1991). In eighteenth-century England the rise of print is said to have formed the basis of a distinctly English 'civil society' (Crowley, 1996, pp. 54–98). Similarly, the twentieth century saw the rise of cinema, radio and television. In the context of language I am particularly keen to stress the importance of national broadcasting as a mechanism for promoting linguistic assimilation. The spread of

You will have noticed that these figures add up to only 95 per cent. This is due to the way that the statistics were originally collected and presented.

radio and then of television ensured that during the 1960s standardized national languages were able to enter the majority of homes across the continent. In the UK, for example, by 1961 some 75 per cent of households had a television set; in 1965, 49 per cent of Italian families owned a television; while behind the 'Iron Curtain' in Hungary a television could be found in 66 per cent of households by 1970 (Marwick, 1990, p. 177; Ginsborg, 1990, p. 240; Romsics, 1999, p. 479). Television has been tremendously popular as a mass medium, and central to popular culture. It has also exposed mass audiences to more-or-less standardized national languages for much of the postwar period, though with the advent of new technologies and deregulation this is changing. For these reasons it must have had an impact on linguistic standardization even if that precise impact is difficult to gauge exactly.

The processes of linguistic assimilation have been many and complex, and not all are related directly to state action. I have not tried to present a comprehensive account of these processes, but simply to outline some of them. I have done this to provide you with an insight and an introduction to some of the complexities of language and cultural identity. I have also sought to relate these to processes that have occupied centre stage during the last 200 years and have shaped linguistic unity and diversity within contemporary Europe.

Conclusion

Because of the complexity of the argument presented in this chapter I want briefly to provide a summary of the ground covered here.

- Language provides a means of representing the world around us, and allows us to articulate both our experiences and our identities.

- Language is part of culture and not easily separable from it: it therefore forms a central part of cultural identity.

- Some have attempted to argue for the primacy of national languages, and thus national identities. I have sought to show that the relationship between language and cultural identity is much more complex.

- This is because, first, nation-states are historical creations, not naturally formed cultural entities.

- There are many different kinds of language community: some are state-based, some are particular, some are based around ethnicity. The patterns of linguistic diversity are very complex.

- Standardized national languages are, like nation-states, historical creations, and likewise linguistic assimilation has been a historical process.

- Linguistic assimilation has not been directed solely by the nation-state, but also by cultural and economic forces that have transformed society during the last two centuries.

- The processes of linguistic assimilation have not created linguistic uniformity even within nation-states. They have instead created new patterns of linguistic diversity.

It is often argued that linguistic diversity represents an obstacle to the achievement of European political unity because of the tremendous loyalty to national language that exists. While the discussion here does underline the importance of a standardized language to a united, national civil society, examples of functioning multilingual and democratic states, such as Belgium and Switzerland, do exist in contemporary Europe. It would be foolish to deny the profound effects of processes of assimilation on linguistic practice and identity, but the argument here suggests that we need to treat claims made about national language with some scepticism. The reasons for this scepticism, however, might be equally disturbing for proponents of greater European cultural unity. Above all I have pointed to the particularism of language, the fact that it is primarily shaped by the contexts in which it is used. This suggests that patterns of linguistic use are socially and historically determined, constantly shifting in response to social change. Language also provides a powerful differentiating force, indicating differences that are based not only on nation but on region ethnic origin, gender and class too.

References

Anderson, B. (1991) *Imagined Communities: Reflections on the Origins and the Spread of Nationalism*, 2nd edn, London/New York, Verso.

BBC news website: http://news.bbc.co.uk/hi/english/world/europe/newsid_434000/434002.stm

Burke, L., Crowley, T. and Girvin, A. (2000) 'General introduction', in L. Burke, T. Crowley and A. Girvin (eds), *The Routledge Language and Culture Reader*, London/New York, Routledge.

Burke, P. (1978) *Popular Culture in Early Modern Europe*, Aldershot, Wildwood House.

Crowley, T. (1996) *Language in History: Theories and Texts*, London/New York, Routledge.

Demetz, P. (1997) *Prague in Black and Gold: the History of a City*, Harmondsworth, Penguin.

Deutsch, K. W. (1953) *Nationalism and Social Communication: an Inquiry into the Foundations of Nationality*, London, Chapman & Hall.

Ergang, R. R. (1966) *Herder and the Foundations of German Nationalism*, New York, Octagon.

Gellner, E. (1983) *Nations and Nationalism*, Oxford, Blackwell.

Ginsborg, P. (1990) *A History of Contemporary Italy: Society and Politics 1943–1988*, Harmondsworth, Penguin.

Gyáni, G. (1995) *Hétköznapi Budapest. Nagyvárosi élet a századfordulón*, Budapest, Városháza.

Hastings, A. (1997) *The Construction of Nationhood: Ethnicity, Religion and Nationalism*, Cambridge/New York, Cambridge University Press.

Hroch, M. [1993] (1996) 'From national movement to the fully-formed nation: the nation-building process in Europe', in G. Balakrishnan (ed.), *Mapping the Nation*, London/New York, Verso.

Labour Focus on Eastern Europe (1979) vol. 3, no. 1.

Lacková, I. (2000) *A False Dawn: My Life as a Gypsy Woman in Slovakia*, recorded, transl. from Romani and ed. M. Hübschmannová, transl. from Czech C. Bulkin, Hatfield, Centre de recherches tsiganes/ University of Hertfordshire Press.

Livezeanu, I. (1995) *Cultural Politics in Greater Romania: Regionalism, Nation Building and Ethnic Struggle*, Ithaca, NY/London, Cornell University Press.

Marwick, A. (1990) *British Society since 1945*, 2nd edn, Harmondsworth, Penguin.

Romsics, I. (1999) *Magyarország Története a XX. Században*, Budapest, Osiris.

Sayer, D. (1996) 'The language of nationality and the nationality of language: Prague 1780–1920', *Past and Present*, no. 151, pp. 164–210.

Sayer, D. (1998) *The Coasts of Bohemia: a Czech History*, Princeton, NJ, Princeton University Press.

Spector, S. (2000) *Prague Territories: National Conflict and Cultural Innovation in Franz Kafka's* Fin-de-Siècle, Berkeley, CA/London, University of California Press.

Tóth, Z. (1998) 'What is melting in the melting pot?', in L. Csejdy and Z. Fejős (eds), *Regio: Minorities, Communities, Society*, Budapest, Teleki László Alapítvány.

Vossler, K. [1927] (2000) 'Language communities', in L. Burke, T. Crowley and A. Girvin (eds), *The Routledge Language and Cultural Reader*, London/New York, Routledge.

Weber, E. (1977) *Peasants into Frenchmen: the Modernization of Rural France 1870–1914*, London, Chatto & Windus.

Williams, T. (1989) 'The Anglicisation of South Wales', in R. Samuel (ed.), *Patriotism: the Making and Unmaking of British National Identity*, vol. 2: *Minorities and Outsiders*, London/New York, Routledge.

Portraying identities, portraying conventions

AUDREY LINKMAN

Visual images, like primary written records, require careful scrutiny and critical analysis when used to investigate cultures and identities. It is particularly easy to think of photographs as truthful and objective because they are generated from light falling on the actual scene or subject. However, all photographs are created by human agency, and photographers legitimately seek to influence viewers' perceptions.

Photographers operate within a context of ideas and adopt working practices which give expression to those ideas. Ideology and method work together to form the generic image. This colour section is devoted to a brief exploration of the ideas and practices which inform one genre within the photographic tradition – early photographic portraiture.

I RICHARD BEARD, Jabez Hogg photographing W. S. Johnston, early 1840s, daguerreotype, 6.7 x 9.2 cm. NMPFT/Science & Society Picture Library

Practical photography was invented in 1839. Portraiture became its first major commercial application because the camera was able to mechanize a well-established, thriving trade in handmade likenesses. Prior to the invention of photography working people bought silhouettes, the comfortable classes purchased miniatures of water-colours on ivory and the rich commissioned their portraits in oils.

2 FRENCH SCHOOL, portrait of a nobleman seated at a desk, c. 1750, oil on canvas, 106.7 x 92.5 cm. Phillips, The International Fine Art Auctioneers/Bridgeman Art Library

Since the Renaissance portrait painters in Europe had evolved a sophisticated professional rhetoric about the form and function of the portrait and the nature of their interaction with the sitter. In order to encourage acceptance of their mechanically produced images early photographers tailored their own practices and products to fit this existing ideology. Painterly ideas influenced every aspect of the photographic portrait, from expression and pose to backdrops and lighting.

3 POMPEO BATONI, John Wodehouse, later 1st Baron Wodehouse (1741–1834), 1764, oil on canvas, 135.3 x 97.8 cm. Allen Memorial Art Museum, Oberlin College, Ohio; Mrs F. F. Prentiss Fund, 1970

Portrait painters observed a fundamental imperative to idealize their sitters – to emphasize their beauties and to omit, shadow or conceal any defects or blemishes.

4 SIR JOSHUA REYNOLDS, Jane Fleming, Countess of Harrington (1755–1824), 1777–8, oil on canvas, 235 x 145 cm. Powerstock/Henry E. Huntington Library and Art Gallery, San Marino, California

Early photographers accepted without question the same obligation to produce a flattering portrait – in spite of the camera's technical capability to capture detail and reproduce it accurately.

'The photographer who understands his art has to hide all the defects and to show more preeminently what is beautiful and perfect' (Antoine Claudet, 1861, 'The art claims of photography', *The Photographic News*, vol. 5, no. 159, 20 September).

5 LADY CLEMENTINA HAWARDEN, photographic study, albumen print from wet collodion negative.
V & A Picture Library

Portraiture was concerned with more than mere external features. The true purpose of the portrait was to reveal the character and soul of the sitter. This gave the painting its moral and spiritual dimensions. In keeping with the theory of idealization, however, painters could depict only those characteristics which reflected well on the sitter and inspired the viewer to moral improvement. Vices, like physical defects, were subject to censorship by the artist.

'If a devil were to have his portrait painted, he must be drawn as abstracted from his own evil and stupidly good' (Jonathan Richardson, essay on the theory of painting, 1715).

6 SIR JOSHUA REYNOLDS, Sir Joseph Banks (1743–1820), 1771–3, oil on canvas, 127 x 101.5 cm. By courtesy of the National Portrait Gallery, London

Photographers proved eager to embrace a rhetoric which enhanced their status. 'To secure a portrait of a man in his completeness, mind and body, instead of a mere mask of his physical presentment, I consider the highest achievement in portraiture, the highest aim of the most skilful portrait painter, the crowning glory of a photographer' ('Hints on character in portraiture', 1876, *The Photographic News*, vol. 20, no. 948, 3 November, pp. 522–3).

For Julia Margaret Cameron, the very act of portraiture was a reverent communion of souls. She wrote of her sitters '… my whole soul has endeavoured to do its duty towards them in recording faithfully the greatness of the inner as well as the features of the outer man' (Helmut Gernsheim, 1948, *Julia Margaret Cameron, Her Life and Photographic Work*, London, Fountain, p. 71).

7 JULIA MARGARET CAMERON, Sir John Frederick William Herschel (1792–1871), April 1869, albumen print, 34 x 26.4 cm. By courtesy of the National Portrait Gallery, London

Facial expression was the vehicle through which the intangible qualities of the mind were made manifest in the painting. Expression was therefore regarded as the most important element of the portrait. Painters sought to achieve the one ideal expression which could represent a synthesis of character and career.

8 ALLAN RAMSAY, Jean-Jacques Rousseau, 1766, oil on canvas, 75 x 64.8 cm. National Gallery of Scotland, Edinburgh/Bridgeman Art Library

Nineteenth-century commercial portrait photographers resorted to the convention of a calm and serious expression as this was thought to project positive qualities such as self-control, proper self-respect, dignity and good breeding.

'The photographer should endeavour to represent his sitters as moderately calm ladies and gentlemen; or, if they are not entitled to the courtesy title, then as decent men and women' (H. P. Robinson [1891] 1973, *The Studio: and What to Do in It*, London/New York, Piper & Carter/ Arno, p. 94).

9 ELLIOTT & FRY, London, John Ruskin, cabinet portrait. Documentary Photography Archive, Manchester: 2375/39

10 LACHLAN McLACHLAN, Manchester, unknown female, c. 1870, *carte de visite*. Author's collection

In painted portraiture the representation of ideal beauty required the suppression of strong emotion 'all of which produce distortion and deformity, more or less, in the most beautiful faces' (Sir Joshua Reynolds [1797] 1975, *Discourses on Art*, ed. Robert R. Wark, New Haven, CT, Yale University Press, p. 78). The avoidance of strong emotion extended to laughter.

Charles Bell, in his *Essays on the Anatomy of Expression in Painting*, was able to define three categories of expression relating to laughter and identify their distinguishing characteristics. Broad laughter was considered 'too ludicrous and too violent a straining of the features' for anything other than the lowest class of Dutch painters and caricature draughtsmen. A smile could convey greater variety of meaning, but a more charming expression was portrayed by 'a certain mobility of the features which indicates the susceptible mind of a lovely woman … an evanescent illumination of the countenance …' (Charles Bell, 1806, *Essays on the Anatomy of Expression in Painting*, London, Longman, Hurst, Rees & Orme, pp. 5–6).

11 SIR THOMAS LAWRENCE, Margaret, Countess of Blessington (1789–1849), oil on canvas, 91.5 x 67 cm. Wallace Collection, London/Bridgeman Art Library

Photographers, too, recognized the vulgarity of laughter. One authority advised 'a look of animation, far short of a smile, which suits nearly all faces', but conceded that ladies could be portrayed with a cheerful expression, and smiles were acceptable for children (H. P. Robinson [1891] 1973, *The Studio: and What to Do in It*, London/New York, Piper & Carter/Arno, pp. 94–5). The exclusion of any reference to male sitters in this context suggests that smiles carried connotations of frivolity and lack of consequence in nineteenth-century consciousness. The absence of smiles in early photographic portraiture was not determined by slow emulsions and prolonged exposures.

12 JOHN INGHAM, Sale, unknown female, 1880s, *carte de visite*. Author's collection

13 F. H. WARLICH, London, Constance and Charles Mansfield, April 1880, *carte de visite*. Documentary Photography Archive, Manchester: 1427/267

The sitter's pose was intended to continue the idealization and echo the limited characterization portrayed by the expression. Physical defects were hidden from view or veiled in shadow. Photographers were advised to aim for a natural, graceful and elegant pose, qualities which characterized the genteel and privileged. Sitters displaying an elegant pose would be viewed as educated and refined. Males were allowed greater variety of movement than females. 'The pose of a lady should not have that boldness of action which you would give a man, but be modest and retiring, the arms describing gentle curves, and the feet never far apart' (A. H. Wall, 1861, 'The technology of art as applied to photography', *The Photographic News*, vol. 5, no. 131, p. 110, 8 March).

14 W. DAMRY, Liège, unknown male, 1860s, *carte de visite*. Author's collection

15 W. H. KENT, unknown male, 1862, *carte de visite*. Author's collection

16 SCHULZE, Heidelberg am Burgweg, Edith Maud Haddon, 1864, *carte de visite*. Author's collection

17 WILLIAM PIPER, Camborne, Ellen Thomas, c. 1865, *carte de visite*. Author's collection

In family groupings position, posture, eye direction and physical contact were all deployed to suggest underlying values such as cohesion, unity, harmony, dignity and stability. In nineteenth-century Europe these were regarded as ideal virtues to which the family would aspire.

18 JAMES BRUCE, Kilmarnock, unknown family group, 1870s, *carte de visite.*
Author's collection

19 ARTHUR HOLBORN, Bristol, unknown family group, 1890s, cabinet. Documentary
Photography Archive, Manchester: D107/1/2

The photographers' debt to portrait painting is most obviously apparent in their choice of backdrops and accessories. Two scenarios featured prominently in their repertoire. Backdrops painted with large windows, wainscoting and flowing drapery were furnished with table, chair and potted plant to suggest elegant interiors, while painted clouds or trees in combination with balustrade, stile or rustic bench conveyed an impression of gracious parkland. These staged settings provided anonymity, hinted at a genteel lifestyle and so subscribed to the overriding concern with idealization. Compare the backdrops in these *cartes de visite* with the paintings by the artist of the French School, Batoni and Reynolds at the beginning of this section (Plates 2, 3 and 4).

20 MAULL & FOX, London, unknown male, 1870s, cabinet. Author's collection

21 D'ALESSANDRI FRÈRES, Rome, unknown male, 1860s, *carte de visite*. Author's collection

22 PORRAL, Gibraltar, unknown female, c. 1870, *carte de visite*. Author's collection

Conventional studio accessories were taken from the painter's repertoire and used to suggest virtues or attributes by association. The book, for example, implied education at a time when many people in Europe were illiterate or uneducated. By arriving at the studio dressed in their Sunday-best outfits sitters signalled their complicity in these make-believe settings and idealized portrayals.

Photograph albums frequently feature as accessories. With their tooled leather covers, metal clasps and gilt edges, photograph albums were deliberately designed to imitate the appearance of Victorian family bibles. Photographers were signalling a connection between the collection of family photographs and the contemporary practice of recording births, marriages and deaths in the flyleaves of the family bible.

A.PEPLOW   HASTINGS.

23 ALFRED PEPLOW, Hastings, unknown female, 1890s, cabinet. Author's collection

The concern with idealization extended beyond the portrait to include the occasion on which the photograph was taken. The family album validated success and achievement and eschewed scandal, setback or failure. Sitters courted the camera to celebrate special occasions or events that reflected well on the individual and brought credit on the family. Rites of passage featured prominently, reflecting the social conformity of the age.

24 JAMES PENNINGTON, Aigburth, christening portrait with unknown woman and child, 1860s, *carte de visite*. Author's collection

25 ANON, William Henry Roberts (born 20 January 1864) and his father (?), c. 1867, *carte de visite*. Author's collection

26 A. LOUVOIS, Brussels, First Holy Communion (?) portrait of unknown female, c. 1900, *carte de visite*. Author's collection

27 SILAS EASTHAM, Manchester, unknown male wearing first pair of long trousers, c. 1863, *carte de visite*. Author's collection

28 J. R. CROSSE, Salop, wedding portrait of unknown couple, 1890s, cabinet. Author's collection

While the majority of early photographic portraits were taken in conventional studios, many were taken in the open air, either by conventional studio proprietors or by itinerant operators. Itinerant photographers worked in suburban streets, in the fairground, at the seaside, at local beauty spots and at those resorts where crowds went for entertainment on Sundays and holidays. Their equipment varied. Minimal necessities included a camera and darkbox to process the negative. Successful itinerants could boast wheeled caravans fitted with glazed studios and darkrooms. Others pitched canvas tents on the fairground or seashore. However basic their facilities, these itinerants worked broadly within the conventions of mainstream portraiture.

29 ANON, members of the Bywater family on holiday at Grange-over-Sands in the 1890s, ferrotype. Documentary Photography Archive, Manchester: 1037/16

30 S. WILLIAMS, Mrs Roberts with her daughters
Hannah (left) and Margaret (right), c. 1900, cabinet.
Documentary Photography Archive, Manchester: 823/7

31 ANON, unknown family group, 1888, cabinet.
Author's collection

Practices relating to portraiture became so conventionalized that they were applied indiscriminately to most subjects taken inside the photographic studio whatever their ultimate purpose. These commercial *cartes de visite* of local and national costume were the precursors of the picture postcard and were sold as novelties to visitors and tourists.

32 A. JAGER, Amsterdam, Costumes des Pays-Bas, La Hollande Septentrionale, Marken, *carte de visite*. The Open University

33 A. JAGER, Amsterdam, Costumes des Pays-Bas, Orpheline Bourgeoise d'Amsterdam, *carte de visite*. The Open University

34 AD. BRAUN, Dornach, Costumes de Suisse,
19, Cantons des Grisons, *carte de visite*. The Open
University

35 ORDINAIRE, Dinard, Breton costume, *carte de
visite*. The Open University

Photography was a European invention pioneered in France and England. As photography spread around the world western practitioners exported not only the technology but also European traditions of portraiture. The British photographer John Thomson travelled extensively in the Far East in the 1860s and 1870s. Among other photographic activities he set up studios in various locations there.

36 JOHN THOMSON, taken in Siam (now Thailand), Siamese nobleman, 1866, from original wet collodion negative. The Wellcome Library, London

37 JOHN THOMSON, taken in Bangkok, former prime minister of Siam, 1866, from original wet collodion negative. The Wellcome Library, London

38 MILTON MILLER, unknown female in ornamental dress. Royal Asiatic Society of Great Britain

39 MILTON MILLER, unknown family group. Royal Asiatic Society of Great Britain

These ideas and practices informed the tradition of photographic portraiture throughout the nineteenth century. Developments in the wider society and within photography itself inevitably brought change and modification. The emergence of the amateur snapshooter in growing numbers from the 1880s marked the beginning of a serious challenge to the dominance of the professional in family photography. The new amateurs inherited this set of ideas about portraiture from the professionals. Aspects of this tradition can still be traced in the photographs we take today and add to our family albums.

40 J. HINCHY, Manchester, group of amateur photographers, c. 1900, cabinet. Courtesy of David Hooper

41 AUDREY LINKMAN, woman photographing bridesmaids at a wedding, 2000, colour snapshot. Author's collection

5

Religion and European identities

DAVID HERBERT

Introduction

> [I]n almost every European country, the twentieth century
> has seen the power, popularity and presence of religion
> decline.
>
> (Bruce, 1999, p. 117)

> There was no outward and visible sign he was a Muslim. He,
> his son and his daughter dressed and acted as Europeans.
>
> (UN negotiator David Owen describes his first meeting with
> Bosnian President Alija Izetbegovič, 1992; in Owen, 1995, p. 39)

> Europe built up its basic outlooks through the rude school of
> the Middle Ages. Despite its coming of age, these childhood
> experiences have never faded from the European mind.
> Religious or non-religious, Europe will always think within the
> Christian alternatives: either [the] Kingdom of God or the
> Kingdom on Earth. Europe will bitterly deny either science or
> religion. No religious movement in Europe will ever be able
> to adopt a social program. Both the European religion and its
> atheism will have a radical and exclusive character.
>
> (Izetbegovič, 1984, p. 211)

A feature of much of contemporary Europe is the relatively marginal
role of religion, whether measured in terms of popular participation,
belief or importance in social systems. Viewed from a global
perspective, Europe is exceptional in this respect:

> certain kinds of overtly religious activity, such as attending a
> place of worship on a week-by-week basis, are in decline, at
> least in Europe ... however, the picture is varied even in
> Europe, and in the USA church-going rates are relatively
> buoyant. They turn from buoyant to booming, however, in
> parts of Latin America, Africa, and the Pacific Rim.
>
> (Lyon, 2000, p. 23)

As Lyon's comment suggests, religious decline is not uniform across Europe, but the fact that here more than elsewhere modernization has brought with it a marginalization of religion is striking. This also has important implications both for European identities in relation to other parts of the world and for religious identities within Europe. In particular, European identity is sometimes defined in opposition to the Muslim identity that is prominent among Europe's Middle Eastern and North African neighbours, as the quotation from Lord Owen illustrates, in spite of the 31 million Muslim inhabitants (see *Britannica Book of the Year 2001*) of Europe. This definition of European identity in opposition to Islam has a long history, running back to the crusades, the Islamic conquest of (and expulsion from) Spain, and the Ottoman occupation of much of the Balkans from the fifteenth to nineteenth centuries.

It is not entirely clear in what respects Lord Owen expected Izetbegovič and his family, as Muslims, to differ from 'Europeans'. Appearance, dress style and manners would all seem to be involved in this. In fact, unlike most Muslims in western Europe, whose presence is due to post-Second World War immigration, the Muslim presence in Bosnia goes back to the fifteenth century . It derives not from immigration but from the conversion of Christian Slavs to Islam, so that Bosnian Muslims, Serbs and Croats are physically indistinguishable. Furthermore, following a combination of communist destruction of most of the cultural means of transmitting religious traditions, and urbanization and industrialization's further disruption of cultural transmission and **ethnic** mixing, Bosnia's Muslims became highly secularized prior to the war and most retained no visible sign of their religious heritage. Yet the conflict that erupted in Bosnia in 1992–5 was to change this, ironically transforming Izetbegovič's appearance in line with Owen's expectations and, more generally, highlighting awareness of religious difference. As a multi-religious, partly secularized European society, Bosnia may provide an important insight into the relationships between religions and European identities in an increasingly religiously plural and partly secularized Europe. In 1991 the population of Bosnia-Herzegovina was 44 per cent Muslim, 31 per cent Serb (Orthodox Christian) and 17 per cent Croat (Roman Catholic Christian), but only 17 per cent of the population were 'religiously active' (Malcolm, 1996, p. 223).

The term ethnic is used here in the sense of a 'shared culture, such as language, customs and institutions' (Abercrombie et al., 1994, p. 150).

Izetbegovič's comments are suggestive of some reasons why Europe may be distinctive in relation to religious identity. He points out that historically Europe has been overwhelmingly Christian, but in particular that the experience of the Middle Ages in which ecclesiastical institutions were dominant has moulded the shape of European modernity, polarizing the religious and secular spheres in a way that has made symbiotic or even peaceful coexistence between the two intensely problematic. This chapter examines the extent to which Izetbegovič's view is justified. I shall begin with a survey of European religious diversity in terms of traditions and the strength of those traditions, attempting to sketch an overview of the relationship between religions and European identities and considering a brief case study of Roman Catholic revival in France, a country with a strong secularist tradition. I shall then examine the issue of religious freedom in Europe in relation to the European Convention on Human Rights (1950), to which states become party when they join the Council of Europe and which now provides a pan-European legal–ethical framework uniting western and eastern Europe, from Portugal to Russia. Finally I shall return to Bosnia, a former republic of Yugoslavia recently torn apart on religious, ethnic and national lines, and now a kind of European laboratory for the construction of a multi-ethnic, multi-religious society.

The European religious landscape

Since the Christianization of the Roman empire – in the third to sixth centuries – western and southern Europe has been predominantly Christian. Northern Europe east of the Rhineland was gradually Christianized from the ninth century (Germany) to the fifteenth century (Lithuania), with the territories to the east of Poland and in the Balkans largely following the eastern rite (style of worship), and the territories to the west the Latin rite. This liturgical division became an ecclesiastical one when the western (Catholic, centred on Rome) and eastern (Orthodox) churches split in 1054. A further rupture occurred with the Reformation in the sixteenth century, when various Protestant churches independent of Rome were established, predominantly in northern Europe. During the seventeenth century conflict between Catholics and Protestants produced major wars, which ultimately led, through the intellectual and cultural movement of the Enlightenment (generally dated around the eighteenth century), to the European imagination of a new kind of society. In such a society fundamental religious differences came to be considered rationally irresolvable, and therefore needed to be contained through various forms of separation of church and state. Arguably, this association of public religion with social and political conflict remains influential in contemporary European attitudes.

Small Jewish communities have also existed throughout much of Europe since the period of Roman occupation. These groups have suffered intermittent persecution and expulsion, most recently as a result of the genocidal policies of Nazism (1933–45), which greatly reduced the population of European Jewry. Moreover, until their expulsion in the fifteenth century there was also a Muslim presence in Spain and, as we have seen in relation to Bosnia, since the fifteenth century Islam has had a presence in the Balkans too, as a result of Ottoman occupation. This has been so not only in Bosnia and other parts of former Yugoslavia, but also in Albania (where Muslims form a majority), Bulgaria and Greece.

The second half of the twentieth century witnessed substantial changes in this religious landscape. Four major factors were:

1   the decline and marginalization of traditional churches (especially in northwest Europe);

2   the impact of communism (which was often militantly opposed to religion) on eastern Europe;

3   increased immigration bringing Muslim, Hindu, Sikh, Buddhist and new kinds of Christian groups to western Europe, especially from former colonial territories;

4   increasing awareness of and interest in new religions and traditions which have not historically been represented in Europe, as a result of the globalization of knowledge.

These factors have led to a diversification of religious practice across Europe, indicated by surveys of church attendance (restricting ourselves to Christian activity for the moment) and levels of belief in God (see Table 5.1). Also, with the exceptions of the republic of Ireland, Northern Ireland and Poland, there is an approximate north–south divide that roughly correlates with the proportion of Protestants in the population (Davie, 2000). (Two factors seem to be important in relation to Ireland and Poland: the lack of a historic established church, and the role of religion in mobilizing national identity against British and Russian occupation respectively.) Thus, generally, southern European and predominantly Catholic countries (such as Italy and Spain) have retained their congregations to a greater extent than northern and predominantly Protestant ones (like Britain and Sweden), although there are exceptions (for example, church attendance in France is low for a mostly Catholic country). Such differences may in part reflect differing priorities in Protestant and Catholic traditions, with the greater Catholic emphasis on the performance of ritual.

Data on other religions is difficult to assess and compare, as these involve much smaller populations and differing patterns of ritual practice. Some divergent trends do appear to be observable, however: assimilation, with its loss of ritual practice, appears to threaten European Judaism, although there is a contrary trend among the ultra-orthodox (Wasserstein, 1996); by contrast, observance among

Europe's Muslims appears to be on the increase (Schiffauer, 1988; Leveau, 1988). Estimates of the proportion of practising Muslims (based on regular *salat* (prayer) attendance at mosque for Friday noon prayers (for men) and fasting during Ramadan) are around 60 per cent of the relevant group in the Netherlands (Sunier, 1995), and 67 per cent in France (Leveau, 1988).

Taken together, the first and fourth factors mentioned above (the decline of traditional churches and growth of interest in non-traditional religions) suggest a shift away from religious identities based on historical identification with a religious institution, often associated with national belonging, towards a religious identity chosen (if at all) by individuals in a consumer-orientated marketplace. Grace Davie (1994) calls this phenomenon 'believing without belonging', the phrase with which she has subtitled her book. However, there has also been an opposite process of identification with a religious tradition without belief in its core tenets. Thus 90 per cent of Swedes declare themselves to be members of the Church of Sweden, a declaration which has real costs, because in doing so they are opting into a voluntary arrangement to pay the church tax (Hamberg, 1992). Yet only 9 per cent describe themselves as practising Christians. How can this be explained? One answer is that 'by so doing [Swedes] identify with a historic community and culture whose symbols and values they lay claim to' (Hervieu-Léger, 2000, p. 160).

Religion can thus sometimes function as a source of cultural identity even when its beliefs are rejected, just as religious beliefs may continue to be held (and endlessly adapted) without recognition of the institutions that have historically transmitted them. In this latter case religion may also become a source of identity, self-chosen, often in association with a group of like-minded individuals or 'elective fraternity' (Hervieu-Léger, 2000, p. 152).

Castells' ideas are discussed in Chapter 1, in the section 'Types of identity'.

In Castells' terms (Castells, 1997) religious identity in the Swedish case seems to be a 'legitimizing identity', in the sense that it serves to identify a connection to a historic and cultural community. However, this is distinct from classic legitimizing identities, because the scope of identification is much less tightly defined – Swedes do not identify with traditional Lutheran sexual ethics, for example; nor does this religious identification legitimize the Swedish state, from which the Lutheran church was disestablished in 2000. In the case of self-chosen religious beliefs forming the basis of (often temporary) social identification, this would seem to be something like a 'project identity' without the ambitions of social transformation. Castells understands project identities as being formed when:

> Social actors, on the basis of whichever cultural materials are available to them, build a new identity that redefines their

position in society and, by doing so, seek the transformation of the overall social structure.

(Castells, 1997, p. 8)

However, it is also possible for individuals to adopt new identities with no interest in transforming the overall social structure. Thus Castells emphasizes the political function of identities, but some identities are not overtly political and may even be deliberately apolitical. Such identities resemble Castells' notion of project identity in that they tend to be self-chosen or reflexive. That is, they arise from individuals' reflection on their own situation, rather than being ascribed or inherited, as is more typical of legitimizing and 'resistance identities'. In such identity construction, it is the individual rather than society which is the object of transformation. Hence I shall refer to them as individually orientated project identities, in contrast to the collectively orientated project identities that Castells identifies.

The second and third factors in the changing religious landscape (communism and immigration) point in a rather different direction. Many communist authorities did their best forcibly to secularize their societies by attacking the means by which religious traditions reproduce themselves: religious schools were closed, religious property confiscated, religious leaders imprisoned. In some cases rival secular rituals were even established, such as the East German *Jugendweihe* (youth dedication) alternative to the Christian rite of confirmation (Burgess, 1997). However, where they weathered these storms, religious institutions and individuals became important channels of resistance to communism in several eastern European countries (such as Poland and East Germany), and hence sources of resistance identity. Similarly, the religious institutions of migrant groups in western European countries have become important channels of community organization and identification. For example, the Rotterdam Migrants' Bureau recognized this in its 1983 plea for municipal authorities to seek closer 'co-operation with the groupings that are closest to the migrants' hearts. For the Turks and Moroccans, these are the mosques' (Feirabend and Rath, 1996, p. 248).

This politicization of religion among ethnic minorities in western Europe has been the source of some unease and perplexity, which may relate to European memories of the bitter historical struggle between the established churches and modernizing forces. Consider the following comments by local councillors in Utrecht on the involvement of Islamic organizations in local politics in the Netherlands. The first concerns the tendency for Muslims to seek practical help through religious networks:

There are also other ways. There exists something in addition to your imam. I am also a member of a church-community,

Table 5.1 Church attendance, religious belief and denominational affiliation in Europe, 1990s

Country	% Attend church 'at least monthly' 1990–3[1] and in () 'at least weekly' 1995/6[2]	% Atheists and agnostics 1992/ 1998[3]	Majority/largest denomination[4]
Ireland	88	4	Catholic
Poland	85	4.6	Catholic
N. Ireland	69	n/a	Protestant/Catholic
Italy	51 (34)	17	Catholic (95%)
Austria	44	–	Catholic
Switzerland	43	–	Protestant/Catholic
Portugal	41	20	Catholic
Spain	39 (22)	19	Catholic (92%)
Slovenia	35	19.2	Catholic
Hungary	34	30.4	Protestant/Catholic
Germany [W/E] (united)	[34/17] (13)	[37/20]	Protestant/Catholic (43%)
Romania	31	3.6	Orthodox
Belgium	31	37	Catholic
Holland	30	39	Protestant/Catholic
Britain	24 (12)	29	Protestant (10% Catholic)
Czechoslovakia (Czech/ Slovak)	21	(43.5, 21.1)	Protestant/Catholic
France	13	35	Catholic
Norway	11	24	Protestant
Finland	11	36	Protestant
Denmark	10	55	Protestant
Sweden	9 (4)	–	Protestant (1% Catholic)
Latvia	9	15	Protestant/Catholic
Iceland	9	–	Protestant

[1] Data from Bruce, 1999, p. 99. Bruce's data is taken from Inglehart et al., 1998.

[2] Data from Bryson and Curtice, 1998, pp. 125–48.

[3] Western European data from Davie, 2000, p. 10. Davie's data comes from Inglehart et al., 1998, and Ashford and Timms, 1992, p. 40. Eastern European data from Tomka, 1999, p. 47.

[4] I have used mixed Protestant/Catholic where the number of nominal adherents of the second largest group is at least half of the number of adherents of the largest group.

that community also has a minister. But what I mean is I will
not address myself to him if I have a housing problem. Then I
go to the housing department, I do not go to my minister.
That is the way things were in the past. I mean those days are
gone.

(Christian Democratic councillor, in Feirabend and Rath,
1996, p. 254)

The second comment explicitly expresses anxiety about a perceived
threat to 'church–state' separation:

The laws of the Morocco-men are interwoven with their
religion, well that is a problem. I do believe it has to be clear
to everyone how Dutch society functions. We keep church
and state separate and I consider that an acquired right that
should not be changed. And that has to be made very clear
[to] mosque organizations. Once that is clear, well I think we
can live together very well.

(Liberal party (D'66) councillor in Feirabend and Rath,
1996, p. 255)

These Dutch politicians are keen to be tolerant, but also to set clear
boundaries on the limits of toleration. In their view, religion belongs
in the private sphere and should not extend beyond it. Furthermore,
both show evidence of a social evolutionary perspective in which the
public role of religion is ascribed to the past and should not be
remobilized ('those days are gone ... an acquired right that should
not be changed').

How do these different factors, and roles of religious identity, relate
to one another? In some ways they appear to point in different
directions. For example, the decline of an association between
traditional churches and national identity and a growth of consumer
approaches to religion in western Europe would seem to point
towards a privatization of religion. However, this is complicated by the
Swedish phenomenon of 'belonging without believing', by which
people choose, through taxation, to identify with a religious tradition
closely associated with Swedish nationhood and history: a collective
religious identity opted into on an individual basis.

The mobilization of religion in opposition to communism in eastern
Europe and as a political identity for migrants in western Europe
would seem to point towards an increased public role for religions,
which might be termed 'de-privatization' (Casanova, 1994). Indeed
these tensions between religion as a private, self-chosen identity and
as a public, ascribed identity are reflected in the European
Convention on Human Rights and other human rights documents;
this is considered in more depth later in the chapter.

One perspective that can help make sense of each of these connections between religion and identity has been developed by the French sociologist of religion Danièle Hervieu-Léger (2000). She argues that religion can be seen as 'a chain of memory' passed across generations which provides an 'imaginative grasp of continuity' (Hervieu-Léger, 2000, p. 132). Such chains of memory, she argues, have important psychologically integrating functions for individuals and socially integrating functions for communities. Modern societies, through such developments as the collapse of traditional families, the loss of connection to a locality, occupational specialization, and the homogenization and attenuation of memory through the mass media, suffer 'a loss of depth and ... unity of collective memory' (Hervieu-Léger, 2000, p. 141). Such an idea links both the privatization and de-privatization of religion, and connects the 'New Age' search to rediscover 'ancient truths' with the Swedish buying into Lutheran tradition, the Polish drawing on Catholicism as the source of continuity for the Polish nation, and the Muslim turning to Islam as a tradition that ideologically transcends religious and ethnic divisions, yet also affirms continuity with previous generations. Thus, as one anthropologist who has studied the development of religious identifications in Southall, London (a predominantly south Asian district) comments:

> Religious identifications will not go away and they may in fact be the most sensitive and creative identifications that people can find and reshape, but they need to be watched for the same reason as national and ethnic identifications: the influence of self-serving elites.

(Baumann, 1999, p. 137)

As Baumann's comment suggests, the idea of religion as a chain of memory reminds us that memory can be manipulated and connects these examples to the mobilization of religion in the conflict in former Yugoslavia, which is discussed below. But although the 'influence of self-serving elites' was an important factor in that conflict, the image of a chain of memory also suggests two other problems with religious identity as a political identity. First, unless the religious community is identical with the political community (and in today's globalized and differentiated societies this is never the case, if it ever was) there is a danger that mobilization on the basis of religious identity will exclude those who are not so identified. This is not a limitation unique to religion, and not necessarily a problem if religion is mobilized as one of a number of cross-cutting bases for political mobilization – such as ethnicity, social class, gender or occupation. But, as with other identities, it becomes problematic where it comes to dominate.

Secondly, the entry of religion into the public sphere, like that of other cultural sources of political mobilization, changes the public sphere. As another anthropologist, Gregory Starrett, explains:

> The standard theory of social action, in which individuals and groups respond to social stress by taking refuge in religion, implies that, were the stress relieved, they would return to the *status quo ante*, rather like the mercury in a thermometer responding to changes in atmospheric pressure ...

> But in thereby treating culture as a dependent variable, the barometric approach ignores the institutional frameworks and social processes through which culture is created and transmitted. Like other institutions, religious ... ones fill not only a social need, but a social space. They take on a very real life of their own with interests, dynamic and potentials that are only incompletely determined by the intersection of forces that have brought them about.

(Starrett, 1998, pp. 227–8)

Hence when seeking to understand the role of religious identity in a situation it is not safe to assume that it is 'just about politics' or 'power', because both politics and power are mediated through culture and are likely to be transformed in the process of transmission. This should be borne in mind when the role of religious identity in the Bosnian conflict is examined later in this chapter.

First, however, I shall consider forms of mobilization of religion that are more typical of the European pattern, taking the case of Catholicism in France. In some ways France is the 'classic' European model on the issue of religion and public identity, with a long history of secular, often anti-religious values in public life stemming from the French Revolution, and one of the most clearly demarcated church–state divisions in Europe. This is embodied in the 1905 law which stipulates that 'the State does not recognize or give subsidies to any religion in France' (Withol de Wenden, 1996, p. 57). It is also a society in which the parish model of 'religiosity rooted in parish, priest and *clocher* (clock-tower)' has yielded to 'a deregulated Catholicism resting on the diffusion of emotional communities and affinity groups' (Hervieu-Léger, 1997, p. 116).

The reading below, an extract from Gilles Kepel's *The Revenge of God: the Resurgence of Islam, Christianity and Judaism in the Modern World* (Kepel, 1994), describes the intellectual and social aspects of a 're-Christianization' movement that has been influential among French Catholics since the late 1970s. 'Re-Christianization' here means the attempt to make society more Christian, though, as you will see, exactly what this means is disputed. The reading locates this movement in the context of, first, the Second Vatican Council, or Vatican II (1962–5), which radically reformed Catholic social teaching, and, secondly, the social upheavals that accompanied the economic crisis in Europe in the 1970s.

Mission Field Europe

In Catholic Europe, the last quarter of the twentieth century opened on a paradox: never before, it seemed, had society been so massively secularized and de-Christianized, and yet re-Christianization movements were springing up everywhere. Some charismatic communities encouraged university graduates to discover the inspiration of the Holy Spirit; others performed scores of miraculous cures. Elsewhere, organizations such as 'Communion and Liberation', aiming to re-create a Christian society after the 'failure of secularism', mobilized hundreds of thousands of young Italians, while in eastern Europe, after the collapse of the Soviet Union, social movements and parties were taking shape which, after forty years of state atheism, based their political identity on a reaffirmation of their Catholicism.

Whereas the Vatican II Council (1962–5) appeared to limit the Church's aim to proclaiming the presence of God in a world grown blind, the pontificate of John Paul II, which began in 1978, has been marked by a reaffirmation of Catholic values and identity. These are now based upon an a priori break with the principles of secular society, and are intended to restore to the 'post-modern' world a meaning, an ethic and an order which, it is claimed, have vanished in the collapse of all its certainties.

In the west, the oil crisis that began in October 1973 enforced economic restructuring which called in question many group loyalties taken for granted in the industrial era, such as trade unionism, while pressing anxieties were developing as to the near future of the planet, under threat from pollution and the arms race. At the same time the electronic revolution, bringing a mass of images and information into every home, was transforming ethical standards as never before. Methods of learning, the transmission of values, the integrity of the family unit and its relationship to the public domain were abruptly transformed in a way which many individuals felt powerless to control.

In eastern Europe the disintegration of communism, which reached the point of no return when the Berlin wall was breached in 1989 and subsequently demolished, freed the minds of millions from strict Marxist control. In Poland the affirmation of their Catholicism by the leaders of Solidarnosc, symbol of the only durable resistance by any civil society to Soviet influence, and the subsequent appointment of a Catholic prime minister in 1989, appeared to show that the collapse of communism would inevitably be followed by a return of religion to the political scene. Poland even seemed to be providing a model or source of inspiration for the 'second evangelization of Europe' – one of the main objectives of John Paul II's pontificate.[1]

Some churchmen saw in these events the end of the modern era, which had begun with the Enlightenment in the eighteenth century when reason, self-confident and emancipated, had been rather too quick to reject religion. Some of the pronouncements at Vatican II, reflecting the social optimism of the 1960s, had attempted to reimpose a Christian logic on the 'progressive values' of secular ideology. The new Christianity of the last quarter-century is different: it has offered a Catholic ethic to a 'world adrift', the only ethic which has any sort of future. 'We are at the beginning of the Christian era', wrote Cardinal Lustiger. 'In our time the West (and probably the whole world) has become such an enigma to itself, is faced by such fearfully unprecedented problems and such terrifying ordeals, that it must at long last consider the possibility that only the coming of Christ will give it the arguments and the strength to assume its destiny ...'[2] ...

The legacy of Vatican II

The Vatican II Ecumenical Council, held from October 1962 to December 1965, set about an *aggiornamento*, or updating, of the Catholic Church at the behest of Pope John XXIII on whose initiative it was convened. Its internal revision of that ancient and complex institution, which engaged the efforts of bishops the world over, resulted in the promulgation of sixteen conciliar documents. They concerned both the reorganization of the Church itself and the redefinition of its relationships with the outside world. The 'dogmatic constitution on the Church' (*Lumen gentium*),[3] and the 'pastoral constitution on the Church in the

[1] See Patrick Michel, 'Y a-t-il un modèle ecclésial polonais?', in *Le Retour des certitudes: événements et orthodoxie depuis Vatican II*, ed. Paul Ladrière and René Éuneau (Paris: Centurion, 1987), pp. 142–57.

[2] Cardinal Jean-Marie Lustiger, 'La nouveauté du Christ et la post modernité', *Revue catholique internationale Communio*, XV, 2 (1990), pp. 13–14.

[3] By tradition these documents are designated by the first words of their Latin text; thus: '*Lumen gentium cum sit Christus ...*' (Christ being the light of the nations ...) or '*Gaudium et spes, luctus et angor hominum huius temporis ...*' (The joys and hopes, the griefs and torments of the men of our time ...).

contemporary world' (*Gaudium et spes*) well illustrate this dual focus.

Each document was the fruit of patient compromise between the forces present in the council – the two successive popes, John XXIII and Paul VI, the Roman Curia, bishops from the west, the east and the Third World, representatives of assorted theological trends – and each left room for interpretation. This made it easier for the texts to be adopted almost without dissent, except from Mgr Lefebvre [the French-born archbishop of Dakar who led a traditionalist group within the church and was later excommunicated] and his friends (who formed only a tiny minority of the Fathers in council). But a few years later the legacy of Vatican II was causing fierce arguments between those who saw it as simply the first step towards opening the Church to the world and those who said 'thus far and no further' ...

Disillusion with secularism and the Catholic 'break'

The re-Christianization that took hold from the mid-1970s onwards started out from a pessimistic judgement on the future of a secularized world. The fear was that scientific and technical progress would escape from man's control and deny his status as a creature of God; that he would be first enslaved and then destroyed. Unlike the 'progressive Catholics' who regarded the classes 'exploited by the bourgeoisie' as the only enslaved creatures of God, the new Christians held that *all* men and women were now endangered, and that no earthly messianism could save them. And compared with the optimistic spirit of Vatican II, they believed much more strongly that conflict with the secular world order was unavoidable. They blamed the supremacy of reason over faith through a period in history that had begun with the Enlightenment and ended around 1975. This Catholic critique of reason utilizes certain trends in the human sciences and in secular philosophy, including psychoanalysis, structuralism and the thoughts of [the twentieth-century German philosopher Martin] Heidegger . But these play only a very minor role; the object is no longer to fertilize theological reflection by the human sciences ... but to point out that they support the challenge to the supremacy of reason which theology poses and, they say, always has posed. Theology then becomes part of a general disenchantment with modernity, a 'disillusionment with secularism'. This theological diagnosis of our contemporary malaise is expressed in formulae – in a whole rhetoric – which is consonant with some of the questionings and anxieties that are surfacing in European societies.

Cardinal Lustiger and Cardinal Ratzinger embody, each in his own way, this consonance of the Church's discourse with post-modernism. The story of Cardinal Lustiger's life could be a perfect example of the relevance of the Christian vocation. He was a Polish Jew, converted during the Second World War, a 'son of secularism', educated at the Lycée Montaigne with the children of the intellectual bourgeoisie of Paris, and gained his degree at the Sorbonne, a secular university. Jean-Marie Lustiger comes from a different world from Father Alexander, the country priest who was made famous by *Horsain* ('The Outsider').[4] His autobiography in dialogue, *Le Choix de Dieu* ('The Choice of God') shows him to be an intellectual who has mastered modern learning, in particular the most sophisticated social sciences, has seen what they can and cannot do, and who finds in the Catholic faith[5] the means of doing what they cannot do.

Now Archbishop of Paris, he says of himself: 'I belong to that generation which has plucked the bitter fruits of Reason's pretensions to unfettered sovereignty.'[6] The end result of this 'arrogance of reason' which ignores God and will answer to nobody but itself was Nazi and Stalinist totalitarianism. It was born in 'the Age of Enlightenment (which engendered) totalitarianism, meaning the divinization of human reason and its refusal to accept any criticism.'[7] Enlightenment thinking becomes the source of all evils, the scapegoat, according to the logic made fashionable by [the German-born US political theorist] Hannah Arendt, who blames the French Revolution for all the totalitarian sins of the twentieth century while endowing that other child of the Enlightenment, the American Revolution, with all the virtues.[8] Cardinal Lustiger, for his part, condemns them all *en bloc*, even blaming this Source of all Ills for the extermination of European Jewry: 'I believe that Hitler's anti-semitism derives from the anti-semitism of the Enlightenment and not from any Christian anti-semitism.'[9]

---

[4] Bernard Alexandre, *Horsain: vivre et survivre en pays de Caux* (Paris: Plon, 1988).

[5] On the arguments raised in certain Jewish circles against the conversion of Jean-Marie Lustiger and the meaning he has attributed to it, see the pamphlet by Raphael Drai, *Lettre ouverte au Cardinal Lustiger* (Alinéa, 1989).

[6] Jean-Marie Lustiger, *Le Choix de Dieu: entretiens avec Jean-Louis Missika et Dominique Wolton* (Fallois, 1987; Le Livre de Poche, 1989), p. 210.

[7] Ibid., p. 161.

[8] See, inter alia, Hannah Arendt, *On Revolution* (New York: Viking Press, 1963).

[9] J.-M. Lustiger, op. cit., p. 101.

Reason, being 'arrogant', makes man the idol of man, with all that that implies of despotism and oppression. But nothing is said here about the class war, the theme of the liberation theologians. Forgetfulness of God is the root of all social evil – a theme that was also common to the theoreticians of re-Islamization and of re-Judaization at that time.

The findings of the human sciences and the life sciences no longer pose a threat to faith (as was alleged when positivism was in vogue). What they do call in question is the autonomy of reason – a reversal of meaning that is also found in contemporary militants of Judaism and Islam. The Cardinal recalled:

> I was born after the nineteenth century, We learned, with Old Father Marx, Freud and Einstein and some others, that all that stuff wouldn't stay the course (...) this chimerical idealization of reason, this 'arrogant' reason that doesn't know its own limitations.[10]

But Freud, Einstein and 'Old Father Marx' have exhausted their historical role once they have seen off the Enlightenment. We should have no use for what they said against religious belief. As regards social organization, whenever politics tries to cut loose from the Christian ethic it inevitably ends in totalitarianism, whose supreme embodiment is communism. Some people thought at the end of the 1960s that that doctrine was about to triumph, but in reality it was obvious to an alert Catholic observer that the revolutionary clamour signified its imminent decline:

> It was the generation of '68 that dared at last to spit in the idol's face. In the Place de la Sorbonne I saw with my eyes and heard with my own ears [student leader Daniel] Cohn-Bendit call [the communist writer Louis] Aragon a 'Stalinist scoundrel'. It was wonderful! In this sea of waving red and black flags, amid all that myth of Marxist revolution! Today, I said to myself, the idol was shattered! May 1968, then Solzhenitzyn and Poland. The new holy scriptures on which the French intelligentsia had fed since 1917, under the magic spell of a new religion and a new eschatology, were demolished. The world was released from the spell and Stalin was dead.[11]

The way was open for re-Christianization; we were about to see the beginnings of the Christian era.

---

[10] Ibid., p. 160.

[11] Ibid., p. 234.

However, in the secularized societies of western Europe, the first obstacle on the road to re-Christianization was that religion had been relegated to the private sphere. In France, legal sanction was given to this process in 1905 with the law separating Church and state. It has been less strictly codified in other countries, but the results have been similar. Hence one of the first tasks in re-Christianization was to campaign for the return of religion to the sphere of public law and, for this purpose, to bring about a 'new secularism' ...

France: charisma, and trouble in the schools

Since the mid-1970s France has been the theatre of a significant re-Christianization movement. But this movement has operated almost entirely 'from below', through a burgeoning of 'charismatic renewal' groups; they have not wished, nor been able, to undertake extensive social action or to enter the realm of politics.

The origins of the 'charismatic renewal' in contemporary European Catholicism are to be found in the United States, among certain groups of American Catholics who had been influenced by the (Protestant) Pentecostals. It was to these groups that the future founders of the European movement looked, in the 1970s, for inspiration and a model. All believers who are committed to 'renewal' begin by experiencing, or desiring, a personal relationship with God, expressed through the Holy Spirit, in the form of an emotional shock beyond human understanding. The Holy Spirit 'descends' upon those whom He chooses, irrespective of their status, lay or clerical, their educational level or their social standing. He bestows upon them 'spiritual gifts' (charisma), of which the most spectacular are 'speaking with tongues' and miraculous healing powers.

In France, this renewed and intense conception of the Catholic faith has enjoyed a significant success since the late 1970s. In 1987 the sociologist Danièle Hervieu-Léger estimated that 200,000 people were involved in the charismatic renewal, either on a regular basis or by way of occasional meetings or retreats.[12] This large number of adherents is spread over a great many prayer groups (nearly a thousand), some of them structured around larger communities. The modes of awareness, forms of vocation and manner of life of the faithful are extremely varied. Members of some of the groups live under the same roof, in town or country

---

[12] Danièle Hervieu-Léger, 'Charismatisme catholique et institution', in *Le Retour des certitudes*, op. cit., p. 223.

(some in former monastic buildings left vacant by a shortage of monks), while others meet regularly but otherwise live what is to all appearances an ordinary life 'in the world'. Some of the communities, like the 'Lion of Judah', have 'specialized' in miraculous healings, and others in caring for mentally handicapped people (L'Arche), dropouts (Berdine) or the destitute (the Bread of Life).[13] In France most of the converts are young educated adults, often graduates, who are 'both most directly imbued with the ideals of progress and the most directly affected, economically and socially, by the disappearance of the certainty of growth that was taken for granted in the 1960s.'[14]

In these cases Catholic identity is affirmed only within the framework of re-Christianization 'from below'. What the charismatic movement wants is to reshape individuals, bring about their inner conversion to Christ. The disciples model their lives on the gospel 'like the early Christians', trying to put the words of Jesus literally into practice. When some of them undertake intensive charitable work, they are not thereby becoming social entrepreneurs after the fashion of the Company of Deeds of Communion and Liberation. Neither has the 'renewal' produced anything equivalent to what the People's Movement represents in Italy, although some of the most powerful communities are beginning to build up networks of friendship and support in political and financial circles.

Nevertheless there are people in France who want re-Christianization 'from below' to lead into a renegotiation of the secular state, as codified by the law of 1905 on the separation of Church and state. The bishops, led by the archbishops of Lyon and Paris, Cardinals Decourtray and Lustiger, want to bring Catholicism out of the private sphere to which the state has confined it, and to give it the 'public legal status' it now demands. From this point of

[13] There are two well documented books on the charismatic movement as a whole: Monique Hébrard's report, very expressive and revised and updated several times, *Les Nouveaux disciples: dix ans après* (Paris: Centurion, 1987) and Frédéric Lenoir's collection of interviews, *Les Communautés nouvelles: interviews des fondateurs* (Paris: Fayard, 1988). These two authors were insiders who were converted to charismatic Christianity by one of the communities about which they write. For an analysis of the charismatic groups in terms of religious sociology, see the articles by Martine Cohen, 'Figures de l'individualisme moderne: essai sur deux communautés charismatiques', *Esprit* (April 1986); 'Vers de nouveaux rapports avec l'institution ecclésiastique: l'exemple du renouveau charismatique en France', *Archives de sciences sociales des religions*, 62, 1 (1986) and 'Le renouveau charismatique en France ou l'affirmation des catholicismes', *Christus* (July 1986).

[14] Daniéle Hervieu-Léger, op. cit., pp. 227–8.

view, the experience of the most vigorous charismatic communities constitutes a French version of the challenge to secularism (*laïcité*). For these communities are making a complete break with the imperatives of *laïcité* and laying the foundations of a 'Christian' social order. But, up to 1990 at least, the charismatic groups had not followed the bishops very far into this battle, preferring to devote themselves to their own particular mode of individual and community mission and not seek contacts among the organs of state.

If the bishops have had some success, it is chiefly in relation to schooling. In 1984 there was a demonstration in defence of private schools which forced the government of the day to withdraw a bill directed against them. Schools, as the place where children's family values came up against social acculturation, were a domain which the Church could never wholly abandon to the secular state. The success of the demonstration, the largest since May 1968, also showed that, in the field of education, the policy of re-Christianization could bring thousands of Catholics on to the streets, indifferent though they might be to other areas of contention such as birth control.

A further episode in the struggle of Christianity to regain 'public legal status' was the 'Islamic veil' affair of autumn 1989. Both the bishops and the chief rabbis expressed active support for the re-Islamization movements, which wanted Muslim girls to be allowed to wear the veil in secondary schools. As schools in France are rigidly secular, holding that religious affiliation belongs to the private sphere and is not to be expressed in school, the supporters of re-Christianization, re-Islamization and re-Judaization made common cause to negotiate a 'new *laïcité*' that would enable them to occupy the public domain, even if initially only in certain institutions – such as schools.

(Kepel, 1994, pp. 47–8, 50–1, 55–8, 76–8)

EXERCISE _____

1   What challenges did the economic restructuring that followed the 1973 oil crisis and other concurrent developments pose to traditional values and legitimizing identities, and in particular to religious ones?

2   In what ways have the teachings of Vatican II differed from those of re-Christianization movements?

3   What have been the manifestations of the re-Christianization movements in France?

4   In Castells' terms, what kinds of identity do those engaged in re-Christianization movements possess?

DISCUSSION

1   The economic restructuring that followed the oil crisis challenged traditional group loyalties such as trade unionism. The arms race and the environment became sources of anxiety, while developments in the social sphere challenged the traditional family. Any challenge to the status quo is a challenge to legitimizing identities, while economic uncertainty and changes in social attitudes in particular challenged the traditional family, and hence Catholicism.

2   Vatican II embraced socially progressive values in tune with the spirit of the 1960s, whereas re-Christianization movements have adopted a much more antagonistic stance in relation to secular values, which they see as having failed. In particular, the Enlightenment faith in reason is seen as having led to totalitarianism and the destruction of humanity's relationship with nature. Secular postmodern ideas are used to support this Catholic critique of modernity, which sees a return to Christian values as the only hope for a modern world that has lost its way. Re-Christianization policies are associated with the papacy of John Paul II, who became pope in 1978.

3   Re-Christianization movements in France have been intellectual (exemplified by bishops such as Cardinal Lustiger), spiritually orientated (such as movements for charismatic renewal) and practically orientated (involved in care for people with learning disabilities and those who are socially excluded). Spiritually and practically orientated movements have on the whole been interested in individual renewal and social care rather than the political change advocated by the bishops, which would involve challenging the French policy of *laïcité*, reasserting the public significance of religion. However, the bishops have had some success in the sphere of education, with a major demonstration in 1984 successful in securing the role of (predominantly religious) private schools, while interfaith (Christian and Jewish) support for Muslims in the 'Islamic veil' affair suggests the possible development of an interfaith alliance reasserting the public significance of religion for French life (although actually the latter involved the wearing of the *foulard,* or headscarf – which does not cover the face and hence is not technically a veil (*hijab*)).

4   One could argue that the re-Christianization movements show
     signs of all three identities described by Castells. At one level
     these movements exhibit a legitimizing identity, in the sense that
     they seek to defend traditional family values and religious ethics.
     At another level they constitute a resistance identity, because they
     challenge the secular status quo based on the policy of *laïcité*. Yet
     they can also be seen as a collective project identity, in that, at
     least in their more intellectual manifestation, they seek to
     transform society from the grassroots upwards. The reluctance of
     many in these movements for charismatic renewal to see their
     groups as in any way political is more reminiscent of the
     individualist form of project identity identified above, which
     tends to emerge when links between communal identity and
     religion are broken. Such an identity also has affinities to the
     French (and more generally European) idea of a strict separation
     of church and state, which may have been absorbed by French
     Catholics.

Religious identity and human rights: a case study of the ECHR

As noted above, even in France, with its long tradition of *laïcité*,
movements for re-Christianization have challenged the privacy of
religious identity. The European Convention for the Protection of
Human Rights and Fundamental Freedoms (to give it its full title), or
ECHR, seeks to protect the right of individuals to choose their
religion (or not). But, on the evidence of the European Court's
judgments, it also seeks to protect religious identity, on the grounds
that religion is an important cultural resource and in the context of
what has been described as 'an emergent right of cultural survival
and flourishment within international law' (Anaya, 1995, p. 325).
This section of the chapter explores the tensions between these
rights, and their implications for the role of religious identity in
Europe.

Context and conceptual tensions in the ECHR

Since 1990 many eastern European countries have joined the Council
of Europe and subsequently ratified the ECHR, with Russia the latest
and most controversial new member (Bowring, 1997, p. 628; Janis,
1997, p. 93). (Russia joined in February 1996. Of the other former
communist countries, Bulgaria, Hungary, the Czech Republic,
Slovakia, Poland, Romania and Slovenia had already joined between
1990 and 1994; see Janis et al., 1995, p. 115). Other human rights

developments, for example relating to the modified role of the Organization for Security and Co-operation in Europe, or OSCE (Evans, 1997, pp. 262–376), together with wider processes of trans-European cooperation on political, economic and security matters, suggest European convergence on human rights issues, and even some kind of developing legal–ethical consensus across the continent. In this process one might expect particular influence to be extended from west to east, since the institutions and instruments adopted in eastern Europe have been developed in a predominantly western European context. However, international human rights legislation is only as effective as its local implementation, and in this case it is further restricted by ambiguities in its conceptualization of religion.

On a liberal understanding religion is essentially a voluntary and ideally a private activity with which one is free to engage (or not) in two senses. First, the individual should be externally free in relation to this choice, so that no one should force or prevent participation. This is the *raison d'être* of most human rights legislation concerning religion, including the ECHR. But, secondly, the individual is also internally free in relation to it, in the sense that, on a liberal understanding, there is no strong human need to engage in religious activity. Such an approach is illustrated in the political philosopher Waldron's comment that 'if a particular church is dying out ... It is like the death of a fashion or a hobby, not the demise of anything that people really need' (Waldron, 1995, pp. 93, 100). Such an understanding of religion fits well with the decline of traditional institutional religion and the growth of consumer models of religious practice in western Europe. This may be described as a 'voluntarist' position.

However, another understanding of religion is common in Europe, and present in the case law developed by the European Court. An example is the Kokkinakis case, where a Jehovah's Witness appealed to the court against his conviction under Greek anti-proselytism laws. Here the court asserted that religion is not only 'one of the most vital elements that go to make up the identity of believers and their conception of life, but it is also a precious asset for atheists, agnostics, sceptics and the unconcerned' (Kokkinakis *vs.* Greece, Series A, no. 260–A, 1993, para. 31). On this understanding, religion is not easily or lightly chosen or discarded, but constitutive of individual and collective identity, perhaps forming part of the cultural fabric from which identity is constructed, even for non-believers. This second understanding of religion receives growing support, as indicated above, from what the American professor of law James Anaya calls 'an emergent right of cultural survival and flourishment within international law' (Anaya, 1995, p. 325). Such support can be found in the United Nations Charter, Article 27 of the Civil and Political

Rights Covenant, the Convention Against Genocide, and the UNESCO Declaration of Principles of Cultural Co-operation (Anaya, 1995, p. 325). This may be described as an 'identity-constitutive' position.

When religion is understood in this second culturally and socially significant sense, there is a danger that challenges to the religious status quo may come to be construed as threats to the stability of society. This can occur even under a convention designed primarily to protect the rights of individual dissenters against state coercion. It is a particular concern for religious minorities when the ECHR comes to be applied in eastern European states where there are strong historic links between religious and national identity, links strengthened by recent history and intensified by post-communist fragmentation. The conceptual tension within the ECHR and its tradition of interpretation between these two understandings of religion has created problems for implementing the convention, especially for religious minorities. I shall now consider these problems with more detailed reference to the interpretation of the ECHR.

Articles relevant to religion and their interpretation

A range of articles has been invoked in cases relevant to religion, but probably the most important are Article 9, covering freedom of thought, conscience and religion, and Protocol 1 Article 2, covering education (Janis et al., 1995, pp. 468, 471, 483 n. 1). Other relevant measures include Article 10, on freedom of expression, Article 11, covering freedom of assembly, and Article 4, which concerns forced labour (Janis et al., 1995). However, each of these is subject to restrictions by national governments in the interests of protecting the public good or national security, and these conditions have sometimes been interpreted in a way that appears to require a duty of respect to majority religious sensibilities that substantially curtails the liberty of dissenting minorities.

Perhaps of most significance are the decisions of the court in the Kokkinakis and Otto-Preminger-Institut cases (Otto-Preminger-Institut *vs*. Austria, Series A, no. 295-A, 1994). Of particular concern here is the circumscription of minority rights to express dissent from the majority religious view, whether by witness to one's religion in the former case, or through satire of an established tradition in the latter. Thus in the Otto-Preminger-Institut case the applicants objected to the confiscation by the Austrian authorities of a film that was held to be 'disparaging' or 'insulting' to Roman Catholic belief (Evans, 1997, p. 285). I shall consider each case in turn.

The Kokkinakis case permits a state to prevent a believer from manifesting their belief if improper means are used (Evans, 1997, p. 335). The state is obliged to demonstrate that improper means have been used, but is given broad discretion to define what is meant by 'impropriety'. Thus the Greek anti-proselytism law was deemed legal by the European Court. This law prohibits:

> any direct or indirect attempt to intrude on the religion or beliefs of others of a different persuasion, with the aim of undermining those beliefs, either by any kind of inducement or promise of inducement or moral support or material assistance, or by fraudulent means or by taking advantage of his inexperience, trust, need, low intellect or naïvety.
>
> (Section 4 of Law no. 1363/1938; Evans, 1997, p. 333)

This would appear severely to restrict the legal scope of missionary activity, and to interpret Article 9 as implying an obligation to respect majority religious views.

This process was extended further in the Otto-Preminger-Institut case when the court ruled that:

> The respect for religious feelings of believers as guaranteed by Article 9 can legitimately be thought to have been violated by provocative portrayals of objects of religious veneration; and such portrayals can be regarded as malicious violation of the spirit of tolerance, which must be a feature of democratic society.
>
> (Evans, 1997, p. 336, para. 47)

Again, the state is given broad discretion to determine the content of this 'respect', the reason given for this being an 'absence of a uniform conception of the significance of religion in society' across Europe (Evans, 1997, p. 336, para. 56). It is notable that this case originated in the predominantly Catholic Austrian Tyrol, while the Kokkinakis case originated in predominantly Orthodox Greece; in other words, these are restrictions on the liberty of minorities in favour of a conservative interpretation of majority sensibilities. The implications of this for eastern Europe are disturbing: dissenting minorities are given least protection where they need it most. Furthermore, the second case suggests that the court will only risk challenging states where it perceives a Europe-wide consensus. This suggests that rapid expansion of the Council of Europe is likely to be followed by a diminution of European Court challenges to states in controversial areas such as religion.

In conclusion, the practice of the court in deferring to perceived regional or national consensus in religious matters, and hence to majority religions in cases involving minority dissent, raises concerns for the rights of religious minorities. Yet national measures to incorporate the ECHR may strengthen enforcement; much depends on the attitude of the court when faced with relevant cases from eastern Europe and on the response of the council community to persistent violation by individual states. All this suggests that wider societal factors will play a large role in the actualization of rights. This leads us to the case study of Bosnia, a society where religious identity has played a prominent and controversial role in recent years.

Religious identity, conflict and reconstruction in Bosnia

> In the world of Omarska [a Serb detention centre], if an inhabitant of Bosnia had a name identifiable as Muslim ... that was considered guilt enough, whatever the beliefs or practices of that individual ... Those organising the persecution, on the other hand, identified themselves through explicit religious symbols. The symbols appeared in the three-fingered hand gestures representing the Christian trinity, in the images of sacred figures of Serbian religious mythology on their uniform insignia, in the songs they memorised and forced their victims to sing, on the priest's ring they kissed before and after their acts of persecution, and in the formal ceremonies that marked the purification of a town of its Muslim population. The term 'ethnic' in the expression 'ethnic cleansing' is a euphemism for 'religious'.
>
> (Sells, 1996, p. 15)

> It is not my belief that the Serbian Insurrectionary War was about religion. When Serbs blew up mosques and Catholic churches and when Croats destroyed mosques and other religious buildings, they were not, in fact, doing so to spread their own faiths, but rather to destroy the architectural artefacts that established other people's history in the area and that helped members of other nationalities remember their past and hold on to their cultural identity. In other words, attacks on religious objects served strictly political purposes; politics was primary, not religion.
>
> (Ramet, 1999, p. 79)

As these quotations demonstrate, opinion on the role of religion in the conflict differs. Thus while Sells argues that the conflict was 'religiously motivated and religiously justified' (Sells, 1996, p. 89), Sabrina Ramet believes that it was *not* about religion (Ramet, 1999, p. 79). She refers to the Serbian–Croatian conflict (1991–2) and the conflict in Bosnia (1992–5) in which Bosnian Serbs were supported by the FRY (Federal Republic of Yugoslavia – i.e. Serbia) as the 'Serbian Insurrectionary War'. This is because she regards both as the result of Serbian expansionism, rather than seeing the war in Bosnia as a separate, civil conflict. As discussed below, there is considerable evidence to support this interpretation. What is not disputed, however, is that religious symbols and discourse were mobilized by all parties in the conflict. The dispute is rather as to the meaning and significance of this mobilization. This section of the chapter seeks to discover what the mobilization of religion in Bosnia in the 1990s can tell us about the role of religious identities in European societies in the twenty-first century.

A chapter in the third volume of this series (Hawkesworth, 2003) considers long-term historical developments in the territories that comprised Yugoslavia until 1991, as well as the relationship between war and the manipulation of memory in the conflict of 1991–5. The present section focuses as far as possible on religious identity, but to do so it is necessary to provide some account of the relationship between religious traditions and other factors in the genesis, course and aftermath of the conflict.

First, some have interpreted the conflict as the re-emergence of ancient religious and ethnic rivalries. Certainly, issues such as the history of the region as a border area (with all the instability that implies) and cultural and attitudinal differences between the constituent peoples of the republic of Yugoslavia when it was first formed in 1921 (especially between Serbs who had fought against the defeated Austro-Hungarian empire and Croats who had been part of it) are important factors in the long-term stability of the republic (Hawkesworth, 2003). But it should also be borne in mind that:

> Muslims, Serbs and Croats lived in peace for most of the five hundred years they cohabited in Bosnia-Herzegovina. The inter-communal violence which accompanied World War II was an important deviation from this pattern, but ... The Serbian Insurrectionary War of 1991–5 was different in that, with the exception of the defenders of Sarajevo, each of the respective sides tended to recruit almost exclusively from the nationality it claimed to represent.
>
> (Ramet, 1999, p. 202)

The recent conflict must therefore be understood as a product of European modernity rather than a relic of Europe's religious past. Recruitment along exclusively ethnic lines and the mobilization of religious identities to create and reinforce those ethnic boundaries thus need to be understood as modern phenomena. Historic tensions require modern means of reproduction – chains of memory – if they are to influence the present.

Secondly, Bosnia's religious diversity requires some introduction. Historically, Bosnia stands at the crossroads of two major world religions (Islam and Christianity) and of eastern and western Christianity (Orthodoxy and Catholicism, respectively). As a result of the **Dayton settlement** which concluded the conflict in 1995, Bosnia-Herzegovina is currently partitioned between the Muslim–Croat (Muslim majority) federation of Bosnia-Herzegovina and the Serb majority Serbian republic (*Republika Srpska*, or RS).

Talks between representatives of the three national groups of Bosnia and the presidents of Serbia and Croatia, brokered by the US, were held at the air base in Dayton, Ohio on 1–21 November 1995. These brought official military conflict in Bosnia to an end.

Figure 5.1 Map of Bosnia and Herzegovina, February 1998. *Current History*

When these two entities are taken together, Muslims form the largest minority, a unique position in Europe (Muslims 44 per cent, Serbs 31 per cent, Croats 17 per cent – see Malcolm, 1996, p. 223), although these figures are from the 1991 census; considerable displacements (and losses) have subsequently occurred. (Note that in Albania Muslims form a simple majority (Clayer, 1997).) However, although reliable figures were not available at the time of writing (May 2002), the displacement of people in the war has probably created an absolute Muslim majority, because although more Muslims were killed and many fled abroad, it is likely that the Bosnian Serb exodus, including to Serbia, has been greater. (Reliable figures are lacking largely because official statistics are distorted by political factors such as the policy of return, discussed below. For example, in the 2000 elections several electoral wards recorded a voter turnout of greater than 100 per cent – for latest details see the OSCE (Organization for Security and Co-operation in Europe) website.)

Thirdly, communism's legacy was highly significant for religious identity. The Second World War proved profoundly divisive in Yugoslavia, but instead of seeking national reconciliation in its aftermath victorious partisan forces under Marshal Tito (originally Josip Broz, 1892–1980), then still a close follower of Stalin, imposed communist power on the country ruthlessly and at a high cost. An estimated 250,000 people were killed as a result of Tito's consolidation of power in 1945–6. In the late 1940s and early 1950s all sources of possible opposition – and that meant any autonomous organizations – were ruthlessly suppressed, mirroring the pattern elsewhere in the postwar communist world. Among these were religious organizations. Between 1945 and 1953 religious schools were closed; religious education in state schools was replaced with classes in atheism; religious professionals were harassed, arrested and in some cases killed; the formation of independent associations on a religious or ethnic basis was banned; and much of the property of religious organizations was confiscated. In tandem with this attack on the influence of religious organizations in society the communist authorities also sought to coopt religious groups, for example by encouraging priests' associations that were independent of the Catholic and Orthodox hierarchies.

This enforced secularization greatly weakened the ability of religious groups to pass on their traditions, as well as limiting their role in public life. Although, as discussed in further detail below, Muslim and Catholic traditions recovered their capacity for the former to some extent, the Orthodox church, whose resources had already been severely depleted by the war, did not, so that throughout the communist period formal religious education was 'virtually unknown' (van Dartel, 1992, p. 278). It should also be noted that the structural impact of communist modernization probably had as large an effect on religion as enforced secularization, for rural religious communities were broken up in the process of urbanization. The widespread ignorance of one's own and others' religious tradition was combined with a nationality policy that had inadvertently highlighted Muslim identity in particular, against which opposition religio-nationalist identities were later to develop.

Indeed, communist policy actually *created* a Muslim national identity (Malcolm, 1996; Glenny, 1999). There had never been a Muslim nation in Bosnia: Bosnian Muslims were Slavs who had converted to Islam during the Ottoman occupation, and had never constituted a majority or even (until the late 1960s) the largest minority in the area. However, since Tito's ideology of 'brotherhood and unity' called for federal unity on the basis of national identity, from 1948 onwards Muslims came under pressure to choose between a Serb and Croat national identity, but repeatedly refused to do so. Eventually in 1968 the Bosnian branch of the Communist party (under internal pressure from secularized Muslims seeking to increase Bosnia's influence in the federation) recognized Muslim 'nationhood' (Malcolm, 1996, p. 199). Thus far, the communist legacy to religious identity was greatly to weaken religious institutions while tying religious identity more closely to secularized forms of national identity. However, in spite of the increased awareness of national identity as economic failure exposed political fault lines through the 1970s and 1980s, in urban areas social integration between the communities continued to increase, so that by the late 1980s the rate of intermarriage was 30 per cent in these areas (Malcolm, 1996, p. 222).

Fourthly, the disintegration of Yugoslavia (1991–5) was crucial. This was a complex process that led to two wars, first in Croatia (1991–2) and then in Bosnia (1992–5). Religious mobilization remained relatively low key until the outbreak of the conflict between Serbia and Croatia in 1991. The main exception was the Serbian church's role in propagandizing the 'genocide' of Serbs by Albanians in **Kosovo** in the early 1980s (in fact, according to Ramet, 1999, p. 307, this constituted relatively minor incidents of harassment of Serbs by Albanians, combined with the Serb fear that higher birth rates among ethnic Albanians would lead to Serbs comprising a smaller proportion of the population). Major internal causes of Yugoslavia's implosion included the cumbersome federal system and weak economy bequeathed by Tito (who died in 1980), Serb dominance of the federal army, government dominance of the Serbian media, and the rise to power in Serbia of Slobodan Milošević (president of the Serbian Communist party 1987–90, president of Serbia and of the Serbian Socialist party 1990–2000), who remained in power until the autumn of 2000. It has been argued that the idea of a 'Greater Serbia', to be established wherever significant Serb populations existed within the Yugoslav federation, fuelled the insurrections which led to the Croatian and Bosnian wars (Ramet, 1999; Glenny, 1999; Malcolm, 1996). This idea was fostered by the Serbian Academy of Arts and Sciences, and made use of by Milošević. In this context, I shall now consider the role of religion in the course of the conflict, taking each major tradition in turn.

Kosovo was given autonomous status as a region within Serbia by the communist government in 1946, and elevated to an autonomous province, but still within Serbia, in 1963. This status was revoked by Milošević in 1987.

Serbian Orthodoxy

In the nineteenth century Serbian nationalist readings of the passion narrative came to identify the death of Prince Lazar (the Serbian leader killed in battle with Ottoman forces in 1389), and Serbia's suffering at the hands of the Ottoman Turks, with Christ's suffering in his passion, while Muslim Slavs were identified with Judas (Sells, 1996). During the late nineteenth century the Orthodox church responded to these nationalist developments by beginning to celebrate the feast of St Lazar. In 1892 this was combined with the feast day of St Vitus, a pre-Christian Slavic god Christianized within Orthodoxy, and appeared for the first time as an official holiday in the church's calendar as 'Prophet Amos and Prince Lazar [St Vitus's] Day' (Sells, 1996, p. 44).

During the 1980s the church again responded to a rising feeling of nationalism, supporting nationalist claims of an Albanian campaign of 'genocide' against ethnic Serbs in Kosovo. The main Serbian theologians of the twentieth century had prepared the church to play this nationalist role, having 'developed their theological concepts on the basis of the idea that Serbian Orthodoxy forms the heart of the Serbian national identity and that from a historical perspective the Serbian nation is under constant threat' (van Dartel, 1992, p. 281).

From 1985 onwards Milošević specifically courted the church's favour. Following the St Vitus's Day celebration commemorating the 600th anniversary of the battle of Kosovo (28 June 1989) – see below – he allowed the church to build and reconstruct churches in previously forbidden areas, while he later (at the turn of the year 1989/90) allowed the church newspaper *Pravoslavje* to be sold at public news-stands and replaced the teaching of Marxism in schools with religious education along Orthodox lines (Ramet, 1999, pp. 112–13). At the anniversary celebrations, the church hierarchy indicated its support for Milošević's policy of revoking the autonomy of Kosovo, describing acceptance of its autonomy as 'only a temporary solution' (Ramet, 1999, p. 36). The celebration of St Vitus's Day in June 1989 illustrates how far the relationship between Milošević and the leadership of the Serb Orthodox church had developed by this stage:

> On 28 June several hundred thousand Serbs assembled at the battlefield site of Gazimestan, outside the Kosovar capital, Pristina, to celebrate the six-hundredth anniversary of the Battle of Kosovo. For many weeks a ferment of national feeling had been created inside Serbia; the bones of Prince Lazar, who died at the battle, had been taken on a tour of the country, becoming an object of pilgrimage wherever they were. In the courtyard of the monastery at Gracanica (south of Pristina), while people queued to pay their devotions to

the Prince's bones inside, stalls sold icon-style posters of Jesus Christ, Prince Lazar and Slobodan Milošević side by side. At the ceremony on the battlefield Milošević was accompanied by black robed metropolitans of the Orthodox Church, singers in traditional Serbian folk costumes, and members of the security police in their traditional dress of dark suits and sunglasses. 'After six centuries', Milošević told the crowds, 'we are again engaged in battles and quarrels. They are not armed battles, but this cannot be excluded yet.' The crowd roared its approval.

(Malcolm, 1996, p. 213)

Clearly, religious symbols were mobilized in the nationalist cause by the highest authorities in the church. However, the Orthodox church should not be regarded as simply the creature of Milošević. On 14 June 1992, at the height of the insurrection in Bosnia, the same Patriarch Pavel who had stood alongside Milošević at the anniversary celebrations three years before led 10,000 people in a march and prayers for peace in Belgrade in protest against his regime. Pavel also voiced criticism of the regime in the autumn of 2000, shortly before Milošević's fall from power. Thus the position of the institutional Serbian Orthodox church is perhaps best characterized as a defensively ethnocentric national church, shaped by a history of suffering and more recent international isolation. The church supported Milošević's plans in so far as these furthered the security of Serbia and Serb control over sacred sites (especially Kosovo), and it also contributed to propagating nationalist mythologies, even though it did not originate these.

The role of the Serbian Orthodox religion more generally in the war – as opposed to that of the institutional church – is difficult to assess. The relationship between the 'folk culture' shared by Radovan Karadzic (Bosnian Serb president) and his Bosnian Serb troops and institutional Serb Orthodoxy is complex. Certainly Christian symbolism was blended with a mixture of folk songs, music and romantic attachment to the countryside, away from the 'impure' mixing of the towns (Sells, 1996, p. 50). Furthermore, the church's own identification with the Serbian nation reinforced such connections. On the other hand, before the war the active membership of the church was probably less than 10 per cent and probably lowest among the young men who were most involved in the war, for religious instruction in schools was not permitted under the communist system, while 'in the Orthodox church, religious education, at least of a systematic kind, was hardly known' (van Dartel, 1992, p. 278). So the chances that such soldiers played an active part in church life or were educated in church teachings are slim.

Therefore much depends on what one means by 'religion'. If the word is used in the rather western sense of a consciously chosen belief system that informs actions in a reflective way, Serbian Orthodoxy had not been very effective in transmitting itself; hence its impact in this sense could not have been great. If, on the other hand, it is used to signify sets of symbols, rituals and stories that may float free of authorizing institutions, but continue to exert influence via other media (such as television or folk songs, or through word of mouth), then Serbian Orthodoxy appears to be have been rather more influential in informing Serbian insurrectionary ideology.

Thus differences between analysts such as Ramet and Sells may perhaps be explained by differences in their understanding of religion. Ramet seems to perceive religion in the former, reflective-systemic sense – what was described earlier as a voluntarist understanding of religion – so that for a war to be religiously motivated and justified, as Sells claims, some substantial argument derived from the tradition must be shown to be involved. Thus Ramet asks, 'Though one can easily cite Serbian bishops who justified the war, is the endorsement of even several bishops tantamount to *religious* justification as such?' (Ramet, 1999, p. 79).

Ramet assumes a characteristically western European understanding of a division between politics and religion, and of their essentially different nature. This understanding is rooted in the church–state rivalries of early modern western Europe, but mediated to the east principally through the distorting lens of communist ideology that claimed to separate church and state, yet sought party domination of both. Furthermore, where religious identity is considered by participants in a situation to be a part of political identity, the utility of such a western European distinction becomes questionable – like human rights discourse, its implementation is only as effective as local cultural mediation can make it. Therefore to perceive religion as essentially something apart from politics is to foreclose on important possibilities for understanding its action, and in this case to obscure its role in the construction of a certain kind of religiously based European identity – something which becomes even clearer in the Croatian nationalist case, as discussed below.

Working with a different understanding of religious identity – described above as 'identity-constitutive' – Sells argues that the widespread use of Christian symbols and discourse by Serb soldiers and leaders, together with insults against the Catholic and Islamic religions, shows that Serbs were in effect 'performing the passion' of the Slavic Christ. They were transforming nineteenth-century folktales based around the 'Kosovo passion' into 'the daily rituals for ethnoreligious purification' (Sells, 1996, p. 51). He gives many

Figure 5.2   Milenko Mihajlovič, Serbian political cartoon depicting a Roman Catholic priest and a Muslim imam fighting over a baby. *The New Combat*, September 1990

examples of this, including the following three. The first (illustrated above) is a 1990 political cartoon depicting a Roman Catholic priest and a Muslim imam fighting over a Serb baby.

Secondly, when the city of Foca was cleared of its Muslim population and all architectural traces of their presence removed, it was renamed Srbinje (Serb place) and the renaming celebrated by visits from high church officials (Sells, 1996, p. 80). Thirdly, Metropolitan Nicolaj, the highest-ranking church official in Bosnia, stood between Radko Mladic and Karadzic at the 1993 Easter service and described the Bosnian Serbs under these leaders as 'following the hard road of Christ' (Sells, 1996, p. 82).

Such examples need to be put into perspective by pointing out that not all Serbs shared such views. In the case of the Bosnian Serbs, the Serb Civic Council formed in Bosnian government (that is, the joint Muslim–Croat federation) areas to articulate the views of Serbs in favour of a multi-religious society noted that as of 1995 less than half of the Bosnian Serb populations lived in the Serb-controlled area of Bosnia (*Republica Srpska*, or Serb Republic). Instead, 150,000 chose to live in Muslim–Croat areas and half a million had fled abroad, including to Serbia (Sells, 1996, pp. 78–9). It should also be remembered that Serbs were not alone in committing atrocities – all sides were guilty of this, as subsequent war crimes trials have shown (Ramet, 1999, p. 286). However, the fact that individuals on all sides committed atrocities does not imply equal collective responsibility. The evidence shows that first Croats, and later Muslims, copied Serb tactics of 'ethnic cleansing' (Sells, 1996, pp. 20–1). But Serb atrocities were distinctive in being committed on a far larger scale as part of an orchestrated and systematic campaign to carve out swaths of Serb-only territory (Ramet, 1999; Glenny, 1999; Sells, 1996).

None of this proves that religion 'caused the war'. Many other factors, as I have noted, were also involved. It should also be remembered that the church did not instigate the policy of ethnic cleansing, nor was it the most powerful propaganda tool of the Milošević and Karadzic regimes; rather, that was provided by the state-controlled media (television, radio and newspapers). As one writer with a long acquaintance with Bosnia concludes:

> Having travelled widely in Bosnia over fifteen years, and having stayed in Muslim, Serb and Croat villages, I cannot believe that the country was forever seething with ethnic hatreds. But having watched Radio Television Belgrade in the period 1991–2, I can see why simple Bosnian Serbs came to believe they were under threat, from **Ustaše** hordes, fundamentalist jihads or whatever. As the independent Belgrade journalist Milos Vasic put it to an American audience, it was as if all television in the USA had been taken over by the Ku Klux Klan.
>
> (Malcolm, 1996, p. 252)

Ustaše was the name of the puppet fascist regime set up by the Nazis in Second World War Croatia. During the conflicts of 1991–5 Serbs and Croats routinely referred to each other as Ustaše/Chetniks (the latter was the name of the Serbian wartime resistance movement). Muslims were called 'Turks', a reference to Ottoman occupation.

Islam

Until 1990 Islamic institutions in Bosnia tended to be politically quietist. However, under attack for what was most distinctive about their identity, that is their religion, many Muslims reacted with a positive affirmation of their tradition. Such an affirmation needs to be put in context: a 1985 survey suggested that only 17 per cent of Bosnians were religious believers (Malcolm, 1996, p. 222). Other work, for example Sorabji's (1989) anthropological study of a Sarajevo suburb, suggests rather higher levels of religious identification and participation among Muslims. Furthermore, in contrast to Orthodoxy (and like the Catholic church), the Muslim community had put considerable efforts into religious education, so that by 1980 across Yugoslavia some 120,000 children were receiving Islamic instruction at primary level (Ramet, 1999, p. 120). Thus, in spite of rather low levels of active participation, it is likely that many Muslims had some basis in their tradition to which to turn in the new situation, both of a formal kind and received via broader cultural transmission. There was, however, little tradition of Islamic political activism on which to draw: 'in spite of [its] formidable institutional base, the Islamic leadership adopted a much lower profile then either the Roman Catholic Church or the Serbian Orthodox Church' (Ramet, 1999, p. 120).

However, in the new context in which their religious identity was under direct attack, Bosnian Muslims reacted in two ways: strengthening their religious identity, for example in the green banners and crescents of Izetbegović's SDA (*Stranke Demokratske Akcije*, or 'Party of Democratic Action', the main Muslim political party); and stressing that they 'stood for the preservation of Bosnia's unique character as a multi-national, multi-religious republic' (Malcolm, 1996, pp. 218–19). There were strong tensions between these two elements, which persisted throughout the war and indeed continue to the present.

Certainly Islamic identity was increasingly mobilized in the war effort, aided in part by the flood of less cosmopolitan rural refugees into urban areas with the tide of Serb ethnic cleansing (Glenny, 1999, p. 644). For example, from late 1993 new exclusively Muslim brigades were established, such as the Seventh Brigade in Zenica:

> The new recruits were men who had been 'cleansed' from their homes, and understandably they did not pay lip-service to the concept of a multinational or multi-ethnic Bosnia. For the first time a strident Muslim nationalism appeared on the scene, rivalling that of the Serbs and Croats. The brigade's officers sported Islamic insignia and beards, and adopted anti-Western positions. Their wives and daughters increasingly adopted Islamic dress and head covering. Shops selling alcohol were attacked, and pigs were slaughtered and their carcasses destroyed.
>
> (Poulton, 1997, p. 233)

Such developments were paralleled in the official public sphere in 1994: the *reis-ul-ulema* (Islamic religious leader) criticized mixed marriages, while journalists committed to multiculturalism were removed from state television (Poulton, 1997, p. 233). However, such religious exclusivism did not go uncontested, and SDA policy has remained officially multicultural both in principle and in practice: Serbs remained in the coalition government throughout the war.

One example from 1996 of the ongoing struggle between religious exclusivism and other tendencies (in this case a secular multiculturalism) concerned the issue of the appropriate form of commemoration for Muslim war dead. When Izetbegovič used Islamic terminology and symbols as official Bosnian forms, the father of a slain soldier objected in an open letter published in the nationalist newspaper *Ljilian*:

> Why do you use the religious term *shehid* [martyr] for my son and other soldiers who have died? My son is not one, and I do not allow you to call him so. Why do you say a *fatiha* [prayer for the dead] for those who have been killed? When it comes to my son, remain silent. It is better not to say anything than to speak a language which neither he nor I understand.
>
> (Osman Tica, reported in *BosNews* (Digest 112), 27 March 1996, in Campbell, 1998, p. 113)

So Islam too was instrumentalized during the conflict, that is used to mobilize a sense of national identity deployed in opposition to other religious nationalisms and implicitly exclusive both of other religious identities and of non-religious identities. This public identification of 'Bosnian-ness' with Islam continued to prove controversial during the 1996 elections, as when Izetbegovič addressed an election rally which featured Islamic religious music and verses from the Qur'ān (Ramet, 1999, p. 283). Furthermore, during the war this identification of Bosnian identity with Islam was rejected by some religious Muslims close to Izetbegovič, who subsequently broke away from the SDA. One example is the academic Rusmir Mahmutćehajić, who is influenced by the Sufi tradition of Islam that has been so significant in Bosnia's history, and strongly critical of the ethnic division of Bosnia enshrined at Dayton. In response he has formed 'Bosnia Forum', an organization for academics drawn from all groups that is aimed at working towards a deeper form of reconciliation premised on the idea of a multi-ethnic, multi-religious Bosnia.

Nonetheless, whether because of the multi-religious and cosmopolitan constituency of Sarajevo or for some other reason, in that city at least Muslim nationalism never spilled over into violence directed against religious property, in contrast to Croatian and Serbian nationalism (Ramet, 1999, p. 255). Furthermore, incidents of this kind outside Sarajevo in Bosnian government-controlled areas were less frequent and severe than elsewhere, although not entirely absent: as late as March 1997 explosives destroyed the Catholic parish church in Humac, a Muslim–Croat area.

These attacks on religious property need to be seen in the context of what Bosnian Muslims describe as 'the war against culture', of which

Figure 5.3 Destroyed mosque at Ahmnici, Bosnia, April 1993. Photo: Roger Hutchings, Network

a key example is the shelling of the historic National Library in Sarajevo that destroyed many historic rare books and manuscripts. Indeed, the Bosnian government has decided to leave several major public buildings unrepaired as monuments to this war, including the parliament building. However, by far the most common form of destruction was that of places of worship. Religious buildings provided the most prominent witness to the long-term settlement of a community that had now been 'cleansed', one that Serbs in particular were keen to eradicate entirely – hence, the destruction of all 211 mosques in Banja Luka, including two of historic importance from the late sixteenth century. By August 1994 Serb forces had destroyed 650 mosques across Bosnia-Herzegovina (Ramet, 1999, p. 255). This has subsequently become one of the most controversial areas of reconstruction, with the international community unable to persuade the local authorities in Banja Luka to grant permission to rebuild. In denying the initial request to rebuild the Ferhadija mosque of 1579 the then mayor of Banja Luka refused Carlos Westendorp, the international community's highest representative in Bosnia, with these words: 'The international community has got to stop insulting the Serbs and asking them to rebuild the monuments from the darkest days of slavery' (quoted in Ramet, 1999, p. 285).

By March 2000 not a single mosque in the Serb republic had been rebuilt. Indeed in the spring of 2001 attempts to lay a foundation stone for a new one on the site of the historic Ferhadija mosque met with strong local protest, and at the time of writing (May 2002) still no progress has been made on this issue. Meanwhile, many new mosques can be seen springing up in the suburbs of Sarajevo. Thus the practical partition of Bosnia is being constructed at the level of religious buildings, as well as in political arrangements, as described further below.

The Catholic church

Although nominally Serbian Orthodox members outnumbered Catholics in Yugoslavia, the Catholic church had the largest active membership of any religious group (Ramet, 1999, p. 80). It was also the most politically active during the communist period, beginning with Cardinal Alojzije Stepinac's criticism of communist policy in the immediate postwar period, which resulted in his imprisonment and internal exile until his death in 1960. A comparison of the leading newspapers of the three major religious traditions illustrates the differences in their political stances. Throughout the communist period *Glas koncila* (a Catholic paper) openly and often took issue with the communist press, publishing interviews and articles on 'state atheism, Christian-Marxist dialogue, proposals to change laws governing religious life in Yugoslavia, and other social issues' (Ramet, 1999, p. 121). In contrast, *Pravoslavje* (an Orthodox paper) did not become active until 1981, after which it became 'ever more strident in its defence of Serbian interests in Kosovo and its advocacy of Serbian Orthodox nationalism generally' (Ramet, 1999, p. 121). *Preporod* (which was Muslim) rarely touched on social issues, focusing instead on mosque building, reports of religious festivals and information about basic Islamic teaching (Ramet, 1999, p. 121).

State oppression lessened after 1970, but several areas of conflict between the Catholic church and the state remained. Issues on which the church continued to challenge the state included the teaching of atheism in schools; the exclusion of believers from the Communist party, and in general their treatment as second-class citizens; the denial of access to broadcasting for religious groups; and human rights. Violations of the latter included wrongful imprisonment and denial of access to religious services for prisoners and military.

The mobilization of religious symbols in the war effort was marked by a division between folk and official Catholicism. Thus the Croat leader Franjo Tudjman's acceptance on behalf of Croatia of the task of 'the Europeanization of Bosnian Muslims' never received the same blessing from church officials as the Serb project did (Sells, 1996, pp. 95–6). By this phrase Tudjman meant the establishment of a Croat state in Bosnian territory 'based on the same ideals of ethnoreligious purity espoused by the Republika Srpska, only in the name of Catholicism rather than Serb Orthodoxy' (Sells, 1996, p. 96). From the beginning of the conflict Pope John Paul II called for peace, and for nationalist passions to be set aside, refusing to take a partisan line. Furthermore, in 1993, when the Croat–Muslim alliance had fallen apart, the president of the council of Islamic elders in Croatia and Slovenia praised the Catholic church's role in non-partisan relief work across former Yugoslavia:

> I am convinced that with this war the Catholic Church has gained lasting [esteem], which we Muslims will know how to foster and develop. That quality is actually the biggest guarantee that it will be possible to resolve the Croatian–Muslim dispute considerably more easily than it appears at this present moment.

> (Quoted in Ramet, 1999, p. 258)

Later in the conflict (September 1994) the pope visited Croatia and tried to visit Serbia and Bosnia, but was refused in the first case by Patriarch Pavel and Milošević, and in the second by UN officials concerned for his safety. Addressing an audience of a million in Croatia on 11 September, he spoke against 'the risk of idolizing a nation, race [or] a party and justifying in their name hatred, discrimination and violence', and went on to call on Croatian Catholics to 'become apostles of a new concord between peoples' (Ramet, 1999, p. 258). However, the limitations of papal authority over religious nationalists were exposed in Catholic-majority Herzegovina, where some Catholic clergy, especially Franciscans, were far more sympathetic to Croatian nationalism (Sells, 1996, p. 111). Medjugorje, the site since 1981 of many reported visions of the Virgin Mary, is situated in Herzegovina, and the Madonna became a focus for Croat religio-nationalist identity in much the same way as Prince Lazar had done for Serb nationalists. For example, the independence of Croatia was announced on the tenth anniversary of the first reported visions (25 June 1991), while in Medjugorje in 1993, 'in the souvenir shops, statuettes of the Madonna were on sale with swastikas, Maltese Crosses and other Nazi regalia' (Sells, 1996, p. 107). Croat militiamen also invoked religious symbolism in explaining their actions: '"It is not enough to cleanse Mostar of Muslims" said a Croat militiaman as his unit worked to destroy the bridge; "the relics must also be destroyed"' (Riedlmayer, 1994, p. 3). Thus nationalist forces harnessed Catholic religious symbols too, contributing to the destruction of civil society.

I now turn to the postwar situation, and especially to the relationship between religion and attempts to reconstruct civil society in Bosnia-Herzegovina.

Religion and postwar reconstruction

> The new Bosnia-Herzegovina was hailed as a triumph of the West's commitment to a multi-ethnic state but in reality confirmed its total partition ... Dayton brought the fighting to an end, in itself a considerable achievement. But as a model for reconciliation and for rebuilding a shattered society, it was and remains severely limited.
>
> (Glenny, 1999, pp. 647, 651)

> Today there is not a single politician in power establishments from any of the 'national bodies', at any level of government, who does not declare himself a hard-line believer in one of the three religions that practically act as if they were state religions, each one of them in 'its own space'. Bosnia-Herzegovina has never had so many pious party-political officials.
>
> (Lovrenović, 2000, p. 77)

The Dayton agreement was thrashed out between Izetbegović, Tudjman and Milošević with American mediation in the first three weeks of November 1995. But the mediators brought a formula of territorial division to the table which had first been proposed by international negotiators in the spring of 1994, a period when Serb forces were in a very much stronger position than during the autumn of 1995. Thus questions have been asked as to why, given the much weakened position of Serb forces, the international community did not bring pressure to bear for a solution which not only established a territorial settlement more closely reflecting the size of the respective populations and pre-war conditions, but also sought to ensure its future unity and multi-ethnicity (Malcolm, 1996; Glenny, 1999; Ramet, 1999).

For the Dayton agreement divided the former republic 51:49 between a Muslim–Croat federation and Serb-administered territory (*Republika Srpska,* or Serbian Republic), with each entity having largely separate institutions (for example police, military, media, parliament and education). There is a combined parliament, with a council of ministers and three-person presidency, but (beyond practical matters, such as air-traffic control) its powers are restricted to foreign and monetary policy, and its procedures such that the veto of any one ethnic constituency can render them inoperative.

This institutional partition is also reflected, as the second quotation above (from Lovrenović) suggests, in the sphere of religion. However, the situation is complex. First, while this quotation suggests that a public show of adherence to religion is universally required, not all public shows are equally welcome; in particular young women who

Information in this section derives largely from interviews and information gathered in Sarajevo, Zenica and Banja Luka in March 2000. My thanks to the British Academy for funding to undertake this research trip, and to Emina Hadžhalilović for translating for me.

have chosen to adopt the Muslim *hijab* (veil) may be criticized, insulted or discriminated against by other Muslims. For example, one woman respondent who runs a secular non-governmental organization (NGO) told of receiving critical comments on her attire from her boss, and even in the canteen at Sarajevo University it was evident that her dress aroused suspicion. The pages of *Dani*, a Bosnian magazine, are also witness to the controversy caused by the small numbers of young women who have adopted Islamic dress. European suspicion of Islam is shared by many Bosnian Muslims too, complicating the relationship there between Muslim and European identities.

Secondly, there is evidence of significant efforts by religious groups to improve intercommunal relations. In Sarajevo representatives from three different kinds of interfaith organization were interviewed in March 2000. The first, *Oci u Oci Interreligijska Sluzba* (Face to Face Interfaith Service), led by the Franciscan (Catholic) Ivo Markovic, aims to promote dialogue among religious leaders and has succeeded in setting up interfaith seminars between trainees at the main Muslim, Orthodox and Catholic training colleges. It has also established an interfaith choir, *Pontanima*, which has toured and released a CD and is seen as a contribution to the 'de-instrumentalization' of religion. The second organization, the Centre for Religious Dialogue, Sarajevo, runs workshops at local level among a range of participants and religious leaders in local politics, aimed at breaking down prejudice and resolving conflict, using conflict resolution methods developed in and funded by the US, but delivered by Bosnians. The third, *Ibrahim/Abraham*, is a more locally focused organization, whose aim is to bring together practising Christians and Muslims in Sarajevo to share aspects of their faith, for example through scripture study and practical (if still, under present conditions, controversial) activities, such as tending cemeteries.

Perhaps not surprisingly the perception of many involved in interfaith organizations is that the role of religion is being wrongly neglected by the international community, which does not fund such initiatives as part of its democratization strategies. This is particularly the case with the main European organizations, such as the Organization for Co-operation and Security in Europe (OSCE). In contrast to the 'religion-blind' position of such agencies, participants in interfaith activities argue that only by being explicit about the role of religion in the conflict, as well as about its potential for reconciliation and building solidarity, is it possible to work towards the kinds of relationship which would prevent the recurrence of the events of 1991–5. Such differences in the understanding of the role of religious identity directly affect the allocation of resources in the reconstruction process.

Figure 5.4 Inter-faith dialogue organized by the Centre for Religious Dialogue, Sarajevo: Serb and Muslim religious leaders meet at Mufti's office in Bihac. Photo: Vjeko Saje

Part of the aim of the OSCE and other international donors is to foster the development of institutions that will ensure the political stability of the state in the long term. As well as government bodies, they seek the development of 'autonomous' local organizations that reflect local needs but also foster relationships across ethnic and religious boundaries. This layer, which includes international NGOs, is known in the literature as 'civil society'. To sponsor civil society building initiatives donors need to be convinced of the 'democratic credentials' of groups. Some such screening process is clearly necessary, but Chandler (1998) argues that the OSCE is too restrictive in its policy and hence, at least up to 1998, had achieved very poor grassroots participation.

One criterion generally applied by donor agencies is multi-ethnicity. This means that groups constituted on a single ethnic or religious basis will not receive funding. According to one study, an example of this is Muslim women's groups, whose 'emphasis on affirming Bošnjak and Muslim identity means that western funding agencies do not see them as encouraging multi-ethnicity in Bosnia – indeed they are often referred to as nationalist – and therefore do not fund them' (Helms, 1999, pp. 4–5). Such groups, whether or not they have an explicit religious basis or purpose, provide vital support to women who are often isolated; as a result of war deaths and emigration, 70 per cent of the adult population of Bosnia is now female, including 80 per cent of refugees.

However, in spite of this isolation from international support,

> some [Muslim women's groups] have begun to combine their affirmation of Bošnjak-hood (*Bošnjaštvo*) with efforts to network with women's NGOs in Serb and Croat areas. And, despite their continued relative isolation from western-sponsored initiatives, these same groups have begun to discuss ideas of women's rights and even feminism without first rejecting them out of hand, weighing these ideas to see which aspects might be applied to Bosnian society.
>
> (Helms, 1999, p. 8)

Rather than specifically religious activities, the majority of religious charities in Bosnia are involved in humanitarian work. For example, the Orthodox International Christians Charity in Banja Luka is involved in supporting Muslims and Croats returning to the Serbian republic (although such non-partisan support has brought some conflict with the local Serbian Orthodox church. The charity gives very practical support, such as providing agricultural equipment and housing materials. With help from these organizations the small number of refugees willing to return to Serbia is gradually increasing. *Pax Christi*, a Catholic charity, is involved in similar practical projects in Zenica and elsewhere.

Religion, then, has become important at the level of symbolic conflict and identity demarcation in contemporary Bosnia. However, mobilization of religious 'resistance' identity does not necessarily condemn groups to reinforce social divisions, even in Bosnia. Some religious institutions and organizations emerged from the war with a strong reputation for non-partisan support, or at least for encouraging toleration. Efforts are now underway to rebuild relationships between communities, from senior to local levels. While there is still much fear and suspicion, it seems that religion can and is making a constructive contribution to the reconstruction process in some respects. Resistance identity can become project identity, although there is also much evidence that it has become legitimizing identity. Evidence of lack of community participation in more highly funded civil society building initiatives suggests that this aspect of the reconstruction process may be worthy of greater attention than it has so far received. It is arguable that the characteristically western European polarization of the religious and secular spheres may contribute to the 'religion-blind' policy that sustains this neglect.

Conclusion

What does the Bosnian case tell us about religion and European identities? On the one hand the Yugoslav case is highly specific, and the factors that led to the federation's disintegration and to ethno-religious genocide in Bosnia are unlikely to be repeated on the same scale elsewhere in Europe. But on the other hand there is evidence that a strengthening of national and confessional boundaries is occurring even in stable and relatively prosperous parts of central and eastern Europe such as southeast Poland (Hann, 1997). Furthermore, as 'Fortress (Western) Europe' proves ever more porous, anti-immigrant and specifically anti-Muslim prejudice may increase, in some cases mobilized on a Christian or post-Christian secular basis against a perceived 'Islamic threat'. In the wake of the events of 11 September 2001 such a perception is likely to be heightened; but even before then, in officially secular France:

> When Jean-Marie Le Pen [leader of the National Front] has a mass celebrated by a Catholic integrist priest before sending in a 'commando' to wreck an Islamic cultural centre near Nevers, he is enacting, with the help of media orchestration, the potential reality of ethno-religious confrontation in a context where the code defining the respective fields of religion and politics, and their interrelationship, no longer operates.

(Hervieu-Léger, 2000, p. 161)

Furthermore, in the Dayton agreement and in earlier 'peace plans' the international community showed that it was prepared both to recognize territorial gains made by aggression and to sanction the creation of ethnically partitioned states. At the same time the ECHR, enshrined in the Bosnian constitution, provides only limited protection for religious minorities in the absence of a Europe-wide consensus on the relationship between religion and society. In this situation, religious identity seems set to play a developing role in social conflict. But that will not be its only role. In spite of the historic process that has led to the marginalization of most religious institutions in Europe, religion as a self-chosen identity remains significant for many Europeans, while the vast majority of religious institutions are orientated towards peacemaking and community building rather than empire building and conflict. The interfaith initiatives of Sarajevo may yet prove a blueprint for a working out of the relationships between religions and European identities that defies Izetbegovič's bleak prophecy on the future of religion in Europe with which this chapter began.

References

Abercrombie, N., Hill, S. and Turner, B. (1994) *The Penguin Dictionary of Sociology*, 3rd edn, Harmondsworth, Penguin.

Anaya, S. (1995) 'The capacity of international law to advance ethnic or nationality rights claims', in W. Kymlicka (ed.), *The Rights of Minority Cultures*, Oxford, Oxford University Press.

Ashford, S. and Timms, N. (1992) *What Europe Thinks: a Study of West European Values*, Aldershot, Dartmouth.

Baumann, G. (1999) *The Multicultural Riddle: Rethinking National, Ethnic and Religious Identities*, London/New York, Routledge.

Borowik, I. (ed.) (1999) *Church–State Relations in Central and Eastern Europe*, Kraków, Nomos.

Bowring, B. (1997) 'Russia's accession to the Council of Europe and human rights: compliance or cross purposes?', *European Human Rights Law Review*, vol. 6, pp. 628–43.

Britannica Book of the Year 2001 (2001) Chicago, Encyclopedia Britannica.

Bruce, S. (1999) *Choice and Religion: a Critique of Rational Choice Theory*, Oxford, Oxford University Press.

Bryson, C. and Curtice, J. (1998) 'The end of materialism?' *British and European Social Attitudes*, Aldershot, Ashgate.

Burgess, J. (1997) *The East German Church and the End of Communism*, Oxford, Oxford University Press.

Campbell, D. (1998) *National Deconstruction: Violence, Identity and Justice in Bosnia*, Minneapolis, MN, University of Minnesota Press.

Casanova, J. (1994) *Public Religions in the Modern World*, Chicago, Chicago University Press.

Castells, M. (1997) *The Power of Identity*, Oxford, Blackwell.

Chandler, D. (1998) 'Democratization in Bosnia: the limits of civil society building strategies', *Democratization*, vol. 5, no. 4, winter, pp. 78–102.

Clayer, N. (1997) 'Islam, state and society in post-communist Albania', in H. Poulton and S. Taji-Farouki (eds), *Muslim Identity and the Balkan State*, London, Hurst.

Cockburn, C. (1998) *The Space between Us: Negotiating Gender and National Identities in Conflict*, London, Zed.

Davie, G. (1994) *Religion in Britain since 1945: Believing Without Belonging*, Oxford, Oxford University Press.

Davie, G. (2000) *Religion in Modern Europe: a Memory Mutates*, Oxford, Oxford University Press.

Evans, M. (1997) *Religious Liberty and International Law*, Cambridge, Cambridge University Press.

Feirabend, J. and Rath, J. (1996) 'Making a place for Islam in politics: local authorities dealing with Islamic associations', in W. Shadid and P. van Koningsveld (eds), *Muslims in the Margin: Political Responses to the Presence of Islam in Europe*, Kampen, Kok Pharos.

Glenny, M. (1999) *The Balkans 1804–1999: Nationalism, War and the Great Powers*, London, Granta.

Hamberg (1992) 'Religion, secularisation and value change in the welfare state', paper presented to the First European Conference on Sociology, Vienna, 26–9 August.

Hann, C. (1997) 'The nation-state, religion, and uncivil society: two perspectives from the periphery', *Human Diversity*, vol. 126, no. 2, pp. 27–45.

Hawkesworth, C. (2003) 'National identity and managing the memory of war: Yugoslavia, a case study', in C. Emsley (ed.), *War, Culture and Memory*, Milton Keynes, The Open University.

Helms, E. (1999) 'Muslim women's NGOs between discourse of secular civil society and religion-based national identity in Bošnjak-majority areas of Bosnia-Herzegovina', unpublished paper presented to Islam and Human Rights in Post-Communist Europe Conference, Sofia, 15–16 March.

Hervieu-Léger, D. (1997) 'Faces of Catholic transnationalism: in and beyond France', in S. Rudolph and J. Piscatori (eds), *Transnational Religion and Fading States*, transl. R. Greaves, Boulder, CO, Westview.

Hervieu-Léger, D. (2000) *Religion as a Chain of Memory*, Cambridge, Polity.

Inglehart, R., Basanez, M. and Moreno, A. (eds) (1998) *Human Values and Beliefs: a Cross-cultural Sourcebook*, Ann Arbor, MI, University of Michigan Press.

Izetbegovič, A. (1984) *Islam between East and West*, Indianapolis, IN, American Trust.

Janis, M. (1997) 'Russia and the legality of Strasbourg law', *European Journal of International Law*, 1, pp. 93ff.

Janis, M., Kay, R. and Bradley, A. (1995) *European Human Rights Law: Texts and Materials*, Oxford, Oxford University Press.

Kepel, G. (1994) *The Revenge of God: the Resurgence of Islam, Christianity and Judaism in the Modern World*, transl. A. Braley, Cambridge, Polity.

Leveau, R. (1988) 'The Islamic presence in France', in T. Gerholm and Y. Lithman (eds), *The New Islamic Presence in Western Europe*, London, Mansell.

Lovrenović, I. (2000) 'Five fragments about implosion', in F. Duve and N. Popović (eds), *In Defence of the Future*, transl. G. McMaster, Vienna, Bolanzo Folio.

Lyon, D. (2000) *Jesus in Disneyland: Religion in Postmodern Times*, Cambridge, Polity.

Mahmutćehajić, R. (1998) 'The downhill path *and* defence, not surrender', in C. Kurzman (ed.), *Liberal Islam: a Source Book*, New York, Oxford University Press.

Malcolm, N. (1996) *Bosnia: a Short History*, 2nd edn, Basingstoke, Macmillan.

OSCE website: http://oscebih.org

Owen, D. (1995) *Balkan Odyssey*, London, Gollancz.

Poulton, H. (1997) 'After Dayton', in H. Poulton and S. Taji-Farouki (eds), *Muslim Identity and the Balkan State*, London, Hurst.

Ramet, S. (1999) *Balkan Babel: the Disintegration of Yugoslavia from the Death of Tito to the War over Kosovo*, Oxford/Boulder, CO, Westview.

Riedlmayer, A. (1994) 'Killing memory: the targeting of libraries and archives in Bosnia-Herzegovina', *MELA Notes: Newsletter of the Middle Eastern Librarians Association*, 61, fall, p. 3.

Schiffauer, W. (1988) 'Migration and religiousness', in T. Gerholm and Y. Lithman (eds), *The New Islamic Presence in Western Europe*, London, Mansell.

Sells, M. (1996) *The Bridge Betrayed: Religion and Genocide in Bosnia*, Berkeley, CA/London, University of California Press.

Sorabji, C. (1989) 'Muslim identity and Islamic faith in socialist Sarajevo', unpublished PhD thesis, University of Cambridge.

Starrett, G. (1998) *Putting Islam to Work: Education, Politics and Religious Transformation in Egypt*, Berkeley/Los Angeles, CA/London, University of California Press.

Sunier, T. (1995) 'Moslems in Nederland, Nederlandse Moslims: sociale integratie in the steer van der Islam', in G. Engborsen and R. Gabriels (eds), *Sferen van Integratie Naareen Gedifferencieerd Allochfonontaleid*, Amsterdam, Boem.

Tomka, M. (1999) 'Religion, church, state and civil society in east-central Europe', in I. Borowik (ed.), *Church–State Relations in Central and Eastern Europe*, Kraków, Nomos.

van Dartel, G. (1992) 'The nations and the churches in Yugoslavia', *Religion, State and Society*, vol. 20, nos 2 and 3, pp. 275–88.

Waldron, J. (1995) 'Minority cultures and the cosmopolitan alternative', in W. Kymlicka (ed.), *The Rights of Minority Cultures*, Oxford, Oxford University Press.

Wasserstein, B. (1996) *Vanishing Diaspora: Jews in Europe since 1945*, London, Hamish Hamilton.

Withol de Wenden, C. (1996) 'Muslims in France', in W. Shadid and P. van Koningsveld (eds), *Muslims in the Margin: Political Responses to the Presence of Islam in Europe*, Kampen, Netherlands, Kok Pharos.

6

'East is east and west is west':

on the fundamentals of the European and eastern world views

ROBERT WILKINSON

Introduction

My aim in this chapter is to try to show, first, that there is a very basic set of assumptions about the world which can properly be called European (and which also in important ways informs cultures, like that of the United States, which are in this respect largely European-derived); and secondly, that this set of assumptions is not the only possible way of structuring human experience. Put another way, the outlook on the world that has been developed in Europe is neither inevitable nor the only conceptual framework on which a civilization may be based. I shall try to demonstrate the truth of these two claims by outlining the chief alternative to this European outlook, a set of assumptions which, as a matter of history, has been associated with several cultures that have developed in the east.

Trying to draw up a list of *general* respects in which European cultural beliefs and practices differ from those of the east is by no means straightforward. I shall leave aside for the moment the assumption that there is a homogeneous tradition we can identify as belonging to Europe, usually said to be a complex blend of Greek and Judaeo-Christian views, modified by the historical unfolding of the cultures of the nations presently making up Europe. Even more difficult to defend is the idea that there is a single 'other', the 'east' or the 'orient', with which we can meaningfully contrast it. For simplicity and as a working hypothesis, for the purposes of this chapter I shall assume that the east begins with the Indian sub-continent. The east will then include the nations which have occupied and presently occupy that sub-continent, together with Tibet, China, Korea and Japan, to name only the major players. Anyone with a nodding acquaintance with the cultures and histories involved will be decidedly sceptical about the possibility of framing universal truths about so vast a geographical area, so vast a number of people, so long a history (in some cases, these cultures were highly civilized while Europeans were still at the woad stage) and so varied an array of beliefs and cultural practices. The one point I intend to stress by means of these generalities is that in advancing some ideas contrasting Europe and the east, as I am about to, these must be interpreted as indications of what one must at best call merely different emphases in the understanding and interpretation of nature and experience, even if (as I believe) these emphases are of considerable depth. They are most emphatically not intended as exceptionless generalizations about an 'eastern world view' that is asserted to be the only world view accepted in the east. Such generalizations (along the lines of the 'mystic orient/scientific west' or 'eastern despotism/western democracy') used to be common, and almost invariably rested on a combination of patronizing ignorance and colonial ambition, a condition which recent scholarship has begun to correct. For every belief and institution I am about to identify a counter-example can be found (just as it can, usually, for similar statements made about Europe). This is because there is in reality no single 'east': what Europeans most inexactly refer to by means of this term is not one culture at all, but many cultures involving a high percentage of all the human beings who have ever lived; cultures which have rich, varied and long histories of their own, which in many ways differ as much from one another as they do from European cultures and which have variously interacted with one another in the course of history. If one ever needed persuading that the world of human culture is not neat, but irreducibly various and untidy, a brief encounter with 'the east' will do all the convincing necessary.

All that said, I should like to argue that we need not give up the attempt to look for these different emphases which might illuminate, first, what it is that makes Europeans not want to give up this idea that there is an 'east'; and secondly, by implication, what is being said about what it is to be in the European cultural tradition as opposed to that of 'the east'. There frequently occur occasions when one wants to say of an event or artefact or practice, 'That must be from the east', or 'No European could have written/painted/composed (etc.) that'. We seem not to be able to do without this idea, and must have something in mind, however inchoate, when we use it. I shall now try to make explicit the facts which justify this intuition. To identify the root of the central difference in emphasis I wish to argue for, I have to begin from a point of great generality and abstraction, which appears profoundly counter-intuitive to many Europeans when they first encounter it. If you find this detour into the fairly rarefied heights of philosophical abstraction unsympathetic, please just be patient: I shall soon come down to its more practical corollaries and manifestations.

Dualism and non-dualism

There is an outlook on the world and experience which occurs far more commonly, and which is far more prominent, in the philosophies and religions of the east than in those of the west, and this is called non-dualism. It embodies so fundamental and so basically different an understanding of the world from the outlook that is commonest in the west, which is called **dualism**, that any culture based on it must be in important ways very different from one which is not so based. I shall argue that dualism and non-dualism entail conceptions of the nature and value of human individuality which diverge in significant ways, and that these contrasting views about individuality lie behind many of the most obvious and commented-on differences in culture between east and west. If there is anything like a consistent east/west difference, it seems to me to be located in a bedrock divergence of view concerning the nature and status of the human individual, derived from the logically ultimate difference between dualism and non-dualism. Once this difference is grasped, much that appears puzzling about eastern institutions becomes intelligible. Granted the viewpoint of non-dualism, many oriental beliefs and practices are seen to be rational workings out of the implications of this basic outlook.

Note that the meaning of the term dualism here is different from that of the mind–body dualism discussed in Chapter 1.

To my knowledge, there is no accepted explanation as to why this difference in philosophies should roughly coincide with the geographical distinction between east and west. Again I must stress that this contrast is far from exceptionless: there are dualist philosophies in the east and non-dualism does occur in the west, notably in the tradition of western mysticism and to some extent in what are called absolute idealist philosophies, which had their heyday in the Romantic period of western cultural history in the early part of the nineteenth century. Yet there can be no doubt that such views are departures from the outlook which is at the core of the European intellectual tradition.

The bedrock assumption of the view I have labelled dualism is so basic and so fundamental to the western way of thinking that westerners probably never even notice that they believe it. It is the assumption that all that exists, in other words reality, consists of genuinely separate individuals. By the term 'individuals' I mean not just human beings and other sentient life forms, but every type of different entity that can be picked out by means of concepts, from sub-atomic particles to clusters of galaxies. Another way of putting this assumption is that separateness is real and not an illusion. Dualism is the view that ultimate reality is more than one entity: its basic assertion is that difference, and so the existence of individual entities, is not an appearance but ultimately the way things are. Let us call this proposition the dualist axiom.

It is important to be clear on how utterly pervasive this dualist axiom is in western thought. I shall give a number of important examples as I go along, but should like to pause here to note one instance which, on reflection, makes the point forcibly. The predilection for dualism underlies almost all of the west's religious thought, at least of an orthodox kind. In polytheistic systems (such as those of ancient Greece or Rome) there are of course multiple gods, and these divinities are discrete, separate from one another. Even in the monotheistic systems of the semitic religions, however, the one god is generally conceived of as a transcendent god: that is, a god who can meaningfully be said to be in some sense distinct from, and free from the limitations of, the created universe. Such a god is an individual, albeit of a very special kind. Moreover, in these religions the anticipated life after death is said to be personal: that is, it is asserted that we survive after death in a way in which some aspect of our individuality continues to exist. Even paradise, then, is a paradise of individuals. It is held to be desirable to be an individual, even in eternity, so deep is the western attachment to this concept.

The basic axiom of non-dualism, by contrast, is the (to western minds) impenetrable assertion that reality is ultimately a unity, a one, or (as is the preferred eastern way of putting it) non-dual. In other words, individuality of all kinds, both among sentient life forms and pertaining to every kind of non-sentient entity, is an appearance only; all division of what there is into individual entities of any kind is in the last analysis an illusion. This assertion, couched in different ways, underlies the view of the world held by Hindus, Buddhists and, to a certain extent, Taoists. Further, when one examines its implications, this explains much that appears to westerners most odd about eastern civilizations, for what the architects of these civilizations have done is to work out the implications of non-dualism with great care and thoroughness. It follows from what I am about to say that it should not be assumed that at the deepest levels eastern civilizations have the same goals as those of the west, but merely set about pursuing them in an odd way. On the contrary, they are not trying to achieve the same deep goals as those of the west at all.

I want now to set out the most central of these implications, using Hindu, Buddhist and Taoist sources. (Naturally I do not claim that these views have everything in common, or that each is monolithic, but I do assert that they have very similar logical structures, as incidentally I hope to show.) By the end of this chapter, you should be in a position to summarize (if very briefly) the contrasts between the dualist (western) and non-dualist (eastern) views of the world: this will give you an idea about the assumptions which lie behind the traditions of thought that are distinctively European and that to this day shape the European view of existence.

I will begin with some points about religion.

EXERCISE _____

State in your own words the basic difference between dualism and non-dualism.

DISCUSSION _____

The basic assertion of dualism is the claim that what exists is a plurality of genuinely discrete individuals: separateness is real and not an illusion. Non-dualism is the thesis that there is an ultimate reality behind the appearance of separate individuals, and that this reality is a unity without articulation. It follows that, for the non-dualist, separateness of any kind is in the last analysis an illusion.

_____

Religion

The essentials of the Hindu religious position are contained in the set of texts called the *Upanishads,* some 108 anonymous works of varying lengths composed over a period of about 500 years, beginning in the eighth century BCE.

It is worth noting that the great eastern religious systems are generally not based on one sacred book, such as the Bible or the Qur'ān, but usually have many sacred texts, even if some are more important than others.

Twenty or so of these texts are philosophically of the first importance and from them a remarkably consistent non-dual view emerges. In this view, the world of ordinary, everyday human experience, of individuals causally related in space and time, is called (in Sanskrit) the *samsara.* The *samsara* is held to be ultimately unreal. Reality is a changeless, eternal, perfect unity referred to as *Brahman.* Moreover, human nature is not made up exclusively of the *samsaric* elements of individual body and individual consciousness or mind (*jiva* – this is what one ordinarily refers to in western languages when one speaks of one's 'self'): there is further present in us an immortal element (which was never born and does not die), our true or original self, *atman.* This *atman* has no form, and whatever is without form is without limit, whatever is without limit is omnipresent, and whatever is omnipresent is immortal, or in other words god. This argument is the basis for one of the most astonishing and at the same time most central of all views associated with non-dualism, the assertion that

Brahman and *atman*, the ultimate reality and the immortal element within us, are identical:

> Containing all works, containing all desires, encompassing this whole world, without speech, without concern, this is the self [*atman*] of mine within the heart; this is *Brahman*. Into him, I shall enter, on departing hence.
>
> (*Chandogya Upanishad*, III.14.4, in Radhakrishnan, 1953, p. 392)

This view is summed up in the Sanskrit phrase *tat tvam asi*, or 'that art thou' – where 'that' refers to *Brahman*.

From this certain further consequences flow which are of the first importance in the present context. One point east and west have in common is the belief that, whatever one's conception of reality may be, wisdom consists in accommodating one's behaviour to it. In the present case, it is asserted that the world of ordinary experience, the *samsara*, is unreal. It is ultimately an illusion, or *maya*. To take it to be real is to be in a state of ignorance tantamount to spiritual blindness, or *avidya* (literally, 'not-knowledge'). The goal of life, in non-dual outlooks, is to escape from this condition of blindness: to pierce the veil of *maya* and to experience directly the unity of *atman* and *Brahman* – in western terms to become one with god. This extremely rare state is called in Hindu thought *moksha*, or release.

What one must be quite clear about is that in the state of *moksha* one is no longer in any meaningful sense an individual. The *atman*, it will be recalled, is distinct from the *jiva*: the latter is the everyday self, the seat of our wants, desires and memories, indeed of everything we would normally call our 'self', everything that makes us individual. But *jivas* are part of the *samsara*: like all apparent individuals, they are unreal. To know reality, to be one with *Brahman*, it is necessary to free ourselves of everything that makes us individual. Salvation (to use the western term for what is being described) in this view is precisely non-individual: indeed, it consists in the *extinction* of individuality. The *jiva* – in western terms the seat of individuality – is in non-dual views something to be *overcome*. The preservation or enhancement of the individual is the road away from the real: it is the highway to *avidya*, and ultimately the road to hell. Paradise here is conceived of as a state in which the *jiva* is, so to speak, dissolved. Personal immortality is *not* desired, even were it conceivable in the terms of this outlook.

A very similar logical pattern appears in the thought of the Buddha (by no means uninfluenced by the Hindu tradition in which he grew up) and survives at the heart of Buddhism in all its manifold forms. The problem which centrally occupied

Siddhartha Gautama (c. 563–483 BCE), the Buddha, was that of suffering. Suffering in all its forms was for him the most important phenomenon in the universe, and he dedicated his life to finding a way to relieve it. After long, ascetic and arduous reflection he had the experience which we refer to as enlightenment, and this (he believed) gave him the solution to the problem of relieving suffering. His revelation was that suffering is the result of desire, and follows both from its satisfaction (which gives rise to further desire) and from its non-satisfaction (which causes frustration). Consequently, he decided that the only way to relieve all suffering is to free oneself from all desires: to be free from all desires is to be free from suffering. That is what it is to be enlightened: to be free from desires is to have achieved the state the Buddha called (following Hindu precedent) *nirvana*. As he put it, a person who is enlightened

> neither constructs in his mind, nor wills in order to produce, any state of mind or body, or the destruction of any such state. By not so willing anything in the world, he grasps after nothing; by not grasping, he is not anxious; he is therefore fully calmed within.

> (*Majjhima Nikaya*, 1888, p. 244)

It is important to grasp what is meant by the concept of *nirvana*, perhaps the most significant single notion among all the concepts one must master to understand the civilizations of the east. In Sanskrit this term literally means 'blowing out' (as of a candle, for example), and in Buddhist texts it signifies 'extinction'. What is extinguished is all desire. As noted above, our desires are a large aspect of what constitutes our everyday self. Accordingly, to achieve or enter *nirvana* involves, in effect, the dissolution of what we ordinarily take to be the core of our individuality. To use an image which recurs over and over again in Buddhist sources, after enlightenment our consciousness is like a mirror, which simply reflects, desirelessly, what is before it. It follows that, in a system of thought such as this, the development of individuality is not only not valued but is seriously disvalued. The more you develop your individual traits, the more you bind yourself on the rack of desire and the further you recede from enlightenment.

There are some reasonably close parallels to these lines of thought in the Chinese philosophy and religion of Taoism (pronounced 'Daoism'), though in its classical version this does not include a metaphysic as developed as that of Hinduism or Buddhism. Here the goal is not to achieve enlightenment or *moksha* but to become what is called a sage or *sheng*. However, when one investigates what it is like to be a sage, certain marked similarities with these other two states become evident. In this philosophy the ultimate reality is called the

Tao (literally, 'the Way'). It is evident that the Tao is not in any meaningful sense an individual at all, as is made clear in the opening lines of the most famous of all Taoist texts, the *Tao te ching* (The Book of the Way and its Power), dating probably from the fifth century BCE:

The Way [Tao] that can be told of is not an Unvarying Way;

The names that can be named are not unvarying names.

It was from the Nameless that Heaven and Earth sprang.

(Lao Tzu, 1997, Chapter 1)

By 'names' here is meant concepts, and what we are being told is that in principle no concepts apply to the Tao. Now the function of concepts is to pick out from the realm of what exists (the universe) individuals of one sort or another; thus what is being asserted is that if any entity can be spoken of meaningfully by conceptual means, it is not the Tao, for the Tao is that which is prior to any discriminations. Though in some way it does give rise to the universe of individuals, it is in fact prior to all individuation. Hence the repeated references to it as the 'uncarved block', namely something which has in it the potential for all forms (see, for example, Lao Tzu, 1997, Chapters 15, 19, 28, 32, 57).

For present purposes, what is of interest is the way in which the Taoist sage is conceived, that is the Taoist equivalent of those who have attained *moksha* or *nirvana*. To help you understand this, the first issue to examine is the concept of action. Some account has to be given by Taoists of how the Tao gave rise to the universe of ordinary experience, the sphere generally referred to in Taoist literature as

Figure 6.1 T'ang Yin (1470–1524), *Dreaming of Immortality in a Thatched Cottage*, handscroll, h. 11 in., ink and colours on paper. The painting depicts a scholar who is dreaming he has gained immortality through Taoist practices. On the right he is shown asleep at his desk in the cottage; on the left as he appears in his dream, floating away to the land of the immortals. Note, in some works on Chinese art you will find this painting attributed to Chou Ch'en (fl. 1500–35). Freer Gallery of Art, Washington DC

'the ten thousand things'. Actions are changes initiated by agents, and agents are individuals seeking to execute their purposes. (Most human action of course is aimed at the satisfaction of our wishes and desires.) Since the Tao is not an individual, it cannot meaningfully be said to act. To give rise to the everyday universe, therefore, the Tao must manifest itself in some other way, and this is called *wu-wei*, or 'actionless activity'. The Tao 'acts without action, does without doing' (Lao Tzu, 1997, Chapter 63). Or again: 'Tao never does; Yet through it all things are done' (Lao Tzu, 1997, Chapter 37). What this means is that the Tao brings about all there is by means of some form of pure spontaneity. (There is a close analogue in Hindu thought: asked why *Brahman* should have given rise to the *samsaric* universe at all – that is, for what possible reason – the answer given is *lila*, which means sport or play, in other words pure spontaneity.)

Now, wisdom consists in knowing what is real and bringing oneself, as far as possible, into accord with it. This is what the sage does. Accordingly, the goal of the sage is to emulate *wu-wei* as closely as possible. To do this one must become as much like the Tao as possible. Since the Tao is not an individual, this means that the sage must become as little like an individual as possible. The actions of ordinary people are largely the product of their desires; accordingly, the fewer desires we have, the less like an individual and the more like the Tao we become. Hence the sage does not strive for any personal end (Lao Tzu, 1997, Chapter 7); diminishes personal desire to the greatest possible degree and so knows 'the contentment that comes simply through being content' (Chapter 46); and day by day subtracts from knowledge (since knowledge of things stimulates desire for them), so arriving at 'inactivity' (Chapter 48). The sage speaks very little, for words embody conceptual distinctions and so lead us further from the Tao (Chapters 17, 23, 56); desires nothing, and so has a mind which simply reflects what it encounters without desire – indeed, such a one may appear to those not seeking the Tao like a child or an idiot (Chapters 10, 20, 49). The further the sage progresses along the path of diminishing the force and role of the ego, the more closely **(s)he** approaches the Tao.

This reference to female sages is not simply an empty politically correct gesture. There is a tradition of female Taoist adepts as ancient as Taoism itself. See Cleary, 1989.

The date of composition of *The Art of War* has been debated for (literally) centuries. Modern scholarship favours a date during the Warring States period of Chinese history, that is 403–221 BCE.

Since the true sage has no desires, whatever such a person does will have no motive and so is not action in the normal sense of the word but *wu-wei*, the purely spontaneous manifestation of the Tao. (These ideas, it must be stressed, penetrated very widely in Chinese thought, even to the at first sight unlikely area of the theory of warfare. Actionless activity is a property of the ideal commander, for example in Sun Tzu's well-known ***The Art of War*** or *Sun-tzu ping fa* – see Sun Tzu, 1998, especially Chapter 6. There is absolutely no analogue to this dimension of Sun Tzu's thought in the European work with which *The Art of War* is regularly compared, Karl von Clausewitz's *On*

War (*Vom Kriege*), first published in 1832 and entirely secular in its approach.)

Let us now draw together the threads from this brief survey of some important eastern belief systems. What I hope is quite clear is that here are three systems which have a very important belief in common, namely that in order to achieve the highest goal in life (*moksha*, *nirvana* or sagehood) we must surrender what we ordinarily take to be the core of our individuality. Moreover, attachment to individuality, especially in the form of our desires and the purposes to which they give rise – let alone the reinforcement of individuality by the strengthening or multiplication of desires – is the major obstacle to what in the west is called salvation. Salvation, in these systems, does not involve in any meaningful sense the continued existence of the everyday ego, of what Europeans call the person in question. What occurs in the state of final release in all these systems is absolute freedom from desire for anything. The minds of those who attain this state are (to repeat) like mirrors, reflecting what is before them entirely without possessive inclination. Such persons are not inert, however. It is agreed in all accounts of this state that it brings perfect serenity and a total and permanent freedom from fear, including fear of death. It also brings endless compassion for suffering in all its forms: those who have obtained release know what to do to relieve suffering in any situation and this is what they do. Such deeds as they perform, however, cannot properly be called actions, since actions are attributes of separate selves and it is merely an abuse of the term to say that these persons are selves. Theirs is *wu-wei*, or actionless activity: it is absolutely spontaneous, like a reflex, and always entirely appropriate to the situation. In these nirvanic systems, then, ordinary selfhood is disvalued and the goal of all spiritual disciplines is to overcome it. I shall for short call systems of thought which conceive of the ultimate goal of existence in this way nirvanic systems, and the values which they advocate nirvanic values.

My contention is that nirvanic values lie behind many features of eastern civilizations, while the contrary values, which I shall call individualistic, lie behind and explain much that is European. In the west people take for granted the absolute finality and reality of the distinction between the individual and the rest of what there is. They are regarded as irreducibly distinct, and individuality is seen as worth preserving – it is *ipso facto* taken to be of value. What makes many features of eastern civilizations so hard for westerners to understand is that they are not based on these assumptions. Rather, they assume that ultimately all distinctions are an appearance, including that between the self and the rest of what there is. If you begin from this very different point of view and develop it both rationally and thoroughly (which is what has happened in these civilizations), then many values, attitudes, beliefs and institutions – logically dependent on nirvanic values – will be different from those in the west. I shall try to show this by looking at some more concrete aspects of both traditions, beginning with attitudes of the self or individual in relation to the rest of what there is.

EXERCISE _____

1   Sum up in your own words what is common to the states of *moksha*, enlightenment and achieving sagehood.

2   What is *nirvana*?

3   What is the principal contrast between nirvanic and individualistic systems of thought?

DISCUSSION _____

1   All these states involve the dissipation of what is normally called our self. Those who attain these states are free from desire. Their minds become mirrors, just reflecting whatever crosses them. Such persons are absolutely tranquil and free from fear.

2   *Nirvana* is the state in which the everyday self is completely extinguished.

3   In a nirvanic system the goal of life is to arrive at a state of being free from all desires. The way to do this is to dissipate the everyday self, which is held in the final analysis to be unreal. By contrast, in an individualistic system the everyday self is held to be ultimately real and of value; hence the satisfaction of its desires is regarded as a legitimate activity.

_____

Self and world

It may seem that the highly abstract philosophical considerations set out above have very little bearing on the way civilizations develop on a practical level: no doubt the descriptions of the spiritual Himalayas set out in these writings are fine as ultimate ideals, but what influence can they have on the way we do things just getting about in the world? The answer is that in fact they have the most direct and dramatic impact on practical matters. It is a mistake to assume that philosophical abstractions have no practical import: on the contrary, they give our whole mode of being its basic orientation and consequently, in a certain sense, set the direction of history, though they do not determine its details. Take the western assumption that self and world are really and irreducibly distinct. There is ourself, and a world of other selves, animate beings and objects. There is, as we say, an **environment**, and it is part of the very concept of an environment that it is something distinct from us, something in which we find ourselves. Further, when something is distinct from us there is *prima facie* no reason not to modify it to suit our own purposes. This is what westerners have being doing throughout their history in a way in which eastern civilizations have not sought to do, though westerners are presently beginning to see that this manipulation of the rest of the world solely in their own interests might not ultimately be sustainable. Again, if we take individual objects to be irreducibly real and different, and we wish to use or modify them to suit the purposes of individuals that are taken to be real and of value, then it is natural to seek to know and describe them as exactly as we can. It is this spirit which lies behind the goal of absolute objectivity of understanding which characterizes western science, probably the most successful of human intellectual enterprises to date. Western science presupposes the dualist outlook. Moreover, it was soon discovered that the pursuit of objectivity brought with it incremental knowledge: one discovery caused new questions to be posed and new answers to be found, and so on. Westerners' understanding of and ability to manipulate the world around them turned out to be progressive. Unsurprisingly, progress itself soon came to be valued: change was accepted in the west as part and parcel of progress and generally has been accepted as a good. (I do not mean to imply that science proceeds simply by accumulating true statements: the matter is much more complex than that. Progress consists rather in working out ever more inclusive explanatory models.)

On the downside, the assumption that the universe is irreducibly separate from us can also, in certain circumstances, produce a feeling of alienation, of being alone in a universe which is simply indifferent to us. This is a feeling common enough in western art, as this example, from the poet A. E. Housman (1859–1936), demonstrates:

It is worth noting that there is no concept equivalent to an environment in Sanskrit, for example, because those who used Sanskrit did not conceive of themselves as distinct from the rest of what there is in the way that westerners do.

> The laws of God, the laws of man,
>
> He may keep that will and can;
>
> Not I: let God and man decree
>
> Laws for themselves and not for me;
>
> And if my ways are not as theirs
>
> Let them mind their own affairs ...
>
> I, a stranger and afraid
>
> In a world I never made.
>
> (*Last Poems,* **XII**, in Housman, 1939, p. 79)

241

The feelings of fear and of the sheer apartness of the individual from what there is, so sharply expressed by Housman, especially in the last two lines quoted, could not occur to an artist or thinker whose beliefs are those of a nirvanic system, for the simple reason that to such a person the universe is *not*, and indeed cannot be, separate from them. In a nirvanic system, since the ultimate reality and the spiritual core of the individual are non-different, human beings must feel themselves, in the last analysis, at one with everything, just more at home in the universe. A couple of examples (Chinese this time) will have to do as evidence. The first is from the poet Wang Shi-ji (fourth century CE). He has been contemplating nature and is in awe at its beauty, variety and order:

> Silent, bright, limitless the vision that remains!
>
> Transient in what I see, World-Order unfolds Itself.
>
> How great is what It does, maker and changer
>
> Of differences many and many, accordant in their arrangements!
>
> Innumerable Its pipes, and though so various
>
> Are ever well met, ever part of us.
>
> (Quoted in Carrithers et al., 1985, p. 163)

Notice that Wang is saying in so many words that the 'World-Order' is *part of us*: he conceives of himself as literally non-different from all there is, when this relationship is properly understood. Similarly, some 700 years later, here is an important philosopher, Chang Tsai (1020–77):

> Heaven is my father and Earth is my mother, and even such a small creature as I finds an intimate place in their midst.
>
> Therefore that which fills the universe I regard as my body and that which directs the universe I consider as my nature.
>
> All people are my brothers and sisters, and all things are my companions.
>
> The great ruler (the emperor) is the eldest son of my parents (Heaven and Earth), and the great ministers are his stewards. Respect the aged – this is the way to treat them as elders should be treated. Show deep love toward the orphaned and the weak – this is the way to treat them as the young should be treated. The sage identifies his character with that of Heaven and Earth.
>
> (Chang Tsai, 'Western inscription' (*Hsi Ming*), in Chan Wing-tsit, 1963, p. 497)

As in Wang's poem, so in this philosophical essay the underlying thought is manifestly that of the ultimate unity of all there is. Many more examples of this thought occur throughout the literature of cultures founded on nirvanic values.

One example of continuity that is of special interest is the Chinese examination system. Throughout most of China's long history, the key to success in life for any man (women had an inferior role) was to enter the civil service by passing the entrance examinations. Their difficulty was legendary, and some men grew old in the attempt to pass them. The examination system was initiated in the Sui dynasty, in 587 CE, and remained in place for over 1300 years, until 1904. The syllabus, astonishingly to westerners, remained much the same throughout, based on the rote memorization of seven classic texts, adding up to 431,286 Chinese characters, plus less detailed knowledge of appropriate commentaries. Education for these examinations began at the age of seven, with the initial memorizing stage taking six years, at 200 characters per day. Even reasonably close western analogues, such as the education of English gentlemen in Greek and Latin, pale in comparison with such a grinding workload and the durability of the system. For a short and accessible account, see Miyazaki, 1976.

If you take this view of the universe as seriously as the individualistic view, then first (to repeat), you will regard yourself as ultimately *at home* in the universe – you cannot be a stranger to something from which you are not even separate; and secondly, you are far less likely to regard the universe as something which is there merely for you to exploit. Westerners have often remarked on and been baffled by the failure of eastern cultures to develop empirical science and technology in a manner analogous to that of the west. For example, as the French writer and thinker Paul Valéry (1871–1945) once observed, the Chinese invented the compass, printing and gunpowder, but did not go on to exploit their discoveries as westerners tend to do: they used the gunpowder for fireworks, not cannon. The Chinese exhibited a moderation in their wishes and the use of their power over nature which to westerners appears inexplicable, for in the west the instinctive habit is to exploit the consequences of discoveries to the full, on every occasion and in every possible direction (see 'Orient et Occident', in Valéry [1945] 1988, pp. 148–9). The bafflement felt by westerners, to which Valéry referred, stems in part precisely from the attitude of respect for the universe that follows from the beliefs of non-dual systems. Moreover, this moderation can also manifest itself as the absence of a deep interest in progress or desire for **change**. One of the facts which staggered the first westerners to know China and Japan well enough to appreciate the fact was the sheer degree of stasis there had been in these civilizations prior to their contact with the west – which, together with certain other assumptions of cultural superiority, caused those travellers to come to the flattering conclusion that they were dealing with societies in need of a hefty dose of western updating.

EXERCISE

1 In a nirvanic system, typically how do individuals regard themselves as related to the rest of the order of things?

2 How does that contrast with the individualistic attitude?

DISCUSSION

1 They regard themselves as in the last analysis not separate from it: they conceive of the universe as a unity.

2 Individualists tend to regard the rest of what there is as ultimately separate from themselves. Since they regard the satisfaction of their desires as a legitimate goal, they are likely to regard the environment as legitimately modifiable to suit their own ends.

Some aspects of moral thinking

The moderation in the exploitation of the environment to which I have referred above is in effect a moral virtue, and it is to some of the features of moral thinking based on nirvanic and individualistic thinking that I wish to turn now, since here also, not at all unexpectedly, there are some characteristic differences. The first concerns the different emphases to be found in the notion of an individual.

The western concept of an individual involves one assumption which is in the present context centrally important, namely that individuality is potentially present to the same degree in all individuals. It is this assumption which lies behind the western belief that each individual is worthy of respect, *simply by virtue of being an individual.* That is, one does not have to be anything more than individual to merit respect. Western philosophers have not been slow to notice that this is so, and have incorporated the notion into their moral thought. Thus when the great philosopher **Immanuel Kant** (1724–1804) sought to find the one principle which (he believed) underlies all moral thought, he arrived at the conclusion that this governing principle is as follows: 'rational beings all stand under the law that each of them should treat himself and all others, never merely as a means, but always at the same time as an end in himself' (*Fundamental Principles of the Metaphysic of Morals*, in Kant [1785] 1948, p. 95). In other words, all individuals are equally valuable simply because they are individuals, and worthy of respect on that account alone.

Kant's definition of enlightenment is discussed in Chapter 2. Note that in the passage quoted there Kant exhorted human beings to use their own reason; in the quotation here he defined human beings as *rational* beings. Note also the radical difference between the concept of enlightenment developed in eighteenth-century Europe (examined in Chapter 2) as the *individual's* use of their own reason, and the eastern concept of enlightenment discussed in this chapter.

This assumption of the equal value of all individuals simply by virtue of being individuals has another characteristic consequence: it leads to a certain emphasis in moral thought on the notion of *rights*. Europe has been in the forefront of developing the concept of moral rights for many centuries, and in so doing the thinkers concerned have in effect been developing (and taking for granted the truth of) this idea of the individual as valuable *per se*. Western thinkers have developed not just the idea of rights within contracts (which are relatively easy to understand and specify) but also the much more problematic notion of *natural* rights, that is rights that pertain to all human individuals, and to some animals perhaps, simply by virtue of their being individuals. Hence the presence in European (and American) history of many works on what used to be called the 'rights of man' and are now called 'human rights': the right to freedom, free speech, life, liberty, the pursuit of happiness and so on. The habit of thought persists of course, as one can see (for example) in the European Union's penchant for drawing up charters of human rights, and in the fact that its supreme court is a court of human *rights*. This is not to say that the west has distinguished itself in inventing social systems which in practice treat all humans (let alone animals) as worthy of respect, but the theory is there nevertheless. It rests on the ultimately dualist assumptions that individuality is real and of value, and so should be safeguarded by means of moral rights and appropriate prohibitions.

When one turns to the corresponding notion of the individual in nirvanic systems there is, entirely rationally, a different emphasis. The core western property of being an individual (in the sense discussed above) is not qualitative: it is not a property you can have to a degree, or which you can develop. You simply are one, and you have the appropriate moral rights by virtue of that. Not so in nirvanic systems: here the core notion of individuality *is* qualitative, as I shall explain. It follows from the basic assertions of such systems that the goal of life for human beings is to bring yourself into as perfect an accord with ultimate reality as you can. Again, broadly speaking there is agreement on what it means to do this: you must by some means seek to shed as many of your personal desires and attachments as possible. *Nirvana* itself, as I have noted, is the condition (attainable to those determined enough) of being entirely non-possessive, and it is a non-reversible state: attaining enlightenment or *moksha* or sagehood is a permanent transformation of the psyche.

Accordingly, in the moral thinking associated with this outlook there tends to be a much greater stress on spiritual development. It follows that individuals tend to be assessed on how far they are along this path towards *nirvana*. Life should be a continuous striving for and evolution towards this goal: you are expected to try to develop in the direction of letting go of as much of your individuality as you can. Hence in nirvanic systems the moral marks are not awarded (as it were) just for being an individual, but for how far you manage to develop along the stated path – in other words, the notion of an individual is qualitative.

The means for doing this, which we cannot go into here, are the many yogas – including work – and meditational techniques and so forth on which there is now a great deal of available literature.

This basic outlook brings with it a characteristic focus in moral thought not on the concept of rights but on the concept of *duty*. One hears almost nothing of this at present in the west, where by far the most frequent kind of moral debate involves individuals claiming some sort of compensation for an alleged infringement of something they claim to be their right. In nirvanic systems, by contrast, the vast bulk of moral thought goes into the specification of duties. In order to see why, it is best to begin with one basic and simple fact about duties, namely that they are an *effort*. This is because they require us to put the demands of our ego second, after a demand or a need of someone or something else. The effect of fulfilling our duties is precisely to help us on the nirvanic path, because this is the path in which the whole everyday ego is put second, as it were, with the ultimate aim of dissipating it entirely. If what westerners call individuality is disvalued (as it is in nirvanic systems), then it is rational, in moral thinking, to focus on moral practices which will stultify rather than develop it.

I should add that both nirvanic and individualistic systems do allow that there can be rare individuals for whom the demands of duty and the promptings of inclination are truly identical: in both traditions they are called saints.

Further, there is a characteristic concern in nirvanic systems with the concept of harmony, such that the bringing about or safeguarding of this state is the aim that underlies much moral thought and legal practice. This notion is closely linked to certain features of the organization of society, as outlined below. In the present context, it is to be noted that the stress on this idea is closely coherent with the non-dual view that true self (post-enlightenment) and reality are identical. I have noted above several times that it follows from this premise that the goal of life is to bring oneself into as close an accord with reality as one can, and 'accord' (a musical metaphor) is just another way of referring to the same state as is denoted by the term 'harmony'. Moreover, in non-dual systems individuals tend to regard themselves as elements of a world whose final goal is an ultimate condition of unity in which all divisions will collapse. In the *samsaric* world, the closest analogue of this desired absolute unity is a state in which all elements coexist as harmoniously as possible, and so harmony is deeply valued.

This concern with ultimate harmony manifests itself in many ways. Let me take examples from Japanese thought and customs. Before Japan was opened to the west in the middle of the nineteenth century, there was in Japanese moral thought no concept corresponding to the western notion of a right, and consequently no word for it in the Japanese language. The reason is that in cases where one person has incurred an obligation to another it is considered improper of the person to whom the obligation is owed to demand its discharge, or (as westerners might say) to demand their rights. Instead, the obliged person who behaves correctly will fulfil the duty voluntarily and (this is important) with particular friendliness. Again, in the case of promises it is not central that the absolute letter of any undertaking should be obeyed (in Shakespeare's *The Merchant of Venice* Shylock's insistence on his pound of flesh and Portia's ingenious get-out clause would both have been considered grossly immoral forms of conduct in such a context), but it is critical to display an appropriate degree of kindness and friendship when discharging the obligation.

246

Figure 6.2 A recent Japanese stamp showing Prince Shōtoku, author of the Seventeen Article Constitution. Tokyo Central Post Office, Postal Service Agency

The goal behind these practices is the achievement of harmony, or *wa*, which was held to be more important than the precise fulfilment of obligations or the formulating of exact moral principles which can be unambiguously applied to the letter. This concern with harmony has been a persistent feature of the moral thought of Japan. It occurs in one of the founding documents of Japanese civilization, the *Seventeen Article Constitution* (*Jūshichijō Kempō*) of 604 CE, traditionally associated with Prince Shōtoku (574–622 CE), who was regent at the time when Japan was just beginning to coalesce into a single state and a figure of the first importance in Japanese cultural history. Article 1 (no less) of this document states that:

> Harmony (*wa*) is to be valued, and an avoidance of wanton opposition to be honoured ... when those above are harmonious and those below are friendly, and there is concord in the discussion of business, right views of things spontaneously gain acceptance. Then what is there which cannot be accomplished?

(Quoted in Aston, 1896, p. 128)

Figure 6.3 Two pages from a modern Japanese edition of the Seventeen Article Constitution of Prince Shōtoku, with headnotes and footnotes amplifying the original text (on the right) in Chinese, and a translation into classical Japanese on the left. Nihon Koteu Bungaku Zenshu/Shogakukan

Again, 1300 years or so later, in the 1930s, when the totalitarian government of Japan then in power sought to curb the (in its view) detestable rise of individualism, a notion which the Japanese had discovered only after the opening up to the west, part of its response was a document issued by the ministry of education (*Monbushō*) called the 'Grand principles of national polity' (*Kotukai no hongi*). What is of interest is the way in which the authors of this document summed up the values they were seeking to defend, the values which they regarded as constitutive of the Japaneseness they wished to preserve. (It is well worth trying to imagine what a European government would produce in like circumstances.)

> In individualism there can exist co-operation, compromise, self-sacrifice, and so on, in order to adjust and reduce contradictions and oppositions, but in the final analysis there exists no real harmony (*wa*) ... The *wa* of our country is not mechanical co-operation, beginning from reason, of equal individuals independent of each other, but the grand harmony (*taiwa*) which maintains its integrity by proper statuses of individuals within the collectivity and by acts in accordance with these statuses ... After all, oppositions of opinions, as well as differences of interests deriving from various standpoints, are integrated into a unity of grand harmony proper to Japan and originating from a common source. Not conflicts, but harmony is final.
>
> ('The status of the individual in the notion of law, right and social order', in Moore, 1968, p. 431)

A great deal of non-European moral thought is epitomized in this short passage. The only point I want to stress here is that this goal of moral harmony, so central in nirvanic systems, is a special case of one of the grand goals of these systems, the bringing of absolute harmony to the universe by the achievement of *nirvana* by all there is.

Sōseki is a major writer. He is rated by the Japanese much as we rate, for example, his older contemporary Thomas Hardy.

The reading below comes from a piece of twentieth-century Japanese literature that is well known in Japan, the essay 'My individualism', by **Natsume Sōseki** (1867–1916). It is an extract from a lecture delivered to students in November 1914. This essay was written roughly seventy-five years after Japan had been opened to the west and accordingly after three generations had had the chance to absorb western influences, among them the notion of the value of the individual as a central moral value. Many Japanese reacted to this idea much as the nationalist government did in the piece cited above – that is, with trepidation.

All such evils [the exploitation of others, described in the passage which precedes this extract] arise because people like that [people with power and money] are incapable of understanding ethical individualism. They try, instead, to aggrandize themselves at the expense of the general public, to use their power – be it financial or otherwise – to further their own selfish ends. Thus it is that individualism – the individualism I am describing here – in no way resembles the danger to the nation that ignorant people imagine it to be. As I see it, individualism advocates respecting the existence of others at the same time that one respects one's own existence. I find that a most worthy philosophy ...

I would like to add just another word to prevent any misunderstanding. Many people seem to think of individualism as something opposed to – even destructive of – nationalism. But individualism in no way justifies such a misguided, illogical interpretation ... Some people nowadays are spreading the idea – and they believe it – that Japan cannot survive unless she is entirely nationalistic. Many go so far as to assert that our nation will perish unless this terrible 'individualism' is stamped out. What utter nonsense! All of us, in fact, are nationalists *and* internationalists *and* individualists as well.

Freedom is the essential substance of individualism, which, in turn, forms the foundation of individual happiness. Each man's share of freedom, however, rises and falls like a thermometer in accordance with the relative security or insecurity of the nation. This is not so much an abstract theory as a generalization determined by the facts; it is the way things happen in the natural course of events. The individual's liberty contracts when the country is threatened and expands when the nation is at peace. No man of character is going to aim solely at the development of his individuality when the very survival of the nation is at stake. [It should be pointed out that Sōseki's audience was entirely male.] On the other hand, do be sure you see that the individualism I am talking about implies a warning against becoming the kind of fellow who insists on keeping his helmet on even after the fire is out, the man who wants to keep in lock-step when that is no longer necessary.

('My individualism' [1914], in Natsume Sōseki, 1992, pp. 309, 311–12)

EXERCISE _____

Even if this extract contained no references to Japan, granted the context given above you might still reasonably conclude that it is by an oriental writer of the period in question. What is the evidence in the text for this view?

DISCUSSION _____

The evidence for the eastern origin of this piece is, first, that the writer is speaking of individualism as something *new* and as something manifestly strange to his audience; and secondly, that he is having to defend it as neither wicked nor prejudicial to the safety of the nation. A major concern in the extract is to show that individualists can be good nationalists at the same time. It would not occur to a western writer to have to justify this notion, which would simply be taken for granted.

_____

Individual and society

One of the aspects of pre-westernized oriental societies which regularly surprises Europeans when they come across it for the first time is the extent to which individuals in these societies were expected to put their own interests second to those of some supra-personal group, often the family (as conceived of in the society in question), or less often but sometimes the state (again, as conceived of in the society in question). This frequently strikes Europeans as intolerably constrictive, but I hope by now it will be clear that this was often not the case for those concerned, since for them the pursuit of individual interest and the development of their own egos were not the fundamental goals they were seeking, while they usually were for those Europeans who voice the criticism. Although it would be simplistic to suggest that nirvanic values were the sole determining ground for this phenomenon (there are good political and pragmatic grounds for it too – it produced a social system that works and endures), there can be no doubt that the disvalue of individualism which is part of the nirvanic outlook does cohere with this emphasis perfectly. I shall give a few examples.

To the Chinese he is K'ung Fu-tzu, the Master K'ung.

I have not yet mentioned one of the crucial formative sources of Chinese civilization, namely the philosophy of the thinker we refer to by the Latinized form of his name, **Confucius** (c. 551–479 BCE). This is because classical Confucianism is not a nirvanic system, but – in the form in which Confucius himself conceived it at any rate – a thoroughly practical system of moral recommendations without a developed metaphysical basis. However, Confucianism in all its forms includes the emphasis on duties already noted as characteristic of a morality based on nirvanic values, and the Chinese have had no real difficulty in blending it with Taoism and Buddhism to produce a uniquely Chinese outlook. The goal of a Confucian is to become a *chŭn tzu*, a term perhaps surprisingly but not inaptly rendered in English as 'gentleman'. Central among the qualities a gentleman had to exhibit are filial piety, or *hsiao* (the more up-to-date phrase 'respect for parents' means much the same) and respect for elder brothers, or *t'i*. Respect for parents meant so conducting oneself as never to cause them anxiety. It did not mean that their views could not be questioned, though it did entail ultimate submission if they were unwilling to change their views (see Confucius, 1997, I.2, 11; II.5–8; IV.18).

The upshot of the practical application of this philosophy, which rapidly attained canonic status in China and retained it until Marxism became the country's official form of belief, is that a Chinese would have regarded him or herself not primarily as an individual in the western sense but as someone's son or younger or elder brother, or wife or daughter. In all these roles there would be duties prescribed and modes of conduct specified. A Chinese was principally a member of a family, and expected to put family first. The individual existed for the good of the family, not the other way round.

The non-development of the concept of moral rights in classical China (and Japan, to a large extent) had a marked impact on the way that legal systems developed. There was no real separation of legal and moral codes: morality specified the norms of conduct and the law punished their violation. The law evolved over a considerable period, from early Han times (206 BCE–8 CE) onwards, but the code which came to form the basis of Chinese law for the longest part of the country's history was written down in the time of the T'ang dynasty (618–905 CE). 'The T'ang Code with annotations' (*T'ang-lŭ su-i*) was completed in 653 CE and contains 502 articles, each divided into a dozen parts and accompanied by annotations. It is (so far as I know) unique among the world's legal systems in making filial impiety (*pu-hsiao*, or inappropriate behaviour by children towards their parents) a punishable crime. Indeed, this is listed at the start of the work as one of the 'ten abominations' (the most serious crimes), together with offences such as sedition, treason, murder and incest (Article 7, in Johnson, vol. 1, pp. 74ff). For example, so long as the parents were living it was illegal for sons, including married sons, to set up separate households (Article 155, in Johnson, vol. 2, pp. 129–30). The head of the family, in law, was owed unquestioning obedience.

Confucius' work is known in English by the unusual term 'analects' ('gleanings'), the name given to one of the first authoritative translations of the text which has just stuck. It is not a direct translation of the Chinese title, *Lun yŭ*, which means 'selected conversations' and is mirrored more closely in the usual French title for this text, *Entretiens*, the German *Gespräche* and the Italian *Dialoghi*. Like Socrates, Confucius wrote nothing down himself. The *Analects* consists of records of his remarks, written down by his followers, in all probability some time after his death.

Mānavadharmasāstra. The term 'laws' in the standard English version of the title is somewhat misleading, largely because there is no one concept in English which approximates to the key Sanskrit term *dharma*. (This conceptual incommensurability is not peculiar to English. For example, the Spanish title, *Las Leyes de Manú*, is misleading for the same reason.) It covers aspects of a number of areas separately conceptualized in the west, notably truth (including religious truth), law, duty and morality. A *dharma* is no less than a complete view of the nature of human life, including its place in the cosmos and its proper goals, and so naturally covers all these areas. A *sāstra* is an interpretative commentary. Accordingly, a *dharmasāstra* is an annotated statement of a view of what human life is and how it ought to be conducted, and this is precisely what *The Laws of Manu* is. The date of the work is disputed by scholars, who have variously put it at between 1250 and 500 BCE. Manu is a mythical figure, the first human being (the Indian Adam, as it were), and the work was almost certainly composed by a number of Brahmins, or members of the priestly caste.

There is a somewhat similar stress on family concerns as the fundamental locus of interests in classical Hindu society, where there is also a clear and direct link to the nirvanic system of values underlying the social order. As described at the opening of this chapter, in classical Hindu philosophy and religion derived from the *Upanishads* human nature is a blend of the biological and the spiritual: each human being has within them (so to speak) a share of the undivided and eternal reality – indeed, since *atman* and *Brahman* are the same, each individual is identical with reality. The whole scheme of Hindu society is designed to provide a way of conducting human temporal existence such that each person may find as much time as possible to attend to the needs of their real (that is eternal) self, or *atman*. The aim is to make the temporal aspect of existence as automatic as possible, to allow maximum time for the pilgrimage towards *moksha* or salvation. It is this belief which underpins all the well-known institutions of Hindu society. If each member of a family fulfils the expected obligations of their role as specified by custom and morality, a stable system will result. As one commentator has put it, the Hindu family system 'dispensed with the need for orphanages, poor houses, old-age pensions and life insurance' (Chand, 1968, p. 413).

The way in which individuals, families and castes should conduct themselves is specified in great detail in a number of Hindu works, of which the best known in Europe is **The Laws of Manu**. In this hugely influential work, every stage and occupation of life then known is described and rules for its proper conduct specified, including the conduct appropriate to members of all castes (the caste system is justified, like everything else, as a means to the desired automatism of the non-eternal aspects of life). Most striking in this context is the vision of life as a pilgrimage whose goal is *moksha*, and which has four definite stages (*āsramas*): studentship and celibacy; marriage and householding; seclusion and withdrawal; and renunciation and world welfare. Each stage has equal value, and each must be performed properly if final release or perfection is to be attained. There can be no doubt that the result is a society and way of life where functions are specialized and behaviour specified in ways which place strict limitations on individual freedom, particularly in respect of an effectively unalterable conformity to the rule of the caste (*jāti-dharma*). What is presupposed is that the surface individual, the *jiva*, ought to be constrained for the sake of the greater good of final liberation.

What most often strikes western readers of this work when they meet it for the first time is the (to them) minute and constricting detail in which appropriate conduct is specified. Here is one example from hundreds, on how a householder should treat a guest:

A guest who comes with the setting sun in the evening should not be turned away by the householder who is a sacrificer; whether he arrives at a convenient time or an inconvenient time, he should not be allowed to stay in his house without eating. (The householder) should not himself eat anything he does not feed to his guest. The revering of guests wins wealth, a good reputation, long life, and heaven. He should present the best seat and room, the best bed, the best farewell and the best service to guests of the highest status, inferior ones to those of inferior status, and middling ones to those whose status is the same as his. And if another guest should come after the ritual to the All-gods is finished, he should give him, too, whatever food he can, but he should not distribute the propitiatory offering (again).

(*The Laws of Manu*, 1991, Chapter 3, stanzas 105–8)

In this volume, all aspects of life are specified with equal precision.

However, the immense detail of this work (it is over 300 pages long in its English versions) should not obscure the basic fact that what we have here is a most striking example of a model for the conduct of an entire life, and the organization of an entire society, where all the rules, practices and institutions are explicitly designed to serve the ultimate goal of spiritual release for all concerned. (I do not wish to imply, any more than with western notions of equality and rights, that the practice always lived up to the theory: it is the *ideals* of the society concerned that matter here.)

EXERCISE

Which feature of the classical organization of eastern societies most strikes European observers when first they encounter it?

DISCUSSION

What strikes the westerner is the extent to which social roles and mores are specified: members of these societies have prescribed for them, far more precisely than is generally the case in the west, powers, duties and responsibilities associated with a particular social role (as father, mother, son, daughter, younger or older brother, priest, warrior, servant, and so on) from which they are not expected to depart and with which they are expected to be content.

Note also that it is not safe to assume that this has necessarily been felt to be oppressive by members of these societies – that would follow only if their goal was the pursuit of European-style individualism.

A few remarks about the arts

काव्यस्यात्मा ध्वनिरिति बुधैर्यैः समाम्नातपूर्व−
स्तस्याभावं जगदुरपरे भाक्तमाहुस्तमन्ये ।
केचिद्वाचां स्थितमविषये तत्त्वमूचुस्तदीयं
तेन ब्रूमः सहृदयमनःप्रीतये तत्स्वरूपम् ॥ १ ॥

Though the learned men of yore have declared time and again that the soul of poetry is suggestion, some would aver its non−existence, some would regard it as something (logically) implied and some others would speak of its essence as lying beyond the scope of words. We propose, therefore, to explain its nature and bring delight to the hearts of perceptive critics.1

Figure 6.4 The opening of the *Dhvanyaloka* or *Light of Suggestion*, a classic work of Sanskrit aesthetics by Anandavardhana, ninth century CE. Edited by Dr K. Krishnamoorthy, Karnatak University, Dhawwar, 1974

It has been shown above that if the ultimate presuppositions of a culture are nirvanic rather than individualistic this will lead to some profound and systematic differences in beliefs, values and attitudes – differences which manifest themselves in all the most important phenomena of the culture concerned. It is to be expected that the arts will also be affected by this divergence, and this is precisely what happens. The ultimate values of any culture, embodied in its religion, moral beliefs and other important institutions, will not only furnish subjects for the arts (as demonstrated in the two poems compared in the section 'Self and world', above), but will permeate the approach artists have to art – that is their beliefs as to what art is and what its functions might be. There is of course not space here to do more than give one or two hints of the far-reaching effects of nirvanic presuppositions in this area, so I shall take just a few examples from Japanese culture to indicate what I have in mind.

This word can also be romanized in the form *noh*.

You have probably heard of the uniquely Japanese form of drama called *nō,* a highly stylized form of play using deliberately anti-naturalistic conventions. All parts are played by male actors using masks and there is virtually no scenery, with what there is symbolic and suggestive rather than realistic. The language used is (and always was) remote from everyday Japanese (as remote, for example, as rhyming couplets are from ordinary spoken English) and is often chanted rather than spoken. The gestures of the actors are also highly stylized, almost ritualized, having as much in common with dance as with any movement one is likely to perform in real life. Not all forms of Japanese drama are like this, and the artists who developed it clearly had a special goal in mind when they did so. What they wished to do was to develop an art form which furnished for its audience an experience that took them out of the world of humdrum human affairs (hence the anti-realism of its conventions), but what they were aiming at is not what we would call escapism – no

Japanese goes to see a *nō* play with this expectation. What is being aimed at is no less than the bringing about of an experience which is as close to nirvanic self-dissolution as can be achieved. This is made explicit in the writings of the man who perfected the art form, Zeami Motokiyo (1363–1443).

Zeami wrote down his reflections on the *nō* in a number of treatises intended for his family (who also made up his acting troupe). He was one of the many Japanese artists profoundly influenced by the form of Buddhism which the Japanese made peculiarly their own, namely **Zen**. Zen involves a number of paradigmatically non-dual beliefs, beginning from the basic assertion that behind the everyday world of human experience, which is ultimately only an appearance, there is an unconditioned reality which is its ground and origin, indicated in Japanese by the term *mu*, or nothingness. This has somewhat misleading connotations in English, since what is indicated by *mu* is not an absolute nothing but rather a somewhat that is absolutely undifferentiated and to which in consequence no descriptions whatsoever apply. To become enlightened as a result of Zen techniques, to experience what is called *satori*, is to come into direct contact with this nothingness. It is quite clear from the way in which Zeami wrote that the goal of the *nō* is nothing less than to bring us as close to this extraordinary experience as possible. When a play or a performance or an actor does this they have the quality Zeami called (untranslatably) *yūgen*. Both the syllables making up this word have similar meanings of dimness, darkness, obscurity or shadowiness. What Zeami meant is that a play (etc.) which has *yūgen* reveals to us a glimpse of the ultimate mystery, an experience whose depth is ordinarily hidden from us by the static or interference that is part of the activity of the surface ego. It is an experience whose depth has no limit. It is interesting to compare this with the most famous of all western accounts of what drama can do for us, namely Aristotle's description of the nature and function of Greek tragedy (another dramatic form using non-realist conventions) in his *Poetics*. Aristotle's answer to the question of why his contemporaries put themselves through the experience of watching tragedies was that this is emotionally beneficial, in that it accomplishes what he called a *katharsis* or purgation of the emotions of pity and fear. We emerge from the experience of tragedy, he claimed, freed from the turmoil and inner upheaval caused by these feelings, and so in a state of inner balance or quietude; but there is no suggestion that we might encounter a hidden ultimate. (You might like to bear this is mind when thinking about the *Agamemnon* of Aeschylus, considered in Chapter 7 by Lorna Hardwick.)

Zen came ultimately from India and was greatly developed by the Chinese as Buddhism spread eastwards: the word Zen is the Japanese way of saying the Chinese *ch'an*, an abbreviation of *ch'an-na*, itself a phonetic transcription into Chinese of the Sanskrit *dhyana*. All these terms mean 'meditation'.

Exactly the same ideas underlie Zeami's use of another of his terms of aesthetic praise, *myosho*. This is sometimes rendered in English as 'peerless charm', but this term tells the innocent reader about as much of what Zeami meant as would translating *yūgen* as 'grace' (as is sometimes done). In his treatise 'Finding gems and gaining the flower' (*Shūgyoku tokka*) Zeami stated, '*Myosho* surpasses verbal expression and lies in the pure realm that lies beyond the workings of consciousness' (Zeami, 1984, p. 132). A consummate actor can

> astonish the heart and senses of the spectators; and in that instant when they are moved without taking cognizance of their reactions, the Flower of Peerless Charm can be said to exist. Such a moment represents Fascination and includes within itself as well the moment of a Feeling that Transcends Cognition. All three of these expressions represent emotional states that transcend the workings of the conscious mind.
>
> (Zeami, 1984, p. 134)

Though he was trying to describe an experience at the very limits of the linguistically describable, Zeami added the following:

> In a state that transcends consciousness, why is it that we can feel a sense of Fascination? It may indeed represent the fundamental quality that is Changeless, never directly visible in any exterior manifestation ... Such matters must be grasped on a more profound level. A smile crosses the face without cognition through the coming of a deep sense of joy.
>
> (Zeami, 1984, p. 134)

The last sentence refers to an incident in the life of the Buddha that is held to be the start of the Zen tradition. According to this, only one of the Buddha's disciples, Kasyapa, understood the Buddha's teaching intuitively, directly and non-verbally, in a manner to which Buddhists refer as direct mind-to-mind transmission. At the moment of having this extraordinary experience Kasyapa smiled, and the Buddha knew at once that he had become enlightened. Zen teaching has been passed on in this way ever since. The point to fasten on here is the non-separation of the aesthetic domain from the main nirvanic concern of the pursuit of enlightenment: recall that Zeami was describing the aim which lies behind *both acting and watching a play*. It is worth pausing to ask how many European dramatists, however exalted their aims, have had quite such a target in mind.

The same non-divorce of the aesthetic from the ultimate goal of life is reflected, as one might expect, in other ways too in Japanese thought. I noted above that Zeami's key terms of aesthetic praise (of which *yūgen* and *myosho* are but two instances) have no real equivalents in English, or indeed in other European languages, and the same is true of other key concepts used by the Japanese in their thought about the arts. Another example is the term *sabi*, for which again there is no word in European languages. *Sabi* is a state which a work of art or a natural scene or event can induce in us, and is a form of aesthetic experience that is highly valued. It means all the following: it is a sense of the transitoriness of all things tinged always with sadness and melancholy; it is felt in solitude; it includes a sense of spontaneity, of all things occurring without relation to others; it is a sense of deep, illimitable quietude; it is more readily felt when we are older, when it comes without being sought. *Sabi* has to do with a particular atmosphere, arising from a scene that need not involve a human being, and this atmosphere occurs when something fulfils its destiny in the vast expanse of the universe. To see a creature experiencing its fundamental destiny of transience gives rise to *sabi*. *Sabi* is not equivalent to the English concept of loneliness, which has connotations of inward drabness or unhappiness; rather it is a state of being alone in which we are not lonely, but in which we and all things interpenetrate. Hence *sabi* can be said to have to do with the merging of the temporal and the eternal, the mutable and the immutable. *Sabi* is akin to seeing the infinite and eternal (or *mu*) in the here and now, and so is akin to *satori*. *Sabi* involves the belief that one attains perfect spiritual serenity by immersing oneself in the ego-less life of nature.

It should be quite clear by now why *sabi* has no counterpart in European thought and languages and is untranslatable: s*abi* is a concept which presupposes *nirvana* as the final goal of aesthetic experience, something that is ultimately not to be differentiated from religious experience, and is just one of a whole framework of concepts that occur in thinking about art only in nirvanic systems. It follows that in a nirvanic system to be an artist it is not sufficient to be technically proficient, nor even to have great imaginative powers: it is necessary also to have some insight into nirvanic states, or in other words to be a spiritual adept. How else can you hope to bring your audience closer to such states? In nirvanic systems, art is a means to salvation: this is a point of view which has occurred only rarely in the aesthetics of Europe (see Wilkinson, 2001).

The main point is that, as in other cases, where human beings have adopted nirvanic values every important aspect of their culture is affected and generally ends up looking very different from those of the west which are derived ultimately from individualistic values.

EXERCISE

In general terms, what is the function of art in a nirvanic system?

DISCUSSION _____

Its function is to bring about an experience as close to that of nirvanic dissolution of the self as is possible. Such art is as remote as can be from a pleasing diversion from or interlude in the main business of life. By contrast, it is another means to the same goal.

_____

Summary, qualifications and conclusions

The argument of this chapter has been as follows. There is a major difference in the world views which, as a matter of history, have underlain the approach to human experience and to the rest of the universe that is characteristic of Europe and European-derived civilizations on the one hand, and of the major civilizations of the east on the other. Unlikely as it may at first seem, the extremely abstract differences I have tried to sum up, which characterize the dominant western metaphysic of dualism and the frequently recurring eastern metaphysic of non-dualism, have been important shaping factors in practical areas of culture, as well as in (for example) the area of religious belief, where such effects would be more readily expected.

The area of divergence which is of most importance concerns the contrasting beliefs about the nature and value of individuality in the dualist and non-dualist outlooks. This affects beliefs about individuality in all its senses, from the abstract issue of principles of individuation applicable to any sort of entity at all, to the type of individuality that concerns humans most centrally, namely our sense of our own individuality and its value. The key single difference is that in the dualist outlook human individuality is regarded as real and of value, whereas in the non-dual outlook it is regarded as ultimately unreal and in the last analysis as something to be overcome.

When there is difference at so profound a level of thought as this, it is to be expected that its effects will be felt throughout the cultures affected – and this is precisely what occurs. It occurs because one of the most important manifestations of human rationality is the capacity to identify and follow through the implications of one's basic ideas. Since both types of culture have done this with considerable thoroughness, it follows that rationality is a transcultural phenomenon. The extent to which it is possible to debate rationally about the first principles of the dualist and non-dualist philosophies is a deep philosophical issue which cannot be gone into here.

I hope it is also clear that I have been concerned throughout this chapter with the logical framework of the beliefs of the cultures concerned: that is with their basic assumptions and ideals, not with their practice. History shows that members of cultures based on non-dual ideals have not conducted themselves in general any better than have westerners brought up in the religion of a loving god: both types of civilization have vied for the title of the most ruthless and bloody sector of humankind. Easterners and westerners have pretty well equally distinguished themselves, within their own cultures and in contacts with each other, by their tendency to display the whole catalogue of human vices. The tendency to moral backsliding is also transcultural. However, that does not invalidate the basic point that these ideals are present, do differ, and do lie behind many of the differences between these two types of culture.

The most significant of these differences have been sketched above. In Europe salvation has been conceived of as the salvation of individuals, but in non-dual cultures it has not: salvation is nirvanic; it consists in the elimination of individuality in any sense that a European would naturally understand the term. This leads to a different sense of the individual's place in the universe. The European belief in the real separateness of individual and universe does not logically entail the assumption that the exploitation of the universe (or environment, if you prefer) is legitimate, but it certainly helps to remove any scruples concerning it that might come to mind. Again, it is manifestly logically coherent with the ideal of objective knowledge, which lies behind the west's scientific method and technology, much of its philosophy, and the thirst for and belief in the value of progress. In a non-dual system, however, individual and universe are alike *samsaric* manifestations of an ultimate from which they are non-different. Accordingly, with such a system it is difficult to feel as alien and lost in the cosmos as has sometimes occurred in the west, and one is far more likely to be moderate in one's manipulation of the rest of what there is. Again, the progress which comes as a result of western science gives rise to the assumption that such change is not only natural but desirable, and that stasis equals stagnation. It is no accident that, in comparison with the social systems of the east, those of the west have exhibited much more by way of change over historical time, at least prior to the westernization of the former.

In moral and legal thought, though the contrast is not absolute, the basic difference manifests itself in European thought in a highly developed theory of individual rights, while in the east the dominant focus of moral thought has always been duty, for reasons explained above. It will no doubt be objected that this is to write as if the semitic religions involve no emphasis on duties, which is manifestly false. Indeed, to take only one example, the words of Jesus of Nazareth as recorded in the gospels are very frequently statements of duties enjoining altruism, of a kind where there are plenty of eastern parallels.

All this is true, and important; but the fact remains that the final ideals of orthodox, exoteric Christianity as developed over time (developed in no small degree by being blended with dualistic Aristotelian logic) are not non-dual, and indeed those (like the **Gnostics**) whose beliefs approached non-dual ideals were branded heretics. As I said above, salvation in the west is conceived of as salvation of the individual. The performance of duties improves individuals, rendering them fit for salvation, but such salvation does not *annihilate* individuality. The aim is not *nirvana*.

It has also been shown how the stress on self-abnegating duties, and the view of life as having a nirvanic goal towards which one should progress, affects the whole structure of society and can shape family relations, other major aspects of social structure and legal practice. Once again, it is characteristic of non-dual beliefs to lead to a conception of the arts which links them directly to the achievement of nirvanic goals, and this has led to some distinctions of an important kind between the two cultures in the way in which artists conceive of the role of art in society.

There are other areas of difference for which there is not space here. For example, beliefs about the nature and role of the state tend to differ in dual and non-dual systems, and there are interesting and complex variations in the area of conceptual elaboration as manifested in language. These differences, like those glanced at above, are of a kind that philosophers call systematic: that is they do not arise from serendipity or whim or individual genius, but are the result of the process of a rational drawing out of the consequences of a basic position.

The difference between the dualist and non-dual outlooks is as basic a contrast in human thought as has yet occurred. Indeed to date it is the most fundamental area in which sectors of the human race have taken a divergent view and it is extremely interesting that it should have coincided, broadly, with the division between east and west. So deep is this difference that it is no wonder that east and west should have felt baffled by the beliefs and customs of the 'other' when finally they met. Beliefs, even of the most fundamental kind, are an important aspect of what constitutes our sense of what and who we are: indeed, if someone undergoes sufficient changes to their beliefs and consequently their modes of behaviour, we often describe the change, tellingly, by saying that they have become *a different person*. My central contention is that the view I have called dualism is and has

Gnosticism, from the Greek *gnosis*, or knowledge, was a form of esoteric Christianity which flourished briefly in the fourth century CE before being outlawed as a heresy. The Gnostics claimed to have knowledge of spiritual truths of a mystical kind, some of which contradicted orthodox belief.

been dominant in Europe throughout its history, reflected in its beliefs, customs and the conceptual formations embodied in its languages. It has shaped and continues to shape Europeans' most fundamental attitudes to the environment, to each other and to other cultures.

Without doubt, the assumptions of dualism and individualism have formed and continue to form the bedrock of the European outlook on human life. Once such assumptions are made, rational animals can proceed only in certain directions and not others: limits and tendencies are set to the way in which human beings can consistently conceive of themselves and the universe, with appropriate suggestions as to attitudes and values. It is not the case that making these assumptions determined the course of European history in detail, any more than making nirvanic assumptions determined the history of the relevant eastern civilizations in detail; but, at a deep level, making these assumptions does set a direction and does limit possibilities. The track has been laid, as it were, and the train has perforce to go along it, even if no one can say how far along it will go, or how fast. European culture, predominantly individualistic, scientific and progressive, would be unimaginably different had it been based on nirvanic assumptions.

References

Aston, W. G. (1896) *Nihongi: Chronicles of Japan*, London, Allen & Unwin.

Carrithers, M., Collins, S. and Lukes, S. (eds) (1985) *The Category of the Person*, Cambridge, Cambridge University Press.

Chan Wing-tsit (ed.) (1963) *A Source Book in Chinese Philosophy*, Princeton, NJ, Princeton University Press.

Chand, T. (1968) 'The individual in the legal and political thought and institutions of India', in C. A. Moore (ed.), *The Status of the Individual in East and West*, Honolulu, HI, University of Hawaii Press.

Clausewitz, K. von [1832] (1998) *On War*, ed. and intro. L. Willmot, Ware, Wordsworth.

Cleary, T. (ed. and transl.) (1989) *Immortal Sisters: Secrets of Taoist Women*, Boston, MA, Shambhala.

Confucius (1997) *The Analects*, transl. A. Waley, intro. R. Wilkinson, Ware, Wordsworth.

Housman, A. E. (1939) *Collected Poems*, London, Cape.

Johnson, W. (ed. and transl.) (1979, 1997) *The T'ang Code*, 2 vols., Princeton, NJ, Princeton University Press.

Kant, I. [1785] (1948) *The Moral Law*, transl. H. J. Paton, London, Hutchison.

Lao Tzu (1997) *Tao te ching*, transl. A. Waley, intro. R. Wilkinson, Ware, Wordsworth.

The Laws of Manu (1991) transl. W. Doniger and B. K. Smith, Harmondsworth, Penguin.

Majjhima Nikaya (1888) vol. 3, ed. and transl. V. Trencker and R. Chalmers, Oxford, Pali Text Society (the standard edition of Pali language Buddhist *suttas*).

Miyazaki, Ichisada (1976) *China's Examination Hell*, New York/Tokyo, Weatherhill.

Moore, C. A. (ed.) (1968) *The Status of the Individual in East and West*, Honolulu, HI, University of Hawaii Press.

Natsume Sōseki (1992) *Kokoro (a Novel) and Selected Essays*, transl. E. McClellan and J. Rubin, Lanham, NJ, Madison.

Radhakrishnan, S. (ed. and transl.) (1953) *The Principal Upanisads*, London, Allen & Unwin.

Sun Tzu (1998) *The Art of War* [*with The Book of Lord Shang*], transl. Yuan Shibing, intro. R. Wilkinson, Ware, Wordsworth.

Valéry, P. [1945] (1988) *Regards sur le monde actuel*, Paris, Gallimard.

Wilkinson, R. (2001) 'Aesthetic virtues in the context of nirvanic values', in G. Marchianò and R. Milani (eds), *Frontiers of Transculturality in Aesthetics*, Milan, Treuben.

Zeami Motokiyo (1984) *On the Art of the Nō Drama*, transl. J. T. Rimer and Y. Masakazu, Princeton, NJ, Princeton University Press.

7

Ancient Greek drama on the modern European stage:

identities and performance

LORNA HARDWICK

Introduction

The purpose of this chapter is to examine ways in which modern performances of ancient Greek drama in Europe relate to key debates in the cultural politics of the present, and to explore how the texts and performance conventions of ancient Greek tragedy have been translated and adapted for the modern stage. The first part of the discussion focuses on comparisons between ancient and modern contexts of production. The second part surveys trends in the cultural politics surrounding modern conceptions of Greek tragedy and raises questions about the ways in which apparently canonical texts and cultural forms can both subvert existing assumptions and generate new cultural readings and attitudes. In modern times politically and culturally interventionist productions of Greek tragedy have moved from their base in avant-garde and experimental productions into the repertoire of national and commercial companies. The third section focuses on the recent performance history of one play, the *Agamemnon*, the first play in the *Oresteia* trilogy by Aeschylus (c. 525–456 BCE), and analyses ways in which productions have mapped crisis points in response to catastrophe, suffering and change. Overall, the study demonstrates that notions of European cultural boundaries and norms are porous and shifting. Modern theatre practice has been refreshed by cultural exchange with non-European performance traditions and re-energized by dialogue with the theatrical practices and texts of the ancient plays, which resist permanent appropriation by any one dominant ideology or aesthetic.

At first sight, the differences in cultural and political context between ancient Greek and modern theatre may make dialogue between the two seem unlikely. Greek drama was at the centre of popular culture. The tragedies which have come down to us originated in the cultural practices of the Athenian democracy which developed in the late

Figure 7.1 Theatre of Dionysus at Athens. (The remains date chiefly from the Roman period.) The special seats for dignitaries are visible in the foreground. Photo: Trip/H. Rogers

sixth and fifth centuries BCE. They were created for competitions at the great festivals in Athens, the Dionysia and the Lenea. These festivals were statements of pride in the power of the democracy, framed within a religious context of public cult. During the height of the Athenian naval empire in the fifth century BCE the major festivals were especially designed to impress the 'allies' (or subject states in the naval empire) and included ceremonies stressing the power of the Athenians, with honours paid to the sons of those killed in battle.

Plays were performed in daylight in the open air. The Theatre of Dionysus in Athens could probably hold over 14,000 spectators. Attendance was thought to be so important for citizens that admission prices here were held very low and even subsidized. Special seats were reserved for the priests of Dionysus, for important officials and for the judges. Theatre was competitive. The names of the winning plays and authors were preserved in official records. So ancient theatre lay at the heart of the life of the community. It was part of a culture of performance and debate, a culture where the law courts and the Assembly were sites of participation and competition and where decisions were taken by vote (Goldhill and Osborne, 1999).

Ancient and modern contexts of production

Identity in Greek society and culture

Concepts of identity were community based. An individual was a member of an *oikos*, or household, which covered extended kin relationships and dependants, including slaves. As a citizen of the democracy a male Athenian (women had no civic rights) was also a member of a community group, or *deme*, as well as a citizen of the *polis*, or city-state. As the early *polis* and then the democracy developed there were inevitable tensions between these identities; some of these are reflected in the plays. The area we now call Greece was divided into a large number of *poleis*. The concept of the nation-state was unknown. There was, however, a cultural sense of shared hellenism, which set Greeks off from other ethnic groups and sometimes took political form in (usually unstable) alliances between Greek *poleis* against, for instance, the Persians. In Greek tragedy, non-Greek characters such as Medea or Cassandra might paradoxically be presented both as outsiders ('barbarians') and as central figures in terms of their achievements or insight.

The subject matter of most of the Greek tragedies is based on stories from mythology and often draws on the tradition surrounding the war between Greeks and Trojans which was supposed to have occurred in the remote past. The playwright Aeschylus drew on stories about the aftermath of the Trojan war as a basis for his *Agamemnon*, for example. Another notable feature of Greek drama is the way that the plays draw on stories about the 'past' of human figures in mythology (Wiles, 2000, pp. 6–11). In the case of the *Agamemnon*, the feuds in the house of Atreus are another feature underlying the action of the play. Because these were part of the cultural framework for the audience, everyone knew more or less what was going to happen. So what was important was how it happened, how it was presented and debated in the play, and any additions or changes in the story. Then there is the relationship between humans and gods, affecting in this case moral and religious concepts such as justice. In terms of group identity across the three plays of Aeschylus' trilogy there is a move from the social unit of the household (the main concern in the *Agamemnon*) to the larger social unit of the embryonic *polis*, which through the law court becomes the source of arbitration in revenge feuds. An important point to note from this use of mythology is that the Greek dramatists were selecting and reworking material from their cultural tradition. The technical term for this is refiguration, and a parallel activity takes place when modern writers and directors refigure Greek plays into new adaptations and versions.

Figure 7.2 Attic red-figure vase, c. 440 BCE. Two women are shown at a tomb marked AGAMEM. National Museum of Denmark, Copenhagen, Department of NE and CI Antiquities

Figure 7.3 The killing of Agamemnon. Attic red-figure calyx krater by the Dokimasia Painter, c. 470 BCE. Agamemnon (right) is shown bleeding, caught in a net-like garment. Aegisthus is about to strike him again. William Francis Warden Fund, Museum of Fine Arts, Boston

Drama as intervention

When writers and directors refigure plays in ways which have implications for their own societies, their political and aesthetic critique is called intervention. I would argue that Greek dramatists were also following a process of intervention in terms of their own society. However, the word is most frequently used to describe the cultural practices in theatre and film of a twentieth-century movement which originated in the left-wing 'committed' theatre of Europe in the 1920s and 1930s, after which it was temporarily crushed by fascism. Among the avant-garde in Germany during the 1920s the notion of an 'engaged' theatre developed. This aimed to alter the consciousness of the spectator through an anti-naturalist aesthetic which often used topical, historical and factual material such as newspaper photos and reports. The 'message' might be communicated by a chorus, spoken or sung, either on the stage or in the auditorium. 'Intervention' occurred through the creation of awareness of the underlying ideology which was ensuring the continuation of the situation being challenged. After the Second World War a new socialist theatre aesthetic formulated along interventionist lines re-emerged and influenced politically engaged theatre worldwide, notably in South Africa in the 1970s (Hardwick, 2000, Chapter 4). Interventionist theatre not only operated in repressive societies but also developed a role in barely censored or liberal contexts where it could reveal and explore fault lines, slipping past the 'censors' of entrenched assumptions and collective amnesia. In this way, drama, poetry and film could open up the possibility of those imaginative shifts of understanding that enable larger-scale transformations of perspective.

Greek drama has been a major source for modern interventionist dramatists and poets. A related feature is the shift in the activities and norms of translation. In verbal terms there has been a move away from the emphasis on 'accurate' or 'faithful' translation and an increased awareness of the processes involved in translation across time and culture as well as language (Hardwick, 2000, Chapter 1). As a result, translations of Greek plays for the modern stage are not primarily conceived as re-creating ancient experience (unless in a limited 'archaeological' context) but instead transplant the dynamics of the ancient play into the consciousness of the modern audience. The result usually directs attention both to the receiving tradition and to that of the Greek source. Feeling for the balance between what is retained, what is adapted and what is newly created shapes the response of the spectators.

Conventions in the production and staging of tragedy in fifth-century BCE Athens

The classical theatre included the following important conventions:

- finance for the production (a wealthy citizen was appointed by lot to bear most of the production costs, including the expense of training, costuming and feeding the chorus);

- selection for entry to the festival (made by a city official);

- the large theatre and acting space (with performances in daylight and outdoors);

- the balance between spoken and sung words, music and dance (the playwright composed his own music, choreographed the chorus dances and directed the production – Aeschylus was also an actor);

- the entire production team, including the actors, were male;

- full face masks were worn and costumes were formal and stylized;

- because of the masks and the size of the theatre gesture and movement of the actor's whole body was important;

- the chorus was central, with a strong identity of gender and social status within the play;

- playing in a chorus was a mark of civic participation and duty;

- the chorus in a tragedy was originally made up of twelve members, later fifteen, who sang lyrics, danced and commented on the action. Although composed of male citizens the chorus frequently represented the collective identity of marginalized groups – such as women, old men, foreigners or captives.

If you add to these features the civic and religious context of ancient theatre summarized above and the fact that ancient Greek is now not widely learned or understood, it is clear that the cultural differences between the contexts of ancient performance and modern translation and reception are very challenging to actors, directors and audiences.

Apart from the socioeconomic aspects, much of the evidence about ancient theatre is drawn from the texts themselves and from vase painting (Taplin, 1997). Furthermore, most of the features summarized above are not easily transplanted into modern theatre. Nevertheless modern productions have drawn on these features of a chronologically distant and sometimes culturally alien tradition in inventive ways. This distance between ancient and modern has brought opportunities as well as challenges. The next section relates these to the impact of intervention in modern theatre in Europe.

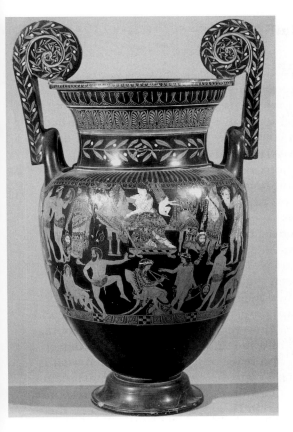

Figure 7.4 The 'Pronomos' Vase, Attic red-figure krater, Pronomos Painter, c. 410 BCE, h. 0.75 m. This is an important source of information about Athenian theatre practice. It depicts a group of actors in tragedy, with costumes, masks and *aulos* player. The chorus is costumed for a satyr play. (Satyrs, costumed with phalloi, were male creatures of the wild, combining human and animal characteristics. The satyr play provided comic relief after the tragedies.) The scene is organized on two levels. On the upper level Dionysus, the patron god of the drama festival, is shown seated, surrounded by actors. To the right an actor represents Heracles, with club and lionskin. (These representations are confirmed by inscriptions on the vase.) In the centre of the lower band is Pronomos, the renowned Theban *aulos* player with another musician (with lyre), a dancing satyr and the playwright Demetrios, who has the scroll in his hand. An important point about the inscriptions on the vase is that while it is the characters played by the professional actors that are named, for the satyr chorus (played by citizens) their own names are given. Museo Nazionale, Naples

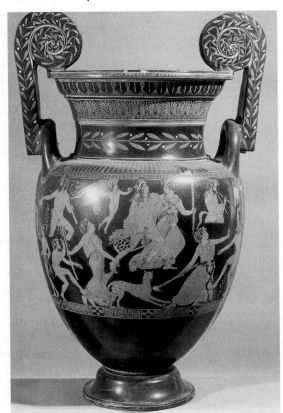

Figure 7.5 Another view of the 'Pronomos' Vase depicts a Dionysian revel, with young gods, meanads and satyrs. In contrast to the previous scene, this emphasizes the imaginary aspects of the mythology associated with Greek drama. Museo Nazionale, Naples

269

The cultural politics of tragedy

Greek drama and political contest

In the twentieth century productions of Greek drama, especially
tragedy, played a significant role in the struggle to reconstruct or
replace political and cultural structures which had collapsed or been
destroyed. In the European context the interventionist role of drama
in politics was by no means always overt or didactic. More often than
not, interventionist productions exploited the element of distance
that separates the contemporary from an ancient culture which is
half-alien to modern consciousness, creating a 'safety gap' that
allowed a performance both to resonate with and yet remain distant
from the world of the audience. This 'distance' could also have the
effect of promoting critique. An audience which is invited by the
production values of a theatrical performance to find or create its
own correspondences between the stage drama and its own
experiences will respond emotionally and intellectually as well as
imaginatively and will perhaps develop a critique of both ancient and
modern practices and values. However, just as distance can encourage
clarity of perspective and so inform critique, by appearing to detach
ancient from modern it can also reassure. Closeness between what is
portrayed on stage and current concerns can make the drama seem
threatening and invoke either hostility or denial in the public response.
According to the ancient historian Herodotus (c. 485–425 BCE), the
Greek dramatist Phrynichos (fl. 511–493 BCE) created in the fifth
century BCE a play called *The Destruction of Miletos*. Unusually for Greek
tragedy, this play focused on a historical rather than a mythological
situation. It moved to tears an audience which was aware of the
sufferings of the Milesians at the hands of the invading Persians. In
spite of this, or rather because of their emotion which reminded
them of their own fears of invasion, the audience then fined the
playwright 1000 drachmas for reminding them of a catastrophe so
close to home and future productions of the play were banned
(Herodotus, *The Histories*, 6.21.2). Phrynichos crossed the safety gap
between theatre and real life and between mythology and civic life.
He narrowed the distance between tragedy and the audience's
troubles, and was attacked for doing this. This happened in a
democratic *polis* which valued tragedy as a civic art form. In repressive
or overtly censored societies the safety-gap provided by an ancient
text that is seemingly remote in place, time, culture and values can
provide a vehicle for the exploration in performance of social,
cultural and political issues which would not be permitted in a
modern work. Furthermore, the fact that Greek tragedy was itself not
overtly didactic so far as the details of contemporary political life
were concerned has meant that its nuanced debates, subtle imagery

and sometimes ironic ambivalence allow translators, directors and designers a good deal of free rein in their interpretation. There is not only scope for creative direction and performance but also room for the audience to activate meaning.

The more oppressive the political and social context of production, the more delicate the balance between the advantages of critical distance and the need for a safety gap. A good example is the version by Jean Anouilh (1910–87) of the tragedy *Antigone* by Sophocles (c. 496–406 BCE), which was staged in German-occupied Paris in 1944. A crude summary of the story might suggest that Antigone (who opposes the civil power and insists on the right to burial of her brother, killed during civil war) would be identified as a resistance supporter and the play banned. Certainly the performance history of the play in the nineteenth and twentieth centuries shows that Antigone has often been played and understood as a martyr figure, representing the individual's stand against the tyranny of the state, while the ruler Creon has been interpreted as a figure representing political expediency (Steiner, 1984). Yet the dynamics of the Greek text allow a case to be made that Creon's arguments are justified. Research into performances staged under the Nazi regime, for example, suggests that the play could be used to demonstrate the futility of resistance to power (Flashar, 1991, Chapter 9, 'Griechische Tragödie unter dem Nationalsozialismus'). The central verbal contest (*agon*) between Antigone and the new ruler Creon (who is her uncle) has Creon putting forward the arguments for supporting the civil power and maintaining good order in the interests of the state and its people. So the classically trained advisers to the censors presumably thought that the play could also be interpreted as a defence of collaboration with the Third Reich, the *de facto* rulers. Such an interpretation is of course transferable to many situations, and the popularity of Anouilh's version of Sophocles' play suggests a strong ideological motive in the selection of plays for performance. In Bulgaria, for example, *Antigone* was a favourite play from the 1940s to the 1980s and was thought to be adaptable to the requirement for drama to present communist ideology in a favourable light and to contribute to the sense of national triumph over fascism. Indeed, the opera *Antigone '43'*, by Lyubomir Pipkov, produced in 1943, specifically relocated the conflict to the time of the struggle against fascism (Protochristova, 1998, p. 75).

In any event, Anouilh's version passed the censors and was staged. It provoked a critical reaction which initially suggested that it was an act of collaboration. Creon was seen as a representative of the pro-Vichy party in France and as the dominant and victorious figure, and the play was attacked by left-wing critics. Yet after liberation the play continued to be performed to large audiences who sympathized with Antigone and regarded the play as a statement about resistance.

Two main points emerge from this. First, if the dynamics of the arguments and contests in the ancient Greek versions of the plays are translated into modern idiom, the performances are not clear didactic statements about 'good' and 'bad' or about winners and losers. Secondly, this fact complicates the politics of appropriation. Not only can there be genuine debate about the interpretation of both ancient and modern versions but Greek plays which are highly politically charged may be permitted by censors, either because they are considered sufficiently remote from modern issues to be 'safe' or because the censors think that their performance may be considered to support the values of the current regime. It follows from this that a comparison between the staging of plays under different regimes and in different countries provides a yardstick for a comparison between different cultural value statements. Such comparisons also serve to direct attention back to the Greek source text, provoking judgements about which aspects of the source have been made more or less prominent, which are problematized or simplified in relation to the original and, especially, which are developed as correspondences to modern situations and how those correspondences are signalled to audiences in the production.

In this respect, the theatrical tradition in different countries is an important influencing factor. For example, Czech theatre since the nineteenth century has, with brief exceptions, been seen as a substitute for repressed political structures. This has led to interpretations of Greek drama which are predominantly political in their emphasis, a phenomenon that has been well documented for the period of German occupation during the Second World War and for the forty years of Soviet domination after that when the repertoire was controlled by censor (Stehlíková, 2000; 2001). During the Second World War many plays were judged 'unsuitable' because of the origin of the author or the democratic ideas expressed in them. (Eventually the plays of all English and French dramatists were prohibited, except those of Shakespeare and George Bernard Shaw.) This meant that the repertoire became thin, so plays by ancient Greek and Roman authors gave an opportunity to enrich it. In addition, however, because they were seen as part of the European humanist tradition their staging could be regarded as an opportunity to express coded resistance.

After 1948 Czech theatre was again subject to restrictions on its repertoire, this time in the interests of 'social realism'. It was laid down that 30 per cent of productions should be Czech works of a progressive kind, while 30 per cent could be Czech and Russian classical plays, 30 per cent from other communist regimes and 10 per cent 'western classics' (which included Shakespeare and Molière as well as Greek plays). However, Greek tragedy was thought to be depressing for audiences and not conducive to a climate of social optimism, so it was not much performed until the middle 1950s. In spite of this restrictive environment, however, theatre practitioners sought to exploit the potential of Greek plays in the treatment of disturbing social and moral questions – for example, in 1958 a production of a Greek tragedy attracted the following comment:

> a striking drama that deals with contemporary crisis in marital relations and loosening of family bonds has been found. It was written by Euripides, it is about two and a half thousand years old and it is called *Medea*.

(Quoted in Stehlíková, 2000, p. 182)

Significantly, the production stressed domestic conflict rather than the conflict between Greek and barbarian and the constraints of political ambition which were prominent in the ancient source text.

The Czech example illustrates how restrictions on repertoire may represent an attempt to set certain parameters of social and political identity and to reinforce them by creating a matching cultural experience. It also shows that a sense of cultural identity may run counter to such impositions, and that the plasticity of theatrical performance may actually allow imposed social and political identities to be probed and challenged. In the case of Greek tragedy there is an additional paradox. The reasons for the selection or permitting of Greek plays as part of a classical repertoire are subtly balanced between pressures for prestige and for subversion. Emergent or insecure theatrical traditions seek prestige; subversion of dominant social or political norms is also desired by creative artists, and the prestige of Greek plays allows this to be pursued as a kind of subversion from within, without recourse to 'alternative' theatre for which funds, venues and large audiences may be lacking or withheld.

Sometimes such difficulties can be publicized in order to draw attention to contemporary problems. For instance a production of Sophocles' *Antigone*, subtitled *A Cry for Peace*, was directed in 1994 by Nikos Koundouros in the no-man's land between northern Greece and the former republic of Yugoslavia. The production was symbolic both of the ambivalence of the political readings of the play itself and of the disarray of the receiving societies. The backdrop consisted of armoured personnel carriers, soldiers and log fires. Since the 1990s Balkan settings have become a major feature of modern productions of Greek drama, adding to the layers of resonance established in the earlier parts of the twentieth century with the struggle for assertion of national and civic identities, the contests between fascism and socialism and the catastrophes of civil war and war between states. It has been suggested that Greek tragedy, because of its preoccupation with catastrophe, fulfils a special role in the response to these horrors (Macintosh, 1997, p. 321).

In addition to their part in the revelation and dissection of human beings' role in and response to catastrophe, Greek plays have also been important in attempts to take positive steps towards healing and resolution. A recent example is the Georgian International Festival of Theatre (GIFT) held in Tbilisi in 1997. The festival was the first of its kind to be held after the collapse of the Soviet Union and the period of terrible civil war between Georgia and Abkhasia in the 1990s. The festival was a conscious attempt to heal the divisions left by the war. Cultural events, especially theatre, were thought of as offerings of gifts which would contribute to the efforts being made to bring about peace and reconciliation (Taxidou, 2000). The festival involved writers, performers, students and critics who worked to create performances that brought together theatre traditions from Europe, the US and South America as well as Georgia. The aim was to redefine the role of civic theatre.

The Greek tragedy chosen for adaptation in this festival was one first performed in 431 BCE: the *Medea* by Euripides (c. 480–406 BCE). The choice was governed partly by the geographical importance of Colchis

Figure 7.6 Keti Dolidze as Medea in Olga Taxidou's *Medea: a World Apart*, performed by the Turmanishvili Film Actors' Studio at the Edinburgh Festival Fringe, 1998. The model of Jason's ship, the *Argo*, symbolizes Medea's history of helping him to success in his voyages and contrasts painfully with her new situation as an abandoned wife in a foreign country. Photo: Ken Reynolds

as Medea's home by the Black Sea in the ancient play (in modern Georgia Medea is still used as a woman's name) and partly by its potential for reworking in the context of modern anxieties about borders, boundaries, 'homes' and ethnicity and nationhood, between which gender can function as an interface. In Euripides' play Colchis is the focus of Jason's expedition for recovery of the Golden Fleece. The place is represented as distant and peripheral to the known world, an alien source of the sorcery and barbarism associated with Medea. Yet it is also a target for exploration and a source of cultural exchange. Euripides used this ambivalence as a means of exploring the images of the outsider and of ethnicity and gender in relation to Greek values. Olga Taxidou's adaptation *Medea: a World Apart* situated these issues in the discourse of the cold war and probed the shifting relationship between notions of civilization and barbarism, presenting the relationship between empire and culture through the filter of the interaction of gender and power. This version of the *Medea* was staged in 1998 at the Edinburgh Festival Fringe and subsequently toured to Sarajevo, Warsaw and Moscow. As the production developed on tour and in response to current events it increasingly focused on the plight of the refugee, which Jason's treatment of Medea could have forced her to become when after bringing her to Greece he abandoned her to make a more politically advantageous marriage. Keti Dolidze, who played Medea, had also been responsible for reviving a medieval Georgian tradition, the White Scarf movement, in which women laid white scarves between the fighting lines in an attempt to stop war. In 1992, when the civil war in Georgia was at its height and the nationalist movement very active, Dolidze appeared on television and called on the women of Tbilisi to assemble in the main square. Over 5000 did so. They went on to travel to the front line, where they stood holding hands in front of the troops to try to stop the fighting.

In its aim of providing a framework for cultural exchange and the promotion of peace, the Tbilisi festival drew on some of the aims on which the poet Angelos Sikelianos and his American wife Eva Palmer had based the Delphi festival in the 1920s. Their festival, first staged in 1927 after three years of preparation, and repeated in 1930, drew partly on the way in which Greek theatre had become an icon of hellenic identity during the 400 years of Turkish domination which lasted until the 1820s. During that period Greek cultural activities that might attract crowds were banned. The Delphic idea aimed at establishing at the *omphalos* (the navel of the earth at Delphi) a university based on the ideal of world peace. The performance style at Sikelianos's festivals was intended to revive the ancient conventions of Greek drama and was criticized in this respect for being inaccessible to the modern public and encouraging cultural nostalgia.

Figure 7.7 Tokusaburo Arashi as Medea in Yukio Ninagawa's production, 1995. Weeping, she holds the children she is about to kill as revenge against Jason who has humiliated and deserted her for another woman. Photo: Photostage/Donald Cooper

In fact some aspects of the ethos of the Delphic festivals still survived in the work of the European Cultural Centre at Delphi. This was founded in 1964 to encourage cultural exchange among nations and has promoted performances of tragedy in Greece which have included an *Antigone* played by an Inuit company, Sophocles' *Oedipus the King* staged by the central Academy of Drama of Beijing, and Japanese productions drawing on **Noh** and **Kabuki** traditions of classical oriental drama. Over twenty ancient theatres have been brought into use with regular summer performances at the Athens and Epidaurus festivals.

Noh and Kabuki are ancient traditions of Japanese drama. Noh originated in the thirteenth century CE and was based on the narrative and dance associated with warrior heroes. Kabuki developed from the seventeenth century CE and was directed at audiences of all classes with popular drama based on erotic and grotesque themes.

The criticisms made of the original Delphic idea demonstrate very clearly the difficulty of combining idealistic and inclusive aims with an emphasis on reproducing the style and conventions of ancient drama. On the other hand, writers and directors who adapt Greek tragedy for modern contexts and audiences often attract criticism on aesthetic grounds. Sometimes this aesthetic critique masks criticism of the perceived political purposes behind the adaptation. A good example is the critical reception accorded to Seamus Heaney's *The Cure at Troy* (1990). This is a version of Sophocles' *Philoctetes*, first

Figure 7.8 Philoctetes nursing his wounded foot.
Attic red-figure lekythos, c. 430 BCE. Philoctetes has
been left alone on an island because of his suppurating
wound. His bow lies beside him. The Metropolitan
Museum of Art, Fletcher Fund, 1956. Photo: © 1982
Metropolitan Museum of Art, New York

staged in 409 BCE (when it won first prize). Sophocles dramatized the
story, alluded to in Homer and the poems of epic cycle, of the Greek
hero who has inherited the bow of Heracles but is abandoned by his
comrades on an island during the voyage to attack Troy because they
cannot bear the stench of his wound, caused by a snake bite.
However, the Greeks subsequently realize they cannot defeat the
Trojans without the aid of the bow and send Odysseus to trick
Philoctetes into rejoining the expedition. By this time Philoctetes has
become totally alienated from his own community. The deception

and persuasion practised by the Greeks govern the action of the play, which in the twentieth century became a significant vehicle for the exploration of political ethics, loyalty and identification with the community. Philoctetes' wound has become a symbol in modern poetry for the suffering created by colonial domination and emblematic of the refusal to leave behind the bitterness caused by affliction (Hardwick, 2000, Chapters 5–6).

Heaney's play is subtitled *After Philoctetes by Sophocles*. The description 'after' applies in two different ways. The play indeed follows the Sophoclean outline, in terms of plot and the imagery of the wound with its pain and noxious effects, both physical and psychological. It also follows many of the Greek conventions, especially in its use of the Chorus as commentator, moral interpreter and guide to the action. Yet of course the play is also 'after Sophocles' in that its creation and its effect on the audience are filtered through modern consciousness. Because of Heaney's language, with its Irish-English rhythms and idiom, and because of the situation in the north of Ireland at the time when the play was written and first performed as part of the Field Day Theatre Company's touring programme (in 1990), critics have been quick to find in *The Cure at Troy* correspondences to the present – for example 'sullen, rancorous, inwardly gnawed by hatred and paralysed by memories of past injustice, Philoctetes is Heaney's unlovely image of the sectarian North of Ireland' (Eagleton [1991] 1998, pp. 374–5). Although Heaney himself has emphasized his intention to preserve something of the formal and ritualistic qualities of Greek tragedy, he has also said that he used the freedom to compose new lines for the Chorus. These lines were used to state specifically modern analogues of suffering inflicted and shared within and across communities – such as these, opening with a reference to a hunger striker's father:

> Stands in the graveyard dumb
>
> The police widow in veils
>
> Faints at the funeral home.
>
> (*The Cure at Troy*, Heaney, 1990, p. 77)

These lines have been described as 'intrusively overt' (Meir, 1991) or even as part of an attempt to create a new mythology (that is a mythology of the commonality of suffering across the barriers of religious and community identity), and they were omitted from the recitation of this choral ode by Liam Neeson for a compilation album, *Across the Bridge of Hope* (1998), which was produced in aid of the Omagh Bomb Memorial Fund. They were also cut from a production staged in the US in 1995. However, a quotation from Heaney's Chorus, 'when hope and history rhyme', was adapted by newspaper headlines and political commentators at the time of the Belfast Agreement (Easter 1998).

> ... once in a lifetime
>
> The longed for tidal wave
>
> Of justice can rise up
>
> And hope and history rhyme.
>
> (*The Cure at Troy*, Heaney, 1990, p. 77)

Certainly Heaney's addition of these lines in an already interventionist play revealed a yawning gulf between the play's attempt at shifting the audience's imagination and empathy across cultural boundaries and the resolutely sectarian response from some on both sides of the unionist/nationalist divide. His concern with war and its effects is also explored in his poem 'Mycenae Lookout' (Heaney, 1996), which draws directly on the opening scene of Aeschylus' *Agamemnon*.

It is clear from these examples that the interventionist role of modern performances of Greek drama in Europe is complex and can provide a significant guide to cultural and ideological shifts. Its various roles have included: the reassertion of national and cultural identity and prestige; acting as a vehicle for political and social critique (sometimes coded), including resistance to external or internal oppression; and providing the means of crossing or commenting on national, cultural, ethnic, gender and class barriers. The particular context for performance (whether state-funded or commercial theatre, arts or festival theatre, experimental or alternative theatre) and the censorship and/or critical reception of the production all offer indications of the directions of cultural resistance, and comparisons between these indicate the direction of shifts as well as providing a yardstick for a comparison between different cultural contexts and theatrical traditions. Within this broad framework, a comparison between recent productions of one play, the *Agamemnon*, can reveal how an ancient cultural artefact can be 'translated' on to the modern stage in ways which both reflect and shape modern experiences and conceptions of identity. To explore this aspect in more detail the next section considers some modern European productions, focusing on comparisons between their approaches to key issues and episodes.

Aeschylus: *Agamemnon*

Aeschylus was the earliest of the three major Athenian tragedians of the fifth century BCE whose works survive in any bulk (the others are Sophocles and Euripides). He is thought to have written some eighty plays, of which about thirteen were victorious in the drama festival competitions. Seven of his plays survive, together with significant fragments of other works. The plays are *Persians* (472 BCE), *Seven against Thebes* (467 BCE), *Suppliant Women* (c. 466 BCE) and the *Oresteia*, a trilogy which consists of the *Agamemnon, Choephoroe* (or *Libation-Bearers*) and *Eumenides* (458 BCE). Also attributed to Aeschylus is *Prometheus Bound* (the date of which is disputed).

Aeschylus is significant as a figure in cultural history for a number of reasons. He came from a prominent family and his tomb at Gela, on the south coast of Sicily, bears an inscription recording that he fought at the battle of Marathon in 490 BCE (when Greeks came together to resist Persian invasion). His play *Persians* was one of the few Greek tragedies to address recent history rather than mythological themes. The fact that his funerary inscription does not mention his career as a dramatist, actor and director of the chorus tells us something about the values attached to the notion of the citizen–soldier in the Athenian democracy. Yet other evidence shows that his works were highly regarded. After Aeschylus' death a state decree was issued giving special permission for his plays to be performed at the dramatic festivals alongside those of living dramatists. Furthermore, the comedy *Frogs* (405 BCE) by Aristophanes (c. 448–c. 388 BCE), which features a mock contest between the three tragedians Aeschylus, Sophocles and Euripides, makes Aeschylus the winner because of the civic value of his plays in the democracy. The relationship between the themes of his plays and civic and political issues in the developing democracy marked him out.

The *Oresteia* is particularly important, not just because of its great theatrical and poetic power but also because it is the only surviving trilogy from the works of the dominant fifth-century tragedians. The trilogy, in which three plays are staged in sequence, allows the development of a theme. In the case of the *Oresteia* the main theme is the development from blood feud, which destroys a family through the exaction of revenge in successive generations, to the establishment of the public law court, which provides a system for the pronouncement of justice and the arbitration and resolution of conflict. This trilogy begins with the mythological setting of the aftermath of the Trojan war when the leader of the Greek alliance, Agamemnon, returns victorious to his home and is murdered by his wife, Clytemnestra, and her lover, Aegisthus. In the next play Clytemnestra is killed by her son Orestes who thus avenges his father. As a matricide Orestes is polluted (to commit a crime which had religious overtones was abhorrent to the gods) and pursued by the Furies, who were spirits of punishment, particularly in respect of murder within the family. (In the *Eumenides* the alternative name for the Furies is 'kindly ones' as they become reconciled.) Orestes is finally exonerated in the third play with the establishment of the court of the Areopagus at Athens. (The Areopagus or 'hill of Ares' at Athens gave its name to the ancient council that met on it.) The trilogy challenged its ancient audience to relate the mythological and remote historical pasts to their own cultural present, and stagings of the play present a comparable challenge today. The drama is a way of constructing, mediating and exploring the implications of the past in a way which interacts with and influences perceptions of the present. The first play in the sequence, the *Agamemnon*, is quite frequently staged on its own. Because of its remote cultural setting it defies simplistic identification with the audience's contemporary situation (for ancients as well as moderns) and therefore requires from the audience just that 'imaginative movement' with which directors of classical plays are concerned. Yet while resisting reductionist approaches it also presents situations and relationships, both private and public, in which the director's lead and the audience's response come together to relate ancient and modern.

The reading below is from J. Michael Walton's *Living Greek Theatre* (1987). It includes an analysis of the dramatic context, staging and theatrical qualities of the *Agamemnon*. The exercise that follows the reading requires you to study this part of the extract carefully. The rest of the reading is concerned with the other plays in the trilogy and is provided as useful information which you can read afterwards if you wish.

AGAMEMNON. 1,673 lines, the longest surviving play of Aeschylus.

Production. 458 B.C. at the Great Dionysia [the largest and most important of the Athenian festivals]. First of the *Oresteia* trilogy: *Agamemnon, Libation-Bearers, Eumenides*. The group, with the satyr play *Proteus*, won first prize, and *Libation-Bearers* and *Eumenides* also survive complete. *Proteus* is lost.

Characters

WATCHMAN.	39 lines
CLYTEMNESTRA, wife of Agamemnon.	338
HERALD.	128
AGAMEMNON, king of Argos.	84
CASSANDRA, daughter of Priam of Troy.	178
AEGISTHUS, Clytemnestra's lover.	64
CHORUS, of old men of Argos.	842

Plot. Being the first play of a trilogy of which the other two plays also survive, Agamemnon is in every way clearer and more easy to appreciate in its full context. The myth of the war against Troy is more familiar today to most and of wider interest than the ramifications of the war between the gods and Titans or the attempt of fifty Egyptian maidens to prove that they are related to a king of Argos [which form the background to other plays by Aeschylus].

For the first Athenian audience Aeschylus' treatment of the homecoming of Agamemnon contained a number of original elements and though this is not the place to discuss prior versions of the story in heroic poetry, it is worth recording that the epic poems of Homer, the *Iliad* and the *Odyssey*, made Aegisthus the villain of the piece. The murder of his mother by Orestes is played down and he is applauded for his actions. In this, at least, Sophocles in his *Electra* is far closer than Aeschylus to the Homeric original.

In brief, the Trojan War was the result of the stealing away of Helen, the wife of Menelaus of Sparta and sister of Clytemnestra, by Paris, son of Priam the king of Troy. Paris claimed this right as the prize for judging Aphrodite the most beautiful of the goddesses. This was no consolation for Menelaus, who commandeered the help of all Helen's former suitors to get her back. Under the leadership of his brother Agamemnon of Argos, the Greek fleet set sail, but was held up at Aulis until Agamemnon sacrificed his daughter Iphigeneia to Artemis to gain a favourable wind.

The siege of Troy lasted for a full ten years and saw the deaths of Patroclus and Hector [Greek and Trojan heroes respectively] before the Greeks gained entrance to the city by the trick of the wooden horse. Victorious they returned to their homes, though not without all manner of trials and tribulations. Clytemnestra in the interim had been seduced by Aegisthus, Agamemnon's cousin, and was plotting to murder her husband.

Agamemnon opens with a Watchman who has been waiting night after night for the sight of a beacon which will be lit to warn the Queen that the war is over. It shines out and he hurries off to tell the news. The Chorus enter, old men left behind when the younger went off to the war ten years before. The old men are full of foreboding as they rehearse the past and speculate about the future. Clytemnestra enters excited at what she has heard and explains how a series of bonfires have been lit all the way from Troy. Soon a Herald arrives full of the privations of the war but confirming that it is indeed over. Clytemnestra greets him in friendly fashion, though his tale of a storm that has split up and weakened the Greek fleet strikes an ominous note which the Chorus echo as they prepare to greet Agamemnon.

The play is almost half over before the title character puts in an appearance, and he is not alone. He has rashly brought with him Cassandra, a daughter of Priam, as his concubine. The meeting between Agamemnon and his wife is formal and tense. She has a red carpet laid out and coaxes him into walking upon it. After some hesitation he removes his shoes before acquiescing. At the last moment before reaching the palace doors he draws her attention to Cassandra, waiting in the chariot. Clytemnestra follows him in, then returns for Cassandra who has neither moved nor uttered. Only after Clytemnestra has again returned to the palace does Cassandra break her silence, pouring out a stream of prophetic utterance which the Chorus fail to comprehend. At last she walks voluntarily into the palace and within minutes Agamemnon's death cries ring out.

The Chorus are uncertain how to react. The doors of the palace open to reveal the bodies of Agamemnon and Cassandra. Clytemnestra justifies her action to the angry but powerless Chorus on the grounds both of the murder of her daughter Iphigeneia and Agamemnon's bringing back of Cassandra. Such protests as the Chorus do make are quelled by the arrival of Aegisthus with an armed band and, after further exchanges, the play ends on a note of discord.

Staging. Compared with the difficulties created by other plays of Aeschylus, the requirements for the *Oresteia* are fairly specific. *Agamemnon* is set firmly in front of the palace of Agamemnon and he returns to the courtyard in the *orchestra* [dancing space] by chariot during the action. The entrance to the palace is clearly in the center of the *skene* [stage building]. Clytemnestra enters from it and through it Agamemnon and Cassandra make their respective exits. Also probable is that a tableau of their dead bodies was displayed on an *ekkuklema* [trolley or platform wheeled out from the stage building]. The only refinement is contributed by the opening scene, in which the Watchman identifies himself as being stationed on the palace roof from which he delivers his speech. Entrances and exits can easily be recreated from the text, so easily indeed that it led some critics to assume that other Aeschylus plays, apart from the *Oresteia* and where details are vaguer, did not employ any *skene*.

Dramatic and Theatrical Qualities. *Agamemnon* is over 50 percent longer than any other Aeschylus play. The opening chorus, after the prologue speech of the Watchman, is over 220 lines and there are other odes of substantial length. Strangely, and something which can easily escape the casual reader, Agamemnon himself has only twenty lines more than the marginal character Aegisthus, considerably less that the Herald and under half of those allotted to Cassandra. Yet the play rightly bears his name. His direct contribution to the action may be slim, but the play revolves around him, both before his arrival and after his death, eclipsing even the importance of Clytemnestra who has four times as much to say.

The construction of the play revolves around this fact. The action is introduced through the lower end of the social stratum in the person of the Watchman, the unfolding of the background and the creation of mood being, as is customary, in the hands of the Chorus. But Clytemnestra is far from negligible as a character. Indeed her strength, compared to that of either of the men in her life, ensures that she wins the battle of wills over Agamemnon's entry into the palace and shows her to have greater determination and ruthlessness than the late-arriving Aegisthus.

Theatrically the play makes use of a number of striking effects. The motionless figure of Cassandra has been present for almost 300 lines before she says a word, but this serves to draw attention to her fate. Cassandra was cursed by Apollo always to prophesy the truth but never to be believed. When she does speak the stream of horror and despair is the relentless preparation for her own murder and that of Agamemnon. She is all victim.

The tempting scene, in which Clytemnestra has the carpet [of valuable tapestries] rolled out to Agamemnon's very feet, is an infallible stroke of pure theatre. Hesitating, aware of his own presumption, Agamemnon is so steeped in hubris as to permit himself to commit an act of which the gods could only disapprove. He removes his shoes first, but in the single action of walking into the house on the scarlet carpet [see above] Aeschylus combines an example of the man's folly and Clytemnestra's temperament, combined with a visual symbol of his past life and actions and the death prepared for him, now only minutes away.

Shortly after, the Chorus contribute another moment, not only powerful in its own right but whose value resides in confirming Aeschylus as a writer and director for whom the chorus was the most malleable of dramatic weapons, physically no less than verbally. Cassandra, reconciled to her fate, enters the palace and the Chorus begin a choral ode. A dozen lines into it Agamemnon's cries are heard from indoors. The Chorus, from a single unit, suddenly split into twelve individuals, each with a different point of view about whether or not to interfere, or indeed how. As a shock effect it has few parallels. As with the red carpet, it captures and condenses a number of meanings into a single sequence. The moment is ended by the entrance of Clytemnestra with the bodies, which serves to reunite the Chorus in their vocal opposition to her and to what she has perpetrated.

The revelations of the dead bodies and the net or robe in which Agamemnon was ensnared in his bath so that he could not fight back have a dual purpose. They serve as a visual focus for the rest of the play which still has 400 lines of virtual inaction to run. They also look forward to the next play in the trilogy, so effectively imprinting the tableau on the audience's mind that when a direct parallel is offered in *Libation-Bearers* the significance of the repetition cannot be missed.

The trilogy deals with a family feud whose destructive quality is its capacity to renew itself apparently indefinitely. Aegisthus' seduction of Clytemnestra is itself an act of revenge for his own brothers, served up in a stew to their father Thyestes by his brother Atreus, father of Agamemnon and Menelaus. The repetition of the curse on the house of Atreus through generation after generation is a major theme of the whole *Oresteia*, reflected in a series of linguistic echoes and parallels. Though some of the means by which they could have been expressed on stage are lost in choreography that is irrecoverable, there is enough remaining to identify a clear if complex scheme which grows out of a perfected sense of dramatic structure.

Other Plays about the House of Atreus

Aeschylus: *Libation-Bearers, Eumenides.*

Sophocles: *Electra.*

Euripides: *Electra, Iphigeneia in Tauris, Orestes, Iphigeneia in Aulis.*

Other Plays in Which Agamemnon Is a Character

Sophocles: *Ajax.*

Euripides: *Hecuba, Iphigeneia in Aulis.*

Other Plays in Which Clytemnestra Is a Character

Aeschylus: *Libation-Bearers, Eumenides* (as a ghost).

Sophocles: *Electra*.

Euripides: *Electra, Iphigeneia in Aulis*.

LIBATION-BEARERS. Greek title *Choephoroi*. 1,076 lines.

Production. 458 B.C. at the Great Dionysia. Second of the *Oresteia* trilogy: *Agamemnon, Libation-Bearers, Eumenides*. The group, with the satyr play *Proteus*, won first prize, and *Agamemnon* and *Eumenides* also survive complete. *Proteus* is lost.

Characters

ORESTES, son of Agamemnon and Clytemnestra.	331 lines
PYLADES, his friend.	3
ELECTRA, Orestes' sister.	170
SERVANT.	12
CLYTEMNESTRA, now married to Aegisthus.	48
NURSE.	40
AEGISTHUS.	15
CHORUS, of slave women.	457

Plot. The play follows on from the *Agamemnon*, but several years have passed. In the intervening period Orestes has been brought up in exile in Phocis while his sister Electra has grown up with their mother Clytemnestra and Aegisthus in Argos.

Orestes enters at the opening of the play and offers prayers to the god Hermes to help him in his quest for vengeance against his mother. His friend Pylades has accompanied him from Phocis, Orestes having been informed by the oracle of Apollo at Delphi that he must avenge his father or suffer the direst consequences. He places two locks of hair at Agamemnon's tomb and then withdraws with Pylades when he sees a group of women approaching.

The Chorus of sympathetic palace servants enter with Electra, bringing libations to lay at the tomb. Electra too prays to Hermes, then catches sight of the locks of hair and suspects that they might belong to her brother. This seems to be confirmed by their color and texture and by her discovery of footprints which match her own, at which point Orestes and Pylades emerge from hiding. After some hesitation and the offer of a third proof, a piece of cloth she wove for Orestes when he was a child, Electra is convinced and brother and sister are reunited.

Together with the Chorus they invoke the help of the shade of Agamemnon and decide on a plan to get Orestes and Pylades into the palace by posing as messengers with news of the death of Orestes. This plan is put into operation. Clytemnestra hears their story, accepts it, and offers Orestes and Pylades hospitality.

All seems set for the act of vengeance, but at this moment an unexpected character arrives in the person of Orestes' old Nurse, who has been sent by Clytemnestra to fetch Aegisthus back to the palace. The Chorus now takes a hand in the plot by persuading her to change her message and inform Aegisthus that he must come without his retinue, though the Chorus dare not at this point tell the Nurse the reason. She agrees and after a short choral ode Aegisthus arrives, is deceived by the Chorus, and enters the palace from which moments later his death cries are heard.

A servant rushes in with news of the murder. Clytemnestra hears the commotion, realizes the significance of a warning dream she had, and reacts characteristically by demanding an axe. Before it can be brought Orestes and Pylades confront her. Faced with his mother and the enormity of the deed he has to do Orestes' resolve wavers and Pylades, in his only speech in the entire play, urges him to act as Apollo has commanded. Orestes agrees and drives his mother indoors to kill her.

The Chorus dance in triumph until the palace doors open again to reveal the dead bodies of Clytemnestra and Aegisthus. Orestes justifies what he has done and no one condemns him, but he suddenly becomes aware of the unseen presence of the Eumenides, the Furies roused by his mother's blood. In torment he runs out and the Chorus rapidly brings the play to its conclusion.

Staging. Though the palace is clearly the background during the latter part of the play, as it was for the first part of the trilogy, there are two complications connected with the staging of *Libation-Bearers*. The first involves the tomb of Agamemnon at which Orestes prays in the opening lines and to which Electra and the Chorus arrive bringing libations. It is clearly a prime feature and forms the centerpiece of the long invocation to Agamemnon's shade. In the second half of the play the tomb is never mentioned and some critics have posited a complete change of setting from tomb to palace. Though the focus changes from foreground to background during the play, there is no reason why both tomb and palace should not be permanently in view, each providing a reminder of the circumstances underlying the action. If, as some believe, an altar which could double as a tomb was a permanent feature of all settings, the entire problem simply evaporates.

There is still some difficulty posed over the number of entrances from the *skene* which represents the palace. From the text it appears that the palace contains separate guestrooms and women's quarters, but any organization of entrances is complicated at the climax of the play when a number of characters come and go in rapid succession. Clytemnestra, for example, may have had her own special entrance, but it is perhaps safest to assume for the purpose of the play that a single central entrance was used from which the various areas could be reached.

Dramatic and Theatrical Qualities. Very much an intermediate play which needs its companion pieces on either side, *Libation-Bearers* is of special interest in any study of Greek tragedy because both Sophocles' and Euripides' *Electras* survive, covering the same ground and providing a unique comparison of styles in tragic writing. Aeschylus' version of the story is recalled, apparently critically, by Euripides in his own recognition scene between brother and sister.

Libation-Bearers splits into three distinct sections of roughly equal length. The first covers the arrival of Orestes and Pylades and the reuniting of Electra with her brother. It is the means of recognition about which Euripides is later to appear skeptical. Orestes has placed locks of his hair at the tomb. Electra compares them to her own hair and finds them similar. She then spies the footprints and discovers that her own feet fit into them exactly. Euripides has his Electra scorn such signs. Why should brother and sister have the same color hair? What man and woman would have the same size of foot simply because they are related? By such literal-mindedness Euripides' Electra gives a real insight into the differing techniques of the two dramatists.

For Aeschylus such things are tokens, no more. The physical gesture of comparing hair to hair – as both actors would originally have been wearing masks with artificial hair anyway – is a conscious piece of pretense related to the gesture it involves. So it is with the comparison of footprints, which relies not at all on an actual print but wholly on Electra's taking up a stance to echo one already taken by her brother.

The moment after Orestes steps from hiding and Electra has a moment of doubt is not an acknowledgment that her judgment may have been faulty but a psychologically sound reaction to the apparent simplicity with which a devout wish has been fulfilled.

The final proof, a piece of woven cloth, is hardly more convincing than the other two, as the Electra of Euripides again is to point out. It is perfectly satisfactory as a token to convert caution into conviction.

This sequence gives the most unequivocal of insights into the manner by which Aeschylus makes his stage work for him and can serve as a yardstick by which to measure solutions to any problems about staging that occur in his plays. It makes it possible, in the present play, to accept that Orestes and Pylades need only give an indication of hiding in order for Electra not to see them or for the slightest of changes to costume or speech pattern, as long as there is some, to work as an effective disguise as Phocian strangers when they first meet Clytemnestra.

The titling of the play by its chorus rather than by Electra, as in the treatments by Sophocles and Euripides, or by Orestes, who has by far the largest individual role, is justified first by the equal part the Chorus share in the long invocation of Agamemnon, which occupies the middle third of the play, and by the information they feed to various characters in the course of the action. They accompany Electra at the beginning, inform Orestes of Clytemnestra's dream, and eventually interfere with the progress of events.

After Orestes has gained admittance into the palace, the ensuing scene with the Nurse serves several purposes. She provides a contrast of real concern over the 'death' of Orestes compared with the feigned distress of his proper mother. She gives time for the suspense to build by introducing a domestic and realistic moment, even a comic one, into a drama otherwise uncompromising. Finally, she provides the opportunity for the Chorus to demonstrate their allegiance when she agrees to take an altered message to Aegisthus. Here is the real nub for the Chorus that identifies their central position in the play when choosing to become coconspirators, however diffident.

Aegisthus' scene is brusque, a calculated contrast to that of the Nurse which precedes it. The flurry of activity leading up to Orestes' confrontation with his mother is again humanized by a subtle touch of doubt. The crucial intervention of the hitherto silent Pylades is a masterly stroke, though a natural extension from the use of the silent figure of Prometheus in *Prometheus Bound* or Cassandra in *Agamemnon*.

The order of the murders, Aegisthus first, then Clytemnestra, is logical here, though it is worth noting that his death cry is audible, while Clytemnestra dies silently and we see only the aftermath in tableau. This tableau is clearly an echo of that at the end of Agamemnon. Orestes draws special attention to it by picking up and displaying, during his speech of self-justification, the snare in which his father died entangled.

Electra takes no further part in the play after the hatching of the plot. This relegation of her to a minor character in the trilogy as a whole throws a proper emphasis onto Orestes and Clytemnestra as the major figures, who exemplify the paradox of required revenge for a dead father. It proves to be a major difference in the handling of the story by the two later playwrights.

Other Plays about the House of Atreus

Aeschylus: *Agamemnon, Eumenides.*

Sophocles: *Electra.*

Euripides: *Electra, Iphigeneia in Tauris, Orestes, Iphigeneia in Aulis.*

Other Plays in Which Clytemnestra Is a Character

Aeschylus: *Agamemnon, Eumenides* (as a ghost).

Sophocles: *Electra.*

Euripides: *Electra, Iphigeneia in Aulis.*

Other Plays in Which Orestes Is a Character

Aeschylus: *Eumenides.*

Sophocles: *Electra.*

Euripides: *Electra, Andromache, Iphigeneia in Tauris, Orestes, Iphigeneia in Aulis* (as a baby).

Other Plays in Which Electra Is a Character

Sophocles: *Electra.*

Euripides: *Electra, Orestes.*

EUMENIDES. (Lit. 'kindly ones.') Also known as *The Furies.* 1,047 lines.

Production. 458 B.C. at the Great Dionysia. Third of the *Oresteia* trilogy: *Agamemnon, Libation-Bearers, Eumenides.* The group, with the satyr play *Proteus,* won first prize, and *Agamemnon* and *Libation-Bearers* also survive complete. *Proteus* is lost.

Characters

PYTHIAN PRIESTESS.	63 lines
APOLLO, the god.	141
ORESTES, son of Agamemnon and Clytemnestra.	103
CLYTEMNESTRA, a ghost.	40
ATHENA, the goddess.	250
CHORUS, of Furies, the *Eumenides*.	434
ESCORT, for the final procession.	16
JURY, of Athenian citizens.	nonspeaking

Plot. At Delphi, in front of the temple of Apollo, the god's priestess prays to the gods in preparation for entering the temple to take her place on her throne. She exits inside, only to return moments later on hands and knees in horror at what she has seen. The temple has been invaded by creatures so foul that she cannot begin to identify them. Asleep though they are, they hold captive a suppliant at Apollo's navel stone.

She departs, to be replaced by Apollo and Orestes as the scene indoors is revealed. Apollo guarantees to support Orestes in his flight from the Furies, though they have been roused from their lair by the act of matricide. That this matricide was less recommended by Apollo than thrust upon Orestes by him is of no concern to the Furies. Apollo ordains Hermes, who may or may not be present in person, to escort Orestes to Athens for a proper judgment of the case and Orestes departs.

The ghost of Clytemnestra appears briefly urging the Furies to wake and accusing them of neglecting their duty to her. Apollo orders the Furies from his shrine, but they, now awake, face him with the basic contradiction that lies behind Orestes' duty to avenge his father's death. Fundamentally opposed to Apollo, the Chorus leave in pursuit of Orestes and the scene moves to Athens.

Orestes arrives and seeks refuge at the statue of Athena. The Chorus are not far behind, vowing that they will never grant him rest. They are checked, at least temporarily, by Athena herself who now enters. She listens to what the Furies have to say but, despite their refusal to entertain the notion of arbitration, hears Orestes' submission too. Athena decrees a proper trial and institutes a court of Athenian citizens, the Court of the Areopagus, to decide the case.

Apollo enters to offer Orestes the promised support and after a verbal skirmish between Orestes and the Furies, argues his case for him. The grounds he chooses seem odd to a modern audience, relating more to the nature of parenthood, it would seem, than to any larger sense of justice. But, when the votes cast are equal, Athena decides, as she has said she will, in favor of Orestes. He leaves the scene a free man.

The remainder of the play, over a quarter of the whole, is occupied with Athena's wooing and eventual conversion of the Furies from nightmare hags to benevolent spirits. This is no simple matter and places her justice in a wider context. The trilogy reaches its conclusion in a mood of reconciliation and concord with a triumphal parade to escort the Furies to their new home as guardians of Athens.

Staging. *Eumenides* has more complicated stage action than any other of Aeschylus' plays. There are two separate locations, one Delphi, the other Athens where Orestes finally takes refuge; there is a chorus who appear to make their first entrance from inside the *skene*, which is a small problem, and while asleep, which is a large one; there is a ghost, though this is not the first time Aeschylus has introduced one (see *Persians*); there is a major trial scene with a jury and the casting of votes, which is followed by the transformation of the Furies and the procession from the theatre.

The opening at Delphi centers on Orestes, who has taken refuge at Apollo's temple, to which the Furies have pursued him. His escape while they are asleep, only for them to be awoken and sent in pursuit by the ghost of his mother, appears to imply that the Chorus departed from the *orchestra* altogether, perhaps to reenter by the other *parodos* [entrance song of the chorus] to indicate the flight to Athens. A similar change of location takes place in Sophocles' *Ajax*, but the departure of a chorus from the scene in mid-action is certainly unusual. Exactly how the sequence was first staged is unknown and there is no direct evidence of how, if at all, the change from Delphi to Athens was shown in the setting. Opinions vary, but some change in the *skene*, whether by means of painted panels or by the substitution of a statue of Athena for that of Apollo, seems at least likely.

The question of how to stage the entry of the Chorus from inside the temple at Delphi while they are asleep, admits of no simple solution, though the entrance was clearly thought of as having shock value to judge by later stories of the effect on the audience. What can be stated with some certainty is that the entrance was sufficiently unorthodox to merit its being remembered in later times as a daring piece of staging.

The trial in Athens includes the introduction of a jury to decide the case and the equipment for the casting of votes. Though the stage is perhaps unusually full during this scene, neither here nor elsewhere in the play is there any sequence to provide the kind of difficulty encountered in a play such as *Prometheus Bound*. All of *Eumenides* could have been comfortably staged within the broad convention that encompasses all the other Greek plays from this time on.

The most intriguing question in *Eumenides* concerns the aspect of the Furies, who are treated by all who encounter them as creatures vile to look at. Their eventual change, which happens in full view, to benign and beautiful deities, offers a challenge to a modern director that is almost beyond solution. Aeschylus had something in mind related to the donning of scarlet robes as enjoined by Athena. Beyond that we can only assume a transformation, surprising without being eccentric, while remaining theatrically of real power.

Dramatic and Theatrical Qualities. It is difficult in a few words to give any adequate sense of the full climactic force of the *Oresteia*. Its stage potential is enormous because it functions at several different levels. There is, for example, a consistency of verbal imagery in the recurrent references to fire, which is finally promoted into the actual fire of the torches to conclude a trilogy that began with a blazing beacon. Similarly the language of the hunt, used by Chorus and main characters alike, has its physical level in the harassment of Orestes by creatures that 'snuffle like dogs' and 'crawl on all fours.'

Rather than itemize the subtleties that emerge from seeing the three plays as a whole, it will be preferable here simply to draw attention to two aspects of the *Eumenides* which relate the *Oresteia* both to the theatre of its time and to the repertoire of the world's stage.

The first of these involves the development of the chorus from its original position as a prime mover in the drama through the growing concentration on character to be found in *Persians*, *Seven Against Thebes*, and *Prometheus Bound*. In *Agamemnon* the Chorus of old men seem to know more about the past than ordinary old men of Argos have any right to know. At the same time they can be quite obtuse about the direct threat to Agamemnon or the ramblings of Cassandra. The two attitudes are compatible because the Chorus have a lyric function, a rhythmic one, and a literal one. These functions may not only overlap but sometimes operate at the same time. Nevertheless, the Chorus of Agamemnon *achieve* nothing and do not alter the outcome.

In *Libation-Bearers* the slaves of the household do effect something when they make a contribution to the plot against Clytemnestra and Aegisthus, without forfeiting their other functions. By the time of the *Eumenides* the Chorus are protagonists but for whom the play would have no purpose. They are the implacable deities whose aspect repels all who come into contact with them, though they are known defensively as 'kindly ones.' But ancient deities they are, with a more venerable claim to authority than Apollo. At the same time the Furies are a stage chorus with the same commission as the choruses of *Agamemnon, Libation-Bearers, Persians,* and *Suppliants,* the last of which in one sense they most closely resemble.

It is because the Chorus can at one and the same time fulfill several roles that the moment of the Furies' conversion is so uplifting. From the oppression and horror that has been a feature of the whole story of the house of Atreus with its generations of bloodletting, there surfaces at last the possibility of relief. From despair emerges hope.

This is closely linked to the other aspect of the *Oresteia* which makes it appear such an achievement, though here the ground is less solid. There is at least a strong argument for considering the *Oresteia* as a composite and comprehensive political statement. It has often been suggested that others of Aeschylus' plays, and indeed those of Sophocles and Euripides, have a level of contemporary reference no more than shadowy after so many hundreds of years. Such a case is more substantial for the *Oresteia* because it is based on the position of the Court of the Areopagus in Athens at the time of writing and the attendant turning point in Athenian democracy that the previous three years had witnessed.

Be that as it may, and this is not the place to review such suggestions, it would be difficult to deny that at least some of the *Oresteia*'s greatness resides in the manner in which Aeschylus transcends the immediate story of Orestes and his family to consider a new vision of justice dependent on the judgment of one's fellow citizens – subject always, that is, to the wisdom of Athena. If the *Oresteia* was not a profound and multilayered declaration about the nature of Athenian democracy, of immediate and pressing relevance to its first ever audience in 458 B.C., then Aeschylus has created a suitable framework for such speculation entirely by accident.

But, of course, there is nothing accidental about the *Oresteia* and the last third of *Eumenides* offers the surest evidence. This question of Orestes' guilt, too large for man to resolve, turns out to be too large for Athena too, and she refers it back. When the verdict of the citizens is declared and, with the casting vote of the goddess, comes down on the side of mercy, though not for mercy's sake, the question remains of what to do with the Furies. Orestes fades out of the scene because in the wider context he is largely irrelevant. The conversion of the Furies can then be seen to be the most, perhaps the only, crucial issue. It may never be possible to reproduce the profound effect of this on a non-Greek audience for whom the progress of Athenian democracy in the fifth century B.C. can hardly be a pressing issue. It should be possible to concentrate on those other aspects of the play that do have a universal context, to touch that hunger for hope and for life that the play applauds. Ultimately, the *Oresteia* is a paean to affirmation.

Other Plays about the House of Atreus

Aeschylus: *Agamemnon, Libation-Bearers.*

Sophocles: *Electra.*

Euripides: *Electra, Iphigeneia in Tauris, Orestes, Iphigeneia in Aulis.*

Other Plays in Which Clytemnestra Is a Character

Aeschylus: *Agamemnon, Libation-Bearers.*

Sophocles: *Electra.*

Euripides: *Electra, Iphigeneia in Aulis.*

Other Plays in Which Orestes Is a Character

Aeschylus: *Libation-Bearers.*

Sophocles: *Electra.*

Euripides: *Electra, Andromache, Iphigeneia in Tauris, Orestes, Iphigeneia in Aulis* (as a baby).

Other Plays in Which Apollo Is a Character

Euripides: *Alcestis, Orestes.*

Other Plays in Which Athena Is a Character

Sophocles: *Ajax.*

Euripides: *Rhesus, Suppliants, Ion, Trojan Women, Iphigeneia in Tauris.*
(Walton, 1987, pp. 53–64)

EXERCISE _____

Having read Walton's description of the action of the *Agamemnon* and his discussion of its qualities, note down the main aspects of the play which seem to you to involve conflicts or problems concerned with identities and relationships. Then consider how these might be explored in a performance. Remember that a performance is not the same as a reading or recitation of a written text. You will need to think about how a performance communicates to the audience through non-verbal means as well as through the words of the play. What might the audience see and hear in conjunction with the words?

DISCUSSION _____

There is no right or wrong answer to this exercise. Your selection of points may well be differently expressed from mine.

The dramatic context of the play – the return of Agamemnon to Argos after the victory of the Greeks in the ten-year war against the Trojans – focuses on the impact of change. Nothing is as it was. Agamemnon is a returning war leader; he has to adjust to ruling his city in peace. He also has to resume his role as a husband. His wife has been ruling in his absence together with his cousin Aegisthus. They have to cede power. The ensuing crisis in relationships operates in a number of spheres – gender, household and city. Power and revenge are agents which determine events.

Crucially, there is the question of Agamemnon's and Clytemnestra's identities as parents. Agamemnon has sacrificed their daughter Iphigenia to appease the army and gain from the gods a fair wind for Troy. An additional layer of identity issues is represented in the figure and role of Cassandra. Brought back from Troy by Agamemnon, she is a captive princess, a victim of war, used by Agamemnon as his sex slave. She is also a prophetess, which further complicates the relationship between past, present and future in the play as well as introducing the concept of offence against the gods (as a prophetess she was dedicated to Apollo and so her rape is an offence against the gods). Furthermore, she is a Trojan, from Asia Minor, and therefore in terms of Greek culture is regarded as an alien, a barbarian.

The fact that Agamemnon actually only enters part-way through the play and that Cassandra is silent for a long period after her entry indicates that dramatically what someone does and how they are perceived can be as important as what they say. Also significant are the other characters, such as the Watchman and the Herald – how they perceive themselves and how they regard the major figures. Their roles round out the awareness of the audience. The Watchman sets the wider scene and hints at the ominous developments to come.

The Herald makes the link between the events of the war and their impact on the homecoming. The Chorus of old men represents a link with the past but can only speculate about the future, whereas Cassandra sees it.

So far as the direction and staging are concerned the set, costume, properties and the atmosphere generated by lighting and music would interact with the verbal tone of the translation and the gestures, movement and body language of the actors to express and draw out the relationships between the characters and to frame the crises of identity which they undergo. For example, how might Cassandra be dressed – as an eastern princess, as a prophetess, as a whore, as a raped and traumatized victim of war? All these perspectives are present in the text. The director has to decide on the emphasis. What might Agamemnon's costume and movement suggest about his self-perceptions as returning warrior? How might the Chorus of Elders and Clytemnestra respond to this? How is the persistence of the image of the sacrificed Iphigenia represented?

In these respects the design and staging might suggest a setting for the play which is modern rather than ancient in time, or they might suggest a geographical location which resonates with the audience's current awareness. The production's anticipation and shaping of audience response are important features in generating acting styles and all the other aspects of staging.

Staging the *Agamemnon*

The richness of possibilities offered by the situations and relationships in the *Agamemnon* has inspired a variety of approaches in recent productions. From these I have selected for particular comment aspects which relate directly or indirectly to the issues of cultural and political identity surveyed in the previous section. The plurality of approaches in recent stagings is part of an international series of revivals of Greek tragedy ushered in by three influential productions of the *Oresteia* in the 1980s. In 1980 John Barton and Kenneth Cavender's *The Greeks* staged for the Royal Shakespeare Company at the Aldwych Theatre, London, a cycle of Greek myth from Homer and Greek tragedy, including the *Oresteia*. Then the focus on the trilogy became tighter and in 1981 Peter Hall's production for London's National Theatre of Tony Harrison's translation of the *Oresteia* showed that Greek tragedy need not be confined to the theatre of protest or to specialized festivals, but could feature in the repertoire of the commercial theatre (Macintosh, 1997, p. 316). As in an ancient production, the cast was entirely male and

Figure 7.9 Masked Chorus of Old Men of Argos in the opening scene of *Agamemnon*, staged as the opening play in Aeschylus' *Oresteia* in the version by Tony Harrison, directed by Peter Hall, National Theatre, London, 1981. Photo: Photostage/Donald Cooper

both the translation and direction reflected the view that Aeschylus' trilogy mapped the emergence and civic acceptance of male supremacy, not only in war but in law. Hall's staging was highly stylized in an attempt to convey ancient theatrical experience. It used full masks and was set in a simple semi-circular playing area with two diagonal approachways and a metal back structure. However, the concept of the production was not limited to the re-creation of ancient conventions. Harrison's English translation was noted (and sometimes criticized) for its dominant single-syllable rhythm, its alliteration and use of Anglo-Saxon compounds like 'she-god'. These served to simplify the verbal and rhythmic complexity of Aeschylus' text. The production was particularly praised for Harrison Birtwistle's musical score (Chioles, 1993), which was thought to be a major factor in shaping the tone and emotional force of the play, but although the Chorus's movements were choreographed its members did not dance.

Masks are also used in Japanese theatre, as is discussed in Chapter 6.

The Harrison/Hall production was also performed in the ancient theatre at Epidaurus, Greece in 1982: a 'first' for a non-Greek production. This was the first of a series of versions of Greek tragedy and myth created by Harrison for performance (usually one-off) in authentic open-air theatres in Greece. Although this production moved across cultural boundaries, both literally in performance and metaphorically in its text, it remained directed verbally by exploration (sometimes ironic) of the gender politics in Aeschylus and in terms of acting style by the theatrical convention of the mask.

More overtly political in terms of contemporary agendas was Peter Stein's 1980 Berlin production of the *Oresteia* in German prose translation. A nationalistic Nazi version directed by Lothal Müthel had previously been performed at the state theatre in Berlin during the Olympic games of 1936. Stein's conception addressed the postwar problems of Germany and was developed through a series of experimental workshops, the *Antikenprojekt*. The script was the result of analysis of over thirty translations (Flashar, 1991, pp. 263–6). The audience was seated on the ground with the Chorus of Elders, dressed in suits, dark glasses and 1940s-style fedora hats, using a central corridor which made it seem as though Chorus and audience were interchangeable. The play was thought to interrogate the then political situation in West Germany, with the new democracy based in Bonn identified with the emergent democracy in the *Eumenides* – and, by implication, sullied along with it when the Eumenides put on the same purple cloth which had been used to wrap the corpses in the earlier part of the trilogy. Stein's approach made the Chorus and spectators complicit in the action and exposed the guilt attached to silence and non-intervention, notably in the Chorus's silent witness in the carpet scene in the *Agamemnon*. Stein's production was revived in 1994. It also toured in Greece and Russia.

A more positive statement about political progress was presented in the staging by Karolos Koun's Theatro Technis in Greece in 1980 and 1982. Koun saw a close relationship between the avant-garde role of theatre and the language and conventions of the ancient Greek theatre. The set, designed by Dionysus Fotopoulos, created a primeval world from which in the final play of the trilogy the community escaped. The production was thought to support the possibility of change for the better in Greece, following the end of the regime of the military junta (the Colonels' regime, 1967–74). Subsequently both interpretative and theatrical debate has continued to focus on the resonances of the plays as comments on political and social change, but such discussions have also broadened to take more direct account of the impact of the theatrical traditions shaping the creation of the performance, the unmasking of issues of culture and identity

Figure 7.10   The Chorus's religious ritual at the tomb of Agamemnon. Karolos Koun's production of Aeschylus' *Oresteia*, Greece, 1982. The Eastern Orthodox religious tradition influenced this depiction of the ritual. Photo: Arguropoulo Photopress

(especially between Greek and non-Greek), and the relationships between Agamemnon, Clytemnestra and Cassandra.

A later production which has also become canonical in its theatrical impact is *Les Atrides*, performed by Le Théâtre du Soleil under the director Ariane Mnouchkine. This toured internationally, including a performance in Bradford in 1992 (in French translation with simultaneous English translation available via head-sets). The company had a background of expertise in oriental theatre and drew on the music, movement, acting styles and costume of Europe, Africa, China, India, the Levant and Japan. The director also took the role of 'auteur' and created a reading of the trilogy which rejected eurocentrism in favour of a multicultural exploration of pathos and suffering.

There were three particularly significant features to *Les Atrides*. First, a shared background experience was created for the audience, who were led to the auditorium through an exhibition that included a huge map of the Mediterranean world showing the voyages of

Figure 7.11   The three-act ballet *Clytemnestra*, choreographed by Martha Graham, was first performed in 1958 and has been revived many times. Photo: Martha Swope/Rex Features

Kathakali is a south Indian performance tradition with complex systems of dance, movement and gesture, in combination with stylized make-up used to convey emotions.

Agamemnon, displays of Greek life and food and an entrance area from where they looked down on a series of terracotta figures similar to the Chinese terracotta army (the ancient models of the Chinese terracotta army at Xian which had recently received a good deal of publicity). Secondly, the production began with a performance of Euripides' *Iphigenia in Aulis*. This put at the forefront of the audience's minds the impact of Agamemnon's sacrifice of his daughter, both in respect of his own torn emotions and in relation to the effect on Clytemnestra. This in turn informed the audience's response to Clytemnestra's hostility to her returning husband in the *Agamemnon*. Thirdly, the director made considerable use of non-European theatre techniques, especially in drawing on parallels between Greek and Japanese Noh and Kabuki drama. After the Second World War a degree of cultural exchange between Japanese and western theatrical traditions had begun to grow. Students in Tokyo in the 1960s, for example, explored Greek tragedy as a source of values associated with freedom and democracy. Subsequently in Tadashi Suzuki's adaptations of Greek tragedy, Japanese traditions of the creative role of the actor gave performance priority over text (Macintosh, 1997, p. 313). Sometimes the performance text itself was not fixed. Even when directors such as Yukio Ninagawa stayed more closely with the text, the dance techniques of Kabuki theatre enabled the Chorus to convey the emotional range of Greek drama. Mnouchkine's *Les Atrides* drew not only on these aspects of Japanese classical theatre but also on Indian theatre, especially in the use of **Kathakali** make-up. For instance, grief is sometimes expressed through formalized make-up, with black tears running down the cheeks of the oppressed. Kathakali heroic make-up, in contrast to the Greek mask, also enabled actors to weep real tears as Agamemnon

Figure 7.12 The Chorus in *Agamemnon* from *Les Atrides*, directed by Ariane Mnouchkine, Théâtre du Soleil, 1990–2. The influences of eastern theatrical traditions are evident in the extravagant costumes and make-up of the Chorus. Photo: Martine Franck/Magnum

did in *Iphigenia in Aulis*. This vigorous non-western register was resented by some critics schooled in narrower approaches to Greek drama. One academic referred to the 'Nipponising' of Greek drama at the hands of Mnouchkine (Golder, 1996, pp. 174–209; the comment was accompanied by equally trenchant criticism of the performance of Greek drama in the British theatrical tradition (Golder, 1996, pp. 176–7). This kind of criticism has a number of bases. In rejecting the inevitable and energizing modern resonances and acting styles it promotes a view of Greek drama as a self-contained vehicle for transmission of an 'authentic' view of the past rather than as a strand in the dialogic processes of reception and refiguration. Yet it also perhaps contains an element of appropriation of Greek drama to the cultural practices with which the critic feels most secure (in this particular case a production that included an American gospel choir was thought to convey appropriately the sense of the sacred which the critic wished to see communicated in modern productions).

These strands of broad cultural awareness and exchange and political intervention, which have been identified in twentieth-century performance history, have converged in recent productions. Cultural categorization and exclusion are significant themes in the *Agamemnon*. In the Craiova Theatre Company of Romania's production directed by Silviu Purcarete, which toured Europe in 1998, this was intertwined in a striking way with the dramatic enactment and scrutiny of political change. The performance was in Romanian translation with English sur-titles, made largely redundant by the visual and aural theatricality of the production. Mime and movement, silhouette and other visual effects and non-verbal sound were major aspects of translation. In the *Agamemnon* the role of the Chorus was crucial to the translation of Aeschylus' play across time and cultures. This Chorus consisted of elderly males wearing baggy grey suits. They carried seat sticks which doubled as walking sticks and were sometimes used like rifles to make synchronized threatening gestures. Described by one reviewer as a 'powerful dramatic presence of fat, wheedling, bald, sexist old male time-servers' (Joyce McMillan in the *Scotsman*, October 1998), they also carried briefcases and shuffled and wandered (as choreographed), with movements to different stage spaces signalling changes in mood, emotion and judgements about the unfolding action. When the Herald returned from Troy the Chorus formed a Soviet-style gerontocracy, welcoming him in frenzied handkerchief-waving rows. The Chorus leader's offer of a towel to the Herald highlighted the total dislocation between the cultural frameworks of the citizen and the exhausted fighter.

Figure 7.13 The Chorus of Old Men, with Cassandra about to leap from her wagon, in the Craiova Theatre Company of Romania's production of Aeschylus's *Oresteia*, directed by Silviu Purcarete (UK tour, 1998). The suits, briefcases and sticks of the Chorus were in sharp contrast to the eastern and Gypsy resonances of Cassandra's entry. Photo: National Theatre of Craiova, Romania

The Chorus was also a main player in a different kind of cultural encounter, this time between west and east, Greek and barbarian (Hall, 1989). The Chorus snoozed on the floor as Cassandra entered in a closed wagon to snatches of eastern music. The wagon could have been a cattle truck or a Gypsy caravan. The Chorus's movements and gestures framed the unfolding of this mysterious arrival. Chorus members pushed the wagon, then beat their breasts and wrung their hands as the captive beat upon the inside walls of the wagon. Terrified by the dive-bomber-type descent of a vulture, they flung themselves to the ground as Cassandra emerged from the wagon, yet rose and caught her as she flung herself in desperation from the top. Then the sticks of the Chorus became alternately phallic symbols and cattle-prods as the elders approached her. They followed Agamemnon in a feeble imitation of his goose-stepping march along the red carpet to his death. After the killing of Agamemnon, the Chorus elders pointed their sticks like guns at Clytemnestra as they called her a carrion-raven. Then the sticks were used to seat the elders as they crouched in mourning in pew-like rows. Cassandra's corpse received different treatment. Like jetsam, she was thrown off the trolley where she had lain with legs splayed. The Chorus's movements also expressed changes of attitude towards Clytemnestra. The Chorus leader stalked her with the sword, the murder weapon, but lowered it when it became clear that she was still mourning her daughter Iphigenia, thus leaving unresolved at this stage in the trilogy the debate about whether Agamemnon or Clytemnestra or both deserved to die. Finally, the Chorus members ceased their abuse when Aegisthus chased them away with a whip. Cowed and powerless, several keeled over and died. Visually the sequence translated the scene into several dimensions – including those of post-Soviet politics and ethnic abuse – and for Romanian audiences must have had a further layer of resonance in the context of debates about political and cultural identity and their relationship to western- or eastern-looking traditions (Verdery, 1991). Of course by the time this performance was developed and toured the Romanian tyranny had fallen (Nicolae Ceauşescu was toppled at Christmas 1989) and the director could be as imaginative as he liked in the translational layering he wished to suggest to the audience.

An analogous and equally searing representation of the denial of fully human status to Cassandra was a major feature of another 1990s production. In the English translation of the *Agamemnon* which toured as a single play in the UK in 1999, directed by David Stuttard, the Chorus moved through several stages of complicity – initially in its visual enactment of the sacrifice of Iphigenia and then in its transformation for a 'locker-room' welcome to the returning Agamemnon. The football chants of Argos ceased at the entrance of

Figure 7.14 Agamemnon, in Nazi-style leather coat, drags Cassandra on a chain to meet Clytemnestra. From the 1999 UK touring production of *Agamemnon* (Actors of Dionysus, directed by David Stuttard). Photo: Adrien Gatie

Clytemnestra, silenced by her contempt. Agamemnon carried a long chain which he jerked periodically. Only gradually was it apparent that cowering behind a wooden pillar and attached to the chain was Cassandra. She then crawled in on all fours, hissing at the Chorus as the elders mocked her in response to Agamemnon's references to 'our guest' and Clytemnestra's taunts that the uncomprehending girl was both an idiot and a barbarian. Cassandra's version of the curse on the house of Atreus was delivered as the rest of the cast retreated, wailing. She became verbally and visually the symbol of the suffering inflicted on Gypsies, refugees and all the displaced.

Several of these features were intermingled in *The Home Guard*, which corresponded to the *Agamemnon* in part one of Ted Hughes's translation of the *Oresteia*, staged at the Royal National Theatre in London in 1999 and directed by Katie Mitchell (Hughes, 1999). The production also toured the US. Here the mythic action was given modern contexts. The Chorus of Elders consisted of retired servicemen in wheelchairs. They were dressed in civilian clothes but wore poppies and, after Agamemnon's death, red berets, and were attended by uniformed Red Cross nurses. The large sliding doors to Agamemnon's palace were used as a screen to project black-and-white film of end-of-war celebrations. Agamemnon returned as a somewhat uneasy hero, dressed as a guerrilla fighter. The background music and snatches of eastern European chants suggested Balkan resonances. The 'carpet' along which Agamemnon walked to enter the palace was made up of the red (blood-soaked) dresses of small children. The programme included photographs, pockmarked with bullet holes, showing children's clothes, shoes and toys, half buried in sand and labelled like exhibits in a criminal investigation. The combination of the staging and the forensic layout of the programme created for the audience a commonality of allusion and understanding of the contemporary didacticism of Mitchell's direction of the play. Agamemnon was represented as a slightly contrary figure, shadowed as he went into the palace by the ghost of his sacrificed daughter, who had sat watching the proceedings and now mimicked his goose-stepping progress inside as he went to his death followed by Cassandra, her clothes still bloody from her rape (a directorial allusion, perhaps, to the Craiova Theatre Company production of 1998).

Agamemnon's ambivalent stance towards Iphigenia's sacrifice, the events of the war and his return has emerged as a key strand in some recent productions which draw on Aeschylus' play, suggesting that previous concentrations on Clytemnestra and her outraged motherhood may have to cede ground to an awareness that Agamemnon also has an identity crisis. In an Edinburgh Festival Fringe production in 2000 Triche Kehoe's version, *Children of Clytemnestra*, used grainy flickering footage from twentieth-century battle scenes to intensify the audience's perception of the underlying effects of war on returning soldiers. In this play the focus is on the relationship between war and responsibility, filtered through the eyes of Cassandra who begins the proceedings by explaining that the actors represent the millions of innocent victims of war. The questions 'Who will stop it?' and 'Why?' are interjected into the narrative of how the Greeks who departed for Troy turned from individuals into monsters. The returning Agamemnon is exhausted and traumatized. The Chorus's powerlessness in Aeschylus's version is

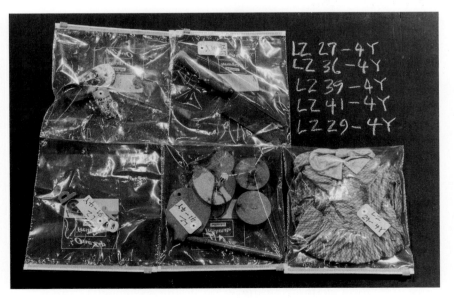

Figure 7.15 The aftermath of children's suffering in war (scattered toys, clothes, shoes, with some items collected and numbered). From the programme of *The Home Guard*, based on Ted Hughes's *Aeschylus: the* Oresteia: *a New Version*, directed by Katie Mitchell, Royal National Theatre, 1999. Photo: Ivan Kyncl

here transmuted into wilful blindness and failure to act: it is not merely complicit in events but actively guilty, and its repeated cry of 'Blot it out' is a powerful expression of denial.

Another aspect of the refiguring of Agamemnon was demonstrated in early 2000 when the play was performed by the Theseion Theatre in Athens as *The Ghost Sonata*, directed by Michael Marmarinos. Here Agamemnon was played as an engaging stranger in his own land, speaking in English which was translated into Greek and projected on to a wall. In contrast to Aeschylus' play, this production opened abruptly with Agamemnon's return and the carpet scene was played as a re-enactment of his entry into the house, as if he were a ghost of his former self. Cassandra's foreignness was communicated by making her a blonde Scandinavian tourist in Greece. The production values and concentration on Agamemnon as a rounded personality meant that the play no longer explored the problems of power struggle but was depoliticized, focusing on what Agamemnon had experienced in his absence. Thus the Chorus was no longer made up of citizen elders and major protagonists but of young people in casual modern dress, analogous perhaps to the audience (Kotzamani, 2000).

Later in 2000 and during 2001 in the US and UK, performances of the Peter Hall-directed adaptation of John Barton's nine-play cycle *Tantalus* took the rehabilitation of Agamemnon even further. Barton's sequence of plays is based on the stories of the epic cycle surrounding the mythology of the Trojan war, with some echoes of Greek drama, especially Euripides' *Iphigenia in Aulis*. This version inverts the content of Greek tragedy, as most of the major episodes (including those from the *Oresteia*) are merely recounted as background. Agamemnon is represented as an unwilling warrior, encouraged by Clytemnestra to perform the sacrifice of his daughter and too weak to prevent the excesses of his comrades in the sack of Troy. *Tantalus* pushes the barriers between tragedy and comedy to the limits, pastiching and debunking the more didactic aspects of cultural and aesthetic intervention which many of the productions discussed in this chapter have displayed. Feminist perspectives are mocked, while rapes are so many as to become trivialized. The protests which the production evoked show the extent to which Greek drama has become associated with serious cultural statements and debates. Yet *Tantalus*, with all its melodramatic and blackly humorous subversion, also explicitly recognizes the role of the *Agamemnon* in the European tradition of drama. (It anachronistically refers to the Greeks as 'the west'.) *Tantalus*, too, is part of the continuing debate about cultural ownership and control (Hardwick, 2001; 2002). It brings to prominence different perspectives on translation for performance, on translation across cultures and on the relationship between translation and invention. In this example the receiving culture is postmodern and fragmented, and *Tantalus* mocks those who would appropriate Greek drama for serious moral and political debate. What is significant, however, is that in order to bring about this shift the production team had to move away from the Greek tragedies and to invent or reinvent an identity for Agamemnon about which Aeschylus was silent.

Aeschylus' play presents a sometimes ambivalent triangular relationship between Agamemnon, Clytemnestra and Cassandra which challenged ancient audiences to recognize and rethink their own conceptions of identity in terms of gender, social status, politics, ethnicity and culture and their shifting interrelationships. Translation of the play to the modern European stage has presented an equivalent challenge to contemporary audiences (Macintosh, forthcoming). The flow of revivals, reinterpretations and adaptations in both national and international theatres demonstrates the continuing importance of the play's role as a catalyst for self-awareness and critique (Patsalidis and Sakellaridou, 1999, pp. 13–14).

References

Chioles, J. (1993) 'The *Oresteia* and the avant-garde', *Performing Arts Journal*, 45, pp. 1–28.

Eagleton, T. [1991] (1998) *News from Nowhere*, no. 9, pp. 93–5, reprinted in S. Regan (ed.), *The Eagleton Reader*, Oxford, Blackwell.

Flashar, H. (1991) *Inszenierung der Antike*, Munich, Verlag Beck.

Golder, H. (1996) 'Geek tragedy? – or why I'd rather go to the movies', *Arion*, 3rd series, vol. 4, no. 1, spring, pp. 174–209.

Goldhill, S. and Osborne, R. (1999) *Performance Culture and Athenian Democracy*, Cambridge, Cambridge University Press.

Hall, E. (1989) *Inventing the Barbarian*, Oxford, Clarendon.

Hardwick, L. (1997–) *The Reception of the Texts and Images of Ancient Greece in Late Twentieth-century Drama and Poetry in English* (database of modern productions), www2.open.ac.uk/ClassicalStudies/GreekPlays

Hardwick, L. (2000) *Translating Words, Translating Cultures*, London, Duckworth.

Hardwick, L. (2001) 'Who owns the plays?', *Eirene*, vol. XXXVII (Greek drama special issue), pp. 23–39.

Hardwick, L. (2002) 'Tantalus staged: anthology, narrative and the audience', *Didaskalia*, vol. 5, no. 2, http://www.didaskalia.net

Heaney, S. (1990) *The Cure at Troy*, London, Faber & Faber.

Heaney, S. (1996) 'Mycenae Lookout', in *The Spirit Level*, London, Faber & Faber.

Hughes, T. (1999) *Aeschylus: the* Oresteia*: a New Version*, London, Faber & Faber.

Kotzamani, M. (2000) Review of *Agamemnon* (*The Ghost Sonata*), *Theatre Journal*, vol. 52, no. 4, December, pp. 576–8.

Macintosh, F. (1997) 'Tragedy in performance: nineteenth and twentieth century productions', in P. E. Easterling (ed.), *The Cambridge Companion to Greek Tragedy*, Cambridge, Cambridge University Press.

Macintosh, F. (ed.) (forthcoming) *Agamemnon Staged*, selected proceedings of the Agamemnon conference 2001, Oxford (includes appendix of modern performances).

Meir, C. (1991) 'Irish poetic drama: Seamus Heaney's *The Cure at Troy*', in G. Genet and E. Hellegouarc'h (eds), *Studies on the Contemporary Irish Theatre*, Actes du Colloque de Caen.

Patsalidis, S. and Sakellaridou, E. (eds) (1999) *(Dis)Placing Classical Greek Theatre*, Thessaloniki, University Studio Press.

Protochristova, C. (1998) 'Attic tragedy in Bulgaria: encounters and insights', in S. Mercouris (ed.), *A Stage for Dionysus: Theatrical Space and Ancient Drama*, Athens, Kapon.

Stehlíková, E. (2000) 'Central European Medea', in E. Hall, M. Macintosh and O. Taplin (eds), *Medea in Performance 1500–2000*, Oxford, Legenda.

Stehlíková, E. (2001) 'Productions of Greek and Roman drama on the Czech stage', *Eirene*, vol. XXXVII, pp. 71–160 (including many illustrations).

Steiner, G. (1984) *Antigones*, Oxford, Oxford University Press.

Taplin, O. (1997) 'The pictorial record', in P. E. Easterling (ed.), *The Cambridge Companion to Greek Tragedy*, Cambridge, Cambridge University Press.

Taplin, O. (1999) 'Greek with consequence', in P. Mavromoustakos (ed.), *Productions of Ancient Greek Drama in Europe during Modern Times*, Athens, Kastaniotis.

Taxidou, O. (2000) 'Medea comes home', in E. Hall, M. Macintosh and O. Taplin (eds), *Medea in Performance 1500–2000*, Oxford, Legenda.

Verdery, K. (1991) *National Ideology under Socialism: Identity and Cultural Politics in Ceauşescu's Romania*, Berkeley, CA, University of California Press.

Walton, J. M. (1987) *Living Greek Theatre: a Handbook of Classical Performance and Modern Production*, Westport, CT, Greenwood Press.

Wiles, D. (2000) *Greek Theatre Performance: an Introduction*, Cambridge, Cambridge University Press.

Acknowledgements

Grateful acknowledgement is made to the following sources for permission to reproduce material in this book:

Chapter 1

Woolf, V. (1977) *Three Guineas.* Chatto & Windus/Harcourt Brace & Company, Inc. By permission of The Society of Authors as the Literary Representative of the Estate of Virginia Woolf.

Pirandello, L. (1990) in Weaver, W. (trans.) *One, No One and One Hundred Thousand.* Marsilio Publishers.

MacInnes, C. (1959) *Absolute Beginners.* Penguin Books Ltd. By kind permission of Virgin Publishing.

Brah, A. (1996) 'Difference, diversity, differentiation', pp. 96–103. *Cartographies of Diaspora: Contesting Identities.* Routledge/Taylor & Francis Books Ltd.

Butler, J. (1997) 'Subject of sex', *Feminisms.* By permission of Oxford University Press.

Bourdieu, P. (1998) 'Conciliation of opposites', in Clough, L. C. (trans.) *The State of Nobility: Elite Schools in the Field of Power.* Polity Press. By permission of Les Editions de Minuit.

Convery, A. et al. (1997) 'Adolescent perceptions of Europe', *Pupils' Perceptions of Europe: Identity and Education.* Cassell. By permission of The Continuum International Publishing Group.

Chapter 2

Meek, R. L. (ed. and trans.) (1973) 'A philosophical review of the successive advances of the human mind', *Turgot on Progress, Sociology and Economics.* Cambridge University Press. © R. L. Meek.

De Condorcet, A. N., Marquis de, (1979) 'The tenth stage: the future progress of the human mind', in Barraclough, J. (trans.). *Sketch for a Historical Picture of the Human Mind.* Hyperion Press, Inc. By permission of Weidenfeld & Nicolson.

Index